ESSENTIALS OF
TOURISM

PEARSON

At Pearson, we have a simple mission: to help people make more of their lives through learning.

We combine innovative learning technology with trusted content and educational expertise to provide engaging and effective learning experiences that serve people wherever and whenever they are learning.

From classroom to boardroom, our curriculum materials, digital learning tools and testing programmes help to educate millions of people worldwide – more than any other private enterprise.

Every day our work helps learning flourish, and wherever learning flourishes, so do people.

To learn more, please visit us at **www.pearson.com/uk**

ESSENTIALS OF
TOURISM

SECOND EDITION

CHRIS COOPER
Oxford Brookes University

PEARSON

Harlow, England • London • New York • Boston • San Francisco • Toronto • Sydney • Auckland • Singapore • Hong Kong
Tokyo • Seoul • Taipei • New Delhi • Cape Town • São Paulo • Mexico City • Madrid • Amsterdam • Munich • Paris • Milan

Pearson Education Limited
Edinburgh Gate
Harlow CM20 2JE
United Kingdom
Tel: +44 (0)1279 623623
Web: www.pearson.com/uk

First published 2012 (print and electronic)
Second edition published 2016 (print and electronic)

ISBN: 978-1-292-08838-9 (print)
       978-1-292-14428-3 (PDF)
       978-1-292-14429-0 (ePub)

British Library Cataloguing-in-Publication Data
A catalogue record for the print edition is available from the British Library

Library of Congress Cataloging-in-Publication Data
A catalog record for the print edition is available from the Library of Congress

10 9 8 7 6 5 4 3 2 1
20 19 18 17 16

Cover image: © Australian Scenics/Getty Images

Print edition typeset in 10/12pt Sabon MT Pro by SPi Global
Printed in Slovakia by Neografia

NOTE THAT ANY PAGE CROSS REFERENCES REFER TO THE PRINT EDITION

BRIEF CONTENTS

CONTENTS

Photograph: Neon Cowboy, Las Vegas © Charles Zachritz/Shutterstock.com

PART 4   TOURISM DEMAND AND MARKETING ESSENTIALS   267

PART 5   TOURISM FUTURES: THE ESSENTIALS   319

Lecturer Resources

For password-protected online resources tailored to support the use of this textbook in teaching, please visit **www.pearsoned.co.uk/cooper**

LIST OF FIGURES AND TABLES

Figures

Tables

PREFACE

This second edition of *Essentials of Tourism* sees a range of updates and new features, not least of which is a range of new, cutting edge, international case studies. The literature and supporting materials have all been brought up to date and I hope that you find this edition even better than the first. As before though, *Essentials* aims to provide the reader with a text covering, literally, the 'essentials of tourism'. The book is structured into 14 chapters to allow tutors and students to complete the teaching and learning of the 'essentials' of tourism in a course over one 14-week semester. As such the book does not assume any prior knowledge of tourism. The structure of the book was arrived at by analysing tourism curricula from leading schools around the world and then distilling those curricula into the 'essential' elements found at the core of every course. Naturally, different institutions and different parts of the world emphasise different aspects of tourism, but the 14 chapters in this book lie at the heart of tourism as it is taught internationally – it is therefore up to you, the reader, to contextualise this material within your own national systems of tourism.

The chapters fall naturally into five parts. Part 1 is designed to establish a framework for studying tourism, a way of thinking that has stood the test of time and, despite the fast moving pace of change that tourism is experiencing, provides a stable analytical framework. Part 2 focuses on the destination, arguably the most important and exciting part of the tourism system. Here we dissect the nature of the destination and examine the critical issues of the consequences of tourism for the destination and look closely at just what is involved in sustainable tourism. Part 3 looks at the tourism sector, both public and private, and analyses the key issues concerning attractions, hospitality, intermediaries, transportation and the public sector in tourism. Clearly each of these sectors is distinct, but in fact they have much in common in terms of how they are managed and their economics. Only the public sector stands out as separate here, simply because it is there to enable and guide tourism rather than to profit from it. Part 4 turns to the tourist in terms of demand and marketing, focusing in particular on the contemporary issues of the marketing's 'service dominant logic' and also how social networking is becoming popular amongst groups of like-minded tourists. Finally, we end with Part 5 examining tourism 'futures' – a term we use because there are so many possible 'futures' and it is impossible to see which one 'future' will prevail.

To aid the use of the book, each chapter has three case studies illustrating contemporary practice in tourism and drawn from destinations and issues around the globe. These cases are international in focus and are designed to highlight important issues of the day. At the end of each chapter a longer case study is provided to draw the chapter together. Each of these cases has discussion points and full sources. In addition, in each chapter we have identified a 'classic paper' – a paper that has acted as a milestone in the thinking of tourism and of the particular topic of the chapter. At the end of each chapter we have provided an annotated list of key sources and a set of discussion questions.

Finally, throughout the book hyperlinks are provided to aid you in going rapidly to the original source of the material.

Chris Cooper
Oxford
2015

CASE MATRIX

Mini	Major	Case No.	Case Title	Destination	Page
	✔	9.1	The Tour Operators' Initiative		218
✔		10.1	The Great Tropical Drive, Australia	Australia	233
✔		10.2	Environmentally and Socially Sustainable Cruising – The Holland America Line		238
	✔	10.1	Low-Cost Carriers: AirAsia		242
✔		11.1	The Hawke's Bay Wine Country Tourism Association, New Zealand	New Zealand	252
✔		11.2	The Policy and Planning Challenges of Diversifying the Tourism Sector in Bulgaria	Bulgaria	258
	✔	11.1	Using Open Innovation to Create a Tourism Strategy for Vienna: An Inclusive Model of Tourism Governance	Austria	264
✔		12.1	TripAdvisor.com – A Celebration of Consumer Power		276
✔		12.2	The Creative Class		280
	✔	12.1	Changing Long-haul Demand: The Case of Barbados	Barbados	290
✔		13.1	Researching Social Media – Turning Market Research on its Head		299
✔		13.2	Branding Challenging Destinations – Greenland	Greenland	305
	✔	13.1	Should Destinations be Marketed?		316
✔		14.1	Virtual Tourism		329
✔		14.2	Networked New Tourists		332
	✔	14.1	Tourism Futures Scenarios		343

PUBLISHER'S ACKNOWLEDGEMENTS

We are grateful to the following for permission to reproduce copyright material:

Figures

Figure 1.1 from Towards a framework for tourism education, *Annals of Tourism Research*, 8(1), 13–34 (Jafari J. and Ritchie J.R.B. 1981), Copyright © 1981 Elsevier Ltd. All rights reserved. Printed with permission from Elsevier; Figure 1.2 from *Tourism Systems Occasional Paper 2*, Massey University Department of Management Systems (Professor Neil Leiper 1990); Figure 1.3 from *Tourism Systems, Occasional Paper 2*, Massey University Department of Management Systems (Professor Neil Leiper 1990); Figure 1.4 from *Data Collection and Analysis for Tourism Management, Marketing and Planning.*, Madrid: World Tourism Organization (2000) ©UNWTO, 9284401711; Figure 1.5 from *Worldwide Destinations: The Geography of Travel and Tourism*, Butterworth-Heinemann (Boniface, B. and Cooper, C. 2009) Copyright © 2009 Elsevier Ltd. All rights reserved. Printed with permission from Elsevier; Figure 1.6 from *Worldwide Destinations: The Geography of Travel and Tourism*, Butterworth-Heinemann (Boniface, B. and Cooper, C. 2001) Copyright © 2001 Elsevier Ltd. All rights reserved. Printed with permission from Elsevier; Figure 1.8 from *Worldwide Destinations: The Geography of Travel and Tourism* (Boniface, B. and Cooper, C. 2009) Copyright © 2009 Elsevier Ltd. All rights reserved. Printed with permission from Elsevier; Figure 2.1 from Destination Networks: Four Australian Cases, *Annals of Tourism Research* 35(1), 169–188 (Scott, N, Cooper, C. and Baggio, R. 2008), Copyright © 2007 Elsevier Ltd. All rights reserved. Printed with permission from Elsevier; Figure 2.3 from *The competitive destination: a sustainable tourism perspective* (Ritchie, J.R.B. and Crouch, G.I. 2003) p.63 CAB International, Wallingford, UK, Fig 3.1, Further details available at www.business.latrobe.edu.au/staffhp/gichp/destcomp.htm, Ch.3, A Model of Destination Competitiveness; Figure 2.4 adapted from The concept of a tourist area cycle of evolution, *Canadian Geographer* 24 (1), 5–12 (Butler, R.W. 1980), Copyright © 2008, John Wiley and Sons; Figure 2.5 from New Forest Tourism; Figure 3.1 adapted from *Economic Evaluation of Special Events. A Practitioner's Guide*, Figure 1 (Jago, L .and

Dwyer, L. 2006) p.4, Common Ground, Altona, Victoria; Figure 3.2 adapted from *Economic Evaluation of Special Events. A Practitioner's Guide*, Figure 2 (Jago, L. and Dwyer, L. 2006) p.7, Common Ground, Altona, Victoria; Figure 5.2 from Host perceptions of tourism: A review of the research *Tourism Management* 42, 37–49 (Sharpley, R. 2014), Copyright © 2013 Elsevier Ltd. All rights reserved. Printed with permission from Elsevier; Figure 5.3 from *Tourism: Change, Impacts and Opportunities* (Wall, G. and Mathieson, A. 2006) Pearson Harlow; Figure 6.2 from *Monitoring for a sustainable tourism transition. The challenge of developing and using indicators* (Miller, G. and Twinning Ward, L. 2005) CAB International, Wallingford, UK, p.32, Box 2.5 Muller's Magic Pentagon, Ch.2 Sustainable Tourism; Figure 6.3 adapted from Sustainable tourism as an adaptive paradigm, *Annals of Tourism Research* 24(4), 850–867 (Hunter, C. 1997), Copyright © 1997 Published by Elsevier Ltd. All rights reserved. Printed with permission from Elsevier; Figure 6.5 from *Monitoring for a sustainable tourism transition. The challenge of developing and using indicators* (Miller, G. and Twinning Ward, L. 2005) p.168, CAB International, Wallingford, UK, Fig 7.5, Management response cycle. Adapted from Noon (2003), Ch7 Implementing Monitoring Systems; Figure 7.1 from *Managing Visitor Atractions: New Directions*, 2nd edition, Fyall, A., Garrod, B., Leask, A. and Wanhill, S. (eds) Chapter 1. The Nature and Role of Visitor Attractions (Leask, A 2008) p.1–2, ©2008 with permission from Butterworth-Heinemann; Figure 7.2 from *Managing visitor attractions. New directions*, 2nd edition, Fyall, A., Garrod, B., Leask, A. and Wanhill, S. (eds) Chapter 2: Interpreting the Development of the Visitor Attraction Product (Wanhill, S.) pp.16–35, ©2008 with permission from Butterworth-Heinemann; Figure 7.3 from *Worldwide destinations: the geography of tourism* (Boniface, B. and Cooper, C. 2009) Copyright © 2009 Elsevier Ltd. All rights reserved; Figure 7.4 from Progress in visitor research. Toward more effective management., *Tourism Management*, 31, 155–166 (Leask, A. 2010), Copyright © 2009 Elsevier Ltd. All rights reserved. Printed with permission from Elsevier; Figure 8.1 from *In Search of Hospitality: Theoretical Perspectives and Debates*, Lashley, C. and Morrison, A. (eds) Chapter 2: An Anthropology of Hospitality (Selwyn, T.)

Photograph: Big Ben & Houses of Parliament © Tony Baggett/Fotolia.com pp.18–37, ©2001 with permission from Butterworth-Heinemann; Figure 8.3 from Hospitality management: an introduction, Longman (Knowles, T. 1998); Figure 8.4 from Six senses virtuous circle., http://www.sixsenses.com, Longman; Figure 10.2 from *Worldwide destinations. The geography of travel and tourism*, Elsevier Butterworth Heinemann. (Boniface, B. and Cooper, C. 2009) Copyright © 2009 Elsevier Ltd. All rights reserved; Figure 12.1 from Demand for accommodation, in *Managerial Economics for Hotel Operation* (Wanhill, S.R.C. and Airey, D.W. eds) (Kotas, R. 1980) Surrey University Press; Figure 12.2 from *Tourism: Principles and Practice*, 4ed. (Cooper, C. and Gilbert, D. 2008) p.45, Pearson Education Ltd. Harlow © Chris Cooper, John Fletcher, Alan Fyall, David Gilbert and Stephen Wanhill, 1998; Figure 13.6 from *Tourism Business Frontiers: Consumers, Products, and Industry*, Buhalis, D. and Costa, C. (eds) Chapter 3: New and Emerging Markets (Cooper, C., Scott, N., and Kester, J.) 2005) pp.19–29, ©2006 with permission from Butterworth-Heinemann.

Tables

Table 1.1 from *Recommendations on Tourism Statistics* Madrid: World Tourism Organization/New York: United Nations (UNWTO and UNSTAT,1994) ©UNWTO, 9284401711; Table 4.1 from *Climate change and tourism: responding to global challenges* UNWTO, Madrid (2007) ©UNWTO, 9284401711; Table 4.2 from Environmental auditing for Tourism, *Progress in Recreation and Hospitality Management*, 4, 60–71 (Goodall, B. 1992), Progress in Tourism, Recreation and Hospitality Management by John Wiley & Sons. Reproduced with permission of John Wiley & Sons permission conveyed through Copyright Clearance Center, Inc; Table 5.2 adapted from When enough's enough. The natives are restless in Old Niagara *Heritage Canada*, 2 (2), 26–27 (Doxey, G.V. 1976), This article first appeared in Heritage Canada magazine, 2 (2) 1976 and is reprinted here with the permission of the Heritage Canada Foundation (www.heritagecanada.org); Table 5.3 from © UNWTO, 92844/13/16 from World Tourism Organization (2011), Tourism 2030-Global Overview, UNWTO, Madrid p.34. and World Tourism Organization (2015), UNWTO Tourism Highlights, 2015 Edition- Global Overview, UNWTO, Madrid p.4; Table 6.2 from A framework of approaches to sustainable tourism, *Journal of sustainable tourism* 5(3), 224–233 (Clarke J. 1997), Reprinted with permission of the Taylor and Francis Group, http://www.informaworld.com; Table 6.4 from *Making tourism more sustainable. A guide for policy makers* UNWTO, Madrid (2005) ©UNWTO, 9284401711; Table 6.5 from *Making Tourism More Sustainable. A Guide for Policy Makers*, UNWTO, Madrid (2005) ©UNWTO, 9284401711; Table 6.7 from *Indicators of Sustainable Tourism* UNTWO, Madrid (2004) ©UNWTO, 9284401711; Table 7.1 from *Worldwide destinations: the geography of tourism* (Boniface, B. and Cooper, C. 2009) Copyright © 2009 Elsevier. All rights reserved. Printed with permission from Elsevier; Table 7.2 from *Managing Visitor Attractions. New Directions*, 2nd edition, Fyall, A., Garrod, B., Leask, A. and Wanhill, S. (eds) Chapter 4: Economic Aspects of Developing Theme Parks (Wanhill, S. 2008) pp. 59–79, ©2008 with permission from Butterworth-Heinemann; Table 9.2 from *The Business of Tourism* (Holloway, J.C. and Taylor, N. 2006) © Pearson Education Limited 1983, 2002,2006; Tables 9.3, 9.4 from *The Business of Tourism* (Holloway, J.C. and Taylor, N. 2006) © Pearson Education Limited 1983, 2002, 2006

Text

Extract on page 34 from © UNWTO, 92844/12/16 based on World Tourism Organization (2002), UNWTO Think Tank, 2-4 December 2002, UNWTO, Madrid; Extract on page 45 from © UNWTO, 92844/15/16 from World Tourism Organization (2007), A Practical Guide to Tourism Destination Management, UNWTO, Madrid p.4; Extract on pages 117-118 from © UNWTO, 92844/14/16 from World Tourism Organization (2004), Tourism and Poverty Alleviation - Recommendations for Action, UNWTO, Madrid, p.15.

Photographs

The publisher would like to thank the following for their kind permission to reproduce their photographs:

(Key: b-bottom; c-centre; l-left; r-right; t-top)

123RF.com: Philip Bird 30, Danil Roudenko 221; **Alamy Images:** Athol Pictures 149, Bigred 206, Corbis Super RF 121, dpa picture alliance 41, Elvele Images Ltd 159, Flirt 99, Gavin Hellier 290, Peter Horree 266, Hisham Ibrahim/PhotoV, LatitudeStock 81, Shivang Mehta 86, Melba Photo Agency 5, Newscast 193b, David Noton Photography 54b, RooM the Agency 57, dov makabaw sundry 237, The Photolibrary Wales 310, Pete Titmuss 253, Maximilian Weinzierl 197, Leon Werdinger 238, Yooniq Images 109; **Corbis:** HO / Reuters 323; **Fotolia.com:** Tony Baggett xviii, doethion 77, hstiver 343, jaranjen 146, lunamarina xiv, M.V. Photography 33, sehbaer_nrw 245, sorincolac 305, supermol100 (Classic Paper Header), dan talson 260, Valeriy Lebedev (Mini Case Study Header), viperagp 293, ian woolcock xxi; **Getty Images:** Adie Bush 74b, Dorling Kindersley / Max Alexander 112, hemis.fr / Gillardi Jacques 2, Moment Open / George Pachantouris 127, Namgyal Sherpa / AFP 124; **Shutterstock.com:** bartuchna@yahoo.pl 269, holbox 218, Inu 318, jpatava 38, Patryk Kosmider 170b, musicman 8, Dmitry Naumov 173, Christina Richards 27, siraphat (Major Case Study Header), Vaclav Volrab 69, Charles Zachritz vi

Cover images: *Front:* **Getty Images:** Australian Scenics

Photograph: Padstow Harbour, Cornwall © Ian Woolcock/Fotolia.com

PART 1
TOURISM ESSENTIALS: AN INTRODUCTION

Tourism is both a victim and a vector of many contemporary trends in the world – climate change, for example, will impact severely upon destinations, but it can be argued that tourism is also a partial cause of climate change. In a complex world of constant and unexpected change, it is important to take a disciplined and analytical approach to the teaching and learning of tourism. This is particularly the case when tourism is the focus of so much media attention – newspaper travel supplements, TV programmes and an explosion of travel literature. Tourism, too, is a controversial activity, not just in terms of climate change, but also there are other consequences of tourism for, say, indigenous peoples. Again it is important to provide a balanced view, taking into account the evidence and the burgeoning literature. It is important, too, to recognise that as tourism matures as a subject area there are new approaches to studying and analysing tourism to complement the more traditional ways of thinking. Examples here include the *mobilities paradigm* and the *critical turn in tourism studies*, based upon taking perspectives of cultural studies, feminism, ethics, postmodernism, power/politics and world-making and applying them to tourism (Ateljevic *et al.*, 2010). This adds up to tourism as an exciting subject to study – after all, most of us have experienced tourism and can relate the material in this book to our own experiences.

In this first chapter, we set out to provide a framework for the book and a way of thinking about tourism. The chapter begins with a historical perspective on tourism before introducing the concept of a tourism system. We go on to outline the role of a tourism system in offering a way of thinking about tourism and in providing a framework of knowledge for those of you studying the subject. This framework is particularly important in the twenty-first century when the world is increasingly complex and experiencing rapid and unexpected change caused by both human and natural agents. In addition, tourism has now become a major economic sector in its own right and we use this chapter to demonstrate the scale and significance of tourism. At the same time, we identify some of the issues that are inherent both in the subject area and in the study of tourism. In particular, we emphasise the variety and scope of tourism as an activity and highlight the fact that all elements of the tourism system are interlinked, despite the fact that they have to be artificially isolated for teaching and learning purposes. Finally, we consider the difficulties involved in attempting to define tourism and provide some ideas as to how definitions are evolving.

CHAPTER 1
TOURISM ESSENTIALS

Learning Outcomes

In this chapter, we focus on the concepts, history, terminology and definitions that underpin tourism. We also provide a framework for the study of tourism to guide you through this book. The chapter is designed to provide you with:

- an awareness of the historical background to tourism;

- an understanding of the nature of the tourism system;

- an awareness of the issues associated with the academic and practical study of tourism;

- an appreciation of vexed terminology associated with tourism; and

- a knowledge of basic supply-side and demand-side definitions of tourism.

Introduction

In a world of change, one constant since 1950 has been the sustained growth and resilience of tourism both as an activity and an economic sector. This has been demonstrated despite the 'shocks' of '9/11', the Malaysian Airlines disasters and the earthquake in Nepal in 2015. Despite these more recent crises, it was the events of '9/11' that triggered changes in both consumer behaviour and the tourism sector itself; changes which impacted on travel patterns and operations around the world. Yet, even with these challenges, the World Travel and Tourism Council (WTTC) demonstrated the tremendous scale of the world's tourism sector:

- The travel and tourism industry's percentage of world gross domestic product is 9.0 per cent.
- The world travel and tourism industry supports 266 million jobs (1 in 11 of world jobs).
- The world travel and tourism industry accounts for 6 per cent of the world's exports.
- By 2015 there were over a billion international tourism trips and up to 6 billion domestic trips.

It is clear that tourism is an activity of global importance and significance and a major force in the economy of the world. It is also a sector of contrasts. It has the capacity to impact negatively upon host environments and cultures – the raw materials of many tourism products – but it can also promote peace, help alleviate poverty and spearhead both economic and social development.

→

As the significance and diversity of tourism as an activity has been realised, increased prominence has been given to tourism in United Nations summits such as the 'World Summit on Sustainable Development' in Johannesburg in 2003, when tourism featured for the first time. International mass tourism is at best only 50 years old, and the 'youth' of tourism as an activity – combined with the pace of growth in demand – has given tourism a Cinderella-like existence; we know it is important, but it is not taken seriously. This has created three issues for the sector:

1. As well as demonstrating sustained growth, tourism has been remarkable in its resistance to adverse economic and political conditions. Natural and man-made events, such as the deliberate crashing of the Germanwings plane in 2015, clearly demonstrate the sector's ability to regroup and place emphasis on a new vocabulary, including words like 'safety', 'security', 'risk management', 'crisis' and 'recovery'. Inevitably, though, growth is slowing as the market matures and, as the nature of the tourist and their demands change, the sector will need to be creative in supplying products to satisfy the 'new tourist'.

2. Technology increasingly pervades the tourism sector. From the use of the Internet to book travel and seek information about destinations, through to the use of mobile technology to revolutionise the way that tourism information can be delivered direct to the user *in situ* at the destination, to the innovative role that the Internet of Things and Big Data play in managing and curating the visit to destinations, tourism is ideally placed to take advantage of developments in information technology. But change has come at the price of restructuring the distribution channel in tourism and in changing the nature of jobs in the sector.

3. International organisations support tourism for its contribution to world peace, its ability to deliver on the Sustainable Development Goals – in particular poverty alleviation, the benefits of the intermingling of peoples and cultures, the economic advantages that can ensue, and the fact that tourism is a relatively 'clean' industry. But an important issue is the stubbornly negative image of tourism as a despoiler of destinations, a harbinger of climate change, and even the employment and monetary gains of tourism are seen to be illusory in many destinations. The International Labour Organization (ILO), for example, views tourism jobs as of low quality, arguing that the sector should deliver 'decent work', not just create jobs of low quality. A critical issue, therefore, for all involved in the successful future of tourism, will be to demonstrate that the tourism sector is responsible and worthy of acceptance as a global activity. The WTTC has been an influential lobbyist in this regard (see www.wttc.org). As the representative body of the major companies in the tourism sector, it has led an active campaign to promote the need for the industry to take responsibility for its actions and for close public and private sector coalitions.

All of these points connect to mean that the tourism sector must take responsibility for the consequences of tourism as an activity. This will involve engaging with the big issues of this century – ensuring that tourism whole-heartedly embraces the green economy and reduces its carbon footprint to help alleviate climate change; that tourism does not exacerbate the global issues of food and water security; and that tourism makes a real contribution to poverty alleviation. And of course, despite the relative youth of international mass tourism, other types of tourism have, in fact, a very long history, dating back thousands of years. In the following section we turn to the historical development of tourism.

The History of Tourism

Early Tourism

Most sources point to the Sumerians' development of trade around 4000 BCE as the birth of travel (Walton, 2015). Trade remained the major motivation for travel with the development of vast trading networks during the fifteenth and sixteenth centuries – the Silk Roads being a prime example. Travel was difficult and dangerous, however, and only conducted when necessary. As well as trade, military and administrative purposes were also motivations for early tourism, although religious festivals and pilgrimage were evident too. Travel for pilgrimage is evident in many Asian countries from an early period when people journeyed to the mountains and rivers to visit ancestral gods and spirits (Sofield and Li, 1998). Indeed from the time of the ancient Egyptians, pilgrimages and festivals have taken travellers across borders but tourism, as travel for pleasure, is evident in Egypt from 1500 BCE onward (Casson, 1994). Travel at this time, however, was still disjointed and a difficult undertaking on treks over long distances.

The building of roads during the Roman Empire facilitated a new, faster medium for travel. As a result, leisure travel across Europe gained popularity in Roman times, but after the collapse of the Roman Empire the roads were not maintained and travel once again became difficult and dangerous. Despite this, pilgrimages continued across Europe during the medieval period with travellers crossing regions to visit religious sites. Consequently, as the main sources of reception along the road, churches and monasteries were early sources of hospitality.

The Grand Tour

From the late fifteenth century, the sons of the upper classes were sent to tour abroad as a means of completing their education. The Grand Tour, as it became known, was seen as part of the process of induction into society, as the 'tourists' expanded their knowledge and experience. Over the course of the seventeenth and eighteenth centuries, thousands of Britons, Germans, French and Russians travelled around the continent, principally to France, Italy, Switzerland and Germany. The term 'tourist' was first coined in the late eighteenth century to describe these travellers. The eighteenth and nineteenth centuries saw travel more through the lens of scientific exploration and expedition, transforming the approach to natural history, and scientists travelled across the world. At this time, travel was still very much a privilege of the upper classes, but this soon changed.

The Nineteenth Century

Cooper (2011) states that the Industrial Revolution's impact on technology and work transformed tourism. The revolution in transportation technology opened up leisure travel to greater numbers of people and the emergence of a tourism industry made the process of travelling much more organised. The railway, in Britain and later in Europe and North America, allowed greater access to a destination at greater speed. Thomas Cook's organised trip from Leicester to Loughborough in 1841 saw the start of mass rail travel for pleasure trips. And in North America, roads and then railways were constructed to facilitate travel across the country as the population spread west over the course of the nineteenth century. Sailing ships were replaced by steamships and allowed greater access to the world, not only for trade and scientific exploration but also for leisure. Other developments of the industrial age, such as the opening of the Suez Canal in 1869, also facilitated this movement abroad.

Jet engine – the jet engine transformed travel by increasing the range and speed of flight.
Source: © musicman/Shutterstock.com

The Twentieth and Twenty-first Centuries

The relative peace in Europe in the late nineteenth century meant that these trends in tourism continued, and a growth in travel occurred up until the First World War. In the years after the war, the car emerged as the new technology to dominate tourism. The first half of the twentieth century saw the car emerge as the main form of transport and the construction of highways and motels facilitated this desire for travel. The popularity of the car for leisure travel began in the United States and moved to Europe by the 1930s, but the car remained much more dominant in the United States. The majority of car travel was domestic, challenging the dominance of the train, while the emergence of passenger air travel in the mid-twentieth century saw a dramatic shift away from surface transport for longer trips.

The aeroplane transformed the way people travelled and opened up new regions, cultures and populations to tourism. Initially used for commercial purposes, aeroplanes began taking passengers in the 1920s. Air travel for tourism took off, literally, after the Second World War. The development of the jet engine, which increased the speed and range of aircraft, made international travel more accessible and with greater affluence on both sides of the Atlantic from the 1950s onward, the tourism industry responded to demand for overseas travel by introducing cheap package holidays. This heralded the industrialisation of the industry and the onset of mass tourism in the second half of the century and into the new Millennium, and the types of tourism that we are familiar with today. It is not just the activity of tourism that has gained attention, but also in the last 50 years tourism as a subject in education has emerged. We turn to that topic in the next section.

The Subject of Tourism

As we have seen, in historical terms, tourism activity is a relatively new development and one which has only recently been considered worthy of serious business endeavour or academic study (Fidgeon, 2010). However, as we have also seen, the tourism sector is of sufficient economic importance and its impact upon economies, environments and societies is significant enough for the subject of tourism to deserve serious academic consideration. There is no doubt in our minds that tourism is a subject area or domain of study, but that at the moment it lacks the level of theoretical underpinning that would allow it to become a discipline. Nevertheless, the popularity of tourism as a subject, and the recognition of its importance by governments, has accelerated the study of tourism.

Tourism as a subject is showing signs of maturity with its growing academic community, increasing numbers of journals and textbooks – which are becoming specialised rather than all-embracing – and its measure of professional societies both internationally and within individual countries. We are also seeing a greater confidence in the approaches used to research tourism as the positivist and scientific approaches are augmented with qualitative and more experimental methods. All of these indicators point to the increasing professionalism of the tourism sector (see Airey, 2015).

Nonetheless, the relative youth of tourism as an area of study creates a range of issues not only for the sector in general but for all of us involved in teaching, researching and studying the subject:

- The subject area itself remains bedevilled by conceptual weakness and fuzziness. We are therefore faced with many questions that would be taken as common ground in other subjects (such as finding our way through the maze of terminology related to the type of tourism which is less destructive – green, alternative, responsible, sustainable, eco!). This results in a basic lack of rigour and focus leaving tourism as a subject area open to criticism by others. Franklin and Crang, for example, are unrelenting: 'The rapid growth of tourism has led researchers to simply record and document tourism in a series of case studies, examples and industry-sponsored projects' (2001, p. 6). This highlights the apparent conflict between 'academic' and 'applied' approaches – which is also an unresolved issue.

- The subject encompasses a number of diverse industrial sectors and academic subjects, raising the question for those studying tourism as to whether or not tourism is, in fact, too diverse and chaotic to merit separate consideration as a subject or economic sector. According to Gilbert (1990), what makes tourism difficult to define is the very broad nature of both the concept as well as the need for so many service inputs. Tourism also envelops other sectors and industries and therefore has no clear boundary, due to the expansive spread of activities it covers (Gilbert, 1990, p. 7). In reality the tourism industry consists of a mass of organisations operating in different sectors each of which supplies those activities which are termed tourism. We would argue, of course, that it should warrant a subject and sector in its own right, but that there is a need for a disciplined approach to help alleviate potential sources of confusion for students. It is therefore important in this respect to provide a framework within which to locate these subject approaches and industries, something that we do in this book.

- As if these problems were not sufficient, tourism also suffers from a particularly weak set of data sources – in terms of both comparability and quality – although the UN World Tourism Organization (UNWTO) (www.unwto.org) has made significant progress in this regard.

- Traditional approaches have tended to operationalise and reduce tourism to a set of activities or economic transactions while more recent authors have been critical of this 'reductionism', stressing instead postmodern frameworks which analyse the significance and meaning of tourism to individuals and therefore provide more explanation of the activity of tourism itself.

- Finally, tourism does suffer from an image problem in academic circles. Nonetheless, many are attracted to it as an exciting, vibrant subject and an applied area of economic activity – which we believe that it is. But to be successful, tourism demands very high standards of professionalism, knowledge and application from everyone involved. This is sometimes felt to be in contrast to the image of jet-setting, palm-fringed beaches and a leisure activity.

But there is light at the end of this tunnel. To quote Coles *et al.* (2006), tourism suffers from the difficulties of location 'in a sea of competing academic territoriality and competing constituencies' (p. 294). They suggest that our approach to tourism should be more flexible and fluid, recognising the inputs and value of differing subjects and disciplines to explanation in tourism. This is termed a 'post-disciplinary' approach, and it differs from the earlier ideas of multi- or interdisciplinary approaches to tourism by being a flexible and creative approach that breaks through the parochial boundaries of disciplines (Coles *et al.*, 2006). It is against this background that an innovative movement has developed known as the 'tourism education futures initiative' (TEFI), which we explore in the case study.

Mini Case Study 1.1
Tourism Education Futures?

It can be argued that tourism education is stuck in the twentieth century, with a tired curriculum that is not fit for the twenty-first century tourism environment. Tackling this challenge head on, in 2006 the tourism education futures initiative (TEFI) set out to create a new and contemporary approach to tourism education, rethinking curricula, values and approaches.

According to its website, 'TEFI seeks to be the leading, forward-looking network that inspires, informs and supports tourism educators and students to passionately and courageously transform the world for the better'. It now comprises a worldwide network of tourism academics and industry practitioners who have come together to develop values-based education. TEFI's major work streams include:

- **TEFI values**

    TEFI believes that values-based tourism education delivers quality and is essential in educating future leaders of a sustainable future. TEFI's five educational values are:

    1. stewardship – sustainability, responsibility and service to the community;

    2. knowledge – critical thinking, innovation, creativity and networking;

    3. professionalism – leadership, practicality, services, relevance, timeliness, reflexivity, teamwork and proactivity;

    4. ethics – honesty, transparency and authenticity; and

    5. mutuality – diversity, inclusion equity, humility and collaboration.

- **Teaching and learning**

    This involves facilitation of innovative, values-based learning experiences for students at all levels. It includes evaluation of curriculum and programme planning and dissemination of good practice in tourism education and the imperative to balance liberal and vocational education incorporating humanities and social sciences.

- **Advocacy for tourism as a field of study and employment**

    This involves creating awareness of tourism as a field of study and promoting its value in global citizenship. The work focuses around raising the stature of tourism in academia and industry so the best and brightest people can be attracted to expand the understanding of tourism and contribute to its transformation.

- **Tourism scholarship**

  This involves advancing the scholarship of teaching and learning in tourism and engaging in tourism in higher education policy and practice.

- **Tourism education futures**

  This is a forum for creative, innovative debate about the impact of future socio-economic, political and environmental trends on tourism education and encourages 'blue sky' thinking about higher education and the tourism curriculum. The work here ensures that tourism educators engage in informed debates about the future of tourism and what kind of graduates should be produced to meet future challenges.

- **Tourism and social entrepreneurship**

  This work focuses around exploring the connections between tourism and social entrepreneurship within the curriculum.

DISCUSSION QUESTIONS

1. Consider TEFI's five educational values. How relevant are they to your tourism education and future career?

2. Do you truly believe that tourism education has failed to keep up with the contemporary environment within which tourism operates?

3. List the skills and competences that you believe are needed in a future leader in the tourism sector. Does your course deliver these?

Source:
www.tourismeducationfutures.org

A Tourism System

In response to the issues identified above, we feel that it is important at the outset to provide an organising framework for the study of tourism. There are many ways to do this. Individual disciplines, for example, view the activity of tourism as an application of their own ideas and concepts, and an approach from say, geography or economics could be adopted. An alternative is to take a post-disciplinary approach as noted above. Figure 1.1 shows one such attempt to integrate a variety of subjects and disciplines and to focus upon tourism.

However, in a book of this nature it is impossible to cover the complete range of approaches to tourism. Instead, as an organising framework, we have adopted the model suggested by Leiper in 1979 and updated in 1990 (Figure 1.2). As Figure 1.2 shows, Leiper's model neatly takes into account many of the issues identified above by considering the activity of tourists, allowing industry sectors to be located and incorporating the geographical element which is inherent to all travel. Finally, it places tourism in the context of a range of external environments such as society, politics and economies. There are three basic elements of Leiper's model:

1. tourists;
2. geographical elements; and
3. the tourism sector.

Tourists

The tourist is the actor in this system. Tourism, after all, is a very human experience, enjoyed, anticipated and remembered by many as some of the most important times of their lives. We deal with definitions and classifications of tourists later in this chapter.

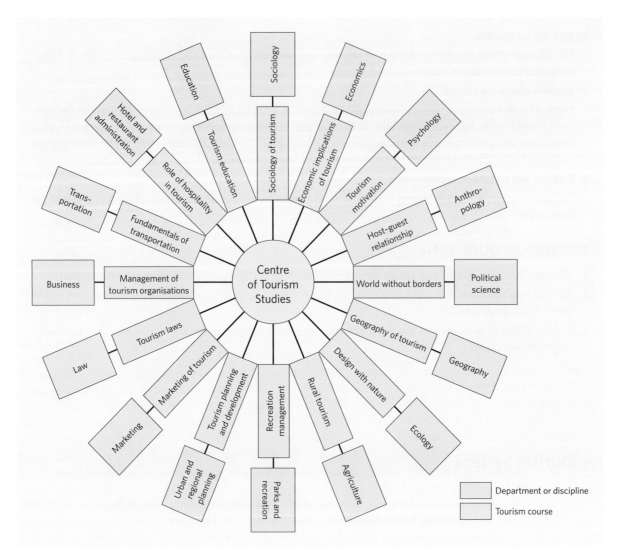

Figure 1.1 A study of tourism and choice of discipline and approach
Source: Jafari and Ritchie, 1981; McIntosh and Goeldner, 1990

Geographical Elements

Leiper outlines three geographical elements in his model as:

1. the traveller-generating region;
2. the tourist destination region; and
3. the transit route region.

The traveller-generating region represents the generating market for tourism and, in a sense, provides the 'push' to stimulate and motivate travel. It is from here that the tourist searches for information, makes the booking and departs.

In many respects, the tourist destination region represents the 'sharp end' of tourism. At the destination, the full consequences of tourism are felt and planning and management strategies are implemented. The destination, too, is the *raison d'être* for tourism, with a range of special places distinguished from the everyday by their cultural, historic or natural significance (Rojek and Urry, 1997). The 'pull' to visit destinations energises the whole

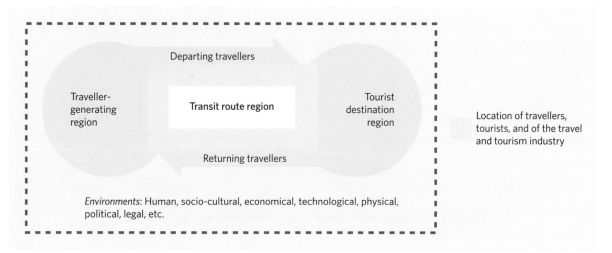

Figure 1.2 A basic tourism system
Source: Leiper, 1990

tourism system and creates demand for travel in the generating region. It is therefore at the destination where the innovations in tourism take place – new products are developed and 'experiences' delivered, making the destination the place 'where the most noticeable and dramatic consequences of the system occur' (Leiper, 1990, p. 23). We analyse the tourist destination in Chapter 2.

The transit route region does not simply represent the short period of travel to reach the destination, but also includes the intermediate places that may be visited en route: 'There is always an interval in a trip when the traveller feels they have left their home region but have not yet arrived . . . [where] they choose to visit' (Leiper, 1990, p. 22). We analyse transport for tourism in Chapter 10.

The Tourism Sector

The third geographical element of Leiper's model is the tourism sector, which we can think of as the range of businesses and organisations involved in delivering the tourism product. The model allows the location of the various industrial sectors to be identified. For example, travel agents and tour operators are mostly found in the traveller-generating region, attractions and the hospitality industry are found in the destination region, and the transport industry is largely represented in the transit route region. We analyse the tourism sector in Part 3 of the book.

Each of the elements of Leiper's tourism system interacts, not only to deliver the tourism product, but also in terms of transactions and impacts and, of course, the differing contexts within which tourism occurs (Figure 1.3). The fact that tourism is also a sector of contrasts is illustrated by examining two major elements of Leiper's model. Demand for tourism in the generating region is inherently volatile, seasonal and irrational. Yet this demand is satisfied by a destination region where supply is fragmented, inflexible and dominated by fixed investment costs – surely a possible recipe for the financial instability of tourism!

The major advantages of Leiper's model are its general applicability and simplicity which provide a useful 'way of thinking' about tourism. Indeed, each of the alternative models that we could consider tend to reveal Leiper's basic elements when they are dissected.

There are also other advantages of this approach:

- It has the ability to incorporate interdisciplinary approaches to tourism because it is not rooted in any particular subject or discipline but instead provides a framework within which disciplinary approaches can be located.

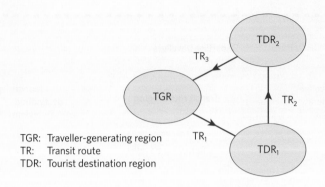

Figure 1.3 Geographical elements in a tourism system with two destinations
Source: Leiper, 1990

- It is possible to use the model at any scale or level of generalisation – from a local resort to the international industry.

- The model demonstrates a highly important principle of tourism studies: that all the elements of tourism are related and interact; that in essence, we are studying a system of customers and suppliers who demand and supply tourism products and services. Inevitably in any textbook or course, Leiper's elements of tourism have to be separated and examined individually, but in reality all are linked and the realisation of their interrelationships provides a true understanding of tourism.

- Finally, the model is infinitely flexible and allows the incorporation of different types of tourism, while at the same time demonstrating their common elements. This shows that the various types of tourism, such as say dark tourism or rural tourism, are simply different blends of the characteristics of Leiper's elements – they are not different tourism systems in themselves. So, for example, ecotourism can be analysed using the model as we show in the mini case study below. Here, we can see that ecotourism does not require a completely new approach, but simply an analysis of each of the particular characteristics of the elements of the ecotourism system.

Mini Case Study 1.2
Types of Tourism: Characteristics of the Elements of the Ecotourism System

We can use Leiper's tourism system to understand how different 'types of tourism' are distinct from each other in terms of the features of the market, the destination and the transit zone.

The distinctive characteristics of each of the elements of the system that make up ecotourism are as follows:

Generating Region

Demand for ecotourism:

- is purposeful;
- is poorly documented;
- desires first-hand experience/contact with nature/culture;
- has the motive to study, admire and/or enjoy nature/culture;

- is tempered by the need to consume tourism responsibly and offset carbon emissions;
- can be segmented in many ways including by level of commitment, level of physical effort, motives; and
- comes from those who are more likely to be well educated, have a higher income and be slightly older than the average tourist.

Destination Region

Destinations for ecotourism:

- are relatively natural areas which are undisturbed and/or uncontaminated;
- have attractions of scenery, flora, fauna and/or indigenous culture;
- allow ecotourism to deliver economic and conservation benefits to the local people, including employment;
- develop ecotourism with a view to conserving/enhancing/maintaining the natural/cultural system;
- apply integrated planning and management techniques;
- apply environmental impact and auditing procedures to all elements of the tourism destination (such as accommodation – a major emitter of carbon, and other facilities);
- attempt to be carbon neutral; and
- encourage local ownership of facilities.

Transit Zone

Transport for ecotourism:

- should monitor emissions and environmental impacts;
- should be of low impact to the environment in terms of noise, carbon emissions, congestion, fuel consumption and waste;
- should promote the conservation ethic;
- should be used as a management tool;
- should encourage use of public transport;
- should encourage the use of locally owned transport companies; but
- reaching a long-haul ecotourism destination may consume large amounts of aircraft fuel and be more damaging to the environment than the tourist realises, and thus defeat the purpose of the trip itself.

DISCUSSION QUESTIONS

1. Do the principles of ecotourism apply equally to each of the elements of the ecotourism system?
2. Should ecotourists be true to their beliefs and offset their carbon emissions when travelling?
3. There is a view that ecotourism is used by developers as a 'soft' medium to access valued natural resources to 'pave the way' for more aggressive tourism development – do you agree with this view?

Definitions of Tourism

We can see from Leiper's model that tourism may be thought of as a whole range of individuals, businesses, organisations and places which combine in some way to deliver a travel experience. Tourism is a multidimensional, multifaceted activity, which touches many lives and many different economic activities. Not surprisingly, tourism has therefore proved difficult to define – while the word 'tourist' first appeared in the English language in the early 1800s, more than two centuries later definitions remain problematic. In some senses, this is a reflection of the complexity and diversity of tourism, but it is also indicative of its youth as a field of study.

As a result, it is difficult to find an underpinning coherence of approach in defining tourism, aside from the need to characterise the 'otherness' of tourism from similar activities such as migration. Yet even this approach is under criticism as both geographers and sociologists increasingly believe that tourism is but one form of 'mobility' and should not be separated out (we examine this in more detail in Major Case Study 1.1 at the end of this chapter). In other words, definitions of tourism have been created to cater for particular needs and situations.

Despite these difficulties, it is vital to attempt definitions of tourism, not only to provide a sense of credibility and ownership for those involved, to justify investment in tourism and tourism education, but also for the practical considerations of both measurement and legislation. Definitions of tourism can be thought of as either:

- demand-side definitions; or
- supply-side definitions.

Tourism definitions are unusual in that, until the 1990s, they were being driven more by demand-side than supply-side considerations. Some writers find this surprising: 'Defining tourism in terms of the motivations or other characteristics of travellers would be like trying to define the healthcare professions by describing a sick person' (Smith, 1989, p. 33). The UNWTO provides the stimulus for developing the measurement of tourism from both a demand and supply side perspective for 'furthering knowledge of the sector, monitoring progress, evaluating impact, promoting results-focused management, and highlighting strategic issues for policy objectives' (www.unwto.org). The benchmark was reached with publication of international recommendations for tourism statistics in 2008. The 1990s saw major landmarks towards this benchmark:

1. **Demand-side definitions.** The UNWTO's 1991 International Conference on Travel and Tourism Statistics was called to tidy up definitions, terminology and measurement issues. The recommendations of this conference were adopted by the United Nations Statistical Commission (UNSTAT) and published as *Recommendations on Tourism Statistics* (WTO and UNSTAT, 1994). The conference and the subsequent publications represent the official 'technical' definitions of tourism.

2. **Supply-side definitions.** In March 2000, the United Nations Statistical Commission approved the adoption of tourism satellite accounts as the method of measuring the economic sector of tourism.

Demand-side Definitions of Tourism

Demand-side definitions have evolved firstly by attempting to encapsulate the idea of tourism into 'conceptual' definitions and secondly through the development of 'technical' definitions for measurement and legal purposes.

From a conceptual point of view, we can think of tourism as: 'The activities of persons travelling to and staying in places outside their usual environment for not more than one consecutive year for leisure, business and other purposes' (WTO and UNSTAT, 1994). While this is not a strict technical definition, it does convey the essential nature of tourism, i.e.:

- Tourism arises out of a movement of people to, and their stay in, various places, or destinations.
- There are two elements in tourism – the journey to the destination and the stay (including activities) at the destination.
- The journey and stay take place outside the usual environment or normal place of residence and work so that tourism gives rise to activities that are distinct from the resident and working populations of the places through which they travel and stay.
- The movement to destinations is temporary and short term in character – the intention is to return within a few days, weeks or months.
- Destinations are visited for purposes other than taking up permanent residence or employment in the places visited.

However, these 'conceptual' approaches do not allow precision for measurement or legislative purposes. As a result, 'technical' definitions were developed by the UNWTO in an attempt to isolate tourism trips from other forms of travel for statistical purposes (Figure 1.4). These 'technical' definitions demand that an activity has to pass certain 'tests' before it counts as tourism. Such tests include the following:

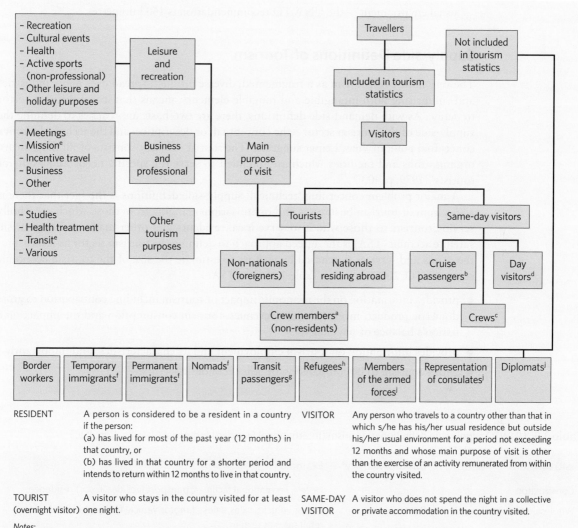

RESIDENT — A person is considered to be a resident in a country if the person:
(a) has lived for most of the past year (12 months) in that country, or
(b) has lived in that country for a shorter period and intends to return within 12 months to live in that country.

VISITOR — Any person who travels to a country other than that in which s/he has his/her usual residence but outside his/her usual environment for a period not exceeding 12 months and whose main purpose of visit is other than the exercise of an activity remunerated from within the country visited.

TOURIST (overnight visitor) — A visitor who stays in the country visited for at least one night.

SAME-DAY VISITOR — A visitor who does not spend the night in a collective or private accommodation in the country visited.

Notes:

[a] Foreign air or ship crews docked or in lay over and who use the accommodation establishments of the country visited.

[b] Persons who arrive in a country aboard cruise ships (as defined by the International Maritime Organization, 1965) and who spend the night aboard ship even when disembarking for one or more day visits.

[c] Crews who are not residents of the country visited and who stay in the country for the day.

[d] Visitors who arrive and leave the same day for leisure and recreation, business and professional or other tourism purposes including transit day visitors en route to or from their destination countries.

[e] Overnight visitors en route from their destination countries.

[f] As defined by the United Nations in the *Recommendations on Statistics of International Migration*, 1980.

[g] Who do not leave the transit area of the airport or the port, including transfer between airports or ports.

[h] As defined by the United Nations High Commissioner for Refugees, 1967.

[j] When they travel from their country of origin to the duty station and vice versa (including household servants and dependants and dependants accompanying or joining them).

Figure 1.4 Classification of international visitors
Source: UNWTO, 2000

- Minimum length of stay – one night (visitors who do not stay overnight are termed **same-day visitors** or excursionists – and are notoriously difficult to measure).

- Maximum length of stay – one year, which is easy to control through immigration and also, as a consequence of being in a destination for more than one year, the behaviour of a 'visitor' may change to reflect that of locals.

- Strict 'purpose of visit' categories, including leisure, business and common interest.

- A distance consideration is sometimes included on the grounds of delineating the term 'usual environment' – the UNWTO recommendation is 160 kilometres.

Supply-side Definitions of Tourism

The very nature of tourism as a fragmented, diverse product, spread over many industries and comprising both intangible and tangible elements, means that it is a difficult sector to define. As with demand-side definitions, there are two basic approaches to defining the supply-side of the tourism sector – the conceptual, or descriptive, and the technical. From a conceptual point of view, Leiper suggests: 'The tourist industry consists of all those firms, organisations and facilities which are intended to serve the specific needs and wants of tourists' (1979, p. 400).

A major problem concerning 'technical' supply-side definitions is the fact that there is a spectrum of tourism businesses and organisations, ranging from those which are wholly serving tourists to those who also serve local residents and other markets. The tourism satellite account (TSA) is the agreed approach to defining the tourism sector as it measures the goods and services purchased by visitors to estimate the size of the tourism economic sector (WTO, 2001) (see also Table 1.1). The TSA:

- provides information on the economic impact of tourism including contribution to gross domestic product, investment, tax revenues, tourism consumption and the impact on a nation's balance of payments;

- provides information on tourism employment and its characteristics; and importantly

- allows tourism to be compared with other economic sectors.

Table 1.1 UNWTO supply side definition of tourism (International Standard Industrial Classification, ISIC)

ISIC divisions	Business activity[a]	Example
Construction	T	Hotels, recreational facilities, transport facilities, resort residence.
Wholesale and retail	P	Motor vehicles sales, sales of motor vehicle fuels, retail food sales, retail sales of textiles.
	T	Retail sales of travel accessories, souvenir sales, etc.
Hotels and restaurants	P	Fast food restaurants, food.
	T	Hotels, camping sites.
Transport, storage and communications	P	Transport via railways, chauffeured vehicles, inland water transport.
	T	Inter-urban rail, airlines, special rail tour service, long-distance bus services, cruise ships.
Financial intermediation	P	Exchange of currencies, life insurance, credit cards.
	T	Travel insurance.
Real estate, renting and business activities	P	Buying or selling of leased property, letting or owning of leased property.
	T	Rental of ski equipment, letting of owned tourism property.

Table 1.1 (*continued*)

ISIC divisions	Business activity[a]	Example
Public administration	P	Translation services, customs administration, fishing regulation, foreign affairs, border guards.
	T	Tourism administration, information bureaux, visa issuance, regulation of private transport.
Education	P	Adult education, driving schools, flying schools, boating instruction.
	T	Hotel schools, tourism education programmes, recreation and park service schools, tourist instruction.
Other community	P	Swimming, scuba instruction, flying instruction, boating instruction, motion picture entertainment.
	T	Visitor bureaux, travel clubs, travel unions.
Extra-territorial organisations	P	OECD, World Bank, IMF, ASEAN.
	T	International tourism bodies.

[a] P = part involvement with tourism: T = totally dedicated to tourism.
Source: UNWTO and UNSTAT, 1994

It is clear from this section that the tourism sector has been late in recognising the importance of supply-side definitions. However, the benefits of doing so are clear. The TSA allows tourism to be compared with other economic sectors, delivers important data for planning and policy, as well as providing an important conceptual framework for studying and researching tourism.

This section has shown that official definitions of tourism have evolved over time and have proved difficult to agree. As we see in the final case study in this chapter, an alternative view of tourism has emerged from the academic community and has the potential to confuse matters even further!

Spatial Interaction Between the Components of the Tourism System: Tourist Flows

The consideration of tourist flows between the generating region and the destination is fundamental to the study of tourism and critical for managing the environmental and social impacts of tourism, securing the commercial viability of the tourism industry and for planning new developments. We can detect regular patterns of tourist flows as they do not occur randomly but follow certain rules, influenced by a variety of 'push' and 'pull' factors:

- **Push factors** are mainly concerned with the stage of economic development in the generating area and will include such factors as levels of affluence, mobility, and holiday entitlement. An advanced stage of economic development will give the population the means to engage in tourism whilst an unfavourable climate will also provide a strong impetus to travel.

- **Pull factors** include accessibility, and the attractions and amenities of the destination area. The relative cost of the visit is also important, as is the effectiveness of marketing and promotion by the destination.

Tourist flows are complex and are influenced by a wide variety of interrelated variables. A number of attempts have been made to explain the factors that affect tourist flows and to provide rules governing the magnitude of flows between regions. An early attempt by

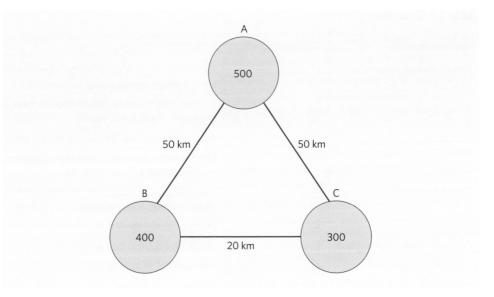

Figure 1.5 The gravity model
Source: Boniface and Cooper, 2009

Williams and Zelinsky (1970) selected 14 countries that had relatively stable tourist flows over several years and which accounted for the bulk of the world's tourist traffic. They identified the following factors:

● distances between countries (the greater the distance, the smaller the volume of flow);

● international connectivity (shared business or cultural ties between countries); and

● the general attractiveness of one country for another.

The 'gravity model' is another way of explaining tourist flows (see Figure 1.5). Push and pull factors generate flows, and the larger the mass (population) of country 'A' or country 'B', the greater the flow between them. The other contributing factor, known as the friction of distance, refers to the cost in time and money of longer journeys, and this acts to restrain flows between the country of origin and more distant destinations.

Classic Paper
Tribe, J. (1997) The indiscipline of tourism, *Annals of Tourism Research* **24(3), 638–657**

John Tribe's classic paper provides valuable insights into the nature of tourism as a subject and how tourism knowledge is created. The paper examines a range of issues, including whether tourism is a discipline or a science, the type of knowledge that exists in tourism and the implications of the very name 'tourism' as unlike, say, physics; it also represents a common activity. The paper begins by stating that tourism is 'conscious of its youthfulness and thus potential lack of intellectual credibility' (p. 638) and goes on to explain that epistemology encourages a systematic review of tourism knowledge and also helps to map the boundaries of the subject.

Tribe says that tourism can be thought of in three ways: (i) as an activity engaged in by people; (ii) as an area of academic interest; and, finally, (iii) as an area of education and training. These multiple perspectives lead to difficulties in defining tourism, as noted in this chapter. Definitions of the subject increasingly draw on business and management viewpoints whilst others come from psychology or behavioural dimensions. Tribe states the following as a definition of tourism:

'The sum of phenomena and relationships arising from the interaction in generating and host regions, of tourists business suppliers, governments communities and environments' (p. 641).

The paper goes on to explain that tourism fails the test of being a discipline due to its lack of theory, as well as not having a coherent knowledge framework or a strong network of academic concepts. Similarly, it fails the test of a 'science' partly because it, rightly, does not confine its research to the scientific method. Tourism can, however, be thought of as a 'field of study' by concentrating on particular phenomena and bringing various disciplines and subject perspectives to bear upon those phenomena.

Tribe's model of the types of knowledge that make up the field of tourism is one of the important contributions of the paper. He thinks of tourism knowledge as:

TF1 – knowledge focused around tourism business studies; and
TF2 – knowledge focused around environmental impacts, tourism perceptions, carrying capacity and social impacts.

Both of these combine to create tourism knowledge itself (TF). He goes on to outline two main ways of generating tourism knowledge:

mode 1 – primarily academic research originating in higher education; and
mode 2 – applied knowledge originating from government industry and other non-academic organisations.

At the time of working (the late 1990s) he felt that mode 2 was economically increasingly important and helped to promote the TF1 part of tourism knowledge, which he felt was becoming dominant.

The paper concludes with a number of observations, notably that tourism is a rather messy subject area, not characterised by a discipline, but rather the 'indiscipline' of the title. Tribe feels that tourism should not be concerned whether it is a discipline or not but instead should celebrate its diversity.

Interrelationships and Classifications

Not only are the elements of the tourism system all interlinked, but also we can see that tourism has close relationships with other activities and concepts. It is therefore a mistake to consider tourism in isolation from these other related activities, as the mobilities case at the end of this chapter demonstrates. For example, most tourism throughout the world is a leisure activity and as such it is important to locate tourism in the spectrum of leisure activities (Figure 1.6). Let us take 'leisure' as an example of one activity to which tourism is related.

Although the Latin translation of leisure literally means 'to be free', defining leisure is, if anything, more problematic than defining tourism. In essence, leisure can be thought of as a combined measure of time and attitude of mind to create periods of time when other obligations are at a minimum. Recreation can be thought of as the pursuits engaged in during leisure time, and an activity spectrum can be identified with, at one end of the scale, recreation around the home, through to tourism, at the other end, where an overnight stay is involved.

Although same-day visits or excursions are a common recreational activity, for tourism to occur, leisure time has to be blocked together to allow a stay away from home. Traditionally, these blocks of leisure time were taken as paid holiday entitlement, though innovations such as flexi-time and three-day weekends have also facilitated tourism.

Tourists

While all-embracing definitions of tourism and the tourist are desirable, in practice tourists represent a heterogeneous, not a homogeneous, group with different personalities, demographics and experiences. We can classify tourists in four basic ways which relate to the nature of their trip:

1. A basic distinction can be made between domestic and international tourists, although this distinction is blurring in many parts of the world (for example, in the European Union). Domestic tourism refers to travel by residents within their country of residence.

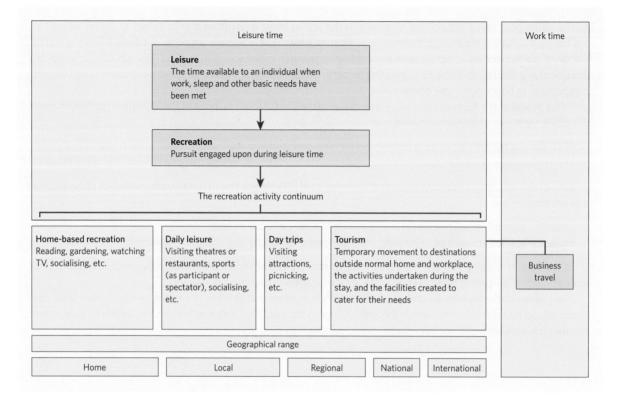

Figure 1.6 Leisure, recreation and tourism
Source: Boniface and Cooper, 2001

There are rarely currency, language or visa implications, and domestic tourism is more difficult to measure than international tourism. As a consequence, domestic tourism has received little attention. In contrast, international tourism involves travel outside the country of residence and there may well be currency, language and visa implications.

2. The type of travel arrangements purchased, such as:
   - an **inclusive tour** where two or more components of the trip are purchased together and one price is paid;
   - **independent travel** arrangements where the traveller purchases the various elements of the trip separately; and
   - **tailor-made travel,** which is a combination of the two and increasingly common due to the use of the Internet to purchase travel.

3. Distance travelled, which is used to make the distinction between long-haul tourism (generally taken to mean travel over a distance of at least 3000 kilometres), and short-haul or medium-haul tourism (involving shorter journeys). This is important in terms of marketing and aircraft operations (and has implications for carbon emissions). Because of their geographical location, Australians and North Americans are more likely to be long-haul tourists than their counterparts in Europe.

4. Tourists can also be classified by 'purpose of visit category'. Conventionally, three categories are used:

   - leisure and recreation – including holiday, sports and cultural tourism and visiting friends and relatives (VFR);
   - other tourism purposes – including study and health tourism; and
   - business and professional – including meetings, conferences, missions, incentive and business tourism.

Not only are these categories used for statistical purposes, they are also useful for the marketing of tourism. Consider, for example, Figure 1.7 where we demonstrate the flexibility of travel for each of the categories from the point of view of airline fare pricing and validity.

There are many other ways to classify tourists. These range from simple demographic and trip classifications, through to their lifestyles and personalities, to their perception of risk and familiarity and postmodern interpretations of consumers and commodities. However, one approach with increasing relevance to contemporary tourism is to classify tourists according to their level and type of interaction with the destination.

Classifications of tourists that adopt this approach commonly place mass tourism at one extreme and some type of alternative, small-scale tourism at the other with a variety of classes in between. It is then argued that mass tourism has a major impact upon the destination because of the sheer scale of the industry and the nature of the consumer. On the other hand, small-scale, alternative types of tourism are said to have a much reduced impact upon the destination, not only because of the type of consumer involved but also because they will shun the travel trade and stay in local pensions or with families. It is argued, then, that the impact of this type of tourism is less disruptive than for mass tourism.

However, some commentators have oversimplified the complex relationship between the consumption and development of tourism resources. This is particularly true of the so-called 'alternative' tourism movement, which is lauded by some as a solution to the ills of mass tourism. Indeed, the tenor of much of the writing about alternative tourism is that any alternative tourism scheme is good whilst all mass tourism is bad. There is, of course, a case for alternative tourism, but only as another type of tourism in the spectrum. It can never be an alternative to mass tourism, nor can it solve all the problems of tourism (Archer *et al.*, 2004). Indeed, 'enlightened mass tourism' may now be the way forward, combining large volumes of tourists, but who have sympathy for, and understanding of, the destination.

These issues, and the fallacy of lauding 'alternative' tourism as a literal alternative to mass tourism, come into clear focus when examined against the frameworks of analysis developed in this book. For example, only by matching appropriate types of visitor to particular types of destination will truly sustainable tourism development be achieved. This leads us to consider the fact that the configuration of the components of Leiper's tourism system combine to create a wide variety of different types of tourism. These types of tourism are created by an interaction with the type of destination and the market. Here, the nature of the destination influences the other components of the tourism system,

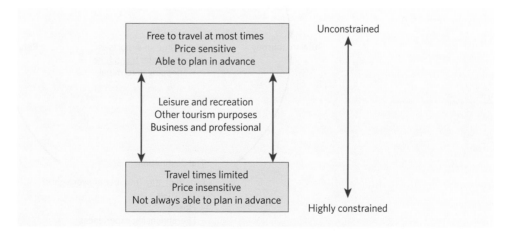

Figure 1.7 Airline pricing and purpose of visit categories

namely the market with its particular motivations to travel, and the means of transport used. Thus we can distinguish many types of tourism including heritage, cultural, urban, rural, eco- and nature-based tourism.

The Tourist Experience

All of the types of tourism noted above are effectively 'experiences'. In analysing tourism, it is easy to forget the tourist as an individual and the extent to which travel and recreation satisfy the need for self-fulfilment through experiences. Tourism is very much a part of the 'experience economy' and the design, staging, marketing and evaluation of the experience has become an important part of tourism product design (Pine and Gilmore, 1999). Every tourism trip can be thought of as an experience with a series of stages:

1. The **anticipation phase** takes place before the trip and involves perceptions and expectations of the destinations as the tourist embarks on making their travel decision.

2. In the **realisation phase** the destination experience is the goal of the trip and is combined with both the outward and return journeys as part of the total experience (Figure 1.8). It is here that the tourist can instantly communicate their impressions of the experience to the world, for instance through blogs or twitter (www.twitter.com).

3. In the **recollection phase** after the trip, the extent to which the quality of these experiences met expectations will influence future travel decisions.

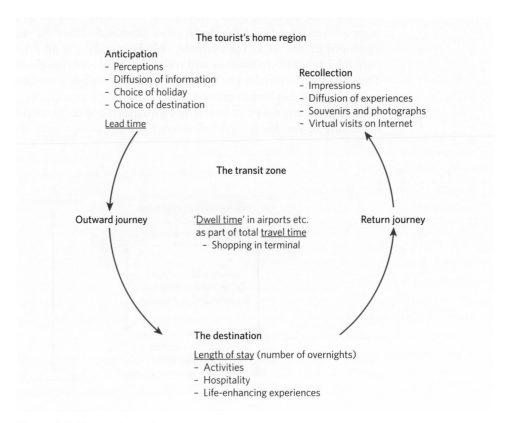

Figure 1.8 The travel experience
Source: Boniface and Cooper, 2009

SUMMARY

Although tourism has long historical roots, mass tourism is a relatively recent activity. As a result, while it has experienced unprecedented growth rates in the past four decades, the study of tourism inevitably lacks the maturity of other subject areas and disciplines. This lack of maturity is manifested in many ways, not least the lack of agreement as to what actually constitutes tourism activity on both the demand and supply side. Nevertheless, the economic importance of tourism has guaranteed increased governmental and international attention. Accompanying this has not only been a growing recognition of the significance and importance of tourism and the need to be able to define and measure all aspects of it, but also a need for the sustainable development and management of tourism. Of course, recent natural and man-made events have checked the inexorable growth of tourism, but overall the sector has demonstrated its resilience to such setbacks.

This introduction provides the basic underpinning framework for the remainder of this book, offering contemporary views on important tourism-related definitions, acquainting the reader with the fundamentals of the history of tourism, the dynamics of the tourism system and how they conspire to create different types of tourism. We believe that in a rapidly changing world it is important to have enduring organising frameworks within which to locate changing practices, world events and their implications for tourism and future trends which will impact on how tourism operates.

Discussion Questions

1. Draft a justification for the introduction of a new tourism programme at your educational institution.
2. It has been suggested that tourism is a fragmented sector in search of an industry. Discuss this assertion.
3. Design a PowerPoint presentation outlining the role of transport in the history of tourism since 1840.
4. In groups, design a table describing as many forms of mobility as you can think of – for example commuting, migration, day-trips. In a second column, identify with reasons those that can be thought of as tourism and those that cannot.
5. Discuss the view that responsible tourism can never be a replacement for mass tourism.

Annotated Further Reading

1. Fidgeon, P.R. (2010) Tourism education and curriculum design: a time for consolidation and review?, *Tourism Management* **31**, 699–723.
   Refreshingly original and interesting take on contemporary tourism education.
2. Goeldner, C.R. and Brent Ritchie, J.R. (2011). *Tourism: Principles, Practices, Philosophies*, 12th edn, John Wiley & Sons, Hoboken, NJ.
   A comprehensive textbook with a strong North American flavour.
3. Hannam, K. and Knox, D. (2010) *Understanding Tourism: A Critical Introduction*, Sage, London.
   A refreshing new approach to tourism.
4. Jafari, J. (2001) *The Encyclopedia of Tourism*, Routledge, London.
   A comprehensive volume with definitive statements on every tourism term written by the leading expert in each field.

5. Lew, A.L., Hall, C.M. and Williams, A.M. (eds) (2014) *The Wiley Blackwell Companion to Tourism,* Wiley, Chichester.
   An excellent and thorough tourism handbook.

6. Page, S. and Connell, J. (2014) *Tourism: A Modern Synthesis,* Cengage Learning, Andover.
   A well-respected and thorough contemporary tourism text.

7. Urry, J. (2000) *Sociology Beyond Societies: Mobilities for the Twenty-first Century,* Routledge, London.
   A refreshingly different approach, focusing on the concept of mobilities and tourism.

8. www.unwto.org
   An all-embracing website providing the official United Nations' view on tourism issues such as pro-poor tourism and providing definitions, definitive statistics and approaches to tourism.

9. www.wttc.org
   A comprehensive website from the private sector's representative body for tourism, with up-to-date statistics and reports on the tourism industry and its contribution to economies.

10. Walton, J.K. (2015) Tourism and history, pp. 31–56 in Cooper, C. (ed.) *Contemporary Tourism Reviews, Volume 1,* Goodfellow, Oxford.
    A state-of-the-art review of tourism history, specialising in the more recent history of tourism.

References Cited

Airey, D. (2015) 40 years of tourism studies – a remarkable story, *Tourism Recreation Research* **48**(1), 6–15.

Archer, B.H., Cooper, C.P. and Ruhanen, L (2004) The positive and negative aspects of tourism', pp. 79–102 in Theobold, W.F. (ed.), *Global Tourism,* Elsevier Butterworth Heinemann, Oxford.

Ateljevic, I., Morgan, N. and Pritchard, A. (2010) *Critical Turn in Tourism Studies: Innovative Research Methodologies,* Routledge, London.

Boniface, B. and Cooper, C. (2009) *Worldwide Destinations: The Geography of Travel and Tourism,* Heinemann, London.

Casson, L. (1994) *Travel in the Ancient World,* JHU Press, Baltimore, OH.

Coles, T., Hall, C.M. and Duval, D.T. (2006) Tourism and post-disciplinary enquiry, *Current Issues in Tourism* **9**(4–5), 293–319.

Cooper, R. (2011) Tourism, pp. 2519–2524 in *The Berkshire Encyclopedia of World History,* Berkshire Publishing, Great Barrington, MA

Fidgeon, P.R. (2010) Tourism education and curriculum design: a time for consolidation and review?, *Tourism Management* **31**, 699–723.

Franklin, A. and Crang, M. (2001) The trouble with tourism and travel theory, *Tourism Studies* **1**(1), 5–22.

Gilbert, D. (1990) Conceptual issues in the meaning of tourism, pp. 4–27 in Cooper, C. (ed.), *Progress in Tourism, Recreation and Hospitality Management* , Belhaven Press, London.

Jafari, J. and Ritchie, J.R.B. (1981) Towards a framework for tourism education, *Annals of Tourism Research* **8**(1), 13–34.

Leiper, N. (1979) The framework of tourism, *Annals of Tourism Research* **6**(4), 390–407.

Leiper, N. (1990) *Tourism Systems,* Massey University Department of Management Systems Occasional Paper 2, Auckland.

McIntosh, R.W. and Goeldner, C.R. (1990) *Tourism: Principles, Practices, Philosophies*, Wiley, New York.

Pine, J. and Gilmore, J. (1999) *The Experience Economy*, University of Harvard Press, Harvard.

Rojek, C. and Urry, J. (1997) *Touring Cultures – Transformations of Travel Theory*, Routledge, London.

Smith, S.L.J. (1989) *Tourism Analysis: A Handbook*, Longman, Harlow.

Sofield, T. and Li, S. (1998) Tourism development and cultural policies in China. *Annals of Tourism Research* **25**(2), 362–392.

Williams, A. and Zelinsky, W. (1970) On some patterns of international tourism flows, *Economic Geography* **46**(4), 549–567.

WTO (2000) *Data Collection and Analysis for Tourism Management, Marketing and Planning*, World Trade Organization, Madrid.

WTO (2001) *Basic Concepts of the Tourism Satellite Account (TSA)*, World Trade Organization, Madrid.

WTO and UNSTAT (1994) *Recommendations on Tourism Statistics*, World Trade Organization, Madrid and United Nations, New York.

Major Case Study 1.1
Tourism and Mobilities – The End of Tourism as we Know it?

An eco-lodge.
Source: © Christina Richards/Shutterstock.com

The social sciences are rediscovering tourism as an area for research by combining social and spatial approaches into a new 'mobilities' approach. This approach challenges the traditional approach taken by tourism academics. Mobilities views tourism as but one form of 'mobility', located within a spectrum ranging from permanent migration to daily shopping where tourism is rethought as a form of 'voluntary temporary mobility in relation to home'. In other words, the mobilities approach views tourism as one dimension of our 'connections' with the world ranging across many different localities. The key message from the idea of tourism 'as a form of mobility' is that tourism is no longer treated as a distinct and special activity, but simply one that is a part of a range of other activities in society.

Larsen *et al.* (2007) argue that the world in the twenty-first century is a highly mobile one and, because tourism is relatively inexpensive and convenient, it blends with other forms of mobility and connections. The reason that this way of thinking has emerged is partly due to 'space–time compression' – the fact that with transport and communication technology it is possible to visit distant places for a day. In Europe, for example, it is perfectly possible to visit Paris for lunch from the UK. This means that we can think of the idea of tourism being part of a 'leisure mobility spectrum' ranging from daily leisure around the home through to tourism where an overnight stay is taken. Here we can see that what may initially be a tourism-related mobility – travelling to and from a second home, for example, may eventually become retirement migration. This does though beg the question as to just how 'new' this thinking is, as there is a long tradition of viewing tourism as part of the 'leisure activity spectrum'.

The Issues

The mobilities approach creates a number of issues for tourism:

- Firstly, the approach foregrounds movement and how we understand the underlying processes driving patterns of tourism movement. These movements are now massive in scale in terms of people, capital and labour, and can be viewed as complex constellations of mobility – multilayered and multi-scaled. The key question, however, is to understand and explain what influences these movements, from micro personal resources, to macro geopolitics.

- Secondly, mobilities blur the distinction between home, work and tourist destinations; and between differing types of traveller – whether they are commuters, shoppers or migrants. This makes reconciling the 'mobilities' approach with drawing up 'definitions' of tourism problematic – particularly when we go back to the definitions of tourism designed by the UNWTO. The UNWTO's definitions see tourism as a distinct activity, taking place away from home and for a period of more than 24 hours. Of course, the formal definitions do now recognise the day trip as an activity, but there is no recognition of the 'spectrum of mobilities' that tourism may embrace, and there is a rigid exclusion of certain types of mobile populations such as migrants, refugees and travellers. So, whilst this chapter has argued the importance of discipline and precision in defining tourism, the mobilities approach takes a more vague and 'fuzzy' stance.

- Thirdly, the approach begs the question as to whether tourism as a subject of study should be a separate and 'exotic' area of study and research (Franklin and Crang, 2001). Instead, there is a case for some elements of tourism explanation to be more closely linked to geography and sociology in the spirit of 'post-disciplinarity' mentioned above. In fact this is most certainly an advantage for tourism as it brings it in from the academic fringes to more be a more mainstream field. The mobilities approach, however, takes this one step further because, by viewing tourism as part of a constellation of movement, it denies the extra-ordinariness and special nature of tourism in people's lives.

- But not everyone can be part of this world of movement. To travel involves mustering the personal resources needed and, yet, some argue that the mobilities approach ignores these inequalities. Only 2 or 3 per cent of the world's population engage in international tourism, and some that do are 'hypermobile', engaging in many trips each year. The less mobile are an important and valuable research area but neglected in the mobilities approach (Hannam *et al.*, 2014).

- A further important contemporary issue is that of mobilities and technology. Mobile technologies such as smartphones and tablets expand and modify the traditional contours of tourism movement, and we are seeing a convergence of people's physical movement and their digital traces on, say, Facebook.

- The mobilities approach demands new research techniques focused around mapping, tracking and mobile forms of research methods such as ethnography. This raises new issues of the ethics of say tracking a visitor's movement around a theme park – not just in terms of ethics but also their complicity in the process.

- Finally, the approach has to be questioned in terms of whether it contributes to the 'big global issues' of the day, such as climate change, poverty alleviation and sustainability. Does it truly embrace the green economy and low-carbon travel, and encourage a change in consumption behaviour within the mobile population who are travelling and creating mobile places – airports, service stations, railway stations and Internet cafes?

DISCUSSION QUESTIONS

1. Is tourism still a 'special' activity or does the mobilities approach devalue it to being a part of everyday life and expectations?

2. Thinking of your own 'mobility' over the last week, how many trips could be seen as 'leisure related'?

3. Social tourism is about removing the constraints preventing the 'less mobile' from travelling. Draft a list of these constraints and how they may be overcome.

Sources:

Franklin, A. and Crang, M. (2001) The trouble with tourism and travel theory, *Tourism Studies* **1**(1), 5–22.

Hannam, K., Butler, G. and Paris, C.M. (2014) Developments and key issues in tourism mobilities, *Annals of Tourism Research* **44**, 171–185.

Larsen, J., Urry, J. and Axhausen, K.W. (2007) Networks and tourism. mobile social life, *Annals of Tourism Research* **34**(1), 244–262.

PART 2
DESTINATION ESSENTIALS

This part focuses upon the tourism destination as a fundamental unit of analysis for tourism. Not only do destinations, their images and their digital traces attract tourists, motivate the visit and therefore energise the tourism system, but they are also at the sharp end of tourism, at the same time suffering and benefiting from visitation. The richness and variety of destinations is a key driver of the success of tourism and they demonstrate a complex pattern across the world where tourism is attracted to the unique, the exotic and the vulnerable. At the same time, tourism destinations are forever expanding as the pleasure periphery reaches ever more distant and remote locations, including the Polar Regions. They are also increasingly represented through tourists leaving digital traces of their visits and memories via online posts and Facebook becomes the new 'postcard'.

The destination is where the consequences of tourism occur – whether they are positive or negative, and it is therefore the focus for planning and management of tourism, all wrapped into a framework of sustainability. We can think of the destination as a loosely formed network of organisations that deliver the tourist experience. Destinations have many common features, but a key distinction is between the 'attractions', which draw the visit, and the 'support facilities', which are essential for tourism but support rather than draw the visit. Sustainability has become the organising concept for destinations and in this part we show how this is delivered through an understanding of carrying capacity and the techniques of destination management and strategic planning. The sustainable destination is a competitive one and we show the features of competitive destination where we also introduce the idea of destination evolution through the notion of a tourist area life-cycle.

There is no doubt that sustainability has become the organising concept for destinations. It is a deceptively simple concept and one with a long pedigree. Sustainability has grown in response to the view that tourism can be very damaging for destinations unless it is effectively planned and managed. In this part we consider the important economic, environmental, social and cultural consequences of tourism at the destination. Of course, tourism brings many benefits but, as we see, it can also destroy the very resources that attract tourists. Gauging the consequences of tourism is difficult. We often do not have a baseline against which to measure the changes wrought by tourism, and often tourism is a scapegoat for changes that may have occurred anyway, or were caused by other factors. We are also dealing with complex environmental and social systems where the relationships between the various consequences of tourism are only just beginning to be understood. There is no doubt that with concerns for climate change we will move to quadruple bottom line sustainability – environment, the economy and the community with the fourth element being carbon. Indeed, throughout this book we stress the vital need for tourism to embrace the low-carbon economy and wherever possible contribute to reducing climate change.

CHAPTER 2
THE DESTINATION

Learning Outcomes

This chapter considers the destination as a crucial element of the tourism system, outlining the key components of the destination, what makes a destination sustainable and competitive and showing how destinations evolve. The chapter is designed to provide you with:

- an understanding of the destination as the focal point of tourism activity;
- an awareness of the individual features and components of the tourism composite and the contribution of each to the destination product;
- an appreciation of the role of destination management and strategic planning in destination sustainability;
- an understanding of destination competitiveness; and
- an awareness of the tourism area life-cycle.

Photograph: Benidorm, Spain © M.V. Photography/Fotolia.com

Introduction

Globally, the richness and variety of destinations continues to contribute to the success of the tourism sector. The supply of tourism demonstrates a complex pattern across the world because it is located in diverse environments and in differing economic and social contexts. The supply of tourism is also continually expanding as the pleasure periphery reaches ever more distant and remote locations. In this chapter we focus on the tourism destination, which we think of as a loosely bounded network of organisations that deliver the tourism experience. The destination represents the third element of Leiper's tourism system (see Chapter 1), but in many respects the most important one because destinations, their images and their digital traces attract tourists, motivate the visit and therefore energise the whole tourism system. The destination brings together all aspects of tourism – demand, transportation, supply and marketing – in a useful framework and we identify these key elements and their contribution to the destination 'amalgam'. In the chapter we show how the concept of carrying capacity contributes to the sustainable planning and management of the destination and identify the elements that contribute to destination competitiveness. Finally, we show how destinations evolve using the framework of the tourism area life-cycle.

Defining the Destination

Despite the fact that the destination can be considered alongside the tourist as the basic unit of analysis in tourism, defining destinations has generated controversy, with some arguing for a geographical definition, whilst others see it as an idea or a concept that cannot be confined within geographical boundaries. Effectively, the destination is a focal point for the generation and delivery of tourism products and experiences and the implementation of management planning and policy. It provides the facilities and services to meet the needs of the tourist. Destinations are also both tangible as physical spaces, and intangible as they generate images, expectations, digital traces and memories. In an attempt to generate some clarity to the debate, the UNWTO held a think tank in 2002 to establish a definition, although this proved more difficult than they expected. The following definition resulted from the meeting:

> 'A tourism destination is a physical space in which tourists spend at least one overnight. It includes tourism products such as support services and attractions and tourist resources within one day's return travel time. It has physical and administrative boundaries defining its management, images and perceptions defining its market competitiveness. Destinations incorporate various stakeholders often including a host community, and can nest and network to form larger destinations. Destinations can be on any scale, from a whole country, a region, or an island, to a village, town or city, or a self-contained centre' (UNWTO Destination Think Tank, Madrid, December 2002).

This definition is more of an all-encompassing list of destination attributes and already seems rather dated. Contemporary thinking now views destinations as loosely bounded networks of organisations that deliver the tourism experience. This immediately recognises the importance of stakeholders and their governance, relationships, and the fact that destinations can nest within each other – Orlando within Florida for example.

Common Features of Tourist Destinations

While destinations are very varied, we can identify five common features of most destinations:

1. Amalgams.
2. Cultural appraisals.
3. Inseparability: that is, tourism is produced where it is consumed.
4. Multiple use of destinations.
5. Destinations as loosely bounded networks of organisations.

Amalgams

Most destinations comprise a core of the following components – the four As:

1. **Attractions** act to pull the visitor to the destination. They include both natural and man-made attractions as well as events.
2. **Amenities** include accommodation, food and beverage outlets, entertainment, retailing and other services.
3. **Access** includes both local transport around the destination and access to and from the destination (air road and sea), through transport terminals.
4. **Ancillary services** come in the form of local organisations.

Of course, each of these components has to be in place before tourism can occur – accommodation alone, for example, will rarely suffice (except perhaps in the case of iconic luxury hotels such as the Raffles Hotel in Singapore: www.raffles.com). The mix of facilities and services at a destination is therefore known as an amalgam – the complete mix has to be present for it to work and the total tourism experience to be delivered.

This amalgamation of the components of a destination comes together in many different ways, and in many different cultural, economic and environmental contexts to create the range of destinations available. The very fact that the destination is an amalgam has a number of implications. In particular, it is important that the quality of each component of the destination and the delivery of the tourism service at these components is reasonably uniform: a poor restaurant can detract from an otherwise satisfactory experience. This *complementarity* of destination components is difficult to control by destination managers given the fragmented nature of enterprises in tourism. Integration of enterprises by larger organisations (tour operators owning hotels and transport carriers) is one means of such control, but for public-sector tourist boards the problem is a critical one.

Cultural appraisals

Visitors have to consider a destination to be attractive and worth the investment of time and money to visit. Because of this we can think of destinations as cultural appraisals. For example, in the nineteenth century the perception of mountains changed from fearsome places to attractive landscapes, which then became popular tourist destinations. An example of this idea is the desire of tourists to visit hostile environments such as Antarctica. As tastes and fashion change, so they are reflected in the destinations that we patronise. This means that, while new opportunities are always available, there is also a constant threat to established destinations, which may go out of fashion. It is, therefore, vital to maintain the difference between the destination and the tourist's home environment through good design and management, and to avoid the development of uniform tourism landscapes.

Inseparability

Tourism is consumed where it is produced as visitors have to be physically present at a destination to experience tourism. Because tourism, by its very nature is attracted to the unique and the fragile parts of the world, destinations are vulnerable to tourist pressure and may suffer alteration. This is exacerbated by the fact that visitor pressure is often concentrated seasonally in time and at specific popular locations.

Like all services, the destination is perishable in the sense that, if it is not used it is lost – the availability of beds, or attraction tickets cannot be stored in the off-season for sale in the peak. Seasonality is a major problem for many destinations prejudicing profitability and rendering them inefficient in terms of the use of their assets. This is because most elements of a destination have a high ratio of fixed to variable costs and therefore, for a highly seasonal destination, the peak (of, say, two or four months) has to make the majority contribution to fixed costs, which are chargeable for 12 months of the year. For example, for many tourist destinations anything up to 80 per cent of total costs are in physical plant, and construction involves long lead times.

Multiple use

Destinations serve residents and workers throughout the year, but at some times of the year they are also used by day visitors or tourists, away from their normal place of residence and work. This multiple use of destinations means that it is possible to classify enterprises according to whether they depend only upon tourism, only upon residents, or a mix of the two. In fact, only purpose-built destinations (such as theme parks) exist purely to serve the tourist. Most destinations have to share tourism with other uses; indeed, tourists are often the most recent and least respected users. For example, tourism in rural areas is shared with nature conservation, agriculture and forestry. Tourism may therefore become a source of conflict in shared destinations, with open antagonism displayed between tourists and other users. Solutions to this problem involve the careful integration of tourism activities in a variety of ways:

- phasing tourism uses in time;
- zoning tourism uses in space;
- management schemes to reduce tension and conflict by intervening in problem situations;
- involving all stakeholders and understanding their differing needs;
- community-driven tourism planning to ensure that tourism develops in harmony with community wishes;
- publicity campaigns to inform local residents of the benefits of tourism;
- information campaigns and codes of conduct targeted at the tourist.

Mini Case Study 2.1
Destinations as Networks

The fifth common feature of destinations is that we can think of them as loosely articulated networks of organisations. The nature of tourism demands collaboration and partnerships to deliver the product and this happens through the creation of inter-organisational networks. Viewing destinations as networks allows us to visualise their network structures in terms of the positions of the organisations and the relationships between them. In turn, these structures can be measured, calibrated, compared and classified. This involves the use of network analysis to understand how destinations function and allows the structure of destination networks – and their shortcomings and inefficiencies – to be identified.

Destination networks comprise two key elements:

1. Nodes of the network – the destination stakeholders. Destination stakeholders are the persons, groups or organisations with an interest in a destination system. Each organisation has a position on the network – with some central and others more peripheral. An organisation's position on the network determines the degree of power and influence that the organisation has within the network.
2. Relationships between the nodes in terms of flows of money, communication, knowledge or other commodities.

Relationships can be measured in terms of their density, connectivity and intensity of the links. Effectively, network analysis allows us to understand how efficient the network is and if necessary, intervention to say, mend broken links, can make the destination more efficient.

The network shown in Figure 2.1 is for the Gold Coast tourist destination in Queensland, Australia. It shows a structural divide between the Gold Coast and its hinterland areas creating two clusters within the network. These clusters relate to the geography of the Gold Coast as well as to the fact that the main markets for the organisations in these two sub-regions are very distinct. This has led to distinct networks of suppliers for the markets with some overlap, but the separation can be clearly seen, with the Coast being a focus of large accommodation organisations and the major operators in tourism, whilst the hinterland tends to more bed and breakfasts and other SMEs.

Viewing destinations in this way is beneficial because the network structure in terms of size, cohesion and shape influences the performance of the destination in terms of communication and relationships between stakeholders. This means that a destination with an efficient network will have more effective communication between stakeholders allowing for more rapid innovation and facilitating development of a 'smart' or 'learning destination'. The network structure can be influenced by the geography of the destination, or by the structure of the industry and government at the destination as we saw on the Gold Coast.

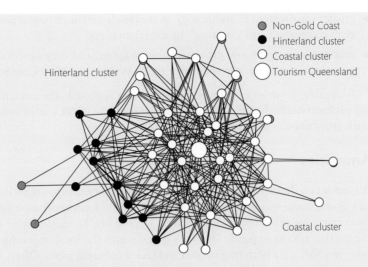

● Non-Gold Coast
● Hinterland cluster
○ Coastal cluster
○ Tourism Queensland

Hinterland cluster

Coastal cluster

Figure 2.1 The Queensland destination network
Source: Scott *et al.*, 2008

DISCUSSION QUESTIONS

1. Examine the network in Figure 2.1 alongside a map of Queensland's Gold Coast. How influential is the geography of the region in determining the structure of the destination's network and relationships between stakeholders?

2. What role should a DMO play in terms of managing networks?

3. What factors will determine whether a destination stakeholder is central or peripheral in a destination network?

Sources:
Scott, N., Baggio, R. and Cooper, C. (2008) *Network Analysis and Tourism: From Theory to Practice*, Channelview, Clevedon.
Scott, N., Cooper, C. and Baggio, R. (2008) Destination networks: four Australian cases, *Annals of Tourism Research* **35**(1), 169–188.
Van der Zee, E. and Vanneste, D. (2015) Tourism networks unravelled: a review of the literature on networks in tourism management studies, *Tourism Management Perspectives* **15**(July), 46–56.

Components of the Destination Amalgam

Before introducing the components of a destination and demonstrating their place in the destination amalgam, we must make the major distinction between attractions and support services. *Attractions* generate the visit to a destination, while *support services* and facilities are also essential for tourism at the destination, but would not exist without attractions. A particular focus of these components is the resort, which we can define as 'a place that attracts large numbers of tourists and that tourism endows with special characteristics, so that revenue produced by tourism plays an important role in its existence'.

Attractions

As we have just observed, it is the attractions of a destination – whether they be artificial features, natural features or events – that provide the initial motivation to visit. Traditionally, attractions have been a neglected sector of the tourist industry owing to their variety and fragmented ownership pattern. However, the sector is now demonstrating maturity with increased professionalism in the management of attractions. This includes a closer match between the market and supply of attractions through:

- the adoption of marketing philosophy;
- better training for attractions personnel;

- greater involvement of technology in the development of new types of attraction and in both co-creating and 'curating' the experience; and

- renewed focus upon and professional management of mega-events, which are emerging as an important sector in their own right, as we see in Mini Case Study 2.2 below.

Alongside this more enlightened management approach, the attractions industry is forming professional bodies and seeking representation in wider tourist industry circles. We deal with attractions in detail in Chapter 7.

Amenities

A tourist at a destination requires a range of amenities, support facilities and services. We can characterise this sector as having a low level of concentration of ownership as these enterprises are often operated by SMEs. On the one hand, this is an advantage because it means that tourist expenditure flows quickly into the local economy. On the other hand, however, SMEs are both fragmented and lack a coherent lobby. Often, too, they lack investment capability and the management/marketing expertise demanded by an increasingly discerning tourism marketplace.

The provision of amenities demonstrates the multi-sectoral nature of tourism supply and the interdependence of the various sectors. For example, the supply of many facilities and services at a resort depends upon the number of bed spaces available; that is, the number of tourists who will visit. For example, provision of around 1000 beds will support up to six basic retail outlets, while 4000 beds will support specialist outlets such as hairdressers. Similar ratios can be calculated for restaurants, car parking or entertainment.

Second World War concentration camp – 'dark tourism' has created destinations from sinister places.
Source: © jpatava/Shutterstock.com

Accommodation, food and beverage

The accommodation/food and beverage sector of the destination not only provides physical shelter and sustenance, but also creates the general feeling of welcome and a lasting impression of the local cuisine and produce. Traditionally dominated by SMEs, the accommodation sector usually offers a mix of type of establishment, and it is important for destinations to adapt and change this mix to meet market aspirations. In some resorts, for example, there is a movement towards flexible forms of accommodation, such as apartments and time-share, and away from more traditional serviced establishments (hotels or self-catering apartments). We must also remember the private informal sector (including second homes and caravans) which is a large, though neglected, part of the accommodation industry (and dealt with in detail in Chapter 8).

Retailing and other services

There is an increasing range of facilities and services available to a tourist as the size of destination increases. These include retailing, security services and other functions, such as hairdressing, banks, exchange bureaux and insurance. These services tend to locate close to the main attractions of a destination, often creating an identifiable 'recreational business district'.

Access

Clearly the development and maintenance of efficient transport links to the generating markets are essential for the success of destinations. Indeed, there are examples of destinations where transport has made, or broken, the tourist industry. Small islands, for example, are dependent upon their carriers to provide market access, while destinations such as Spain and Mexico are ideally situated to take advantage of international tourism from Europe and North America respectively. In international terms, developing countries have particular problems attracting a share of the market because they are generally distant from the generating markets.

Catchment areas will also vary according to the drawing power of the destination. Tightly drawn geographical catchments will characterise smaller resorts without a major distinguishing attraction. However, major destinations, such as the theme parks of Orlando, can draw upon an international catchment.

We can therefore see that physical and market access to the destination are important, just as is the provision of services such as car rental and local transport, in order to service excursion circuits and provide transfers to accommodation at the destination. An increasingly creative approach to transportation at the destination adds to the quality of the tourist experience, and there are many examples of innovative transport provision in this respect including:

- scenic drives;
- park and ride schemes;
- shuttle buses for walkers;
- cycle ways; and
- innovative vehicles such as aquaducks or citycats.

Ancillary services

Most major destinations provide ancillary services to both the consumer and the industry through a destination management organisation (DMO) (Pike and Page, 2014). These services include marketing, development and coordination activities. The DMO may be in the public sector, may be a public/private sector cooperative or, in some cases, may exist totally within the private sector. Such organisations are often linked to regional and national tourist boards and provide the framework within which tourism operates at the destination. A particular issue for DMOs is to prove their effectiveness in terms of marketing and competitiveness as noted by Morgan *et al.* (2012).

The main services normally provided by the DMO are as follows:

- promotion of the destination;
- coordination and control of development;
- provision of an information/reservation service to the trade and the public;
- advice to and coordination of local businesses;
- provision of facilities such as catering or sports; and
- provision of destination leadership and partnership building.

Infrastructure and Superstructure

We can consider infrastructure and superstructure as alternative ways of looking at the components of a destination. Infrastructure represents all forms of construction above or below ground needed by an inhabited area, with extensive communication with the outside world as a basis for tourism activity in the area. Adequate infrastructure is essential for destinations and is mainly in the form of:

- transportation (road, railway, airport, car-parks);
- utilities (electricity, water, communications); and
- other services (health care and security).

Infrastructure is normally shared by residents and visitors alike. There are examples where lack of adequate infrastructure has prevented the growth of tourism (such as restricted water supplies on the Kenyan Mombassa coast). Infrastructure does not normally generate income and is treated as a public investment in most tourist developments. Seasonality is a major problem for infrastructure development and most construction is planned to meet a percentage of peak load rather than peak.

Whereas infrastructure tends to be provided by the public sector, *superstructure* is normally a private-sector activity, as it is the profit-generating element of the destination. It includes accommodation, built attractions and retailing and other services. We should remember, however, that in many countries the public sector is active in providing financial incentives (grants, loans, tax holidays) for private sector tourism investment. Although the norm is for the public sector to provide infrastructure as a prerequisite for private sector development of the superstructure, in many cases combinations of public and private sector finance are used to develop destinations.

Types of Tourism

The particular combination and features of the destination amalgam characterises various 'types of tourism' such as say heritage tourism, pink tourism or ghetto tourism. For example, destinations delivering the type of tourism known as dark tourism are characterised by sites of death, disaster or where something dark has occurred. These may be battlefields, sites of assassination, or sites such as concentration camps. Of course, these could hardly be called attractions and their interpretation and display for the dark tourists demand sensitivity. Another type of tourism, adventure tourism also demands particular configurations of destination components. Here, the destination is often surveyed to create an adventure tourism 'template' where particular sites and resources can be identified for activities such as, say, mountain biking, bungee jumping, white water rafting or mountaineering. Adventure tourism is a rapidly growing type of tourism as tourists seek out the unusual and the dangerous at the destination; growth which has been facilitated by innovations in technology such as GPS on mobile phones and social networking. For all the many 'types of tourism' it is the combination of these destination components with the particular wants and needs of the market that define each 'type'.

We now turn to the next mini case, which focuses on another particular type of tourism, that of event tourism.

Mini Case Study 2.2
Events and the Destination

Large crowd at a Formula One Grand Prix.
Source: © dpa picture alliance/Alamy Images

Introduction

Events are now an integral part of the destination mix (Sharples *et al.*, 2014). As once only or infrequently occurring activities, they contrast with the destination's fixed plant such as attractions. Events have a long history, with the first Olympic Games in 776 BC thought to be the first ever special event (Jago and Dwyer, 2006). Since the 1980s, events have grown in prominence; Whitford (2015) for example, estimates that in Europe alone there are over 4 million events annually. This has led to the emergence of the global events as an industry sector in its own right. Events come in all types and sizes, but can be thought of as 'hallmark events' where the event is defined by the location – the Cannes film festival for example; 'mega events' which are international and huge in scale – the Football World Cup is an example here; as well as the array of 'major international events' and 'minor local and regional events'.

Advantages of Events for Destinations

For destinations there are clear benefits in holding events and hence many destinations now have event plans and strategies. Mega events in particular can bring global publicity, attract significant visitation, stimulate urban development and help to reposition destinations. Other benefits include use of events to:

- reduce seasonality;
- attract media attention and place promotion of the destination;
- generate economic benefits (employment, revenue generation and investment);
- generate the social benefits of building or rejuvenating communities and social capital; and
- attract regional development.

Defining and Categorising Events

It is important to define events so that we can measure their scale and impact, and also for planning and policy reasons. Yet there is no real agreement over definitions of events. Whitford (2015) defines an event as:

> 'Something of significance that occurs such as a celebration, an important occurrence or a ceremony or any mutually beneficial activity involving the local population in a shared experience'.

Getz (2012) goes on to classify events into a number of categories:

- **cultural celebrations,** which include festivals, religious events and art/cultural events;
- **business events,** which include meetings, conferences and exhibitions; and
- **sporting events,** which can range in size from local events to the mega events of say, the Olympics.

The Future

Events are an integral part of destinations, but they are not without controversy. Particular issues concerning events are their economic, social and environmental impacts and their legacy effects – in other words, what are the consequences for the destination of holding an event, and how lasting will be the benefits of the event (Holmes *et al.,* 2015)? Here, the Olympic movement has been particularly concerned with the legacy effects of the stadia and other sporting venues that are constructed for the Games.

Whitford (2015) summarises the issues for the future as follows:

> 'events should not be seen as quick fix economic development tools. Nor . . . as a panacea to societies' socio-cultural and/or environmental quandaries or as vehicles for political grandstanding' (p. 12).

She sees the future of events as promoting sustainable options for the economic and social well-being of the destination.

DISCUSSION QUESTIONS

1. Identify a recent mega sporting event. How did the destination use the event for place promotion?
2. There is real concern that the events industry is not as 'green' as it should be. For a local event that you are familiar with identify initiatives they could take to be a 'green' event.
3. List the possible economic consequences – both positive and negative – of holding a mega event.

Sources:
Bowdin, G.A.J., Allen, J., O'Toole, W., Harris, R. and McDonnell, I. (2011) *Events Management,* 3rd edn, Routledge, London.
Gerritsen, D. and van Olderen, R. (2014) *Events as a Strategic Marketing Tool,* CABI, Wallingford.
Getz, D. (2012) *Event Studies Theory, Research and Policy for Planned Events,* 2nd edn, Routledge, London.
Holmes, K., Hughes, M., Mair, J. and Carlsen, J. (2015) *Events and Sustainability,* Routledge, London.
Jago, L. and Dwyer, L. (2006) *Economic Evaluation of Special Events: A Practitioner's Guide,* Common Ground, Altona, Victoria.
Page, S. and Connell, J. (2014) *The Routledge Handbook of Events,* Routledge, London.
Sharples, E., Crowther, P., May, D. and Orefice, C. (2014) *Strategic Event Creation,* Goodfellow, Oxford.
Whitford, M. (2015) Event management, pp. 227–266 in Cooper, C. (ed.) *Contemporary Tourism Reviews, Volume 1,* Goodfellow Publishers, Oxford.

THE SUSTAINABLE DESTINATION   43

Destination Stakeholders

A final way of viewing the components of destinations is by looking at the fact that tourism destinations comprise a mosaic of different actors that we can term stakeholders. A truly sustainable destination will recognise that it must satisfy all of its stakeholders in the long term. This can be achieved by a strategic planning approach which balances a marketing orientation focused on tourists, with a planning orientation focused on the needs of local people. We must also remember that the tourist experience is made up of a series of small *encounters* with many stakeholders and that these encounters strongly influence the success or otherwise of the visit. In every destination there are several stakeholders, which have a wide range of both compatible and conflicting interests:

- **The host community** is the most important stakeholder as they live and work at the destination and provide local resources to visitors. It is therefore important to involve the local community in decision-making, and to ensure that tourism does not bring unacceptable impacts upon the local people and their homes.

- **Tourists** are looking for a satisfying experience, through properly segmented and developed products. They seek a high quality of service and a well-managed and organised destination.

- **The tourism industry** is to large extent responsible for the existing development of tourism and the delivery of the tourism product. It seeks an adequate return on investment. The industry can be through of as polarising between global and niche players. The global players tend to be multinational well-resourced with capital, expertise and power. Often they have limited interest and commitment to destinations. Niche players are traditionally small, family-based enterprises lacking capital, expertise, qualified human resources and influence at the destination.

- **The public sector** sees tourism as a means to increase incomes, stimulate regional development and generate employment. The public sector is an important stakeholder, often taking a destination leadership or governance role.

- **Other stakeholders** include pressure groups, chambers of commerce and power brokers within the local, regional or national community.

The Sustainable Destination

Clearly the components of the tourist destination can be effective only if careful planning and management deliver a sustainable tourism product, and in so doing ensure that one or more of the components does not surge ahead of the others. We explore the concept of sustainable tourism in detail in Chapter 6. It is clear that the concept of sustainability demands a long-term view of tourism and ensures that consumption of tourism does not exceed the ability of a host destination to provide for future tourists. In other words, it represents a trade-off between present and future needs. In the past, sustainability has been low priority compared with the short-term drive for profitability and growth, but as pressure has grown for a more responsible tourism industry, it is difficult to see how such short-term views on consumption can continue. To understand how to deliver sustainable tourism destinations we need to consider three key concepts:

1. Carrying capacity.
2. Destination management.
3. Strategic planning.

Carrying Capacity

Central to the concept of sustainability is the idea of carrying capacity. Carrying capacity is a deceptively simple idea – quite simply, the carrying capacity of a destination refers to its ability to absorb tourism use without deteriorating. In other words, capacity intervenes in the relationship between the tourist and the destination. As we can see in Table 2.1 carrying capacity comes in a variety of forms.

Mathieson and Wall (1982) define carrying capacity as:

'The maximum number of people who can use a site without an unacceptable altera-tion in the physical environment and without an unacceptable decline in the quality of experience gained by visitors' (p. 21).

The main problem with carrying capacity is that the concept is easy to grasp but very difficult to put into practice because it is a management decision. Managers of the tourist destination, as well as the tourists themselves, decide what is *unacceptable* and when the quality of experience has declined. Indeed, any destination can be managed to a high or low capacity, a level that is determined as much by management as by the innate characteristics of the resource and its culture.

Destination Management

Destination management is about 'place making' to deliver a high-quality experience to the visitor and to manage the consequences of visitation at the destination. It provides the tools to produce sustainable and competitive tourism at a destination going one step beyond destination marketing to take a more holistic and integrative approach to man-aging the 'whole destination'. Destination management tends to be led by the relevant DMO through the medium of policy, planning legislation and partnership building with destination stakeholders. It also reflects contemporary thinking that the local destination is the most meaningful building block for marketing, development, and engagement with stakeholders.

Table 2.1 Types of carrying capacity

Physical Carrying Capacity

This relates to the amount of suitable land available for facilities and also includes the finite capacity of the facilities (such as car parking spaces, covers in restaurants or bedspaces in accommodation). It is the most straightforward of all capacity measures and can be used for planning and management control (by say, limiting car parking spaces at sensitive sites).

Psychological Carrying Capacity

The psychological capacity of a site is exceeded when a visitor's experience is significantly impaired. Of course, some people are crowd tolerant and enjoy busy places, whilst others shun them. Psychological capacity is therefore a very individual concept and difficult to influence by management and planning, although landscaping can be used to reduce the impression of crowding.

Biological Carrying Capacity

The biological capacity of a site is exceeded when environmental damage or disturbance is unacceptable. This can relate to both flora and fauna, for example, at picnic sites, along paths or in dune-ecosystems. More research has examined the capacity thresholds of vegetation than has looked at the tolerance of animals or birds to tourism (at, say, whale watching locations). It is also important to consider the total ecosystem rather than individual elements.

Social Carrying Capacity

The concept of social carrying capacity is derived from ideas of community-based tourism planning and sustainability. It attempts to define levels of development, which are acceptable to host community residents and businesses and may use techniques that attempt to gauge residents' threshold *limits to acceptable change* (LAC).

The UNWTO (2007) define destination management as:

'The coordinated management of all of the elements that make up a destination. Destination management takes a strategic approach to link up these sometimes very separate entities for the better management of the destination. Joined-up management can help to avoid duplication of effort with regards to promotion, visitor services, training, business support and identify any management gaps that are not being addressed' (p. 4).

As shown in Figure 2.2, destination management combines the practices and principles of:

- development planning;
- marketing; and
- management.

The key to effective destination management is to encourage cooperation and collaboration to strengthen partnerships between all stakeholders at the destination. This delivers a shared vision and an integrated, holistic approach to managing the destination. The benefits of destination management are as follows:

- it ensures that the destination is competitive;
- it ensures that the destination is sustainable;
- it ensures that tourism delivers economic benefits to the host community;
- it ensures the delivery of quality experiences to the visitor;
- it delivers an over-arching destination vision; and
- it promotes continuous destination improvement.

The case study at the end of this chapter outlines a particular destination management model known as the VICE model.

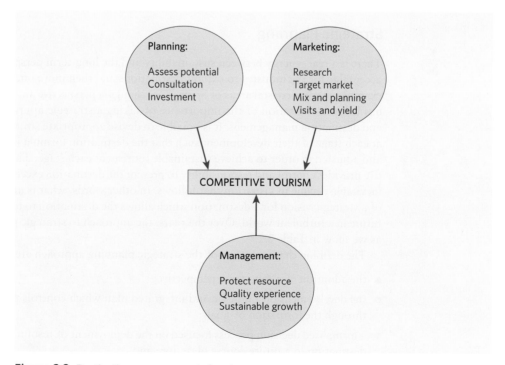

Figure 2.2 Destination management planning concepts

Table 2.2 Strategic planning – from the traditional approach to experience strategies

Traditional Strategic Planning

In the early years of destination strategies, managers tended to adopt a traditional and rather rigid sequential approach. This consisted of a series of stages typically:

- situation analysis/environmental scanning;
- objectives and goals;
- strategy formulation;
- marketing, positioning and mix; and
- implementation and monitoring.

By the late 1990s, this approach had become less relevant to the changing operating environment of destinations in a world of continuous and unexpected change.

The Visioning Approach

In the late 1990s, a number of destinations began to adopt a 'visioning' approach to strategy. Here visions are crafted that present a practical and achievable picture of where the destination sees itself in the future.

Visioning is a dynamic and engaging process, very much a bottom-up, allowing the destination to be flexible and responsive to changing circumstances. It is focused upon bringing together stakeholders in a collaborative and participative goal-setting approach to generate a 'shared vision'. Visions are inspiring, imaginative and reflect the shared aspirations of the destination.

Experience Strategies

In the new millennium, a small number of forward-looking destinations have developed experience strategies in recognition of tourism as an experience. This approach accepts that visitors are accustomed to high-quality entertainment experiences and so, to be competitive, destinations must engineer memorable, personal and transforming experiences to match the expectations of the visitor.

This approach recognises that meaningful experiences cannot be guranteed, but they can be managed. Tourism Tasmania's Experience Strategy is a leading example here.

Strategic Planning

There is a real synergy between sustainability and the long-term perspective. It is no longer acceptable for the industry to exploit destinations and then move on, as has happened, for example, in some coastal areas of Spain. This changing perspective away from the short term has led to a realisation of the importance of taking a strategic approach to both markets and destination management. It is possible to devise appropriate strategies for destinations at each stage of their development such that the destination formula is constantly reviewed and adjusted in order to achieve sustainable tourism at each stage. This long-term perspective provides control and responsibility to prevent the destination exceeding capacity and the inevitable decline in visitation that follows. In other words, what is involved is the crafting of a strategic vision for a destination which allows the destination to take control of its own future in a turbulent world. Over the years, the approach to strategic planning has evolved, as we show in Table 2.2.

The defining characteristics of the strategic planning approach are:

- the adoption of a long-term perspective;
- the development of a holistic and integrated plan which controls the process of change through the formation of goals;
- a formalised decision process focused on the deployment of resources, which commit the destination to a future course of action; and
- the political process at the destination is critical to success.

The benefits of the strategic approach to the destination are clear:

- It provides a common sense of ownership and direction for the myriad stakeholders, while at the same time sharpening the guiding objectives of the destination.
- The coherence provided by the approach provides a framework for joint initiatives between the commercial and public sectors and demands the clear identification of roles and responsibilities and provides a sense of ownership for all.
- Finally, the approach delivers a range of performance indicators against which the destination's performance can be judged.

However, the introduction of a longer-term strategic planning perspective by destinations is problematic. Simply, the adoption of strategic planning at the destination is not as straightforward as in a commercial organisation where responsibilities and reporting lines are well defined. As we have seen, destinations comprise a constantly shifting mosaic of stakeholders and value systems. Each of these groups has a different view of the role and future of tourism at the destination and therefore the adoption of strategies becomes a political process of conflict resolution and consensus, all set within a local legislative context and where power brokers have a disproportionate influence. The power of this political process should not be underestimated. Politics influences those who are responsible for the planning process, and lack of political support commonly leads to the failure, or non-implementation, of plans. In addition, the tourist sector at destinations is characterised by fragmentation and a dominance of small businesses, which often trade seasonally. This has led to a lack of management expertise at destinations, a divergence of aims between the commercial and public sectors and a short-term planning horizon which in part is driven by public sector, 12-monthly budgeting cycles, but also by the tactical operating horizon of small businesses. At the same time, the stage of the destination in the life-cycle influences the acceptability of a destination-wide marketing exercise. In the early stages of the life-cycle, for example, success often obscures the long-term view, while in the later stages, particularly when a destination is in decline, opposition to long-term planning exercises may be rationalised on the basis of cost.

Finally, the performance indicators adopted in such exercises can be controversial since tourist volume is the traditional, and politically acceptable, measure of success in many destinations. Yet, from the point of view of sustainability more appropriate measures are likely to be the less tangible ones of environmental and social impacts. Of course, to be competitive a destination must be sustainable – it is all too easy to go for growth and at the same time destroy the very resource that the tourist wants. We turn to destination competitiveness in the next section.

The Competitive Destination

An imperative for all destinations is to be competitive in order to deliver benefits to all stakeholders. In the bigger picture, it is in fact destinations that compete with each other rather than the individual businesses within the destination. To be competitive demands that destinations thoroughly understand their positioning against their competitors' offering and constantly innovate in terms of their product offering and their marketing. In other words, destinations must research their own characteristics, product offering and markets as well as those of their competitors. Ritchie and Crouch have published widely on the issue with a comprehensive framework for analysing destination competitiveness (Figure 2.3), and we base our classic paper on their work.

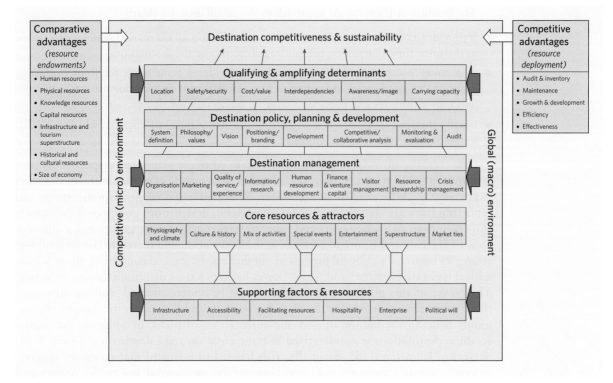

Figure 2.3 Conceptual model of destination competitiveness
Source: Ritchie and Crouch, 2003

Classic Paper

Ritchie, J.R.B. and Crouch, G.I. (2000) The competitive destination: a sustainable perspective, *Tourism Management* 21, 1–7

This paper by Brent Ritchie and Geoffrey Crouch forms the introduction to a special issue of *Tourism Management* on the competitive destination. The paper is based on a major long-term research project aiming to define the elements that influence the competitiveness of destinations and is one of a series of papers that began in 1993. As such it not only contributes in a major way to the tourism research agenda, but it also assists us in understanding how destinations function and compete. The authors recognise that the destination is the fundamental product in tourism and that, effectively, competition in tourism occurs between destinations and their relative features. This explains why many of the leading destinations in the world commit significant resources to promotion and the quality management of their products. It also explains why many of the world's major cities see themselves as tourism destinations and aggressively compete for custom.

The paper is a classic for two reasons:

1. It systematically maps out a model for destination competitiveness based upon a considerable amount of research, as well as discussion and refinement through debates and focus groups with students and destination managers. For example, the 2000 version of the model introduces tourism policy as an important influence upon competitiveness. Here, Ritchie and Crouch see policy as comprising three parts – the structure of the policy in terms of umbrella guidelines, the content of the policy, and policy process in terms of how the policy is delivered.
2. It provides a useful framework for defining the tourism destination. Ritchie and Crouch emphasise the importance of coming up with an agreed definition of the destination – not simply from an academic point of view, but also from the practical point of view of destination managers who need to share their understanding of the destination with their stakeholders. Their model of a destination has four key features:

(a) It distinguishes between the *physical resources* of a destination – such as beaches, and *the processes and activities* that occur around them to create tourism;

(b) It distinguishes between *natural resources* (climate for example) and *human elements* such as buildings, technology and culture;

(c) It identifies and defines the *actors* who create the destination; and

(d) It defines *destination governance* 'vertically' by tier of government and 'horizontally' by partnerships.

The paper goes on to identify the following key components of destination competitiveness:

- **Core resources and attractions** – the main attractions that draw tourists to a destination.

- **Supporting factors and resources** – the facilitating resources that sustain and support the visit, although they are not the main reason for visiting – they include access, accommodation and food and beverage.

- **Qualifying and amplifying determinants or situational conditioners** – these determinants limit or nurture the ability of the destination to compete. They include factors such as the size and scale of the destination and levels of security. Of course these may be outside the control of the destination itself, for example, the unrest in the Middle East renders many otherwise highly desirable destinations as almost no-go areas.

- **Destination policy, planning and development** – we will see later in this book how effective and coordinated 'whole of destination' policy and planning can influence the competitiveness of a destination. In contrast, a badly planned and managed destination will always find it difficult to be competitive.

- **Destination management** – as we have seen, effective destination management delivers the visitor experience on the ground and ensures quality management and coordination of the destination products, again this can make or break a destination.

- **Comparative versus competitive advantage** – in their model, Ritchie and Crouch make the distinction between the *comparative advantage* of a destination, which comes from its endowed resources of say natural beauty or cultural heritage, and *competitive advantage*, which is linked to how effectively the comparative resources are employed. This will very much depend upon the local DMO.

- **Global (macro) versus competitive (micro) environment** – here the model recognises that all destinations exist within a global environment and will be subject to forces outside their control – examples here could be demographics or global economic cycles. Equally, there are micro-level influences upon the destination which come from the tourism system itself, including say changes in distribution methods of the product, or changes in transport provision to the destination. Both sets of factors influence destination competitiveness.

This paper deserves to be read because of its wide-ranging nature, its clarity of thinking about the destination and its contribution to our understanding of the structure and functioning of tourism destinations.

The Evolving Destination

There is no doubt that the evolution of tourism has been closely linked to the evolution of destinations and, in particular, resorts. As markets also develop and change, resorts have had to respond in terms of their tourist facilities and services, for example through adaptation to climate change. A more formalised representation of this ideas is expressed by Butler's (1980) tourist area life-cycle (TALC) (see Figure 2.4). This states that destinations go through a cycle of evolution similar to the life-cycle of a product (where sales grow as the product evolves through the stages of launch, development, maturity and decline). Simply, numbers of visitors replace sales of a product (Table 2.3). Obviously, the shape of the TALC curve will vary, but for each destination it will be dependent upon factors such as:

- the rate of development;
- access;

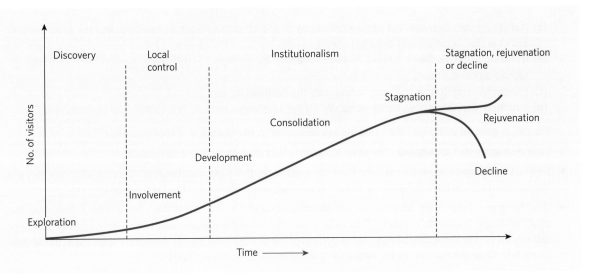

Figure 2.4 The tourist area life-cycle
Source: Butler, 1980; Boniface and Cooper, 2009

Table 2.3 The tourist area life-cycle

Exploration Stage

Here the resort is visited by a small volume of the explorer-type tourists who tent to shun institutionalised travel. The natural attractions, scale and culture of the resort are the main draw, but volumes are constrained by lack of access and facilities. At this stage, the attraction of the resort is that it remains as yet unchanged by tourism and contact with local people will be high. Parts of Latin America and the Canadian Arctic are examples here.

Involvement Stage

At the involvement stage, local communities have to decide whether they wish to encourage tourism and, if so, the type and scale of tourism they prefer. Local initiatives will begin to provide for visitors and advertise the resort, which may lead to an increased and regular volume of visitors. A tourist season and market area emerge and pressures may be placed on the public sector to provide infrastructure and institute control. At this point, it is important to establish appropriate organisation and decision making processes for tourism. Here, involvement of the local community should ensure that locally determined capacity limits are adhered to and that sustainable principles are introduced. The smaller, less-developed Pacific and Caribbean islands are examples here, as are countries such as Yemen.

Development Stage

By the development stage, large numbers of visitors are attracted, at peak period perhaps equalling or exceeding the number of local inhabitants. By this stage, the organisation of tourism may change as control passes out of local hands and companies from outside the area move in to provide products and facilities. These enterprises may have differing aims and timescales from those of the local community in terms of sustainable development. It is therefore at this stage that problems can occur if local decision taking structures are weak. Control in the public sector can also be affected as regional and national planning may become necessary in part to ameliorate problems, but also to market to the international tourist-generating areas, as visitors become more dependent upon travel arrangements booked through the trade. This is a critical stage as these facilities, and the changing nature of tourism, can alter the very nature of the resort and quality may decline through problems of over-use and deterioration of facilities. Parts of Mexico and the north African coast exemplify this stage.

Consolidation Stage

In the later stages of the cycle, the rate of increase of visitors declines, though total numbers are still increasing and exceed permanent residents. The resort is now a fully-fledged part of the tourism industry with an identifiable recreational business district (RBD). Many Caribbean and Mediterranean destinations are examples here.

Stagnation Stage

At stagnation, peak tourist volumes have now been reached and the destination is no longer fashionable, relying upon repeat visits from more conservative travellers. Business use of the resort's extensive facilities is also sought, but generally major promotional and development efforts are needed to maintain the number of visits. Resorts in this stage often have environmental, social and economic problems and find that competition for visits is fierce and coming from a number of well-entrenched, mature resorts. A number of Spanish resorts (such as the Costa Brava) exemplify this stage.

Table 2.3 (*continued*)

Decline Stage

Visitors are now being lost to newer resorts and a small geographical catchment for day trips and weekend visits is common. However, resorts should not await decline as inevitable but should look to revitalise visits by seeking new markets, repositioning the resort or finding new uses for facilities.

Rejuvenation Stage

Destination managers may decide to rejuvenate or relaunch the destination by looking at new markets or developing the product. Introduction of new types of facility such as casinos is a common response. Here a destination should seek to protect its traditional markets, whilst also seeking new markets and products such as business, conference or special interest tourism. This helps to stabilise visitation, may combat seasonality and reduces dependence on declining market segments.

Rejuvenation strategies are difficult to implement as managers are dealing with the built fabric of tourist destinations rather than with a consumer product. Indeed, it is at this stage that the analogy of a product life-cycle and the destination cycle breaks down, simply because tourism is so closely woven into the very way of life of resorts and supports jobs, services and carriers. The classic examples of this stage are Atlantic City, USA; Scheveningen, the Netherlands; and a number of Spanish destinations – Benidorm and Majorcan resorts – and Welsh destinations – Rhyl and Llandudno.

- government policy;
- market trends; and
- competing destinations.

Each of these factors can delay or accelerate progress through the various stages. Indeed, development can be arrested at any stage in the cycle, and only tourist developments promising considerable financial returns will mature to experience all stages of the cycle. In turn, the length of each stage, and of the cycle itself, is variable. At one extreme, instant resorts such as Cancun (Mexico) (www.cancun.com) move almost immediately to growth; at the other extreme, well-established resorts such as Scarborough (England) (www.scarborough.co.uk/) have taken three centuries to move from exploration to rejuvenation.

We can see that one particular benefit of the tourist area life-cycle is as a framework for understanding how destinations and their markets evolve (see Butler, 2015). The shape of the curve varies depending upon supply-side factors such as:

- investment;
- capacity constraints;
- tourist impacts; and
- planning responses.

Indeed, it could be argued that an understanding of the cycle aids the development of community-based and sustainable tourism strategies at the involvement stage. To implement such approaches in later stages may be inappropriate and certainly are more difficult. In other words, tourist destinations are dynamic, with changing provision of facilities and access matched by an evolving market in both quantitative and qualitative terms, as successive waves of different numbers and types of tourists with distinctive preferences, motivations and desires populate the resort at each stage of the life-cycle.

The TALC is best utilised as a conceptual framework, although other writers have suggested that it can be used to guide strategic planning at destinations, or as a forecasting tool. There are, however, significant problems with these approaches:

- The difficulty of identifying stages and turning points.
- The difficulty of obtaining long runs of visitor arrivals data from which to assemble the curve.
- The danger of planners responding to (possibly false) warning signs, which can be influenced anyway by management intervention.
- The danger of a tailor-made strategy for each stage.

- The level of aggregation is open to many interpretations. After all, there will be a life-cycle for nested destinations – a hotel, a resort and a region – as well as differing curves for each market segment.

The TALC has many critics, in part drawn by its very simplicity and apparent deterministic approach. Some argue that, far from being an independent guide for decisions, the TALC is determined by the strategic decisions of management and is heavily dependent on external influences. However, as a framework within which to view the development of destinations, albeit with hindsight, and as a way of thinking about the interrelationship of destination and market evolution, it provides many useful insights.

SUMMARY

This chapter has focused upon the tourism destination as a fundamental unit of analysis for tourism. The chapter has demonstrated the various approaches to defining and thinking about the destination and recommends viewing destinations as networks of organisations that deliver the tourist experience as we saw in the first case study. The chapter went on to identify the common features of destinations, including events (focus of the second case study), and the fact that they are amalgams, and showed how this has implications for destination management as well as understanding the different types of tourism. The chapter showed that sustainability has become the organising concept for destinations and that this is delivered through an understanding of the carrying capacity and the techniques of destination management and strategic planning as we see in the final case study on the VICE model of management. Sustainability delivers a competitive destination and we showed the various influences on destination competitiveness. Finally, the chapter introduced the idea of destination evolution through the notion of a tourist area life-cycle.

Discussion Questions

1. In class discuss the various approaches to defining the destination. Decide your preferred approach and justify it.
2. Taking a destination of your choice identify the key components of the destination and consider the implications of the 'amalgam' concept.
3. There are a number of types of carrying capacity – discuss which should be the ultimate limiting factor for tourism at a destination with which you are familiar.
4. Using the Internet, identify a destination strategy and write a critique of its approach.
5. Taking a destination which you know well, research the history of demand and plot visitor numbers against time on a graph – can you identify any of the TALC stages on the graph?

Annotated Further Reading

1. Butler, R.W. (2015) Tourism area life cycle, pp. 183–226 in Cooper, C. (ed.) *Contemporary Tourism Reviews, Volume 1*, Goodfellow, Oxford.
   Authoritative and up to date review of the life-cycle.
2. Boniface, B., Cooper., C and Cooper, R. (2012) *Worldwide Destinations: The Geography of Travel and Tourism*, Routledge, London.
   Comprehensive coverage of every destination in the world.

3. Hall, C.M., Gössling, S. and Scott, D. (2015) *The Routledge Handbook of Tourism and Sustainability*, Routledge, London.
   Comprehensive handbook on sustainability and the destination.

4. Getz, D. (2014) Timing tourism: MICE, events and mega events, Chapter 32 in Lew, A.L., Hall, C.M. and Williams, A.M. (eds) *The Wiley Blackwell Companion to Tourism*, Wiley, Chichester.
   Contemporary account of event management at the destination.

5. Leiper, N. (2000) Are destinations 'the heart of tourism'? The advantages of an alternative description, *Current Issues in Tourism* **3**, 364–68.
   A lively discussion of the idea of the destination in tourism studies.

6. Page, S. and Connell, J. (2014) *The Routledge Handbook of Events*, Routledge, London.
   Comprehensive and contemporary handbook of events at the destination.

7. Ritchie, J.R.B. and Crouch, G.I. (2000) The competitive destination: a sustainable perspective, *Tourism Management* **21**, 1–7.
   The full version of their competitiveness model in a comprehensive volume.

8. Scott, N., Baggio, R. and Cooper, C. (2008) *Network Analysis and Tourism: From Theory to Practice*, Channelview, Clevedon.
   Complete coverage of all aspects if networks and destinations.

9. Smith, S.L.J. (1996) *Tourism Analysis: A Handbook*, 2nd edn, Longman, Harlow.
   Provides one of the best discussions of the various analytical methods that may be brought to bear in the analysis and identification of tourism destinations.

10. UNWTO (2007) *A Practical Guide to Destination Management*, UNWTO, Madrid.
    A thorough manual on how to manage the destination.

References Cited

Boniface, B. and Cooper, C. (2009) *Worldwide Destinations: The Geography of Travel and Tourism*, Heinemann, London.

Butler, R.W. (1980) The concept of a tourist area cycle of evolution, *Canadian Geographer*, **24**, 5–12.

Butler, R.W. (2015) Tourism area life cycle, pp. 183–226 in Cooper, C. (ed.) *Contemporary Tourism Reviews, Volume 1*, Goodfellow, Oxford.

Crouch, G. and Ritchie, J.R.B. (2012) *Competitiveness and Tourism*, Elgar, London.

Mathieson, A. and Wall, G. (1982) *Tourism: Economic, Physical and Social Impacts*, Longman, Harlow.

Morgan, N., Hastings, E. and Pritchard, A. (2012) Developing a new DMO marketing evaluation framework: The case of Visit Wales, *Journal of Vacation Marketing* **18**(1), 73–89.

Pike, S. and Page, S. (2014) Destination marketing organizations and destination marketing: a narrative analysis of the literature, *Tourism Management* **41**, 202–227.

Ritchie, J.R.B. and Crouch, I. (2003) *The Competitive Destination: A Sustainable Tourism Perspective*, CABI, Wallingford.

Scott, N., Cooper, C. and Baggio, R. (2008) Destination networks: four Australian cases, *Annals of Tourism Research* **35**(1), 169–188.

UNWTO (2007) *A Practical Guide to Destination Management*, UNWTO, Madrid.

Major Case Study 2.1
The VICE Model of Destination Management – The New Forest National Park, UK

The contested New Forest landscape is carefully managed.
Source: © David Noton Photography/Alamy Images

The New Forest

The New Forest is an environmentally sensitive area with a unique landscape in the south of England. The whole area is under severe pressure, not only from tourism and recreation, but also from other developments such as housing and transport and as a result it was designated as a national park in 2005. The New Forest landscape comprises areas of open heathland, interspersed with woodland. Its status as Crown land has protected it from development over the centuries. This case study outlines the Forest's renowned VICE approach to destination management which balances the needs of different stakeholders.

The New Forest is a significant natural resource that faces many competing demands. Recreation and tourism create major impacts on both the resource and the local community, although the economy does benefit. This has been complicated by national park designation. The national park covers an area of 56,651 hectares designed to conserve the New Forest landscape, flora and fauna and to promote its enjoyment by visitors.

Tourism and Transport in the New Forest

The New Forest is a very popular destination for both staying and day visitors. Visitor pressure in the Forest arises from the fact it is easily accessible through the national motorway network and that over 15 million people live within a 90-minute drive. Tourism in the New Forest is estimated to:

- support almost 2,500 jobs in the area;
- contribute £72 million annually to the local economy; and
- attract 13.5 million day visitors and almost 3 million overnight visitors.

A key issue is the management of traffic. Most visitors arrive by car, and a comprehensive traffic management plan includes a 40 mph (65 kilometres/hour) speed limit on unfenced roads, and the use of landscaped verges, ditches and ramparts to prevent off-road parking. Visitors are directed instead to over 150 designated parking zones. Other forms of transport include the ever-popular horse riding, cycle hire (although mountain bikes have caused damage in certain areas), horse-drawn wagon rides, and regular bus and coach services. These alternatives to the car are coordinated in a series of networks in an attempt to reduce the number of car-borne visitors to the Forest.

Destination Management

Managing the New Forest as a destination is critical given the combination of an environmentally sensitive area and large numbers of visitors. The New Forest is fortunate in having developed a visionary set of destination management plans which, in Crouch and Ritchie's (2012) model, can be said to have enhanced the destination's competitiveness. Destination management in the New Forest is based upon the principle of partnership, hence the title of their management strategy – *Our Future Together* (NFDC, 2003). This followed an earlier strategy *Making New Friends* (NFDC, 1996) and a consultation document, controversially entitled *Living with the Enemy*, which mapped out the challenges for the New Forest tourism industry (NFDC, 1994). A further complication in the management of the New Forest is the plethora of agencies, committees and other bodies involved in the management of the Forest under its national park status, underscoring the need for a partnership approach. The lead tourism agency is the New Forest Tourism Association (NFTA) formed in 1989 to promote the New Forest as a quality year-round holiday and business destination.

The New Forest destination management approach has become known as the VICE model (see Figure 2.5) based on:

1. Visitors.
2. Industry.
3. Community.
4. Environment.

The model is 'built into' the destination rather than 'bolted on' and stresses the interdependence between the four elements and has turned a problematic set of relationships into mutually beneficial partnerships by smart communication, and partnership building with stakeholders. The strengths of the approach are:

- developing a clearly identifiable destination and brand;
- strong leadership from the NFTA;
- ensuring continuity of stakeholders;
- long-term commitment to the strategy;
- a positive local profile for tourism;
- strategy and administrative structure work together;
- securing trust – changing the culture; and
- good regional and sub-regional relationships.

Beyond the New Forest

The VICE model has proved so effective that other UK regions have adopted its guiding principles for destination management. Cornwall has embedded the VICE model into its local sustainability plans whilst the Cotswolds region is using the VICE model to evaluate sustainability principles across the region (see Cornwall Destination Management Organisation, 2007 and Cotswolds Tourism Partnership, 2009).

DISCUSSION QUESTIONS

1. Draft a communication plan to help the New Forest Tourism officer convince local residents that tourism is of economic benefit to the Forest.

2. Other destinations are now adopting the VICE model. How transferable is this approach to other destinations?

3. A key issue for the Forest is the dominance of day visitors and the relatively small number of overnight visitors (around 3 million nights annually). As a result, the tourist authorities in the New Forest are concerned that much of the economic benefit from tourism is lost. Draw up a strategy to increase the number of overnight visitors in the Forest.

Sources:
Cornwall Destination Management Organisation (2007) *Destination Audit*, Roger Tym and Partners, Exeter.
Cotswolds Tourism Partnership (2009) *Cotswolds and Forest of Dean Destination Management Organization Sustainability Plan*, Cotswolds Tourism Partnership, Cirencester.
Crouch, G. and Ritchie, J.R.B. (2012) *Competitiveness and Tourism*, Elgar, London.
New Forest District Council (1994) *Living with the Enemy*, NFDC, Lyndhurst.
New Forest District Council (1996) *Making New Friends*, NFDC, Lyndhurst.
New Forest District Council (2003) *Our Future Together*, NFDC, Lyndhurst.
www.forestry.gov.uk/forestry/
www.nfdc.gov.uk
www.nfta.co.uk/
www.thenewforest.co.uk
www.newforestnpa.gov.uk
www.visitengland.org

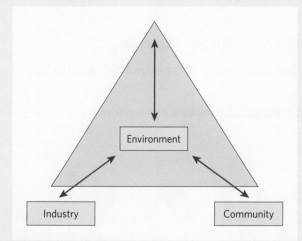

Figure 2.5 The VICE model
Source: New Forest Tourism

CHAPTER 3
THE ECONOMIC CONSEQUENCES OF TOURISM

Learning Outcomes

This chapter considers the economics of tourism, taking into account the unique characteristics of the sector and both the positive and negative consequences of tourism for a destination. The chapter is designed to provide you with:

- an understanding of the unique characteristics of the tourism sector;

- an awareness of the importance of economic evaluation of tourism and events;

- an appreciation of the tourism multiplier concept and its development;

- an understanding of the ways that tourism can bring economic benefits to a destination; and

- an awareness of the economic costs of tourism to a destination.

Introduction

Tourism is often described as one of the world's largest industries. It employs millions of people, has a turnover in billions of dollars and encourages millions of people to travel. In other words, it is a substantial economic sector and economists bring a level of discipline to its analysis. There is no doubt that economics has made a fundamental contribution to the study and understanding of tourism, evidenced by the establishment of the journal *Tourism Economics* in the 1990s. Economic analysis based upon tourism statistics is vital for decisions in the tourism sector whether for investment, marketing or planning (Dwyer *et al.*, 2015); after all, there is little point in embarking on the expensive process of collecting statistics and economic modelling if it does not inform policy. Sometimes though, economists have been accused of developing a bewildering array of technical terms, models and approaches – indeed there is no simple recipe for assessing the economic contribution of tourism and economists themselves often disagree about techniques. For example, there is currently a debate about how to assess the economic contribution of events to a destination as we see in a case study later in the chapter. Nonetheless, it is important for the language of economists to be clear, transparent and able to inform policy. An example here is the classic paper for this chapter by Sinclair *et al.* (2003), which shows how economists can make a clear and unambiguous contribution to understanding tourism.

The Supply Side of Tourism: Definitions and Characteristics

Economists remain in dispute as to whether tourism is really an industry and, if so, how to define and measure it (Dwyer *et al.*, 2015). In part, these problems arise because many industries are involved in delivering the tourism product as a service or 'experience' and tourism has distinctive characteristics that we have to take into account. As a result, Sinclair *et al.* (2003) state that research on tourism supply has focused on individual sectors rather than the structure of the sector as a whole. Leiper (1990) is clear in his view that tourism is in fact only *partially* an industry as governments, communities and others are involved in delivering the tourism product. Tourism is therefore an industry that challenges conventional economic paradigms. Yet it is important that we understand how its complex system functions if we are to manage tourism effectively. Debbage and Ioannides (1998) speak of the commodification of tourism that has created such a machinery of production:

> 'Although changes in consumer demand and the evolution of increasingly more sophisticated consumer preferences can play substantive roles in shaping the tourism product, it is the actual 'machinery of production' that helps to manipulate and facilitate origin-destination tourist flows across the world' (p. 287).

They go further by saying that tourism economists have tended to neglect the supply side of tourism. This is despite the fact that tourism is an increasingly important focus of policy intervention, and of development in many countries, as economic strategies focus on the revenue and employment generating potential of tourism. There is no doubt that the dilemma of analysing the supply side of tourism from an economic point of view has arisen because of the unique characteristics of tourism. These include:

- The sector is an invisible export as there is no tangible product to show in a balance of payments account.

- It comprises both tangible and non-tangible elements.

- It is produced where it is consumed. In other words, it is one of the few industries where the consumer has to physically visit the site of production in order to consume it. As a result, the producer does not bear any transport costs as they are borne by the tourist.

- Tourism is not a single product but a diverse range of products and services that interact. This means that although the sector is fragmented, for the product to be delivered there has to be collaboration at the destination across the various enterprises that deliver aspects of the product – such as accommodation, transport and attractions. As a result, unless there is considerable integration of these aspects within a destination there is scope for substantial leakage of income away from the destination.

- Tourism is also a fragmented sector in that it comprises many different types of provider and has no single voice to represent it – indeed Leiper (1990) terms it a set of businesses in search of an industry.

- The tourism industry is highly diverse – from size of establishment (SMEs to corporations); business type (IT to service provision); sector (air transport to accommodation); organisation (public and private sector); and process. It is therefore more a collection of industries than a single industry.

- The sector is characterised by very unstable demand, which makes it a risky investment prospect from a financier's point of view.

- Tourism is a traditional industry that is slow to accept change, yet it is also one that promotes travel and thus contributes to climate change through carbon emissions. As a result, there is a constant need to innovate and adapt to new technologies.

Mini Case Study 3.1
Measuring the Size of the Tourism Sector:
Tourism Satellite Accounts

Background

Measuring the size and scope of the contemporary tourism industry has traditionally been a major challenge, in terms of developing a coherent and shared view of just what comprises the supply side of tourism, and how to measure it. Development and implementation of the *Tourism Satellite Account* (TSA) methodology has proved to be a major breakthrough in supply-side measurement and for the credibility of the tourism sector. The TSA allows the tourism component of the economy to be identified as explained below.

A satellite account is a term developed by the United Nations to measure the size of economic sectors that are not defined as industries in national accounts. By the conventional definitions used by economists for an industry, tourism would not qualify – there is not a single production process, the product is fragmented and varied and there is no geographical catchment for the market. The concept of the satellite account is based upon the fact that the tourist (the demand side) receives a single product in the form of the visit, and all the consumption associated with that visit. Effectively then, the TSA is a sub-set of a nation's accounts that involves expenditures by individuals defined as a tourist by the UNWTO.

The Tourism Satellite Account

The TSA allows tourism to be compared for the first time with other industries, as well as allowing economists to compare tourism sectors between different countries. The TSA measures:

- tourism's contribution to GDP;
- tourism's ranking compared to other economic sectors;
- the number of jobs created by tourism;
- the amount of tourism investment tax revenues generated by tourism industries;
- tourism consumption;
- tourism's impact on a nation's balance of payments; and
- characteristics of tourism human resources.

Using the Tourism Satellite Account

The potential uses of the TSA are really significant. They encourage planners and economists to increase and improve knowledge of the relative importance of tourism in a country or region. As a result, it is also an important instrument for politicians wishing to advocate support for the sector and provides support for designing more efficient policies relating to tourism and its employment aspects. The data from the TSA can be used to create awareness among tourism stakeholders of the economic importance of tourism and its contribution to the wider economy. Current and future work on the TSA is focusing on the regional level, human resources, culture and the environment (see Jones, 2013).

DISCUSSION QUESTIONS

1. Draft a two-page briefing paper for a newly elected tourism minister explaining the benefits of the TSA concept.
2. Using the Internet, examine a set of TSA for a country of your choice. How 'user friendly' is the report for policy makers or politicians?
3. Visit the World Travel and Tourism Council website (www.wttc.org) and look at the way that they use TSA data. How credible is their approach?

Sources:
Jones, C. (2013) Scenarios for greenhouse gas emissions reduction from tourism: an extended tourism satellite account approach in a regional setting *Journal of Sustainable Tourism* **21**(3), 458–472.
Statistics Canada (2006) *Human Resource Module of the Tourism Satellite Account 1997–2002*, Statistics Canada, Ottawa.
UNWTO (2001) *The Tourism Satellite Account as an Ongoing Process: Past, Present and Future Developments*, UNWTO, Madrid.
UNWTO (2009) *Tourism Satellite Account Data Around the World: Worldwide Summary*, UNWTO, Madrid.

The Demand Side of Tourism: Measurement Issues

The measurement of tourism demand is important for two key reasons:

1. Estimates of the number of tourists to a destination drive the economic models that assess the role of tourism in an economy.

2. Governments are keen to monitor and attach measures to the movement of people within, into and out of their countries. Measures of incoming tourism are particularly important because of the economic benefits.

Most statistics of tourism demand represent the best estimates available rather than an absolute value. They have the following broad benefits:

- They often provide valuable trend data, where information is produced over a number of time periods.
- Information about the origins of visitors, their trip and attitudes can be used in marketing or planning.
- They enable the effects of decisions or changes to be monitored.
- They provide a means of making forecasts.
- They allow economists to measure the contribution of tourism to the overall economy.
- They assist in providing a platform of data to inform policy.
- Commercial organisations use tourism statistics for marketing purposes.

In addition to the above, local and regional tourism organisations and individual businesses make use of domestic tourism statistics as an aid to decision making.

The measurement of demand normally includes statistics of volume, value and profiles. In addition, during the collection of such data from visitors, questions are also often asked that relate to visitor opinions and attitudes.

Measures of Demand

Volume statistics

The total number of international tourist arrivals, the total number of international tourist departures and domestic tourism are the three key measures of demand. These measures are actually of trips and not counts of individuals. A serious weakness in using tourism arrivals, as far as most tourism suppliers are concerned, is that the length of stay is not taken into account. The length of stay is important for accommodation establishments. A better measure of volume for many purposes is therefore total tourist nights. This also acts as a measure of likely impact on a tourist destination.

Value (Expenditure) Statistics

Total visitor expenditure is a simple measure of the economic value of visitors to a destination. It normally includes spending within the destination, and excludes fare payments made to international passenger carriers for travel into and out of that country.

Visitor Profile Statistics

Profile statistics are made up of statistics relating to the visitor and include trip characteristics and demographics.

Measurement methods

Tourism statistics are normally estimates rather than exact values. The reasons for this mainly centre on the fact that monitoring and measuring what are at times complex movements of people is not easy and is a process subject to error.

Volume statistics are often obtained using counting procedures at entry and exit points to a country or (for inbound tourism) sometimes through the use of registration forms at accommodation establishments. Nevertheless, there are many countries that do make counts and collect information at frontiers for tourism-related purposes. Clearly, islands have an advantage in this respect, since there are likely to be fewer entry/exit points. A major problem with using counts made by accommodation establishments alone is that they give only partial coverage as they omit those staying with friends or relatives.

Expenditure statistics are notoriously difficult to collect. We can derive them using foreign currency estimates from banks, or from suppliers of tourism services and facilities such as hotels or attractions. These methods are cumbersome and normally not satisfactory as they require the cooperation of these organisations and often are only provided as estimates. Increasingly, therefore, information is collected directly from the tourists themselves, through sample surveys of foreign tourists as they leave the country, and from nationals as they return from a foreign trip, either on entry to the country or through household surveys.

Household surveys are used to measure domestic and outbound tourism. A structured sample of households is constructed and interviewers are employed to collect information using a questionnaire. Questions normally relate to past behaviour, covering trips already made, although studies of intentions are sometimes undertaken.

En route surveys are surveys of travellers during the course of their journey. Strategic points are selected on key surface transport routes to stop or approach people, who are then either interviewed or given a questionnaire or other documentation, to complete in their own time for return by post. A major problem with this type of work is that the representativeness of the sample can be in doubt because of incomplete knowledge of traffic movement within a country.

Surveys are often conducted at popular tourist destinations or in areas where there are high levels of tourist activity. They typically lead to estimates of the volume and value of tourism to the destination, and to profiles of visitors and their visits. Questions are also asked to elicit opinions about the destination and associated attitudes.

Surveys of suppliers of tourism services are sometimes undertaken in order to gain information on topics such as occupancy rates or visitor numbers.

Using Tourism Statistics

There are a number of points to bear in mind when using tourism statistics:

- For measurements which result from sample surveys, in general the smaller the sample size, the greater is the probable error.
- Even though the sample size for data relating to a region or country may give rise to acceptable levels of error, an analysis of a subset of the data, pertaining to a smaller area or region, may not be feasible owing to the much reduced sample size.
- Sample size is not everything. The true random sampling of tourists who are, by their very nature, on the move is not normally possible. A sample has to be formally and carefully constructed.
- Where methodology in collecting data changes (even when it is for the better), it is dangerous to compare results.
- There are serious problems involved in attempting either to compare or to combine figures collected by different countries or organisations.

The Economic Consequences of Tourism

Introduction

As an activity of global significance, tourism has economic consequences for enterprises, communities, destinations, regions and countries. Quite simply, the economic significance of tourism is due to the fact that tourists earn money in their place of residence but spend it at the destination. Economic impact analysis then tracks and aggregates these monetary payments as they move through the destination's economy (Dwyer *et al.*, 2010). As a result, tourism generates significant revenues, estimated at US$1159 billion in 2013 from international tourism, and generates significant numbers of jobs globally, estimated by the World Travel and Tourism Council at almost 266 million jobs in 2014. One of the key areas of research has been upon the way that the money and jobs generated by tourism circulate around the destination economy and 'multiply' to create further income and jobs (Dwyer *et al.*, 2015). We deal with this aspect of the economics of tourism later in this chapter.

An important development is the conceptualisation of the tourism-related sector of the economy as the 'visitor economy', encompassing not only the economic significance of tourism, but also allowing the analysis of the supply chain and policy-related decisions which may impact upon the sector (Deloitte, 2008).

In the past, research focusing upon the economic consequences of tourism was more commonly done at the national scale rather than the regional or the local. As Wall and Mathieson (2006) state, there are a variety of reasons for this:

- Economic consequences of tourism are more readily measurable than say environmental or social impacts. As a result, data are available, and these are more commonly collected at the national level.

- The methodologies for assessing the economic consequences of tourism are well established. Indeed, contemporary econometric models and in particular 'computable general equilibrium (CGE) models', allow us to estimate the impact of policy changes or changes in demand upon the economic value of tourism by modelling the whole economy within which tourism lies (Dwyer *et al.*, 2015).

- Research funding agencies and tourist boards believe that results of investigations into the economic value of tourism will deliver *positive* results that can be used for political purposes, whilst studies focusing on the environment or host communities will tend to be more *negative*. It is interesting to note, however, that the contemporary approach of the CGE model does not always place tourism in a positive economic light.

Wall and Mathieson (2006) observe that the consequences of tourism for a destination will depend upon:

1. The type of tourism generated to the destination. For example international tourists tend to spend more than domestic tourists, and sectors such as business or conference tourism spend more than leisure tourists. The consequences will also differ according to the length of stay of the visitor and the generating regions of the tourists.

2. The ability of the national economy to leverage from the economic consequences of tourism in terms of the capacity to invest in tourism, and whether the level of tourism development is sufficient to allow economies of scale for suppliers.

3. The organisation of capital at the destination in terms of how much foreign investment is present and the capacity of the domestic economy to generate capital to support tourism. In many destinations, the hotel sector is a popular form of investment for foreigners.

The greater the level of foreign capital, the greater the 'leakage' of profits on the investment back to the foreign company. This is a common issue for destinations dependent upon international tour operators for their market and developments – Cyprus is a good example here.

4. Attributes of the destination in terms of the structure of the market, the degree of dependence upon intermediaries, and the degree of seasonality.

5. The setting of the destination in terms of whether it is in a developing or developed economy, the political structures and its geographical location in terms of being peripheral or more central in a region.

Mini Case Study 3.2
Evaluating the Economic Effects of Events

Introduction

As one-off occurrences, events present a unique and particular context for evaluating economic consequences. Economic evaluations take place to ensure that events are contributing to the destination and living up to the expectations of sponsors and organisers. Ideally events should be evaluated in the round, including environmental impacts and the impacts on local residents (see Ma, 2013), but in practice economic evaluation is the most common. (See Figure 3.1 for a summary of the approach.)

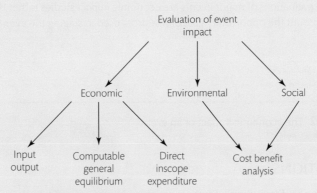

Figure 3.1 Evaluating the impact of an event
Source: Jago and Dwyer, 2006

Why Evaluate Events?

It is important to evaluate the economic consequences of events as often their organisers have to seek funding and sponsorship, and to do this they need to justify the benefits of the event both for its duration and its legacy. It is also important to recognise that events can have economic costs as well as benefits. These costs can be in the form of opportunity costs, revenue losses and leakages, and the reputation of the destination. As such, there needs to be thorough evaluation of the economic costs and benefits generated by an event to justify the funding assistance they may receive, as well as to assess their overall impact. In other words, comprehensive and robust approaches to event evaluation are important. Jago and Dwyer (2006) are clear:

'Economic evaluations of special events reveal important information about events to stakeholders and enable the new expenditure and employment created for the host region to be measured' (p. 2).

Economic Evaluation of Events

Economic evaluation of events has been the subject of many different, and inconsistent, methods over the years. These have often exaggerated the positive economic impact of the event, overstating the benefits by not counting the cost of staging the event, or by including expenditure that would have occurred anyway, without the event. Jago and Dwyer (2006, p. 3) include other evaluation 'myths':

- all special events create economic benefits;
- the construction of new facilities is always a benefit;
- all visitor expenditure is the same;
- events generate substantial employment; and
- all spending by event participants counts in calculating economic benefit.

The two most common methods of economic evaluation are input–output models and computable general equilibrium (CGE) models. In a definitive report on economic evaluation, Jago and Dwyer (2006) clearly favour the CGE method. Such methods are driven by the data on expenditure at the event. This is determined by:

- the number of visitors;
- the types of visitors;
- the type of event;
- the trip duration of visitors;
- costs at the host destination; and
- spending by organisers and sponsors.

Finally, most economic evaluations of major events are economic *impact* studies rather than *evaluation* exercises, as they do not take into account the opportunity cost of resources used in staging the event (see Figure 3.2).

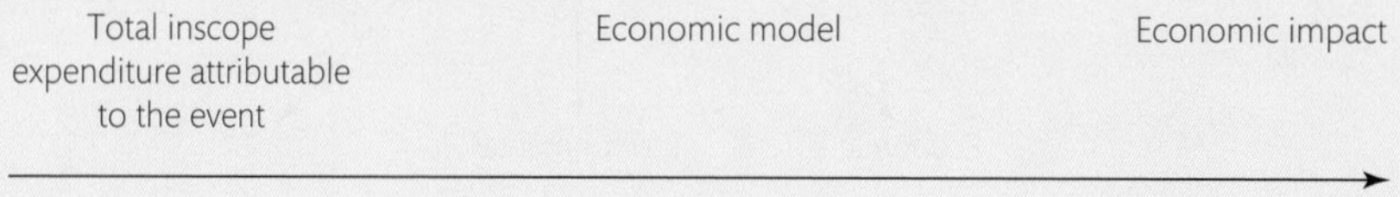

Total inscope expenditure attributable to the event	Economic model	Economic impact

Figure 3.2 The economic impact of an event
Source: Jago and Dwyer, 2006

DISCUSSION QUESTIONS

1. Taking an event that you are familiar with, list the main categories of expenditure that would determine its economic impact.

2. As an event organiser, how would you use information about the economic 'benefits' of your event?

3. Why do you think that the environmental and community consequences of events is relatively little researched?

Sources:
Jago, L. and Dwyer, L. (2006) *Economic Evaluation of Special Events: A Practitioner's Guide*, Common Ground, Altona, Victoria.
Ma, S.G., Mab, S.M., Wuc, J.H. and Rotherham, I.D. (2013) Host residents' perception changes on major sport events, *European Sport Management Quarterly*, **13**(5), 511–536.

The Concept of the Tourism Multiplier

Tourism economists have focused much of their research upon the fact that tourist expenditure at the destination increases the income of the destination by an amount greater than that which was originally spent. In other words, expenditure 'multiplies' as it circulates around the destination. This is known as the 'multiplier effect'. The actual multiplier itself is the numerical coefficient indicating how much destination income will increase due to the initial injection of tourist spending – the higher the multiplier, the greater the amount of additional income generated. In other words an income multiplier of 1.5 means that for every $10 spent at the destination by the tourist, $15 will be generated as the tourist initially pays for accommodation, and the hoteliers themselves purchase food and other services and their suppliers pay out, say, wages or rent to stay in business. This is an example of the 'dynamic' nature of destination economies and shows that the initial spending by the visitor is only the first stage of the economic consequences of tourism for a destination (Figure 3.3).

The tourism *income* multiplier is the most commonly used coefficient, but it is also possible to calculate tourism *employment* multipliers and *government revenue* multipliers.

Multipliers give different values according to the type of consequence desired:

- **Direct effects** – the actual expenditure or jobs generated by spending on tourism commodities.

- **Indirect effects** – the secondary effect of tourist spending as money is paid to traders and other suppliers by the primary recipients of the revenue. In other words, hotels pay the laundry companies to clean the bed linen and, in turn, they generate jobs.

- **Induced effects** – created by the contribution of tourist spending as it feeds into the general health of the economy in terms of income, jobs and government revenue.

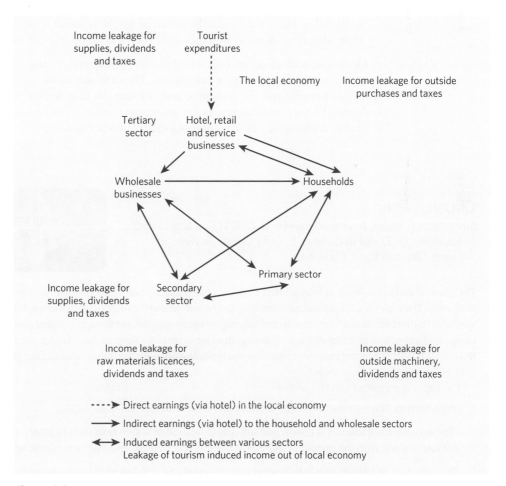

Figure 3.3 The economic impact of tourism in a locality and leakage effect
Source: Page and Connell, 2009

Tourism multipliers have generated a large and sometimes controversial literature, in part because the calculation of the multiplier coefficient is so important for supporters of tourism at a destination. In summary, the size of the multiplier depends on three key factors:

1. **The economic self-sufficiency of the destination.** The more self-sufficient a destination, the higher will be the multiplier as the linkages between the different sectors of the economy will be closer. This means that the indirect and induced effects will be greater and there will be less 'leakage' of income and jobs out of the destination. Leakages occur when spending or jobs are lost to other sectors, or income is taken out of the economy by placing it into savings. Of course, self-sufficiency is closely linked to scale – a small destination will be less self-sufficient than a larger one and so the size of the multiplier tends to increase with scale (Figure 3.3).

2. **The econometric technique used.** Tourism economists use different multiplier techniques, and as computing power has increased, these 'econometric techniques' have become increasingly complex. The current debate is between 'input–output models' and the more contemporary 'CGE models' (Dwyer *et al.*, 2003). The development of Tourism Satellite Accounts has been possible due to the CGE models and gradually they are being used as best practice.

3. **The sources of data for the multiplier.** One point that is often overlooked is that all of these techniques are only as good as the data that they use. For multipliers, data at the national level are reasonably reliable, but as we consider multipliers for ever smaller geographical areas – regions and individual destinations, for example – the data become less reliable and often have to be collected by the research team. For example, we saw above that most demand statistics – the fuel of multipliers – are estimates only.

Of course, multipliers are only a tool to allow policy makers and politicians to assess the economic value of tourism to a destination. The next section of this chapter considers the economic benefits and the economic costs of tourism to a destination. It is important to understand these consequences, as any defence of tourism as an activity tends to use positive economic arguments, whilst minimising the economic costs.

Classic Paper

Sinclair, M.T., Blake, A. and Sugiyarto, G. (2003) **The economics of tourism, pp. 22–54 in Cooper, C. (ed.)** *Classic Reviews in Tourism,* **Channel View, Clevedon**

Thea Sinclair and her colleagues have written a 'classic' review paper covering all the main elements of the economics of tourism. The paper is a 'classic' because not only is it complete and thorough in its coverage, but it is also written by specialist tourism economists who are technically highly accomplished, yet write in a highly accessible style. As with all review papers, one of its strengths is its provision of an extensive reference list. This list reads like a road map of the development of tourism economics with names including Brian Archer, John Fletcher, Stephen Wanhill, Stephen Witt, Haiyan Song and Larry Dwyer.

The paper is organised into five sections:

1. **Introduction.** The introduction is authoritative and clear. It begins with a definition:

   'The economics of tourism is concerned with the allocation of scarce resources to satisfy consumers' demand for tourism and with the impact of tourism at the macroeconomic and microeconomic levels' (p. 22).

   The introduction stresses that literature on tourism supply has tended to focus on certain sectors such as transport and accommodation, but the authors rightly point out that demand for tourism has much more coverage.

2. **The demand for tourism.** The authors state that demand analysis is:

   '**useful for increasing our understanding of the relative importance of different economic determinants of demand for forecasting and for related policy formation' (p. 23).**

   In this section of the paper they analyse the various approaches taken by economists to tourism demand based upon the technical approaches offered by different models.

3. **The supply of tourism.** Supply-side issues have long been neglected, mainly due to the complexities of tourism and also the lack of data. However, the development of Tourism Satellite Accounts is redressing this imbalance. We consider Tourism Satellite Accounts in Mini Case Study 3.1.

4. **The wider impacts of tourism.** Tourism has wide economic impacts at both the macro and the micro level, but the strength of this paper is that it considers the relationship between economic impacts and others, such as environmental considerations.

5. **Conclusions.** The authors conclude that demand studies have dominated the study of tourism economics and that there is a need for more policy-related work. They observe that whilst the demand work is analytical, the work required on the supply of tourism is more descriptive. Work on tourism impacts has changed in focus as different techniques have been used, but work linking economic impacts with others, such as the environment, are less common.

   This is a thorough, technically adept and wide-ranging paper written in an accessible authoritative style – a deserved classic.

The Economic Benefits of Tourism

The economic benefits of tourism to a destination can be summarised into three areas – income, employment and regional development.

Income

One of the most significant economic consequences of tourism is the spending generated by tourists at the destination. We have already seen how this 'multiplies' through the destination to generate additional income and contribute to the gross domestic product of regions and countries. The World Travel and Tourism Council estimates that tourism contributes on average 9.5 per cent to the gross domestic product of countries worldwide (www.wttc.org).

At the national scale, income from spending by international tourists counts as an invisible 'export' as it is income that was earned overseas in country A and then spent on products at the destinations of country B. This means the income counts as part of the balance of payments of a country on the travel account. The balance of payments is a country's financial account. Tourism earnings are an 'invisible' export because no tangible goods are involved. This *earned* income is set against income *spent* by residents of that country when they travel abroad. This income spent abroad counts as an 'invisible import' for country A. For countries that have a highly successful inbound tourism industry – such as Spain – this means that the travel account is in credit, whilst for countries such as the UK or Germany, which are major generators of international tourism, the travel accounts are in debit. For the major destinations of the world the scale of their export income is highly significant for the travel account. In contrast, for the major generators of tourism or importers their impact on the travel account is much less significant. Countries with significant international tourism spending and receipts are shown in Table 3.1.

Table 3.1 The 10 leading generators and destinations for international tourism

The leading generators of international tourism (based upon spend)	The leading destinations for international tourism (based upon volume)
China	France
USA	USA
Germany	Spain
UK	China
Russian Federation	Italy
France	Turkey
Canada	Germany
Italy	UK
Australia	Russian Federation
Brazil	Mexico

Source: based on data from UNWTO

The travel account of the balance of payments is based upon direct spending by international tourists. The categories of spending are normally:

- expenditure on tourism commodities such as accommodation, food and beverage and retail;
- tourist expenditure on capital goods – such as antiques;
- imports and exports of goods for tourism (such as wine or equipment);
- payments to carriers for fares;
- money transfers, often by expatriates;
- interest, profits and dividends; and
- foreign capital investment (often in accommodation).

In the future, tourism will be increasingly important in the developing world and many countries are now using tourism as a development option to stimulate their economies. Whilst in the past this was more the case for countries that did not have other forms of income, tourism is increasingly used as a way to diversify economies, as in the oil rich countries of the Middle East.

Of course, the economic benefits will reduce if the country imports many of the goods and services needed to support the tourism sector. For example, in the early years of the development of tourism in many Asian and African countries, expatriate managers and senior staff dominated the hotel sector and governments were prompted to develop strategies to reduce the level of expatriate labour in favour of locally-trained managers. In part, this influx of expatriate labour was caused by a second problem for the countries themselves: a dominance of foreign investment and ownership in the hotel sector.

Finally, tourism spending acts to stimulate investment in the sector and also contributes to government tax revenues, most commonly through indirect taxation of spending but in some countries through a tourism tax on arrivals, departures or beds.

Employment

Tourism is favoured as an economic sector due to its ability to generate and sustain significant levels of employment. As we see in Major Case Study 3.1 at the end of this chapter, tourism generates employment across a wide range of sectors, from accommodation to transportation and guiding, and at a range of levels from the unskilled to the highly trained – such as pilots.

Using multiplier analysis, tourism manpower planning calculates the number of jobs required to support tourism at a destination using the level of tourism expenditure. In other words, there is a threshold of expenditure required to generate each tourism job. Of course, this will depend upon the scale and maturity of the tourism industry at the destination, as well as the level of imported labour for tourism. In the Maldives, for example, levels of imported labour in the island resorts is very high.

Despite the fact that tourism is lauded for its ability to generate significant numbers of jobs quickly, there are major issues relating to the 'quality' of tourism jobs as we see in the case study.

Regional Development

One of the major roles of tourism in an economy is for regional development, particularly in areas where other types of economic activity are difficult – such as mountainous areas or small islands. As a result, tourism development has become an important part of national economic strategies. Tourism is often used as a leading economic sector for development, to be followed by other sectors and investment. Yet the strongest lesson learned from experience around the world is that to be successful as a development option, tourism must be integrated into the rest of the economy and society and have strong public sector leadership, often through a development agency or tourism board. It is also true that the role of tourism is important in the early stages of development but with time, this influence diminishes as the economy develops and other sectors grow.

As an economic development tool, tourism is an important agent of economic change, bringing significant advantages:

- it generates rapid injections of expenditure into the local economy;
- it is a major job creator with jobs that do not require high levels of training. tourism can generate twice as many jobs as other economic sectors such as say oil production;

Alpine landscape – tourism development is often the only viable option for remote rural areas.
Source: © Vaclav Volrab/Shutterstock.com

- it allows for rapid improvements in living standards and creates demand for goods and services;
- for the developing world, tourism delivers the ability to earn foreign currency;
- it creates an infrastructure and facilities of benefit to the local economy and society;
- it encourages the development of an entrepreneurial culture;
- it reduces dependence on primary economic sectors such as mining, oil production and agriculture;
- it helps to maintain the viability of enterprises at the destination; and
- it creates a stimulus for the domestic tourism industry.

These advantages are particularly valuable for two particular types of destinations:

1. Those in the developing world where many countries have low incomes, an uneven distribution of wealth and high unemployment. The economies of these countries are often dependent upon the primary sector and have high levels of economic leakage to the developed world. Here, tourism can be used not only as a development tool but also one of poverty alleviation (as we see in Chapter 5).

2. However, whilst the developing world is often seen as the primary focus for tourism development, we must not forget that in the developing world tourism is a major contributor to the economies of peripheral coastal, mountainous and remote islands where other activities such as agriculture may be marginal – and, of course, tourism is attracted to these areas as they are often of natural beauty.

As we turn to the economic costs of tourism to destinations in the next section, we must remember that both developing country economies and those of peripheral areas tend to have structurally weak economies. Here there is a tendency for significant levels of imports, and tourism development comes with costs involved and leakages through imports of goods and labour.

The Economic Costs of Tourism

As it is the economic dimension which tends to favour tourism in any assessment there is much less work done on the economic costs of tourism. Where work has considered these costs, they have tended to focus only upon the 'direct' costs of tourism rather than the indirect or induced effects. It can be argued, for example, that employment generated by tourism is not 'decent' work – as we outline in the case study at the end of this chapter. We can think of the economic costs of tourism falling into three categories.

1. opportunity cost;
2. overdependence/lack of diversity; and
3. inflation and externalities.

Opportunity Cost

Any tourism development will divert labour and investment resources away from the opportunity for other developments – such as, say, schools or health care. Similarly, government revenues used to enter the tourism market or to promote their destinations will not be available for other uses. This is a key issue for poorer countries justifying tourism development as a means of poverty alleviation. It explains why tourism needs to be integrated into other social and economic strategies for development to ensure a balanced approach. Finally, income spent on tourism is not available for consumers to spend on other goods – such as, say, cars or electrical products.

Overdependence/Lack of Diversity

There is always a danger that a destination will become too dependent upon tourism and therefore exposed in a downturn of demand; tourism demand is, after all, highly volatile, price elastic and prone to changes in fashion and taste. Demand in many parts of the world is also seasonal and this can mean that previously year-round economic activity becomes highly seasonal. In 2015, for example, Egyptian tourism suffered a collapse in demand due to the bombing of a Russian holiday charter plane flying out of Sharm el Sheikh and on-going security problems in the country.

Where a country is dependent upon one or two economic sectors – such as, say, agriculture or mining, the introduction of tourism can reduce activity in those sectors by taking labour and resources away. As a result, the addition of tourism does not help to diversify the economy but is simply a substitute for another sector.

Inflation and Externalities

Tourism can be a cause of inflation in destinations where there is high demand for products. The spending power of tourists may exceed that of the locals and lead to inflation in the price of goods, property and land. This is a common issue in many areas of outstanding natural beauty or cultural heritage destinations such as national parks and heritage towns. This can eventually mean that the local community is unable to afford local housing or to purchase local goods. This has long been a problem in the English Lake District and Snowdonia national parks. In such popular tourism destinations, externalities of tourism as an activity become evident as residents suffer from additional traffic, queues for services and competition for local goods.

SUMMARY

This chapter has mapped out the key dimensions of the economics of tourism. The chapter began by demonstrating the unique characteristics of tourism as an industry, including its highly fragmented nature, the fact that it is an 'invisible' industry and that it is produced where it is consumed. This has meant that economists have struggled to come up with accurate measurements of tourism supply and to define it. However, the development of the Tourism Satellite Account has been a breakthrough in the analysis of the supply side of tourism and is now used to measure the size and scope of the industry and to make credible comparisons with other industries as we saw in the case study. The chapter then went on to outline the economic consequences of tourism, pointing out that this work has a long history, partly because it tends to show tourism in a positive light. Here, the case study showed how the economic consequences of events are an important dimension of event planning. The chapter went on to outline the concept of the tourism multiplier as an important tool for assessing the economic value of tourism to a destination. Quite simply it is a coefficient that represents the extra income or employment earned by an injection of tourism spending into a destination. It is, however, dependent upon accurate statistics of tourism demand, a topic examined in detail in the chapter. The chapter then outlined the main areas where tourism can benefit a destination, focusing on income, employment and regional development. The chapter closed by considering some of the economic costs of tourism, an area that has received less attention until recently. The main costs are related to the nature of tourism jobs, the risk of overdependence, inflation and opportunity cost.

All of these issues are elegantly captured in the classic paper chosen for this chapter on the economics of tourism by Sinclair *et al*. (2003). The chapter closes with a major case study examining the controversies around tourism employment.

Discussion Questions

1. In class, debate whether tourism is an economic force for good or evil at a destination of your choice.
2. Using UNWTO statistics create a table of the top 10 country spenders and earners from international tourism for 2015, 2005, 1995 and 1985. Highlight the changes over time and explain why these have occurred.
3. Draft a briefing document for a regional planning minister outlining the benefits of using tourism to lead investment into a remote coastal region.
4. Research the concept of opportunity cost and discuss its significance when considering tourism in a developing country of your choice.
5. Why has tourism proved so difficult to define and measure on the supply side?

Annotated Further Reading

1. Dwyer, L., Forsyth, P. and Dwyer, W. (2010) *Tourism Economics and Policy*, Channel View, Bristol.
   The most comprehensive text on tourism economics set to become a classic.
2. Dwyer, L., Forsyth, P. and Papatheodorou, A. (2015) Economics of tourism, pp. 13–30 in Cooper, C. (ed.) *Contemporary Tourism Reviews, Volume 1*, Goodfellow Publishers, Oxford.
   An advanced and thorough treatment of all aspects of tourism economics.
3. Dwyer, L. and Forsyth, P. (2008) *International Handbook On The Economics Of Tourism*, Edward Elgar, Cheltenham.
   Comprehensive volume covering all the main topic of tourism economics.
4. Ioannides, D. and Debbage, K.G. (eds) (1998) *The Economic Geography of the Tourist Industry: A Supply Side Analysis*, Routledge, London.
   Excellent and comprehensive edited volume on the supply side of tourism.
5. Riley, M., Ladkin, A. and Szivas, E. (2002) *Tourism Employment: Analysis and Planning*, Channel View, Clevedon.
   Thorough text examining all aspects of tourism employment.
6. Smith, S.L.J. (1996) *Tourism Analysis: A Handbook*, 2nd edn, Longman, Harlow.
   Thorough text on supply-side definitions and measurement.
7. Song, H., Dwyer, L. and Li, G. (2012) Tourism economics research: a review and assessment, *Annals of Tourism Research* 39(3), 1653–1682.
   Advanced review of the tourism economics literature.

8. Stabler, M.J., Papatheodorou, A. and Sinclair, M.T. (2010) *The Economics of Tourism*, Routledge, London.
   Readable and comprehensive coverage of tourism economics.

9. UNWTO (2001) *The Tourism Satellite Account as an Ongoing Process: Past, Present and Future Developments*, UNWTO, Madrid.
   Excellent summary of the development, concept and use of the TSA.

10. Wall, G. and Mathieson, A. (2006) *Tourism: Change, Impacts and Opportunities*, 2nd edn, Pearson, Harlow.
    Excellent second edition of the key text examining the consequences of tourism.

References Cited

Debbage, K.G. and Ioannides, D. (1998) Conclusion: the commodification of tourism, pp. 287–292 in Ioannides, D. and Debbage, K.G., *The Economic Geography of the Tourist Industry: A Supply Side Analysis*, Routledge, London.

Deloitte (2008) *The Economic Case for the Visitor Economy: Final Report*, Deloitte/Visit Britain, London.

Dwyer, L., Forsyth, P. and Dwyer, W. (2010) *Tourism Economics and Policy*, Channel View, Bristol.

Dwyer, L., Forsyth, P. and Papatheodorou, A. (2015) Economics of tourism, pp. 13–30 in Cooper, C. (ed.) *Contemporary Tourism Reviews, Volume 1*, Goodfellow Publishers, Oxford.

Leiper, N. (1990) Partial industrialisation of tourism systems, *Annals of Tourism Research*, 7, 600–605.

Page, S. and Connell, J (2009) *Tourism: A Modern Synthesis*, Cengage, Andover.

Sinclair, M.T., Blake, A. and Sugiyarto, G. (2003) The economics of tourism, pp. 22–54 in Cooper, C (ed.) *Classic Reviews in Tourism*, Channel View, Clevedon.

Wall, G. and Mathieson, A. (2006) *Tourism: Change, Impacts and Opportunities*, Pearson, Harlow.

Major Case Study 3.1
Contemporary Tourism Employment Issues

Tourism employment has become a major issue for the twenty-first century.
Source: © Adie Bush/Getty Images

Introduction

The International Labour Organization is campaigning for all jobs to be *decent jobs* (www.ilo.org). One criticism of tourism employment is that the quality of the jobs is poor. This impacts upon the ability of tourism destinations to deliver the tourist experience as enterprises find it difficult not only to find employees, but also those with the right skills. Tourism is in a trap – as more tourism is demanded, more jobs are created, increasing the pressure on the supply of skilled manpower in both the long and the short term (Baum, 2007).

The Role of Tourism Employment

Tourism is a powerful instrument for development because the travel and tourism sector directly and indirectly employs large numbers of people, generating jobs across a broad spectrum of economic activity. In addition, employment in the tourism sector is considerably varied and the variety of opportunities makes the sector attractive to new entrants into the labour market and groups prone to unemployment, such as young people, women or those with minimal education.

Tourism employment contributes in a major way to the long-term sustainability of destinations, where locals are employed and trained and the income flows directly to the local economy. Tourism employment also goes some way to alleviating poverty by giving families the economic wherewithal to break out of the poverty trap and transcend issues of poverty and gender. Tourism employment in the twenty-first century is, however, characterised by a range of issues.

Contemporary Tourism Employment Issues

Image and Working Conditions

The image and working conditions of tourism employment make jobs within the sector seem particularly unfavourable. As a result, the sector suffers from high labour turnover, which comes at a cost for the employer. This is exacerbated by the working conditions in tourism, which are characterised by low wages, temporary and part-time employment and anti-social hours. Naturally, employers adopt these strategies to match their labour supply with the periods of demand for tourism – for example, catering companies covering meal times.

To move towards *decent work* in tourism, there is a need to change the mindset of both governments and communities towards employment in tourism. The mindset needs to change to one that values people, their skills and knowledge, develops them, rewards them and treats them as valued resources. This will demand innovative responses to human resources practice, reward systems, working conditions and skill development that are crucial to offset further supply shortages. In other words, what is needed is a change in human resource practice that both develops talent and invests in the work force.

Understanding Tourism Labour Markets

These issues cannot be resolved if we are unable to assess the scale and scope of the problem. Until recently, tourism labour markets were difficult to measure and to monitor – for a variety of reasons. In particular, estimations of jobs generated by tourism have proved elusive and complex to measure because many jobs in the sector are indirect, seasonal and informal. With the TSA methodology it is possible to understand and measure labour markets, to diagnose the problems and to act. This will allow planners to view an accurate picture of the pyramid that comprises tourism jobs (with unskilled labour at the bottom and executives at the top). Approaches such as labour market observatories, with their local and regional monitoring of labour markets, mean that this information can be fine-grained and allow for rapid decision-making and creative approaches to manpower planning and policy. In other words, governments will be able to plan for future labour and training needs from a platform of knowledge rather than guesswork.

Destination Employment

Whilst some issues relating to tourism employment are universal, others are specific to particular types of destinations – such as high labour turnover in urban areas, or isolation of workers on island destinations. Development of localised solutions to respond to tourism and labour market characteristics at the destination level are therefore important. These include developing skills for new and emerging niche products such as nature-based tourism and the challenge of skills for technology and the new digital world of marketing.

Human Capital Issues

As with other sectors, tourism faces issues of human capital in the future. These include an ageing workforce in many destinations, the changing attitudes to work of Gen X and Gen Y, and the real issue of competition for labour from other economic sectors. Tourism also creates real issues relating to the mobility of labour, mutual recognition of qualifications across borders and the imperative to develop skills to encourage future labour mobility across trading blocs such as the EU or ASEAN.

To solve these issues, sector leadership will be required to change the image of tourism employment as low paid and servile, and awareness programmes for communities will need to be designed to show young people the value of a career in tourism. This will help to make tourism more attractive as a career choice and help people to build a career in the sector, a sector which must be seen as offering 'decent work'.

DISCUSSION QUESTIONS

1. Using job vacancy websites, compare the conditions and wages of a catering position with other positions in IT, finance or retail. Draw up a table comparing the jobs and in class debate the most attractive positions.

2. As a regional manager of a large fast food franchise, draft a strategy to retain your entry-level staff.

3. In many countries, awareness campaigns are being designed to showcase the benefits of a career in tourism – draft the outline approach to such a campaign in a country that you are familiar with.

Sources:

Baum, T. (2007) Human resources in tourism: still waiting for change, *Tourism Management* **28**, 1383–1399.

OECD (2014) *Supporting Quality Jobs in Tourism*, OECD, Paris.

Riley, M., Ladkin, A. and Szivas, E. (2002) *Tourism Employment: Analysis and Planning*, Channel View, Clevedon. www.ilo.org

CHAPTER 4
THE ENVIRONMENTAL CONSEQUENCES OF TOURISM

Learning Outcomes

This chapter considers the major issue of the consequences of tourism for the environment. This is a complex area as, whilst tourism is dependent upon environmental quality to attract and support visitors, it also can have a detrimental effect upon those very environments – and their climate. This chapter is designed to provide you with:

- an understanding of the historical dimensions of tourism and the environment;

- an awareness of the importance of a disciplined approach based upon carrying capacity;

- an appreciation of both the negative and positive consequences of tourism for the environment;

- an understanding of the techniques of environmental impact assessment and environmental auditing; and

- an awareness of the broader issues relating to tourism and the environment.

Photograph: Penguins on an iceberg © doethion/Fotolia.com

Introduction

In this chapter we adopt a broad interpretation of the environment to include not only the natural environment, but also the built environment of historic and archaeological sites and destination landscapes. In other words, we consider the environment in all its forms and the ecosystems within that environment. Gössling (2002) is clear on the need to maintain the integrity of ecosystems as they provide services essential to the survival of humanity, yet we know little about how much stress ecosystems can endure, or how they function. An essential component here is to understand the role of tourism within the ecosystem. We must also recognise that the consequences of tourism for the environment are substantial, but that in fact these consequences are associated with only a small percentage of the world's population – those that can afford to travel. Wall and Mathieson (2006) identify the most critical ecosystems for tourism as:

- coastlines;
- oceanic islands and marine ecosystems;
- mountains;
- polar ecosystems; and
- tropical rainforests.

The Developing Relationship Between Tourism and the Environment

Since the 1970s, the relationship between tourism and the environment has been in the headlines, although the debate goes back much further in history. Many forms of tourism depend upon the environment, and its quality, for their resource base and attractions – think, for example, of areas of scenic natural beauty such as the Canadian Rockies, or the national parks of Africa where the wildlife resources are the key draw for tourism. The environment, too, figures large in much tourism promotion and many destination images – the 100% Pure New Zealand campaign being an obvious example here (www.tourismnewzealand.com/). In the twenty-first century it is the issue of climate change that has dominated, and there is no doubt that tourism is a 'climate sensitive' sector. Of course, tourism can also benefit the environment, not only by providing economic support and investment, but also in terms of educating tourists to understand and protect the environment. Ultimately it is the unique and special places on the earth that attract tourism, and in turn these ecosystems are the most fragile and vulnerable to change. But, as we have stressed in other chapters, it is the fact that tourists have to visit the resource itself to consume it, and that this visitation is focused in space and time, that leads to the potential pressures on the environments visited. Add to this the fact that environmental costs are rarely built into the price of tourism, and the classic conflict between the long-term horizons of sustainable development and the short-term view of developers, and the stage is set for a constant tension. Holden (2009) takes this one step further, arguing that the sustainability debate has had little impact on the practical 'business' of tourism and that, if it is to do so, then we need to understand how tourism markets function. This tension is now part of a global debate on how to address climate change, where tourism and mobility have become a key part of the discussion.

The relationship between tourism and the environment is therefore a complex one and one that has evolved over time. Before 1945 the scale of tourism was such that there were few major issues, aside from hot spots of activity such as the English Lake District where in the late nineteenth century measures were being taken to protect it from excessive visitation. Indeed, early commentators on tourism saw it as a flawless industry – without smokestacks – that can benefit the environment. With the rise of mass international tourism in the 1960s, however, and excessive resort developments in areas such as coastal Spain, the relationship became more problematic, leading to real conflict between tourism and the environment. The full-blown development of mass tourism in the 1970s lead to a wave of environmental concerns and the call for new approaches to address the situation; new models of tourism and planning were required which eventually emerged in the form of sustainable tourism. We deal with these developments in Chapter 6.

An important development was the promotion of alternative, responsible or ecotourism products. Newsome *et al.* (2012) note that whilst there are many forms of alternative or allegedly 'low-impact' tourism, the term 'ecotourism' is the most commonly used. Ecotourism, or more strictly nature-based tourism, is often seen as the solution to negative environmental impacts. Ecotourism is seen as low-impact, encouraging responsible and 'environmentally friendly' visitors, and utilising low-impact developments and forms of transport. Ecotourism is also dominantly 'non-consumptive', i.e. it does not involve killing or harming the fauna and flora; rather it is seen as having a strong educational component. A major critic of this approach is Brian Wheeller, who dismisses ecotourism as 'ego tourism', vociferously stating that all forms of tourism are damaging to the environment – ecotourism and other forms of alternative tourism are simply smokescreens for tourism developments that can be pushed through under the cloak of 'self-righteous virtue' (Wheeller, 2003). Nonetheless, ecotourism continues to grow without challenge and is legitimised through societies and organisations. We now turn to an important concept that mediates the relationship between tourism and the environment.

Carrying Capacity

The relationship between tourism and the environment is determined by the carrying capacity of the resource in question. Quite simply, the environment becomes stressed when visitor capacity is exceeded. However, whilst this seems a deceptively simple concept, to operationalise carrying capacity is much more difficult. This is because, at the end of the day, deciding upon when an environment becomes stressed is a subjective judgement. It is interesting, for example, that different groups – planners, residents and visitors – may perceive this 'threshold' of stress differently.

The concept of carrying capacity has a long pedigree. It was originally developed by resource managers in agriculture and forestry to determine the cropping levels that plots of land could sustain without nutrients and other food sources being depleted. In tourism, carrying capacity refers to the ability of a destination to take tourism use without deteriorating in some way. In other words, it defines the relationship between the resource base and the market and is influenced by the characteristics of each.

One of the best definitions is by Mathieson and Wall (1982):

'The maximum number who can use a site without unacceptable deterioration in the physical environment and without an unacceptable decline in the quality of experience gained by visitors' (p. 21).

This definition raises three key points:

1. Carrying capacity can be managed, and there is no absolute number for any destination. For example, a beach can appear crowded with very few visitors present, while a wooded area can absorb many more visitors.

2. There are two sets of influences upon carrying capacity for any environmental system: the tourist, and the resource itself, as shown in Figure 4.1.

3. Carrying capacity is determined by managers who decide when the decline in the visitor experience becomes 'unacceptable'.

Regarding environmental impact, we can think of five types of carrying capacity:

1. **Physical carrying capacity** refers to the number of facilities available, such as aircraft seats or car parking spaces. It is easy to measure and can be calculated on a simple percentage basis.

2. **Environmental or biological carrying capacity** is more difficult to measure and refers to limits of use in the ecosystem. There is increasing interest in the capacity not only of the vegetation cover to take tourism use but also of animal life, such as whale or dolphin watching, or tourism in the African game reserves.

Figure 4.1 Influences upon carrying capacity

3. **Psychological or behavioural carrying capacity** refers to the point at which the visitor feels that additional people in the environment would spoil the experience. This is less straightforward than may appear at first sight. Completely empty spaces are just as problematic as crowded ones, and the type of tourist also has an effect on perceptions of crowding.

4. **Social carrying capacity** is a measure of the ability of the host community to tolerate tourism. It is a more recent addition to typologies of capacity but is becoming an important issue. Indeed one of the most important tests of a sustainable tourist destination is the level of involvement of the local community in plans and decisions relating to tourism development.

5. **Economic carrying capacity** refers to the point at which the investment needed to sustain environmental quality becomes prohibitive.

Carrying capacity is a pivotal concept when we are considering the consequences of tourism for the environment. We now turn to the positive and negative consequences of tourism for the environment.

Consequences of Tourism for the Environment

Mutual Benefit

Whilst the headlines capture the 'hotspots' of conflict between tourism and the environment, there are in fact, three key areas where tourism can benefit the environment:

1. **Conservation.** The cause of tourism has been influential in encouraging the conservation of areas of natural beauty and their built heritage. National parks, marine reserves, historic monuments and archaeological sites all benefit economically from tourism. Tourism also encourages good practice in terms of planning and management, and drives the motivation for interpretation and visitor education which in turn help to protect fragile environments and monuments. This is practiced internationally by UNESCO and locally by national governments (www.unesco.org). Indeed tourism can be a motivation for the rehabilitation of built and natural environments – historic warehouses on the dock side in cities as far apart as Oslo and Yokohama have been saved by converting them into retail and food & beverage outlets for a dominantly tourism-driven market. Given these successes, tourism can then be used as a persuasive argument for continued protection of a site if it is threatened. It also makes the case for vibrant historic town centres beloved by the 'creative class' which leads to civic prosperity (see case study in Chapter 12).

2. **Environmental education.** Environmental education of visitors as a way of raising awareness of environmental values has become a major activity in many protected areas and sites of historic interest. Using the varied media of interpretation – including museums, trails, guides and new technology to curate the experience – visitors learn about the unique characteristics of their destination and can, in turn, be moved to protect it, and often police it. Here, the concept of 'visitor payback' works in favour of the environment with the visitor remitting monies back to the destination for conservation long after the visit. Of course, education of visitors has a long history, with the Victorians learning about different environments and landscapes through painting and literature, but it is the contemporary, though undervalued, technique of interpretation and guiding which has made a major contribution here. Gössling (2002) observes that tourism and travel have therefore initiated changes in the relationship between humans and the environment in terms of knowledge, attitudes and behaviour. Here, we can think of the environment as a 'social or cultural construction', such that attitudes towards the environment in Mediterranean countries, or in China, are very different to those in the Western world of say, the USA or the UK.

3. **The built environment.** Tourism does, of course, bring a range of benefits for the built environment, some of which were noted above. Where buildings and landscapes have been designed for tourism and pleasure – such as coastal resorts or the historic landscaped gardens of the UK – tourism leaves a valuable legacy in terms of architecture, landscapes and urban detailing. Think, for example, of the resort landscapes of San Sebastian in northern Spain (www.sansebastianspain.info) or of Brighton in the United Kingdom (www.visitbrighton.com/). Tourism also provides the economic lifeblood of resorts and increasingly is seen as a means of supporting new 'mixed' developments for both tourists and residents. The central area of Manly, a resort in the Sydney suburbs, does this well.

Conflict

Whilst there are many beneficial effects of tourism for the environment, the list of negative consequences is easier to draft and to describe. The scale and significance of environmental impact depends both upon the type of tourism involved and the nature of the resource. New forms of tourism are beginning to introduce new impacts – geo-tourism, for example, is seeing an increase in the collection of minerals and fossils at important geological locations. In the next section we outline the main negative consequences of tourism, beginning with possibly the most significant of all, that of climate change.

Climate change

We can think of climate change as 'significant changes in long-term average weather patterns, which in turn shifts the climatic characteristic of a region over time to new conditions' (Dwyer *et al.*, 2007). It is only in recent decades that the consequences of travel for air quality, and particularly for climate change, have been realised. As a result, tourism is now both 'a victim and a vector' of climate change. The additional activity of transportation due to tourism increases carbon emissions with estimates suggesting that tourism accounts for around 5 per cent of the world's total emissions. Aircraft are particularly damaging as

Urban warehouse district with shops and cafés – tourism provides a viable use for derelict industrial heritage.
Source: © LatitudeStock/Alamy Images

Table 4.1 Emissions from international and domestic global tourism (including same day visitors), 2005

	Carbon dioxide (Mt)
Transport	517
Other transport	468
Accommodation	274
Activities	45
Total tourism	1304
Total world	26 400
Share	4.95%

Source: UNWTO, 2007

their emissions take place at high altitude, but accommodation is also a major contributor to greenhouse gas emissions. Research is only now beginning to examine this issue – long-haul tourism, for example, has very high emissions, contributing 17 per cent of global tourism-related carbon dioxide emissions, but it only represents 2.7 per cent of all tourist trips (see Table 4.1).

Climate change is a complex issue that we are only now beginning to understand and model. As a result, it has been realised that tourism development and activity as 'business-as-usual' is not sustainable for the environment, or for future economic development. Indeed, tourism decision-making and decision-makers are already impacted by climate change (see Buzinde *et al.*, 2009). This means that we are facing 'new realities' of tourism in a time of climate change, and these have begun to dominate international policy debates, fuelled by forecasts of economic and social disruption to life styles, health, social well-being and political stability – indeed destinations such as Venice, the Maldives and some Pacific islands are in danger for their very existence and will generate 'climate refugees'.

There are two linked processes of climate change at work:

1. **Global warming.** With the accumulation of greenhouse gases in the atmosphere generated by transportation, air conditioning and other processes, solar radiation is prevented from escaping from the earth and therefore leads to a warming effect. this has consequences for tourism destinations including:

   - coral bleaching in iconic destinations such as the Great Barrier Reef;
   - retreat of the snowline for winter sports resorts in, say, the European Alps;
   - excessive temperatures at beach resorts;
   - rising sea level threatening destinations such as the Pacific islands;
   - more extreme weather events such as hurricanes, heavy precipitation, typhoons and heat waves;
   - changing climate zones impacting upon wetlands and deserts, creating water shortages; and
   - changing tourism consumer decision-making and demand patterns as transport costs and taxation increase – long-haul destinations in particular are vulnerable to these changes in demand patterns. This is an area that has yet to be researched in detail.

2. **Depletion of the ozone layer.** Release of certain gases into the atmosphere from devices such as air conditioning units and fridges has reduced the effectiveness of the ozone layer to filter out harmful UVB sunrays. These rays can cause eye cataracts and skin cancer and have led to many beach resorts having to adjust their products to 'beach plus' where

additional products such as sports and theme parks have been developed as visitors no longer want to spend all day in the sun.

Addressing Climate Change

There are three key ways that the tourism sector can address climate change:

1. **offset** the carbon emissions created by tourism, for example by tree planting;
2. **mitigate** the impact of tourism on climate change by changing industry practices and consumer behaviour; and
3. **adapt** destinations and consumer behaviour to climate change.

To address these pressing needs, the world's two leading agencies for tourism, the UNWTO and the WTTC, have both developed strategies that fast track the response of tourism to slow climate change.

The UNWTO has held a series of meetings to discuss the issue of tourism and climate change. These began in Djerba, Tunisia in 2003 and now include side events at international climate change conferences, such as the Copenhagen UN Climate Change conference in 2012. One of the most significant meetings was in Davos, Switzerland in 2007. It led to the 'Davos Declaration' (UNWTO, 2009), which states that all tourism stakeholders – governments, the industry, destinations and research networks – need to harness their energies to address climate change focusing in particular on the following points:

- Climate is a key resource for tourism and the sector is highly sensitive to climate change and global warming.
- Given the importance of tourism in the global challenges of climate change and poverty alleviation there is an urgent need to consider policies that encourage truly sustainable tourism, reflecting a quadruple bottom-line of environmental, economic, social and climate responsiveness. This recognises that these global challenges are linked and reinforcing and must be addressed within the framework of the Sustainable Development Goals (SDGs).
- The tourism sector must respond to climate change and progressively reduce its greenhouse gas emissions. This will need action to mitigate the greenhouse gas emissions of tourism, especially from transport and accommodation.
- Tourism businesses and destinations must adapt to changing climate conditions (an issue we deal with in Chapter 14).
- Existing and new technology must be applied to improve energy efficiency.
- Financial resources to help poor regions and countries in these actions must be secured.

The WTTC is committed to reducing greenhouse gas emissions and underlines the need for partnerships between the tourism industry, consumers, employees and government. Their strategy (WTTC, 2009) calls for:

- clear communication for tourists on climate change;
- finance and investment to encourage low-carbon tourism operations;
- practical tools to help businesses reduce their carbon footprint such as WTTC's 'Hotel Carbon Measurement Initiative' or Accor's 'Earth Guest' research; and
- market-led policies to drive innovation in mitigation and adaptation.

It is clear that tourism has to tackle climate change in tandem with other tourism-related development issues including poverty alleviation. If tourism continues 'business as usual' then carbon emissions from tourism will increase by 130 per cent by 2035. In order not to threaten the economic and employment benefits that tourism can bring to the developed world, greenhouse gas targets will need to be applied differentially to different parts of the tourism industry, and to different destinations so as not to jeopardise tourism-related poverty alleviation projects.

Mini Case Study 4.1
The Challenge of Communicating Climate Change

Introduction

Communication is at the cutting edge of thinking about how the tourism sector can address issues such as climate change. Communication is the key to altering opinions about climate change and therefore to changing behaviour by translating passive awareness into active concern. The question is simple:

> **'How can such a complex issue as climate change be communicated to the tourism sector and to tourists themselves in order to stimulate behaviour change?'**

The real challenge for communicators is how can they make climate change 'real' when the phenomenon itself is invisible. Giddens (2009) is clear on this, saying that the dangers faced by global warming are not tangible, immediate or visible in everyday life and so many sit on their hands and do nothing. There is no doubt that tourism is guilty here – do tourists care about climate change and, if not, what should be done? And does the tourism sector care? Here the answer increasingly is yes.

Communicating Climate Change

There are three possible approaches to communicating the challenges of climate change to both the tourism sector and the tourist:

1. **Public education.** This will require a wave of public awareness programmes to ensure that climate change makes sense to people's lives and the reality of climate futures is made real. This involves enhancing public awareness of the basics of the science, the realities of possible climate risks and what the solutions should be (Abbasi, 2006).

2. **Education and training.** This approach is essential to educate and inspire new generations about climate change; after all they will be at the forefront of the transition to a low-carbon economy. This can be done through equipping them with the skills and knowledge to understand climate change through active learning packages, Internet portals, desktop models of the earth's climate system, and changing the curriculum in schools and higher education. On this last point, we also have to recognise the long lead times involved in changing the curriculum and also possible resistance from teachers who may be 'climate sceptics'.

3. **The tourism industry and its consumers.** Here, the tourism sector is already developing climate portals, and destinations have a range of tools available to help them adapt to new climates. Climate change, too, is becoming part of industry training run by consultants and human resources departments. Communicating with small businesses is more of a challenge but working with industry associations is a good strategy here. Communicating with the tourists themselves is also being done by intermediaries and destinations as well as through guidebooks, interpretation and the media.

This case study has shown that communication about climate change is as complex as the science of climate change itself. Yet, the imperative is to persuade industry and consumers that climate change affects 'them'. This will need deeper engagement and understanding of audiences and very smart communication techniques if behaviour change is possible.

DISCUSSION QUESTIONS

1. In class, debate whether tourists think about the realities of climate change when they book and take a flight.
2. Devise an outline training programme for destination managers focusing on climate change adaptation for destinations.
3. What communication approaches can you think of that will make the realities of climate change tangible and concerning for the general public?

Sources:
Abassi, D. (2006) *Americans and Climate Change: Closing the Gap Between Science and Action*, Yale School of Forestry & Environmental Studies, New Haven, CT.
Giddens, A. (2009) *The Politics of Climate Change*, Polity, Cambridge.

Flora

The study of the impact of visitors on vegetation has a long history dating back to work in national parks and protected areas. The dominant consequence of tourism on vegetation is through the process of 'trampling' where visitors walking on or brushing past vegetation crush and damage it. Camping has a similar effect. This has a number of negative effects on the local ecosystem:

● Trampling compacts soil making it difficult for new seeds to germinate or for soil organisms to live and aerate the soil. It also reduces the effectiveness of drainage leading to flooded paths and the natural instinct of visitors to give them a wide berth so creating new areas of impact.

● Trampling eventually kills off the more 'sensitive' plants leaving the 'trample resistant' ones to thrive. This means that presence or absence of certain plants can be used as an indicator of environmental stress. This process significantly reduces species diversity.

● Trampling means that replacement plants find it difficult to establish, and people passing by accidentally knock off flower heads and buds so exacerbating the process. This means that well-used paths or picnic sites become bare and unsightly. Re-establishment is particularly difficult in harsh environments such as the high trekking paths in the mountains in New Zealand and the Andes, or in sand dune environments. Sand dune environments receive many visits as they are a coastal ecosystem, often found between access roads and the beach. Here the plants that are at risk are the very ones that stabilise the dunes, so any loss of vegetation can have a severe impact. In the Netherlands for example, these dune environments are intensively managed.

Of course, much of this damage by visitors is unintentional, as is the case for vegetation on the side of rivers, lakes and canals damaged by the wash of recreational boats or fires from campsites. Deliberate impacts come from activities such as plant collecting or deforestation of landscapes to provide timber for tourism developments as has occurred in Nepal. Here, tourists on trekking trips can use up to 5 kg of wood per day. Equally, the winter-sports industry has a major impact on delicate tundra and high-altitude environments as ski runs and their associated superstructure and infrastructure destroy vegetation which is slow to recover, often not before the next season. In the mountains, walkers and climbers leave spent equipment and litter on the mountains, whilst in all ecosystems, 'off road recreational vehicles', mountain bikes and horse riding can also have severe effects on vegetation.

Fauna

Wildlife has become a major resource for tourism, not just on land but also in marine environments with scuba diving on reefs, whale-watching tours and activities such as swimming with dolphins or visiting loggerhead turtle nesting sites. Yet, many of these activities cause unintentional stress on the fauna, an issue that as yet is little understood.

Tourism can have intentional and direct impacts upon wildlife through activities such as hunting, poaching or trophy collecting (ivory is an example here), or indeed wildlife observation that interferes with the species being watched. There is increasing evidence in Australia, for example, that whales are migrating further from the coast to avoid the whale watching boats and there are many stories of injuries to turtles and dolphins from boat propellers. We still do not know enough about the consequences of tourism upon wildlife and it is an area in need of further research. Nonetheless, the UNWTO (2015) estimate that wildlife watching represents 80 per cent of the total annual sales of trips to Africa.

In most cases, tourists do not intend to have a harmful impact upon wildlife. Yet, it is the unintentional impacts that can be the most severe. These range from the taming of bears in Canada who now feed on the rubbish of campsites rather than in the wild, to hand feeding of dolphins in Queensland, Australia; through to the impact on the mating and hunting habits of predators in Africa's national parks. National park designation and resort and infrastructure development can also disrupt migration patterns and, in the case of national parks, the balance of the ecosystem can be disrupted when some species are favoured at the expense of others. Development of infrastructure such as roads through wildlife areas also increases the numbers of animals accidentally killed in road accidents, whilst beach developments and noise disrupt seabird breeding and feeding success. Attempts to solve these issues are complex and involve destination communities, as the following case study shows.

Mini Case Study 4.2
The Sunderbans Jungle Camp

Sunderbans mangroves.
Source: © Shivang Mehta/Alamy Images

The Sunderbans Area

The Sunderbans Jungle Camp is in the state of West Bengal, India. It is located in the Sunderbans mangrove ecosystem, a network of waterways and islands in the Ganges river delta, extending from India into Bangladesh. Much of the area is protected under UNESCO World Heritage listing and its other listings date from the nineteenth century including a Tiger Reserve, National Park, Biosphere Reserve, and Reserve Forest, which when combined account for 15 per cent of the area. There are settlements on the islands in the delta, and the local economy is based upon agriculture and fishery. The local population is in excess of 50,000.

The area has a rich ecosystem with fauna that includes the royal Bengal tiger and other jungle cats, wild boars, spotted deer, rhesus monkeys, dolphins, estuarine crocodiles, monitor lizards, turtles and many snakes. There is also abundant birdlife with storks, ibis, kingfishers, egrets, herons, terns, owls, raptors and eagles. The area also has an extensive man-made heritage with ruins dating back to 200 CE.

However, the Sunderbans ecosystem is vulnerable to a range of threats including climate change and man-made hazards – the area was subject to a major oil spill in 2014. It is also under environmental pressure, with conflicts between the wildlife of the region, particularly tigers, and man. This can be in the form of tiger attacks, but also tiger poaching for valuable body parts. In response, the Sunderbans Jungle camp was established as a conservation measure and a demonstration project to show how tourism can benefit the environment and the local community and so be replicated elsewhere.

Sunderbans Jungle Camp

The Sunderbans Jungle Camp is a low-cost tourism development with close involvement of the local villages. The Camp is based on an island in the delta – Bali Island – with the intention that it will be copied by other developments to create a sustainable flow of tourism into the region. This will provide an alternative source of income to lessen dependence on the fragile environmental resource of agriculture and fishing and reduce poaching. By providing an alternative livelihood for the poachers they have become conservators and interpreters of the natural history of the area.

The Camp consists of six bungalows and a dining hall designed on local principles. There are decks for wildlife observation, boats for transport and cruises and an interpretation centre. The Camp supports 18 jobs as well as income for guides and fishermen. Food is locally sourced and based upon Bengali cuisine. Entertainment is provided by the local community using local traditions, many of which were dying out until revived by the Camp.

The Camp supports a number of social development programmes for the local community including:

- a medical treatment camp for the islanders;
- monitoring studies on climate change, lesser cats, and migratory water birds;
- book and garment banks; and
- an evening school.

The Camp has been developed with 'Help Tourism', which specialises in the region and the use of tourism as a tool for conservation and sustainability. The values of Help Tourism are based upon both providing alternative livelihoods for the communities that have depended on the natural resources of protected areas and to deliver 'purposeful travel to natural areas to understand the cultural and natural history of the environment without concealing actual threats'. Their mission is to:

> **'Link protected areas and World Heritage Sites with people's livelihood by giving them ownership through tourism as a first step towards meaningful and sustainable conservation'.**

This is achieved through the company's vision to:

1. Involve local people in community tourism initiatives between the protected areas of the East Himalaya, and helping them to create extension forests.
2. Gradually mature these initiatives with wildlife management by creating community reserves, to be used as migration corridors for wild animals between the protected areas.

DISCUSSION QUESTIONS

1. In class, debate whether small-scale projects such as the Sunderbans Jungle Camp can be effective in overcoming the environmental challenges of regions such as the Sunderbans.
2. Draft a press release for the international tourism media explaining the benefits of the Sunderbans development.
3. Help Tourism is a new generation of responsible tour operators utilising the Internet as a marketing and communication tool. Assess their website from the point of view of communicating effectively to the ecotourism market (www.helptourism.com).

Sources:
www.helptourism.com/social-ecological-tourism-conservation-village-community-eco-tourism-projects-initiatives/westbengal/sundarban-jungle-camp.html

Water Supply and Quality

In the twenty-first century, many parts of the world are suffering from water stress (Gössling *et al.*, 2015). As a result, tourism development will be constrained in some destinations – particularly in Africa, the Middle East, South Asia and China. Tourism development places pressure upon scarce water resources simply because tourism shifts demand for water from the tourist's origin to their destination. This is exacerbated by the fact that the tourism industry uses more water per person than the local residential population and, in particular, demands high consumption for golf courses and swimming pools.

Tourism also depends upon the water resources of lakes, the oceans, rivers and canals for many activities, yet tourist activity can have an adverse effect on water quality. This can be through:

- Developments along the shore line which pump waste, litter and detergents into the water, releasing nutrients and creating algal blooms, which impacts upon water quality. This is particularly an issue for water bodies that are not tidal such as lakes or the Mediterranean. Waste also releases pathogens into the water, which kills fish and other species and reduces diversity. Cruise ships in the Caribbean, for example, deposit large amounts of waste annually.
- Petrol and oil from outboard motors and other recreational boats is slow to break down in the water.
- The movement of boats and jet skis constantly stirs up water.
- Major developments such as resorts and marinas can disrupt tidal regimes, shift currents and divert sediment flow.

Land Use

Gössling (2002) sees the use and conversion of land to tourism uses as one of the major consequences of tourism globally. This is not simply for the development of resorts or attractions, but also for the supporting developments such as infrastructure. This means that the area affected by tourism is in fact significantly greater than the resort itself. Changes in land use due to tourism are a significant initiator of reductions in biodiversity and habitats. The use of land for tourism takes it out of agricultural production; clearing encourages invasive species; and deforestation reduces the area available for carbon sinks and results in soil erosion and increases in salinity.

Energy

Tourism is a voracious user of energy, not simply for transportation, but also at the destination itself. Until the world moves to a low-carbon economy, the use of traditional sources of energy – those that are based on fossil fuel such as oil – will increase. Tourism, of course, is dependent upon transport by definition and this means that it is vulnerable to energy price rises and to taxation upon energy use.

The Built Environment

We often gloss over the consequences of tourism for the built environment, but in fact these are significant for certain environments such as say resorts or historic cities. Tourism can be associated with negative consequences for the built environment, not just in terms of catering for visitor needs but also in terms of poor design. We can summarise these consequences as follows:

- Tourism can be associated with congestion both within resorts or historic towns and their route of access. Most tourists are car-borne (as we see in Chapter 10) and this brings both noise and the danger of accidents. Car-led development leads to sprawl and ribbon development around resorts – Orlando in Florida is a classic example here as development has grown around the magnet of the theme parks. Even the simple fact that many resorts have a promenade that acts as a major road artery creates a barrier between the recreational business district and the beach as we can see in the Spanish resort of Benidorm (www.alicante-spain.com/benidorm.html).

- There is a need for traffic management at many destinations, an approach that has come late to tourism, but one that is essential to raise the overall visitor experience (see Chapter 10).
- There are many examples of inappropriate developments, often at the coast, which are out of scale with the environment and fail to use local design principles. The Mediterranean and both the Canary Islands and Balearic islands were early culprits here.
- Catering for tourism in resorts, at attractions and in heritage towns has a reputation for attracting low-quality food and beverage outlets, tacky retailing and shambolic planning, leading to a type of 'architectural pollution'. The danger here is that these developments, often in the recreational business district of resorts, can drag down the overall environmental quality of the destination not just for visitors, but also for residents.
- Where planning has lagged behind tourism demand, the infrastructure of resorts can be overloaded, as is the case in Byron Bay in Australia where new development has been halted until the water and sewerage system can be upgraded (www.byron-bay.com/). The other issue to remember is that tourism is seasonal so any infrastructure is not fully utilised throughout the year.
- The way that many resorts and historic towns have developed means that the local population is often segregated into other parts of the town, partly because businesses in the recreational business districts do not cater for locals and partly due to the price of car parking and access.

Environmental Impact Assessment and Auditing

The tried and tested techniques for assessing the environmental consequences of tourism developments are 'environmental impact assessment' (EIA) and 'environmental auditing' (EA). Both are effectively procedural frameworks to aid decision-making and the distinction is clear:

- Environmental impact assessment takes place before a development is begun and during its construction; and
- Environmental auditing takes place during construction and operation of the development.

Environmental Impact Assessment

Environmental impact assessment is a legislative or policy-based concern for possible positive or negative effects on the total environment attributable to a proposed or existing project, programme or policy. EIA was initially formalised in US policy in the late 1960s, requiring the impacts of a development to be disclosed in an 'environmental impact statement'. At the time it was heavily criticised as expensive and a means to delay or cancel development, but supporters see it as a means to formalise environmental concerns into decision-making. Since its introduction in the USA it is now used worldwide.

The main stages of an EIA are to:

1. identify all impacts of a development, including secondary ones;
2. measure the relevant variables, their magnitude and interactions with sources of information;
3. interpret the findings;
4. communicate findings to all stakeholders in a clear non-technical style.

Approaches to an EIA vary from the very simple checklist where a tick box method is used, through to more complex network or matrix analysis of the relevant ecosystem to capture interactions between the environmental variables themselves.

Environmental Auditing

Environmental auditing is a management tool providing a systematic, regular and objective evaluation of the environmental performance of a tourism organisation, plant, building process or product (Goodall, 2003). In the twenty-first century a key variable of these audits revolves around carbon emissions. Audits are now an important part of sustainable tourism. Normally, they are self-administered, though often externally policed, as they can lead to eco or green labels being applied to the development or organisation. As the approach has matured there are a range of types of audit (Goodall, 2003) as shown in Table 4.2.

There are, of course, pros and cons and issues with both approaches. On the plus side, they ensure that environmental concerns are taken seriously and can lead to cost savings for the organisation. Increasingly the environmental credentials of a tourism organisation or development are used in promotion and both EIA and EA assist in this process. There are some problems, however, not least the fact that the environmental impact of a development does not assess the wider impact of the plan or policy within which that development plays a part. For example, in Table 4.3 whilst the EIA may assess the environmental 'footprint' of the hotel development, it does not assess the higher-level programmes, plans and policies that supported that development. The approaches also encourage the quantification of environmental variables, often using dubious methods; and there may be a minimum size of development that is required to undergo an assessment such that smaller developments escape scrutiny.

Table 4.2 Types of environmental audit

Type of audit	Characteristics
Activity	An overview of an activity or process which crosses business boundaries in a company such as staff travel by employees of a hotel change.
Associate	Auditing of firms within the supply chain of a company, for example tour operators' hotels and airlines.
Compliance	Simple regular checks to ensure the organisation complies with current environmental regulations such as airline checking noise levels.
Corporate	An audit across the whole company to ensure that agreed environmental policy is understood and carried out throughout the firm.
Issues	Focuses upon a key issue such as carbon emissions.
Product	Ensures existing and proposed products meet an organisation's environmental policy. For example, tour operator designs holiday based on walking using local, vernacular designed accommodation and services.
Site	Audit directed at spot checks of buildings, plant and processes, known to have actual or potential problems. For example, hotel energy efficiencies or airport authority checking noise and emissions on take-off.

Source: Goodall, 1992

Table 4.3 The issue of scale with EIAs

	Policies	Plans	Programmes	Projects
National plan	National tourism policy			
Regional plan		Regional tourism plan		
Sub-regional plan			Investment programme	
Local plan				Hotel development

Over-arching Issues

We finish this chapter by considering some of the wider issues involved in assessing the relationship between tourism and the environment, beginning with Richard Butler's classic paper on the topic.

Classic Paper
Butler, R.W. (2000) Tourism and the environment: a geographical perspective, *Tourism Geographies* **2(3), 337–358**

This paper is a classic for two reasons. Firstly, it provides an excellent review of the literature and contemporary thinking on the relationship between tourism and the environment. But more than this, the paper provides a new perspective on many elements of the 'received wisdom' of this relationship. As a result, we have a paper which is stimulating to read, but also solid in its scholarship and coverage.

Butler begins by challenging current thinking on the relationship between tourism and the environment, questioning the very dependence of tourism upon the environment as a resource. Butler says that this dependence is taken for granted, but challenges whether it is accurate in all cases – for example, much of beach tourism has little relationship with a pristine quality environment and other forms of tourism such as VFR and business/conference tourism are only tangentially dependent upon the environment. Butler concludes that the statement about the dependence of tourism upon the environment needs to be carefully re-examined. He goes on to challenge the fact that it is actually very difficult to disentangle the environmental elements of the attractiveness of a destination from other elements; in other words, are we attracted to the destination and its environment as whole, or to specific parts of it?

Butler then goes on to critique the tourism and environment literature. He argues that researchers should be more concerned with understanding the 'processes' of environmental change than to assigning blame for the impacts of tourism. He also rehearses the argument found in this chapter that it is sometimes difficult to disentangle the human agents of environmental change from the natural ones. The paper has an excellent section on managing the environment for tourism and Butler clearly believes that there has to be a willingness on the part of all destination stakeholders to do this if it is to be successful.

The paper concludes with some specific research issues, which Butler feels should form the future agenda for tourism and environmental research. These include:

- A better understanding of the relationship between tourism and the environment in varied settings and for a variety of forms of tourism.

- A better understanding of the elements which make up environmental attractiveness and how these change over time due to cultural perceptions.

- A stronger link between physical science research and the processes of planning and managing destinations. This will be an important issue for regions such as the Antarctic.

- More attention should be paid to the processes and causes of impacts rather than the end result.

- An acceptance of the need to manage the volume of tourists at destinations and a recognition of the value of carrying capacity as a concept and tool, as we discussed earlier in this chapter.

- A greater focus on less glamorous destinations, such as mass tourism resorts, rather than simply upon environmentally-sensitive areas.

- An increase in funding for longitudinal studies that will allow us to understand long-term environmental change.

Butler concludes 'The relationship between tourism and the environment in which it occurs is complex, poorly understood and should be of crucial concern' (p. 354).

There is no doubt that an imperative for researchers is to understand the structure and processes of how ecosystems work if we are to effectively reduce the consequences of tourism upon the environment. Here it is important that we consider the totality of the consequences of tourism for all elements of the ecosystem, and how these elements are related to each other. Indeed, whilst researching the relationship of tourism and the environment has come a long way since the 1960s, Wall and Mathieson (2006) identify a number of issues of concern:

- Research is uneven with few studies examining the impact of tourism upon species such as birds or fish, whilst a huge amount of work has been done on vegetation. Similarly, research has tended to focus on the temperate climate zones and only now is research turning to the Antarctic environments for example, or the tropics.

- Many studies do not reach the policy makers, planners or, indeed, developers who could benefit from the knowledge.

- Simply because ecosystems are so complex, research tends to focus on one aspect of the environment – fauna or flora, for example – and fails to examine the impact upon the whole ecosystem. Worse, the study of the consequences of tourism tends to be pigeon-holed into environmental, economic and social, with few studies looking at the interaction of these elements. In the African national parks, for example, designation has a major impact on the local population in terms of their ability to farm and hunt.

- Much research is done after the consequences of tourism have occurred with less work examining the conditions before tourism arrived. However, with sustainable tourism indicators being developed this situation is changing (as we show in Chapter 6). It is equally difficult to disentangle the actual effects of human intervention in ecosystems against the natural processes of environmental change.

Finally, a new strand of research is emerging, mainly due to climate change. This is based upon the impact of changing tourist behaviour, driven by environmental concerns, upon the tourism sector itself. Reduction of the desire to fly long-haul is an example here – an issue of concern to tourism authorities in long-haul destinations such as New Zealand and Australia.

SUMMARY

One of the most reported issues in the world is the consequences of tourism and travel for the environment and particularly for climate change. In this chapter we have seen that this is a complex relationship which has developed over the last century, from a position where tourism was seen as relatively benign, to one where there are real concerns about the consequences of tourism for the environment. Here there is much confused thinking about just what constitutes environmentally-responsible tourism. We showed that it is important to understand the underlying concepts, which include the need to consider the whole ecosystem when we look at the consequences of tourism and attempt to manage for them, and to utilise tried and trusted concepts such as carrying capacity, EIA and EA.

Of course, the negative consequences of tourism for the environment make the headlines, but it can also be a force for good, including the economic contribution that it makes, encouragement of conservation and environmental education (as we saw with the Sunderbans case study) and the development of attractive resort towns and landscapes. Nonetheless, tourism also is problematic for the environment for many reasons, particularly in terms of carbon emissions – estimated at 5 per cent of global emissions and the consequent impact upon climate change. We deal with this issue at length, including a study on communicating climate change, and also the approaches of the UNWTO and the WTTC in developing an agenda to address climate change. Other negative consequences are for flora and fauna, and for water energy and land use. We have seen that the management of these impacts employs a range of techniques including environmental impact assessment and environmental auditing. Finally, we must recognise that the relationship between tourism and the environment is complex and we must consider issues such as whether all effects are man-made, how to disentangle tourism effects from others and ensuring that we understand the degree of change caused by tourism across the whole ecosystem. The chapter closes with a major case study on the challenges of tourism in the Galapagos Islands.

Discussion Questions

1. As a newly hired manager of a national park, draft a memo to your staff explaining the benefits of carrying capacity for managing visitors to the park.

2. In class, debate the negative and positive consequences of tourism for the environment. Divide the class into two groups and come up with three key arguments on each side.

3. Take a destination which you know well, and draft a checklist of the negative consequences of tourism for the environment, using the headings in this chapter.

4. Take a typical inclusive tour to a mass tourism destination and identify the 'hot spots' of environmental impact. Consider how they can be monitored by an environmental audit.

5. We know that there is confusion about terms such as ecotourism, responsible tourism and alternative tourism. Consider all of these terms and come up with your own preferred term and justify it.

Annotated Further Reading

1. Cater, C.I. and Garrod, B. (2015) *Encyclopedia of Sustainable Tourism*, CABI, Wallingford.
    Thorough handbook with a focus on the environment and tourism.

2. Fennel, D. (2008) *Ecotourism. An Introduction*, Routledge, London
    Excellent overview of the key issues of ecotourism.

3. Gössling, S. and Hall, C.M. (2006) *Tourism and Global Environmental Change*, Routledge, London.
    Comprehensive and advanced text examining the impact of climate change across the tourism system.

4. Hall, C.M. and Higham, J. (eds) (2005) *Tourism, Recreation and Climate Change*, Channel View, Clevedon.
    Excellent and wide ranging edited volume on all aspects of tourism and climate change.

5. Hall, C.M. (2014) Tourism and the environment, change, impacts and response, in Lew, A.L., Hall, C.M. and Williams, A.M. (eds), *The Wiley Blackwell Companion to Tourism*, Wiley, Chichester.
    Authoritative introduction to destination issues.

6. Holden, A. and Fennell, D. (2012) *The Routledge Handbook of Tourism and the Environment*, Routledge, London.
    Comprehensive handbook covering all aspects of the relationship between tourism and the environment.

7. Lew, A.L., Hall, C.M. and Williams, A.M. (eds) (2014) *The Wiley Blackwell Companion to Tourism*, Wiley, Chichester.
   A thorough and well-researched compendium containing a range of chapters dealing with the environmental consequences of tourism.

8. Newsome, D., Moore, S.A. and Dowling, R.K. (2012) *Natural Area Tourism Ecology Impacts and Management*, 2nd edn, Channel View, Bristol.
   A classic text detailing the consequences and management of tourism in natural areas.

9. UNWTO (2009) *From Davos to Copenhagen and Beyond: Advancing Tourism's Response to Climate Change*, UNWTO, Madrid.
   An authoritative and well-researched contemporary account of the thinking of the UNWTO on climate change.

10. Wall, G. and Mathieson, A. (2006) *Tourism: Change, Impacts and Opportunities*, Pearson, Harlow.
    Excellent second edition of the key text examining the consequences of tourism.

References Cited

Abbasi, D. (2006) *Americans and Climate Change: Closing the Gap Between Science and Action*, Yale School of Forestry & Environmental Studies, New Haven, CT.

Buzinde, C.N., Manuel-Navarrete, D., Yoo, E.E. and Morais, D. (2009) Tourists' perceptions in a climate of change eroding destinations, *Annals of Tourism Research* 37(2), 333–354.

Dwyer, L., Edwards, D., Mistilis, N., Scott, N., Cooper, C. and Roman, C. (2007) *Trends Underpinning Tourism to 2020: An Analysis of Key Drivers for Change*, STCRC, Gold Coast, Australia.

Goodall, B. (1992) Environmental Auditing for Tourism, *Progress in Recreation and Hospitality Management* 4, 60–71.

Gössling, S. (2002) Global environmental consequences of tourism, *Global Environmental Change* 12, 283–302.

Gössling, S., Hall, C.M. and Scott, D. (2015) *Tourism and Water*, Channel View, Bristol.

Holden, A. (2009) The environment-tourism nexus influence of market ethics, *Annals of Tourism Research* 36(3), 373–389.

Mathieson, A. and Wall, G. (1982) *Tourism: Economic, Physical and Social Impacts*, Longman, Harlow.

Newsome, D., Moore, S.A. and Dowling, R.K. (2012) *Natural Area Tourism Ecology Impacts and Management*, 2nd edn, Channel View, Bristol.

UNWTO (2009) *From Davos to Copenhagen and Beyond: Advancing Tourism's Response to Climate Change*, UNWTO, Madrid.

UNWTO (2015) *Towards Measuring the Economic Value of Wildlife Watching Tourism in Africa*, UNWTO Madrid.

Wall, G. and Mathieson, A. (2006) *Tourism: Change, Impacts and Opportunities*, Pearson, Harlow.

Wheeler, B (2003) Alternative tourism – a deceptive ploy, pp 227–234 in Cooper, C. (ed.) *Classic Reviews in Tourism*, Channel View, Clevedon.

WTTC (2009) *Leading the Challenge on Climate Change*, WTTC, London.

Major Case Study 4.1
Managing the Consequences of Tourism in the Galapagos Islands

The Galapagos Islands

The Galapagos Islands lie in the Pacific Ocean. The unique wildlife of the Galapagos is a world-class attraction, which has been given international recognition as a World Heritage Site and Biosphere Reserve. The best-known animals are the marine iguanas and giant tortoise and most of the animals have no fear of man, as there are no natural predators. Traditionally, the Galapagos were protected by their remoteness, and the human impact was relatively slight. Since the 1970s the growing popularity of ecotourism has focused public interest on the islands, providing support for conservation but posing a greater threat to the fragile ecosystems. In addition, the islands' environment is vulnerable to invasive species, demographic growth and shipping accidents – such as the 2015 incident of a cargo ship running aground with a cargo of hazardous materials.

Managing the Environmental Resource

National Park Designation

In 1959, when the number of visitors was less than 1000 a year, the Ecuadorian government designated 97 per cent of the archipelago as a National Park, excluding only those areas already settled. In 1968, the Charles Darwin Foundation, an international non-profit organisation, was established to protect the islands' ecosystems in cooperation with the Galapagos National Park Service (GNPS), a government agency. The Foundation became the Galapagos Conservancy in 2002 with a focus on education. Organised tourism began in the late 1960s, and in 1974 a master plan for the national park set a limit of 12,000 visitors a year, later expanded to 40,000 for economic reasons, with a maximum visitor stay of six days. By 2007, the park had a new strategic plan.

Zoning

The National Park is divided into five zones to give varying degrees of protection and balance the needs of tourists against the primary objective of conservation. Access is also controlled by price; it is expensive to reach the Galapagos by air or cruise ship from the mainland of Ecuador and international visitors to the National Park pay a substantial entrance fee. The majority of tourists find accommodation on the cruise ships and yachts that tour the islands, although land-based hotels are opening on four inhabited islands.

Tourists are restricted to 54 land sites and 62 underwater sites designated by the GNPS. Small groups are allowed to visit in 2–4-hour shifts to limit environmental impacts. At each visitor site a rough way-marked trail provides the only access to wildlife, unusual plants and volcanic landforms. Tourists are always accompanied by a licenced naturalist-guide with a maximum of 20 visitors per guide. Itineraries for tourists on cruise ships visiting a large number of sites, or on day excursions based at island hotels, are arranged well in advance by the tour operator. Those arriving in chartered yachts and other small vessels are allowed some flexibility in organising their own itineraries subject to a maximum number of sites per boat.

Visitor Impacts

Ecotourism in the Galapagos is a valuable economic resource for Ecuador. Tourism is one of the few commercial uses of the islands' limited resource base – various attempts at agricultural development in the past have met with failure, due mainly to problems of water supply. Most international visitors are high-income, middle-aged Europeans and North Americans. Conservationists are concerned that this controlled 'educational tourism' could grow to become conventional tourism. There are no clearly defined limits on the annual number of visitors, and the planned limit of 40,000 has long been exceeded and now exceeds 170,000. The number of tour vessels has not increased since the mid 1990s, but tour companies are now tending to use larger, more luxurious ships than before, with some holding 100 tourists. More controversial are the occasional visits of large cruise ships to the islands, as it is difficult to impose quarantine regulations on passengers. There is some evidence that the environmental capacity has already been reached in the most-visited areas, with disturbance to nesting birds and path erosion.

It is now generally acknowledged that the islands have reached some kind of crisis point in terms of conservation. In 2007 the President of Ecuador declared the Galapagos 'at risk' and a national priority for Ecuador, and an action plan was put into effect. A new governor was appointed to implement stricter immigration measures, and quarantine systems have been planned in Quito and Guayaquil. There are also plans to develop renewable sources of energy to make the islanders more self-sufficient.

The Stakeholders

Conservation is also vital for the surrounding seas, and tourism has to share use of this resource with the important fishing industry; this includes both small-scale local operators and large, well-equipped ships based on the mainland and supplying international markets. In 1986 the government established the Galapagos Marine Resources Reserve, reputedly the world's largest, covering an area of over 130,000 square kilometres. In 1995 a concerted effort was made to ban commercial fishing. In protest, islanders threatened the staff of the GNPS and the Charles Darwin Research Station, causing deliberate damage to wildlife habitats. In the Galapagos, the government has taken on board the principle of local involvement. The 'Special Law for the Galapagos', passed by the Ecuadorian Congress in 1998, recognises the importance of sustainable development.

It remains to be seen how effective the Special Law will be in practice. Like other developing countries, Ecuador takes pride in its heritage, but has limited financial resources to set aside for conservation when there are more pressing economic and social problems. It may also be difficult to find experienced professional workers to enforce the regulations in the face of opposition from local politicians, an inefficient bureaucracy, and multinational corporations. It is clear that there are many interests in the management of the islands' environment of which tourism is an important, but not the only, stakeholder. Nevertheless, schemes to train young islanders in conservation and catering are cause for optimism for the future of the Galapagos.

DISCUSSION QUESTIONS

1. Draft a list of ways to manage visitors in national parks. Which of these do you feel is effective – and which measures are being used in the Galapagos Islands to prevent any contamination and disturbance to the wildlife?

2. Thinking of the various stakeholders involved in the Galapagos, devise a chart that shows each stakeholder and their major interests in the tourism sector. Where do the potential conflicts lie?

3. Devise a list of the positive and negative effects of tourism upon wildlife generally – how many of these effects would you expect to find in the Galapagos?

Sources:
Crowley, P. (1999) *The Galapagos: Tourism at the Crossroads*, Tourism Concern, London.
www.galapagosonline.com
www.galapagos.org
www.igtoa.org

CHAPTER 5
THE SOCIAL AND CULTURAL CONSEQUENCES OF TOURISM

Learning Outcomes

This chapter considers the social and cultural consequences of tourism and considers how these originate from the 'encounter' or 'contact' with the tourist. The chapter also outlines the theoretical frameworks which have been developed to explain these consequences. The chapter is designed to provide you with:

- an understanding of the role of the tourist, the host and the encounter;

- an awareness of the importance of the concept of the demonstration effect;

- an appreciation of the theoretical frameworks developed to understand the relationship between hosts and guests;

- an understanding of the consequences of tourism for host societies; and

- an awareness of the process and result of cultural change brought about by tourism.

Photograph: Tourist taking pictures of Ndebele women © Flirt/Alamy Images

Introduction

As tourism reaches out to ever more distant and exotic locations, often in lesser-developed countries, the consequences of visitation upon the host community and their culture has become an important issue. Of course, tourism can support communities economically through employment, spending and infrastructure development. However, tourism can also bring less desirable consequences for host communities, prompting both social and cultural changes within those societies. In part, this is because the contrast between affluent tourists and residents in the poorer countries of the world can be startling in terms of behaviour, language and culture – contrasts that can lead to significant, and irreversible, changes in the host society. This has been termed by the well-known travel writer Jan Morris as 'contact!' We also must not dismiss the impact of outbound tourism on the generating market as tourists bring back new cuisines and customs, which are slowly adopted. The issue, as with all consequences of tourism, is that societies and cultures are constantly evolving and often tourism can be a scapegoat for inevitable change that would have occurred without tourism.

   This area of study is known as host/guest relationships, an emergent research area where the methods of approach are now becoming well developed, although many of the researchers view the issues from the standpoint of their part in the developed world. To date, research on social and cultural consequences of tourism tends to be

→

written from a negative point of view, and certainly there is little evidence to support the rose-tinted views of earlier commentators that bringing cultures and societies together broadens people's horizons and promotes peace and understanding. Here though, on the positive side, it could be argued that tourists do become sensitised to other cultures and ways of life.

One of the most interesting aspects of this research relates back to the fundamental fact that tourists are strangers in the destination and can be the target of xenophobia. Their behaviour, language and way of dress are often significantly different from the host leading to the idea of social or cultural distance. This means that whilst the tourist can act as a catalyst for change in the host society, the tourists themselves are vulnerable to crime and exploitation, simply by their status as strangers who are less aware of local behaviour and habits. Early commentators on these issues were Krippendorf (1987) and Emanuel De Kadt, whose paper we have chosen as the classic paper for this chapter as it covers all the key issues and is still relevant today.

Classic Paper
De Kadt, E. (1979) Social planning for tourism in the developing countries, *Annals of Tourism Research* 6(1), 36–48

De Kadt's paper is a classic because, whilst it was written in the late 1970s, it demonstrates a thorough understanding of the social and cultural consequences of tourism and links them closely to 'development' issues. As a result, the paper remains just as relevant today.

The paper begins by stressing that planners and policy-makers have not addressed the social and cultural impacts of tourism in the developing world. He argues for planners to take much more account of the non-economic costs and benefits of tourism and shows how planners and policy-makers act within specific socio-political contexts. These contexts and the various power relations at local and national levels influence how tourism policy is formed and plans are created. The paper is particularly forward looking here in its discussion of the role of tourism in poverty alleviation – a topic now at the top of the agenda of all tourism and development agencies, and the subject of the end of chapter case study. The heart of De Kadt's argument is that the usual perspectives on tourism planning have been economic and that the social and cultural costs of tourism have been ignored. On page 40 he sums up these impacts clearly:

> 'The main "real life" impacts of tourism are experienced by the people who live in the communities of the tourist destination areas. Some get wealthy, others do not: often all see outsiders make the richest pickings. Employment opportunities emerge, and the structure of the local labor force changes with women and young people tending to benefit most. Life styles come under pressure, new adjustments may have to be found to ancient concepts of hospitality.'

De Kadt argues that community empowerment is needed to overcome some of these impacts, but at the time he was writing – the late 1970s – the notion of community-based tourism was in its infancy and barriers, both social and political, were more evident. He is accurate in his observation that these impacts will vary by destination and that rapid development tends to heighten the impact of tourism.

In the second half of the paper, De Kadt argues that foreign penetration into the tourism sector of developing countries through transnational enterprises is a major source of negative impacts because of their strong bargaining power at international level, their ownership, employment of expatriate labour and acculturation.

In the main areas of this paper, De Kadt's views and analysis are well ahead of his time of writing, particularly those relating to the issues of poverty alleviation and the impact of foreign ownership upon destinations. De Kadt has continued to influence the development of the sociology of tourism and this paper is clear evidence of his forward-thinking approach.

Hosts and Guests

Mathieson and Wall (1982) structure their discussion of the social and cultural consequences of tourism into three parts:

1. **Tourists** – responsible for change in the host society by 'demonstrating' their difference in terms of language, culture and affluence. The travel experience also changes both the tourist and their society.

2. **Hosts** – deliver the tourism experience at the destination and are exposed to the tourists through working and living at the destination.

3. **The encounter or 'contact' between tourist and host** – when the two groups meet there are contrasts of behaviour and expectations which trigger long-term changes and consequences in both societies. In addition, the 'social distance' between the two groups and the experience during the trip will influence the tourist's attitude towards the host. Here tourism changes:

   - firstly, the social systems of the destination in terms of value systems, individual behaviours, family relationships, life styles, language, religion and moral behaviour (for example, tourism is often associated with gambling and prostitution); and
   - secondly, the culture of the destination in terms of living culture (ceremonies and events) and cultural artefacts.

Although we discriminate between society and culture for the purposes of this chapter, in practice they do overlap.

Tourists

In this part of the book we have seen that the consequences of tourism can range from the beneficial to the disruptive and that this depends not only upon what happens at the destination, but also upon the characteristics of the tourist themselves. Tourists influence the degree of impact in terms of their types and number. In the past tourists were stereotyped as wealthy, boorish and high spending, effectively the 'enemy' of the host and their culture. But these stereotypes are unhelpful and have been replaced by more analytical approaches. For example, Smith (1977) has drawn up a classification system for tourists that attempts to show their potential impact on the host destination by considering the numbers of each type of tourist, their motivations to visit and their degree of adaptation to local norms. Although the classification was drawn up in the late 1970s, before many changes in the tourism system, it has stood the test of time (Table 5.1). Indeed, it was Smith's approach that initiated the alternative/low impact tourism movement. We argue that if the type of tourist can be matched to appropriate types of destination, then the negative consequences of tourism will be minimised, simply because the destination and the visitor will have similar expectations (see Figure 5.1). For example, using Smith's classification, we can see that it is at the incipient mass stage that problems begin as greater numbers of visitors trigger changes and the destination has to adapt in terms of supplying facilities and standardising delivery of the experience. To ensure that Smith's classification remains relevant we have added 'enlightened mass tourism' representing a twenty-first century phenomenon of mass tourists sensitised to the destination by industry-led corporate social responsibility and consumer-led behavioural transformative experiences curated by interpretation and information (Weaver, 2014).

Recently researchers have developed a broader view of the tourist as a person, recognising that tourists have a particular way of looking at the world. Urry's (1990) seminal work on the tourist 'gaze' is important here. Urry (1990) contrasts the middle classes and their 'romantic gaze' seeking authenticity to the 'collective gaze', which is more representative of mass tourism.

Table 5.1 Smith's classification of tourists

Type of tourist	Characteristics	Adaptation to local conditions	Numbers
Explorer	These are academics or explorers, totally accepting of local conditions and self-sufficient in terms of food and equipment. They are virtually unnoticed by the destination.	Adapts fully	Small
Elite	A group who has seen the world and is now looking for something different, such as Antarctica or the Amazon. They adapt easily to local conditions.	Adapts fully	Small
Off-beat	This group is more conventional tourists who look for some added extras to a holiday. They adapt well to local conditions. Their money is welcome and they are not disruptive.	Adapts well	Increasing numbers
Incipient mass	Here there are greater numbers but they visit in small groups or as individuals – they are seeking the comforts of home but do not demand them – if they are absent then it is put down to experience. They are more dependent on the services of a tour operator. Nonetheless, it is at this stage that problems begin to emerge as expectations between the visitor and the destination differ.	Seeks their own amenities	Steady flow
Mass	Here there are large numbers of tourists, bringing with them their own uncompromising values and expectations. They expect multilingual guides, their own language and their own food.	Expects their own amenities	Continuous influx
Enlightened mass	A growing group of twenty-first century tourists who are sensitised to the destination by corporate social responsibility initiatives, interpretation, guiding and information, and transformative experiences at the destination.	Sensitised to the destination community and culture	Growing numbers of arrivals
Charter	This is the full-blown, somewhat down-market, mass tourism group, arriving in large numbers, often highly seasonal but demanding of their own culture, food and facilities. They have travelled but do not want the character of the destination to interfere with their enjoyment. They are totally dependent on the services of the travel trader.	Demands their own amenities	Large numbers of arrivals

Source: adapted from Smith, 1977

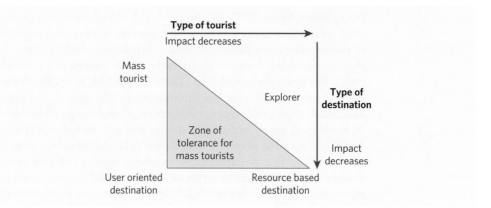

Figure 5.1 The relationship between tourist, destinations and tolerance levels

Hosts

Of course, hosts can be impacted by tourism even if they never come into contact with a visitor. This is because they are part of a host society that deals regularly with tourism and therefore attitudes and opinions pervade the destination. Sharpley (2014) has provided an extensive review of how host societies perceive tourist impacts at the destination. He concludes that there are one set of factors that relate to the destination itself – 'extrinsic' factors, and a second set of factors that relate to the individual host – 'intrinsic' factors.

Extrinsic factors include:

- extent/stage of tourism development;
- nature/type of tourism/tourists;
- density of tourists/tourism development;
- seasonality; and
- national stage of development.

Intrinsic factors include:

- economic/employment dependency on tourism;
- community attachment;
- distance from tourism zone;
- interaction with tourists;
- personal values;
- social identity/social status; and
- demographic – age, gender, education.

The main issues of concern to the hosts are often traffic congestion, litter and overcrowding, as well as perceived impacts upon religion, crime, language and the general way of life of the destination. Residents respond to tourism through particular 'coping' behaviours in the tourism season, such as changing their shopping habits.

The Encounter

Many of the consequences of tourism upon the host community are attributable to the 'encounter' or 'contact' – when the tourists and the host meet (Sharpley, 2014). Here, the degree of impact upon the host will depend upon how the encounter occurs, the level of tourism development in the community and the social carrying capacity of the host population. De Kadt (1979) states that contact can happen in a number of ways:

- simply by being in the same place, in the street, or on the beach;
- through commercial transactions such as shopping; and
- through spontaneous meeting and chatting, which is what is meant when people talk of travel broadening the mind.

If you think of your own travels you will remember that the first two encounters are the most common and have certain characteristics (UNESCO, 1976). For example, such encounters tends to be brief – being served a restaurant meal or buying souvenirs in a gift shop. This type of encounter is also temporary, something novel for the tourist that they will remember, but routine for the shopkeeper or waiter, just another encounter with another visitor. In other words, the encounter is not an equal one and is characterised by certain time and space constraints:

- On the one hand, tourists are at leisure, mobile, have money to spend and are being served whilst on holiday. The tourist has expended considerable resources to spend time at the destination and so is impatient of delays or inefficiencies.
- The host, on the other hand, is working hard, catering to the needs of the tourist, tied to their workplace and at times therefore tempted to exploit the relationship.

In contrast, a spontaneous encounter between host and tourist, by say meeting to talk about the weather, is very rare. The encounter is more commonly a commercial transaction. There is, of course, a trade-off here as these spontaneous encounters carry greater risk than the managed, transaction-based ones. It is interesting that few studies have focused upon how hosts 'cope' with the 'encounter'. Dogan (1989) found that a host's patterns of 'coping behaviour' can include resistance to tourism through hostility to development, a retreat away from the tourism zone or maintenance of a strong boundary between themselves and the visitors. Figure 5.2 summarises the main types of encounter.

The Demonstration Effect

During the encounter, tourists often 'demonstrate' to the host that they are different by their dress, behaviour, manners and language, and come from a culture which the hosts should aspire to. This is known as the 'demonstration effect'. Effectively, the demonstration effect is about copying behaviours and transferring values from one culture to another, often in terms of economic aspirations. For it to happen, the 'social distance' between the hosts and guest has to be sufficiently different and the transfer of behaviour has to be sustainable over a long period. Fisher (2004) notes that tourists are more likely to influence the behaviour of the young generations of the host society. Of course, the demonstration effect can be positive – for example, in changing behaviour towards particular groups in society, such as indigenous peoples. It is interesting that different forms of tourism will dictate the degree of 'exposure' of the hosts to their guests. For example, low-impact, alternative forms of tourism encourage the spontaneous type of encounter where hosts and guest meet as equals, perhaps using home-stay as their accommodation – yet in some respects this type of encounter is the most damaging in terms of triggering change. In contrast, resort, or 'enclave' type tourism minimises the encounters to commercial ones, with the tourists travelling through the destination in a 'bubble' of hotels, escorted tours, coaches and managed, routine encounters – sometimes referred to as tourist ghettoes. Here, the local people that the tourist meets are 'culture brokers' who understand both the host and guest culture and act as a buffer between the two societies.

The notion of the demonstration effect, however, whilst intuitively attractive, has been criticised as vague, used uncritically and at times patronising (Fisher, 2004). Fisher argues that the demonstration effect fails to recognise the other influences on the hosts, such as mass media, which can be more important than contact with tourists in changing behaviour and values.

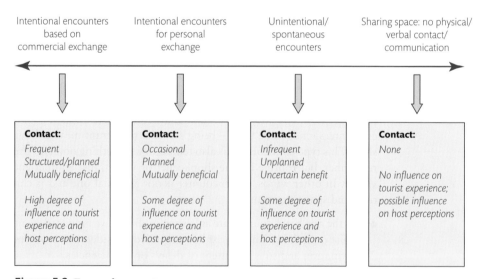

Figure 5.2 Types of encounter
Source: Sharpley, 2014

Table 5.2 Doxey's irridex

The level of euphoria	People are enthusiastic and thrilled by tourist development. They welcome the stranger and there is a mutual feeling of satisfaction. There are opportunities for locals and money flows in along with the tourist.
The level of apathy	As the industry expands, people begin to take the tourist for granted. Tourists rapidly become the target for profit taking and contact on the personal level begins to become more formal.
The level of irritation	This will begin when the industry is nearing saturation point or is allowed to pass a level at which the locals cannot handle the numbers without expansion of facilities.
The level of antagonism	The irritations have become more overt. People now see the tourist as the harbinger of all that is bad. 'Taxes have gone up because of the tourists.' 'They have no respect for property.' 'They have corrupted our youth.' 'They are bent on destroying all that is fine in our town'. Mutual politeness has now given way to antagonism and the tourist is 'ripped off'.
The final level	All this while people have forgotten that what they cherished in the first place is what drew the tourist, but in the wild scramble to develop they overlooked this and allowed the environment to change. What they now must learn to live with is the fact that their ecosystem will never be the same again. They might still be able to draw tourists but of a very different type from those they so happily welcomed in the early years. If the destination is large enough to cope with mass tourism it will continue to thrive.

Source: adapted from Doxey, 1976

Modelling the Encounter

The consequences of the encounter will depend upon both the type of tourist and the level of development of tourism at the destination, as well as the characteristics of the host community. Sociologists have been criticised for failing to come up with analytical models of host/guest relationships, seeming rather to devise somewhat descriptive models (Mathieson and Wall, 1982). The literature provides three well-known models of the encounter.

1. The first is by Doxey (1976), who designed an index of tourist irritation (Table 5.2). Doxey's index is superficially attractive, effectively saying that the more tourists that visit a destination, the greater the level of disruption and thus, irritation. However, his model suggests a one-way direction of the consequences of tourism, closely linked to the idea of Butler's (1980) tourism area life-cycle.

2. Attractive though it is, Doxey's model fails to take into account the dynamics of the host community. Bjorklund and Philbrick's (1972) attitudinal model is therefore more realistic (Figure 5.3) because it recognises that at any one point in time there will be various opinions of tourism amongst the host community – and indeed these opinions and their vociferousness will change as tourism develops.

3. Finally, MacCannell's (1973) idea of staged authenticity is based upon Goffman's idea of all daily activities being equivalent to a staged performance. MacCannell adapts Goffman's idea of a 'front and back region' for tourism:

   - The front region is the meeting place of hosts and guests and includes hotel reception areas, shops and restaurants. Here performances are staged and the host is acting out a part.
   - The back region is where the local people play out their daily lives or where the staff in the hotel relax in the canteen or staff room, out of sight of the guests. This is the intimate and 'authentic' region of the destination – the part of the destination that the 'new' tourist is most interested in.

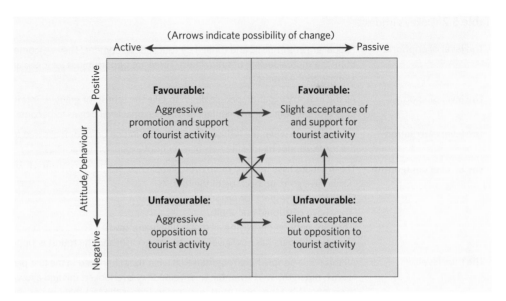

Figure 5.3 Host attitudinal/behavioural responses to tourist activity
Source: Wall and Mathieson, 2006; Bjorklund and Philbrick, 1972

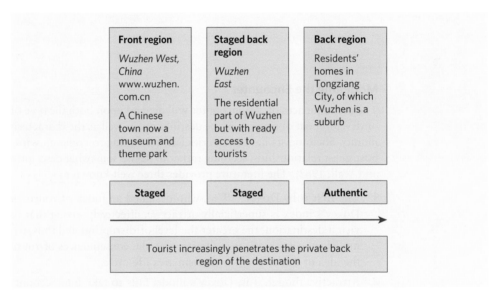

Figure 5.4 Levels of cultural penetration, Wuzhen, China

MacCannell argues that in order to protect the back region from visitors, destinations design 'staged' back regions, such as creating a village to look like an authentic one, or staging a festival as if it is part of everyday life (Figure 5.4).

The Consequences of Tourism for the Host Community

In Chapter 4 we introduced the concept of carrying capacity. Social carrying capacity relates to community acceptance of tourism – where a destination exceeds social carrying capacity then tourism development has become unacceptable. The consequences of tourism that can lead to this level are many and varied and demonstrate that it is misguided to dissect the consequences of tourism into economic, environment and social/cultural factors. For example, the employment consequences of tourism would normally be thought of as economic consequences but, as we show below, they also have significant social consequences for the destination. The consequences of tourism for the host community include the following.

Social Structure

When tourism is introduced to traditional societies it can have significant consequences for social structures. For example, where coastal tourism is developed, it acts as a magnet for employment, often attracting the young and female from the rural hinterland to work in the resorts. This leads to rural depopulation and by giving females economic independence, it can undermine traditional, male-dominated societies. This also has the effect of diverting labour from the land, and from more traditional craft-based enterprises, threatening their existence, as has happened in Corsica. Of course, we have already seen that there are other issues linked to jobs in tourism including (i) the quality of jobs and seasonality and (ii) the socially divisive issue of immigrant labour.

Relocation of Hosts

In some extreme cases, local people may be relocated to make space for tourism development as has happened with the relocation of Bedouin from the historic monument of Petra in Jordan, or villagers from Ayia Napa in Cyprus.

Politics

If tourism is to be beneficial to the host community it is important that control remains at the local level. This is best achieved if tourism grows slowly and the locals control the pace of growth so that it is kept within social carrying capacity. If this is not achieved, there is the danger of economically powerful groups emerging as has happened in Bulgarian resorts.

As tourism grows and the destination begins to attract an international clientele, the awareness and recognition of the destination is enhanced and both the locals and the industry will be exposed to ideas from other countries and international good practice. However, where a destination has outgrown local control and is dependent upon inclusive tours, the balance of power can shift from local decision makers to national and international players. Quite simply, large tour operators will tend to want to deal at a higher level than with local politicians if they are seeking development or incentives, so by-passing local political groups. Decisions relating to development, marketing and promotion of the destination will be made in London, New York or Frankfurt rather than at the local or regional level – prompting the accusation of 'neo-colonialism' or 'imperialism' towards tour operators.

This means that locals are not in control of tourism at the destination and are therefore unable to control many of the negative consequences such as inflated prices in the shops and high land or property prices. It also implies that many of the benefits of tourism flow back to the headquarters of the tour operators and are not captured at the local level. Finally, it is possible that the local community can be manipulated to support the economic ambitions of local or national politicians in terms of tourism.

Morals

Historically, tourism has been associated with low moral standards including prostitution, crime and gambling, although of course tourism is an easy target to blame here. Away from home, tourists see themselves as anonymous and therefore are more likely to engage in these activities which, as a result, tend to be found at tourism destinations. Some destinations have legalised both prostitution and gambling – indeed the development of casinos is a classic strategy for the rejuvenation of tired destinations, expanding their tax base and attracting a new type of visitor. However, there is evidence that casinos change the nature of the destination and can attract organised crime.

Sex tourism is a controversial consequence of the fact that tourists are strangers in the destinations where the moral climate of home is absent. Sex tourism is also known to spread disease such as AIDS. Wall and Mathieson (2006) identify a number of factors that link tourism to the sex industry:

1. Tourism creates spaces where sex tourism can flourish.

2. Tourism employment for women liberalises them from home and they may then choose to enter the sex industry.

3. Tourism is attracted to the poorer countries of the world where locals may be forced into the sex industry to survive.

4. Some destinations, such as Thailand, have become recognised locations for sex tourism.

Finally, there is evidence that tourism encourages crime and vandalism, partly because there are more people around the destination but also because, as strangers, tourists are easy prey to criminal activity. Residents, too, become targets and both vandalism and threats to personal safety are also an issue with tourism, creating the types of locations where these activities can flourish. In response, destinations become burdened with the extra cost of policing, often drafting in special 'tourist police' – as happens in the resorts of Spain, and in Australia during 'schoolies' weeks – and for any destination crime is bad publicity. Finally, tourism has become the target of major crimes such as terrorism and hijackings.

Language

The demonstration effect is partly responsible for the fact that tourism can lead to the standardisation of language at destinations, threatening minority languages and driving through languages such as English and Spanish. In part, too, this is due to economic development where these languages dominate and become the language of choice of the industry, often influenced by expatriate workers. This leads to the necessity of the hosts learning the language if they are to engage with the tourism industry. Of course, in many destinations a different language is seen as an attraction with bilingual signage, as we see in Wales or the Isle of Man.

Residents' Lifestyle

Much of the research into the social consequences of tourism has focused upon the impact on resident's lifestyle and quality of life. This will depend on the ratio of hosts to guests, and scales have been developed to measure this (for example, the ratio of tourists to the host population). On the positive side, tourism can foster pride in local communities and enhance community spirit and values (as, for example, in the English community of Wirksworth – www.derbyshire-peakdistrict.co.uk/wirksworth.htm – and in Tasmania) as well as assisting in community renewal (Blackstone Valley, USA – www.tourblackstone.com/). Tourism brings increased opportunities to residents through festivals, events and additional facilities, and this does enhance the quality of life of the local community. The following case study showcases a community development initiative by a tourism company which has had a significant impact.

However, despite positive initiatives such as Myths and Mountains, there is no doubt that tourism can be disruptive of the local way of life, whether it be through increased congestion on the roads, more people in the shops, increased crime levels or noise from

Mini Case Study 5.1
Myths and Mountains

Global village library.
Source: © Yooniq Images/Alamy Images

Introduction

The tour company 'Myths and Mountains' have created a community development initiative that is at the cutting edge of sustainable development. The company offers adventure-travel tailored tours and experiences to up-market travellers in the mountain regions of South East Asia. In 1991, their founder decided she wanted to give something back to the communities they visited, and founded READ (Rural Education and Development) global to develop a network of village libraries to foster rural prosperity. The libraries are for the whole community and not just a part of it; they become the heart of a community, educate future generations and are a community asset. The project is not imposed upon the communities – instead, the essence and success of the project is the partnership with 'rural communities in South Asia, where a majority of women are illiterate, and most families live below the poverty line' (http://readglobal.org/).

The READ Global Project

The project takes the initiative to the villages. Villages that want a library have to put in a proposal, supply the land, and provide at least 10 per cent of the cost themselves. READ now has 79 library centres serving 2.1 million rural villagers in 222 villages. To ensure sustainability, a local business is established to support and sustain it – to date over 100 businesses have been established, ranging from cloth-bag making to an ambulance service. Each library centre:

- offers knowledge, information, and educational opportunities to the villagers;
- is owned and operated by the local community;
- is often the only resource of its kind in rural villages; and
- has a library, computer room, women's section, children's room, and training hall.

Community development programmes have been established in the villages, focused around the libraries. The key platforms are:

1. **Education.** The libraries provide education for villagers of any ages or background. The key areas are literacy, health, children's programmes and youth support.

2. **Economic empowerment.** The libraries provide education and training to create livelihoods and foster financial literacy. This allows villagers to earn a living without having to move to cities and to invest in their families. Training includes livelihood and small business skills, whilst initiatives include savings co-operatives.

3. **Technology.** The libraries provide free access to computers and the Internet and technology training as few villagers have access to computers.

4. **Women's empowerment.** The libraries offer women and girls a safe, neutral space to gather, learn, and advocate. This helps women build their confidence and decision-making power. Training includes leadership development, women's and family health and gender awareness whilst initiatives include self-help groups.

READ global is a cutting-edge sustainability initiative, working in partnership with rural communities and providing community development projects designed to foster individual economic independence and community rural prosperity. In 2015, READ global was assisting with disaster relief following the Nepal earthquake.

DISCUSSION QUESTIONS

1. Why is the partnership approach with communities preferable to imposing an initiative upon them?

2. Visit the two websites below. This project began as the initiative of a tour company but do you think the project has grown apart from its tourism roots?

3. Assess the four community development platforms. Is there anything that you would add?

Sources:
http://mythsandmountains.com
http://readglobal.org/

entertainment at night. Where tourism development has exceeded social carrying capacity it is often through factors such as the commercialisation of local attractions and culture, loss of open space and community facilities to serve tourism, and the separation of locals from the recreational business district of the resort. The degree of disruption experienced by residents and their attitude towards tourism development will depend upon three key factors:

1. the location of their home in relation to tourist activity at the destination;

2. the length of time they have lived at the destination; and

3. whether they work in tourism, or have close family who do so.

It will also depend upon:

- **The type of tourism** – for example, racial tensions can arise where the cultural distances are great and there are obvious differences between host and guest as has happened in some Caribbean islands.

- **The type of destination** – for example, in traditional mass tourism resorts much of the tourism activity takes place in and around the recreational business district and there is a separation of tourism activity and local residents. In rural areas the consequences of tourism are more subtle as tourists are dispersed throughout the destination. Nonetheless, the consequences for local residents in rural areas can be severe, not only in terms of interference with traditional rural activities such as farming, but also through the change in the level of services as shops that used to serve the local population become gift shops and tea rooms.

Here, one of the most severe set of consequences, yet one that is almost hidden, is that of second home development. Second homes deliver little economic benefit, yet their impact upon services and community spirit is severe because second homeowners are only present in the destination for a few weeks of the year. This impacts upon health, education and other services, reducing the level of support that they receive and so reducing the quality of life of the local community. Not surprisingly, it is second home development that attracts the most hostile reaction from local people, in some cases turning to violence, and has promoted authorities to attempt to limit the level of second home development in some destinations (Muller, 2014).

Processes of Cultural Change

The culture of a destination has long been an attraction for visitors, dating back at least as far as the grand tour of Europe in the eighteenth century. Yet, it is interesting that whilst culture is a major attraction, it is also changed irreversibly by tourism itself, particularly as tourism often demands 'instant culture' at the destination. Brunt and Courtney (1999) view cultural impacts as:

'those which lead to a longer-term, gradual change in a society's values, beliefs and cultural practices' (p. 496).

As an attraction, culture can be viewed along three dimensions:

- material culture, which includes architecture, monuments, buildings, souvenirs, crafts, literature and paintings;
- normal daily life, which includes local cuisine, everyday life in the destination and the lifestyle of the local people; and
- animated forms of culture that include theatre, festivals and events, some of which may be re-enacted or specially staged for the visitor.

The inevitable consequence of the culture of an international tourist coming into contact with a traditional culture is the danger that the traditional culture is changed or even destroyed. Whenever there is an encounter between two cultures, the cultures tend to borrow from each other, a process known as acculturation or 'cultural drift'. In tourism, it tends to be the weaker culture that borrows the most, particularly as that culture may have to change simply to cater for the tourist. Of course, it is difficult to know just to what extent tourism is responsible for this borrowing, as in the twenty-first century most cultures are also exposed to the mass media, and will evolve and change despite the influence of tourism. The danger here is that the constant process of borrowing leads to uniform cultures and destinations across the world. This is a significant issue for tourism and despite the fact that, as we have seen, the encounter is a brief temporary one, when grossed up, encounters with tourists lead to irreversible, permanent, cultural change. At the end of the day, the degree of change will depend upon the strength and confidence of the host culture.

Cultural change from tourism occurs through:

- the demonstration effect through the intermingling of hosts and guest;
- employment of expatriates in the tourism sector;
- visibility of undesirable activities such as gambling; and
- erosion of local culture and sometimes language.

The main negative consequence of tourism for culture is commercialisation, and whilst this is prevalent in the developing world we also observe it in the developed world – take, for example, the commercialisation of the British Royal family for tourism or indigenous peoples in Canada or the USA; and the commoditisation of religion in many destinations where religious monuments, churches and sites have become tourist attractions rather than places of worship. Here, the contrast between the principles of some religions such as Islam, and the behaviour of visitors to countries where the religion is dominant, can be problematic.

Cheap souvenirs can diminish the value of heritage sites.
Source: © Dorling Kindersley/Max Alexander/Getty Images

Material culture is commonly cited as vulnerable to commercialisation through the cheap reproduction of crafts – often known as 'airport art' – where the original craft has been changed to unsophisticated and poor quality copies. However, whilst we have all experienced this type of souvenir, there is an argument that tourism can help to preserve these traditional crafts if tourists then seek to buy more authentic, original versions. This keeps craftspeople at work, and may even revive dead crafts. The same argument can be applied to festivals, events and customs. We must also remember that some destinations use their culture as a marketing tool to attract visitors and to stamp a sense of identity on the destination – Australia uses its indigenous culture effectively for this purpose (www.australia.com/), whilst Hawaii's culture is a key brand value in its promotion (www.hvcb.org/).

Indigenous people

Butler and Hinch (1996) are clear in their view that whilst indigenous cultures and people are a potential tourist attraction, the process is fraught with danger. The curiosity of tourists to see how others live can easily become voyeurism and there is the danger of the 'encounter' being reduced to viewing the 'savages' of, say, African tribes or South Pacific islands with hints of old colonial relationships. Even the most well-meaning of visits to see how others live can introduce subtle changes into traditional societies through the demonstration effect and the acts of the hosts to accommodate tourists. The concept of homestay, for example, where the visitor stays with a local family, ticks all the boxes of low-impact and sensitive encounters in theory, yet if the hosts are not trained and prepared for the behaviour and customs of the visitors, then it can create major changes in the host society.

Effectively, tourism reduces the 'encounter' with indigenous people to an economic transaction. To be successful, the local community must take ownership and control of the process to ensure that it occurs on their terms and that the benefits are distributed fairly. If this can occur, then the economic benefit of tourism stays within the host community. Examples of successful projects here include:

- Home Valley Station in Australia, a cattle ranch owned and run by indigenous Australians and open to tourists (www.hvstation.com.au/);

- Sarara Camp Kenya, a game reserve and luxury safari camp owned by the Samburu community (www.sararacamp.com/); and

- Huaorani, Ecuador, guest cabins on the Amazon rain forest owned and run by the Huaorani people (www.huaorani.com/).

Here Tao and Wall (2009) have developed the 'sustainable livelihoods' approach, which shows how local populations can benefit from tourism through multiple activities rather than single jobs so that tourism complements rather than displaces existing activities. The approach is centred on people and assesses how their capabilities, activities and assets can enable them to earn a living from tourism. It is based on the idea that tourism can complement existing activities such as agriculture and hunting and that these activities themselves can grow their markets through tourism. Here we begin to touch upon the principles of pro-poor tourism, which is dealt with in the final case study of this chapter. The next case study shows how the relationship between tourism and local tribes people is managed through partnership and establishment of a foundation.

Mini Case Study 5.2
Isoitok Camp Manyara and the African Roots Foundation

The Camp

The Isoitok Camp Manyara is a tented camp located on the Maasai Steppe in Tanzania. It offers 'a grass roots cultural experience and a true look behind the scenes into Maasai culture' (http://isoitok.com/). The camp is set in a rich wild savannah bush location and was founded in 2007. The camp has a close partnership with the local tribes people, the Maasai, and aims to have a low impact on the area through the use of initiatives such as solar energy.

The camp's unique partnership with the local Maasai people provides the opportunity to offer a menu of cultural and lifestyle activities that allows tourists to understand the tribes people's way of life. Local English-speaking Maasai guide scouts take tourists on walks and to various real (not staged) Maasai activities and ceremonies. These include:

- Maasai medicine walk – covering root and plant extracts still used by the Maasai;
- Maasai boma (dwelling) visit – meetings with the Elders, warriors, women and their children;
- traditional goat sacrifice; and
- viewpoint walk with bush refreshments.

The local Maasai community not only has the unique partnership with the camp but also has its own foundation, the 'African Roots Foundation' (ARF).

The Foundation

The ARF is a not-for-profit community development organisation, created in 2007, based on small-scale, sustainable projects which aim to improve the daily life of the communities surrounding the camp. To quote the website the ARF is:

> 'an initiative of Bush2Beach Safaris to create a platform for inter-cultural experiences through which Western and African cultures combine their strengths to increase the self-support opportunities of local rural communities through the initiation of integrated, community based development projects that are actively and physically supported by eco-tourism' (http://africanrootsfoundation.org).

The ARF is involved on a range of projects, including:

- education on the conservation of the environment and wildlife, health and HIV awareness;
- promotion of cultural traditions and practices;
- fair trade of locally manufactured cultural crafts;

- health awareness and improvement programmes;
- water management and sustainable use of natural resources; and
- natural environment and wildlife, eco- and low-impact tourism.

These projects are designed to meet the agreed immediate needs of the communities and 'must provide additional income and employment through the promotion of fair trade and sustainable tourism' (http://africanrootsfoundation.org/).

The ARF continually monitors the success and outcome of the projects and is in constant touch with the elders and representatives of the communities.

DISCUSSION QUESTIONS

1. How comfortable are you with the tourists of the Isoitok camp visiting intimate parts of the lives of the tribes people? Is it voyeurism?

2. Visit the two websites below. Who really controls the activity with the Maasai – the ARF or the tour operators?

3. Ecotourism is the economic basis for the community development initiatives – is this a sustainable model?

Sources:
http://africanrootsfoundation.org/
http://isoitok.com/

Assessing the Social and Cultural Consequences of Tourism

Whilst the methodology of assessing both economic and environmental consequences of tourism are well developed, much less work has been done on developing methods to assess the social and cultural consequences of tourism on the quality of life of the local people. In part, this is due to the difficulty of 'quantifying' these consequences and often the lack of agreement at local level as to just what is 'acceptable change'. Of course, environmental impact assessments now take into account social and cultural impacts, but often the local population is excluded from the process. Here, recent work on the development and monitoring of sustainability indicators (discussed in Chapter 6) has gone some way to assist in this approach. There are also tried and tested techniques of surveying local communities as to their views of tourism development and the degree of change they are prepared to accept due to tourism development. This also has the advantage of assessing acceptable levels of change before tourism develops, rather than the more common approach of assessing consequences after the event.

SUMMARY

This chapter has outlined the social and cultural consequences of tourism for the host population. It began by outlining the tripartite framework needed to analyse these consequences, namely the tourist, the host and the encounter or 'contact'. The chapter has shown that the social and cultural consequences of tourism depend upon the type of tourism development and its pace, as well as the type and number of tourists and the characteristics of the local population at the destination. The concept of social carrying capacity was introduced to explain how destinations could suffer from excessive development in the eyes of the local population. The chapter stressed the importance of the 'encounter' with the tourist and how this encounter occurs in different ways and has certain characteristics. An important aspect of the encounter is the 'demonstration effect' – a process whereby the hosts may copy the behaviour and values of the tourist. Theoretical frameworks to help understand these processes were then outlined, namely those of Doxey, Bjorklund and Philbrick and MacCannell.

The chapter then went on to outline the various social consequences of tourism for the host destination and examined influences upon the hosts' perception of tourists and tourism development. The main social consequences were identified as impacts upon the political and social structures of the destinations, negative impacts on moral behaviour through crime, gambling and sex tourism, impact upon language and negative host attitudes brought about by changing lifestyles through experiencing crowding and congestion at the destination. The chapter included two case studies showing how tourism development can benefit host societies if well managed. Finally, the chapter considered processes of cultural change brought about when a dominant tourism culture comes into contact with a host culture. Here the process of acculturation, or 'borrowing', was identified. Cultural consequences of tourism include the commoditisation of culture and the impact on indigenous peoples. The chapter closed by considering frameworks for assessing social and cultural consequences of tourism and included a case study on the mechanism of tourism as an agent of poverty alleviation.

Discussion Questions

1. In class, debate the proposition that there is little evidence to support the rose-tinted view that bringing cultures and societies together promotes peace and understanding.

2. For a destination with which you are familiar, draw up a balance sheet of positive and negative social consequences of tourism.

3. Analyse the process of the 'encounter' from your own holiday experience – how accurate is the statement that true 'equal' encounters between host and guest are rare?

4. Assess the impact of tourism on the host culture of a destination with which you are familiar.

5. Taking a destination with which you are familiar, map the various interest groups onto Bjorklund and Philbrick's matrix.

Annotated Further Reading

1. De Kadt, E. (1979) *Tourism – Passport to Development?*, Oxford University Press, Oxford.
   Classic coverage of the social and cultural consequences of tourism.

2. Hopkins, D. and Becken, S. (2014) Socio-cultural resilience and tourism, Chapter 39 in Lew, A.L., Hall, C.M. and Williams, A.M. (eds) *The Wiley Blackwell Companion to Tourism,* Wiley, Chichester.
   Contemporary coverage of the socio-cultural consequences of tourism.

3. Krippendorf, J. (1987) *The Holidaymakers. Understanding the Impact of Leisure and Travel,* Butterworth Heinemann, Oxford.
   One of the first books to raise concerns about the social and cultural consequences of tourism.

4. MacCannell, D. (1973) Staged authenticity: arrangements of social space in tourist settings, *American Journal of Sociology* 73(3), 589–603.
   Classic and highly influential paper.

5. Sharpley, R (2014) Host perceptions of tourism: a review of the research, *Tourism Management* **42,** 37–49.

6. Smith, V. (1977) *Hosts and Guests: The Anthropology of Tourism*, University of Pennsylvania Press, Philadelphia, PA.
   A further classic text examining hosts and guests through anthropological eyes.

7. Urry, J. (1990) *The Tourist Gaze: Leisure and Travel in Contemporary Societies*, Sage, London.
   Influential book on the postmodern tourist.

8. UNWTO (2011) *Manual on Tourism and Poverty Alleviation – Practical Steps for Destinations*, UNWTO, Madrid.
   Authoritative coverage of tourism and poverty alleviation with good examples.

9. Wall, G. and Mathieson, A. (2006) *Tourism: Change, Impacts and Opportunities*, Pearson, Harlow.
   Excellent second edition of the key text examining the consequences of tourism.

10. The websites of IIPT (www.iipt.org) and ECPAT (www.ecpat.net) provide contrasting views of the social consequences of tourism, one seeing tourism as an agent of peace, the other a campaign against the involvement of children in sex tourism.

References Cited

Bjorklund, E.M. and Philbrick, A.K. (1972) *Building Regions for the Future*, Department of Geography, Lowal University, Quebec.

Brunt, P. and Courtney, P. (1999) Host perceptions of sociocultural impacts, *Annals of Tourism Research* **26**(3), 493–515.

Butler, R.W. (1980) The concept of a tourist area cycle of evolution, *Canadian Geographer*, **24**, 5–12.

Butler, R and Hinch, T (1996) *Tourism and Indigenous People*, Routledge, London.

De Kadt, E. (1979) *Tourism – Passport to Development?*, Oxford University Press, Oxford.

Dogan, H. (1989) Forms of adjustment: sociocultural impacts of tourism, *Annals of Tourism Research* **16**(2), 216–236.

Doxey, G.V. (1976) When enough's enough: the natives are restless in old Niagara, *Heritage Canada* **2**(2), 26–27.

Fisher, D. (2004) The demonstration effect revisited, *Annals of Tourism Research* **31**(2), 428–426.

Krippendorf, J. (1987) *The Holidaymakers: Understanding the Impact of Leisure and Travel*, Oxford, Butterworth Heinemann

MacCannell, D. (1973) Staged authenticity: arrangements of social space in tourist settings, *American Journal of Sociology* **73**(3), 589–603.

Mathieson, A. and Wall, G. (1982) *Tourism: Economic, Physical and Social Impacts*, Longman, London.

Muller, D. (2014) Progress in second home tourism research, Chapter 31 in Lew, A.L., Hall, C.M. and Williams, A.M. (eds) *The Wiley Blackwell Companion to Tourism*, Wiley, Chichester.

Sharpley, R. (2014) Host perceptions of tourism: a review of the research, *Tourism Management* **42**, 37–49.

Smith, V. (1977) *Hosts and Guests: The Anthropology of Tourism*, University of Pennsylvania Press, Philadelphia, PA.

Tao, C.T.H. and Wall, G. (2009) Tourism as a sustainable livelihood strategy. *Tourism Management* **30**, 9–98.

UNESCO (1976) The effects of tourism on socio-cultural values, *Annals of Tourism Research* **4**(1), 74–105.

Urry, J. (1990) *The Tourist Gaze: Leisure and Travel in Contemporary Societies*, Sage, London.

Wall, G. and Mathieson, A. (2006) *Tourism: Change, Impacts and Opportunities*, Pearson, Harlow.

Weaver, D.B. (2014) Asymmetrical dialectics of sustainable tourism: toward enlightened mass tourism, *Journal of Travel Research* **53**(2), 131–140.

Major Case Study 5.1
Tourism as an Agent of Poverty Alleviation

Defining Poverty

Poverty has become one of the world's major challenges and defeating it is the first of the UN's Millennium Development Goals (MDGs) – to 'eradicate extreme poverty and hunger' – and forms a core element of many of the other MDGs. The World Bank defines poverty as anyone living on less than one US dollar per day. This is not the same as *relative poverty* experienced by many people in the West, meaning insufficient income to afford a holiday or consumer goods, but the inability to meet more basic needs such as food, water and shelter. However, poverty is much more than just an economic condition, it relates to the very way of life of people and includes living conditions, access to resources and intangibles such as pride and self-esteem.

The UNWTO (2004) states that poverty alleviation is an essential precondition of peace, environmental conservation and sustainable development. Indeed, the UNWTO goes further, saying that addressing poverty is an ethical obligation for the developed world. Tourism has been recognised as a sector that can make a significant contribution to poverty alleviation, especially in rural areas. Yet surprisingly, the role of tourism in poverty alleviation is a relatively recent initiative. In the past, economic, regional and environmental issues dominated thinking on tourism development. Following the UN Johannesburg World Summit on Sustainable Development in 2002, poverty alleviation emerged as a central issue for tourism in the future – the role of tourism development as a means of reducing world poverty and in 2005 the UNWTO convened a conference to examine how tourism can contribute the MDGs.

Tourism as an Agent of Poverty Alleviation

Since Johannesburg, tourism has been recognised as a means of alleviating poverty. This new agenda has been enthusiastically embraced by the developing world and international agencies (including the UNWTO, UNCTAD and the World Bank). The UNWTO, for example, has developed a programme, 'sustainable tourism – eliminating poverty' (ST-EP).

Treating tourism as an agent of poverty alleviation results in increased net benefits for poor people. The critical issue is how to channel visitor spending and investment into improved income and quality of life for people in poverty.

The UNWTO state that tourism has many advantages as a sector for poverty alleviation:

- Tourism is produced where it is consumed – it brings tourists to the destination allowing opportunities for economic gain from contact with visitors.

- Tourism is easily accessible to the poor – it is labour intensive, employs a high percentage of women and young people, and mainly comprises SMEs (small and medium-sized enterprises). It also spreads economic benefits both geographically and to other sectors such as agriculture and handicrafts due to its 'connectivity'.

- Tourism is naturally attracted to remote, peripheral areas where other economic options are limited, and to the lesser developed countries of the world where there are significant natural and cultural attractions.

- Tourism is one of the few development opportunities for the poor and encourages entrepreneurial development.

- The infrastructure required to develop tourism benefits poor communities.

- Tourism is significant and growing in the developing and least-developed countries. These include China, Vietnam, Laos, Cambodia, Myanmar and a number of Pacific islands. Indeed, the UNWTO (2014) forecast that tourism to emerging economies will exceed that of advanced economies before 2020 (Table 5.3).

Table 5.3 Tourism arrivals and forecasts by type of economy (IMF definition) (millions)

Type of economy	1980	1995	2014	2020 forecast	2030 forecast
Advanced	194	334	619	643	772
Emerging	83	193	513	717	1037
World	277	528	1133	1360	1809

Source: UNWTO, 2014

Principles of Poverty Alleviation through Tourism

The UNWTO (2004) has defined the overarching principles of poverty alleviation through tourism as:

- Mainstreaming to ensure that sustainable tourism development is factored into poverty elimination programmes and also that poverty is considered in tourism plans and strategies.

- Partnerships between all destination stakeholders are vital to achieve effective poverty alleviation.

- Integration with other economic sectors ensures that overdependence on tourism is avoided.

- Equitable distribution of the benefits of tourism is vital, as we see below.

- Acting locally at the destination level ensures community involvement and an appropriate scale of development.

- Retention of economic benefits by close management of the supply chain to avoid leakages.

- Viability of the projects should be assured through sound financial management and feasibility.

- Empowerment of the local community, and of women, is essential to enable them to have access to information and control decisions.

- Human rights are vital to avoid discrimination, particularly against women and children.

- Commitment and monitoring involves planning for the long term and developing indicators to monitor success.

Strategies for Poverty Alleviation Through Tourism

There are a variety of approaches to poverty alleviation. Here, we can identify three key approaches:

1. Delivering economic benefits, which include:
   - creating jobs for the poor which underpin and secure household income;
   - providing opportunities for entrepreneurs to both directly and indirectly supply tourists with goods such as handicrafts – the beach operators of Mombassa in Kenya are an example here;
   - development of local co-operatives;
   - voluntary giving and donations by visitors; and

   - increasing the economic benefits for the whole community – by renting communal land for camping, for example.

2. Delivering improved living conditions such as infrastructure, training and education, reducing the environmental impacts of tourism, reducing competition for natural resources, and improving access to services such as schooling, health care, communications.

3. Delivering participation and involvement benefits by changing the relevant policy and planning framework to allow participation by local communities, increasing their contribution in decision-making and developing partnerships with the private sector.

   Of course, the effectiveness of tourism as an agent of poverty alleviation demands that the relevant approach is selected from the menu above appropriate to the particular destination. The approaches are highly dependent upon the particular destination in question. We can therefore think of two further approaches:

4. Destination-based strategies work well for poverty alleviation in particular groups, encouraging economic linkages between, say, tourism businesses and local farmers to reduce leakage through imports, boosting partnerships, developing local enterprises and increasing community pride.

5. National policy-based strategies are preferred for objectives such as changing systems of land tenure, improving planning procedures, training and education, and infrastructure development.

   Successful implementation of these strategies will depend upon some key principles, recognising:

- the sustainable livelihoods approach mentioned in this chapter;
- the imperative of local ownership and control;
- the need for capacity building in the community;
- that tourism is a system demanding access to transport, accommodation and a wide range of support services and products – good destination level planning and management is therefore essential;
- that the principles of poverty alleviation through tourism are the same everywhere, but that their

implementation will vary according to the type of tourism product from, say, small-scale ecotourism to mass tourism – product development and quality control are an important aspect of this point;

- the need to ensure that consumers are aware and support the project;
- the need to develop partnerships with the private sector on an equitable footing;
- the reality that not all the poor will benefit equally; and
- the focus must be on delivering benefits, not just cutting costs.

Nonetheless, there are barriers to the implementation of tourism strategies to alleviate poverty and tourism itself can be problematic. For example:

- a perception by aid agencies that tourism is for the wealthy;
- significant economic leakages out of the local community to buy imported goods for tourist consumption, thus reducing the net benefits of tourism;
- lack of education, training and understanding about pro-poor tourism;
- lack of investment and low-interest loans to allow local tourism enterprises to get under way;
- lack of infrastructure and basic services in very poor areas;
- the seasonal and unpredictable nature of demand for tourism.

But despite these barriers, the idea of pro-poor tourism as a mechanism for alleviating poverty is gaining momentum and should be central to the agenda of tourism development in the future.

DISCUSSION QUESTIONS

1. Using the Internet and other media sources, identify a tourism project that is designed to alleviate poverty. Identify the type of pro-poor strategy that is being used and draft a list of possible issues that may affect the success of the project.

2. Design a brochure for a tourism experience that contains a significant pro-poor element. Think carefully about how you should communicate the benefits of the tour to the visitor.

3. Draft a report to the sceptical head of a large charity justifying why you feel tourism could play a role in the charity's key objective of reducing poverty in Africa.

Sources:

Ashley, C., Boyd, C. and Goodwin, H. (2000) Pro-poor tourism: putting poverty at the heart of the tourism agenda, *Natural Resource Perspectives* **51**(March), 1–12.

Rogerson, C. (2014) Strengthening tourism-poverty linkages, Chapter 48 in Lew A.L., Hall, C.M. and Williams, A.M. (eds) *The Wiley Blackwell Companion to Tourism*, Wiley, Chichester.

UNWTO (2004) *Tourism and Poverty Alleviation: Recommendations for Action*, UNWTO, Madrid.

UNWTO (2011) *Manual on Tourism and Poverty Alleviation – Practical Steps for Destinations*, UNWTO, Madrid.

UNWTO (2014) *Tourism Highlights, 2014 Edition*, UNWTO, Madrid.

www.adb.org/Documents/Policies/Poverty_Reducation/default.asp

www.propoortourism.org.uk

www.worldbank.org/poverty

www.world-tourism.org

CHAPTER 6
SUSTAINABLE TOURISM

Learning Outcomes

This chapter considers the background and approaches to sustainable tourism as an organising concept for tourism in the twenty-first century. It outlines the evolution of the concept and shows how it can be effectively implemented. The chapter is designed to provide you with:

- an understanding of how the idea of sustainable tourism has evolved;

- an awareness of the various concepts and definitions of sustainable tourism;

- an appreciation of the different types of sustainable tourism;

- an understanding of the underpinning principles of sustainable tourism; and

- an awareness of contemporary approaches to implementing sustainable tourism.

Introduction

As tourism continues to grow across the world, reaching ever more remote and sensitive places, it has placed increased pressure upon the environment and host communities of those destinations – as we have seen in the previous three chapters. A pioneer of sustainable tourism, Jost Krippendorf (1982) states the matter clearly:

'Unrestricted tourism growth could lead to the positive economic effects of tourism being outweighed by significant social and environmental disadvantages' (p. 135).

Tourism is unusual in that its core product depends upon the successful management of the resources upon which tourism depends. To respond to the challenges that this implies for tourism in the twenty-first century, there is an imperative for the sustainable development of tourism. These challenges include four key priorities:

1. To plan and manage tourism growth to minimise negative impacts and promote the positive impacts of tourism. This is particularly important for vulnerable destinations such as coasts, wetlands, mountains, deserts, the Polar Regions and areas of significant cultural heritage.

2. To use tourism to help alleviate poverty in the world.

3. To take action on climate change, as climate change will impact upon tourism in two ways – firstly, demanding adaptation on the part of destinations and, secondly, shifting patterns of demand by stressing tourists' individual responsibility for their behaviour.

4. Ensure that sustainability is financially attractive by developing new ways of operating as a sector including public/private partnerships, embracing the principles of the 'green economy' and developing environmental accounting techniques.

Here contemporary thinking is based upon two principles:

1. Scientists accept that ecosystems are complex adaptive systems, with natural, social and economic elements. For tourism, this means that it is essential to take a 'whole of destination' approach to sustainability, managing the system by determining thresholds of acceptability and monitoring the system through the use of indicators (which are dealt with later in the chapter).

2. The challenge of sustainability is closely linked to economic development. As such, not only should we consider the issue of tourism sustainable development, but also the means by which tourism itself can contribute to sustainable development in economies across the world. Indeed, the challenges posed by sustainability are allowing the tourism sector to be both innovative and adaptive to rethink the way that it operates. This is known as the 'higher level approach' to planning and contrasts with the 'lower level approach' based upon property development. The 'higher level approach' has been driven by the imperatives of climate change, environmental pressures and demands from the consumer.

Background to Sustainability

The concept of sustainability itself has a long pedigree, rooted in resource management and agriculture dating back to ancient times, and reflecting shifting priorities in society. It is also a concept that continues to evolve (Liburd and Edwards, 2010). From the 1960s onwards there was a growing interest and concern for the environment, fuelled by media coverage, the emergence of 'green' consumerism and the establishment of powerful NGOs. For tourism, the concept has come late, growing in awareness throughout the 1980s, supported by international conventions, declarations and initiatives that reflected the mood of the times (see Table 6.1). It is interesting, for example, that in the UN's Earth Summit in Rio the word tourism did not appear, yet in the next decade, in the second Earth Summit in Johannesburg and Rio+20 in 2012, tourism was seen as an important player with its own section of the report. Sustainable tourism has also matured over the decades moving from idealism to reality. Examples here include the way that leading companies such as Accor and Tui are showing leadership in sustainability. However, Buckley feels there are exceptions and that the sector is not yet mature in this regard, relying on regulation rather than the market for sustainable initiatives (Buckley, 2012).

The concept of sustainability has, and continues to evolve, perhaps away from a sole concern with the environment to a broader concern for society. Here, the development of the United Nations 'Millennium Development Goals' (MDGs) in 2000 was pivotal in broadening the agenda (www.undp.org/mdg/). The goals include targets for poverty reduction, increasing education levels, empowering women, reducing child mortality and combating diseases such as HIV/AIDS and Malaria (see Saarinen *et al.*, 2012). The MDGs are important as they act as the framework for the development agencies of the developed world to intervene in the developing world. However, by 2012 the UN's Conference on Sustainable Development, Rio+20, supported the redevelopment of the MDGs into Sustainable Development Goals (SDGs) to redress the criticism that the MDGs neglected the environment. As the debate has matured we have moved from a position of tourism being either sustainable or not, to one where the effort is focused upon moving all forms of tourism towards sustainability (Clarke, 1997). In other words, sustainable tourism development should not be seen as an end goal in itself, but instead

Table 6.1 Milestones of sustainable tourism development

Date	Initiative
1962	Publication of Rachel Carson's *Silent Spring*
1968	Publication of Hardin's *Tragedy of the Commons*
1972	Club of Rome Report *Limits to Growth* UN Stockholm Conference on the Human Environment – no mention of tourism
1973	Publication of Schumacher's *Small is Beautiful*
1980	World Conservation Strategy published by the International Union for the Conservation of Nature (IUCN)
1987	Brundtland Report, *Our Common Future*, published
1992	Rio Earth Summit – very much with *environment* as the focus Agenda 21 UN Commission on Sustainable Development
1993	Establishment of the *Journal of Sustainable Tourism*
1999	UNWTO Global Code of Ethics for Tourism
2000	Tour Operators Initiative for Sustainable Tourism Development Millennium Development Goals
2002	Johannesburg World Summit on Sustainable Development developed idea of Agenda 21 – shifting the emphasis from *environment* to *people* International Year of Ecotourism Quebec Declaration on Ecotourism
2003	European Commission Tourism Sustainability Group established
2006	Marrakech Task Force on Tourism Sustainable Development
2007	UNESCO/UNWTO Collaboration for World Heritage Davos Processes on Climate Change Global Sustainable Tourism Criteria Publication of European Union's 'Action for a More Sustainable European Tourism'
2008	Sustainable Tourism Stewardship Council
2009	Copenhagen Climate Conference aiming to deliver a holistic framework to stabilise global warming by 2050
2010	UN Framework Convention on Climate Change, Cancun, Mexico
2012	Rio+20, Rio, Brazil, shifting the emphasis from MDGs to Sustainable Development Goals (SDGs) to readdress environmental concerns UN Climate Change Conference, Qatar

as part of a dynamic process of change, encouraging new initiatives to take tourism along a path towards sustainability. Miller and Twining-Ward (2005) see this evolution as the 'sustainability transition', where sustainable tourism evolves to adapt to society and its particular sites and destinations. Essentially, we can view sustainable tourism as a continuous process of improvement that has become the organising concept for much of tourism.

Everest – clean-up tourists leave the destination in a better condition than they found it.
Source: © Namgyal Sherpa/AFP/Getty Images

The Pillars of Sustainability

We can think of three key pillars that support the triple bottom line approach to sustainability (Figure 6.1). These pillars are interlinked and mutually reinforcing:

1. **Economic sustainability** revolves around the concept of the enterprise supporting jobs and delivering income to communities in the long term. Without this, destinations and their communities cannot survive. Increasingly environmental considerations will impact upon the economy as we move to a 'greening' of the economy.

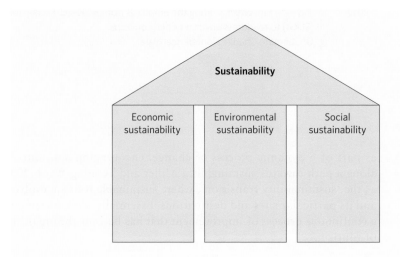

Figure 6.1 The three pillars of sustainable tourism

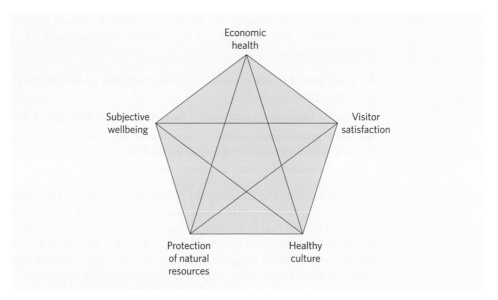

Figure 6.2 Muller's sustainability pentagon
Source: Muller, 1994; Miller and Twining-Ward, 2005

2. **Social sustainability** focuses upon sharing benefits fairly and equitably and respecting the quality of life of communities and of human rights. It will increasingly involve 'living within our means'.

3. **Environmental sustainability** focuses upon stewardship of resources and managing and conserving the environment, and will involve the notion of 'limits to growth'.

Some commentators suggest that there should be a fourth pillar based upon carbon, but this is not yet generally accepted. Tourism is a key player in each of these pillars, not only as a private sector activity, but also as one that impacts upon destination communities and utilises the environment as a resource to attract tourism. At the same time, it is in a strong position to educate the tourists themselves about the imperative for sustainable development and appropriate behaviours. There is therefore a delicate balance to be struck between the pillars, as environmental damage to a destination will reduce visitation and so jeopardise the viability of local enterprises that depend it. The Great Barrier Reef in Australia is a good example here (www.gbrmpa.gov.au/). Muller's (1994) conceptualisation of sustainability is useful as it diagrammatically illustrates the 'pillars' of sustainability, and in his pentagon he extends them to five (Figure 6.2). The centre of the pentagon represents a harmonious situation of balanced development where all forces are balanced – for destinations this is easier said than achieved!

Concepts and Definitions

There remains confusion and a lack of agreement over exactly how to conceptualise and define sustainability, sustainable development and sustainable tourism – indeed the terms are used rather loosely and interchangeably. Generally, the most commonly cited definition for, and accepted thinking about, sustainable development is from the Brundtland World Commission on Environment and Development (1987). They define sustainable development as 'a process that meets the needs of the present without compromising the ability of future generations to meet their own needs'. The Brundtland report neatly linked the concept of economic development with the notion of environmental and social sustainability, concluding that it is impossible to separate them. The Brundtland definition comprises three parts:

1. **development** – here the issue is the compatibility of sustainable development with economic growth;
2. **needs** – focusing around issues of equity and distribution of resources; and
3. **future generations** – where the issue is that the income of future generations should not be less than the current generations and that current generations have a responsibility of stewardship for both social and natural 'capital'.

At the heart of the Brundtland Commission's concept of sustainable development was the apparent paradox between economic development and environmental quality. The Commission has been highly influential in subsequent thinking on sustainability and its report has shaped the agenda. They stated that sustainable development should address the maintenance of ecological integrity and diversity, meet basic human needs, address the needs of future generations, reduce injustice and increase self-determination. In stating this, the Commission laid the early bases for the UN MDGs.

There continues to be a debate over just what sustainable tourism encompasses and how it should be defined. For example, some commentators confuse it with ecotourism or nature-based tourism, or feel that it is only about small scale, niche forms of tourism. This is not the case – sustainable tourism encompasses all forms of tourism and indeed, is as much a process as an approach as we saw above. The UNWTO (2005) developed a set of paragraphs to act as conceptual definition:

> **'Sustainable tourism development guidelines and management practices are applicable to all forms of tourism in all types of destinations . . . Sustainable tourism principles refer to the environmental, economic and socio-cultural aspects of tourism development and a suitable balance must be established between these three dimensions to guarantee its long term sustainability . . . Sustainable tourism development requires the informed participation of all relevant stakeholders as well as strong political leadership to ensure wide participation and consensus building. Achieving sustainable tourism is a continuous process and it requires constant monitoring of impacts, introducing the necessary preventive and/or corrective measures . . . Sustainable tourism should also maintain a high level of tourist satisfaction . . . raising their awareness about sustainability issues' (p. 11).**

This definition can be shortened to:

> **'Tourism that takes full account of its current and future economic, social and environmental impacts, addressing the needs of visitors, the industry, the environment and host communities' (p. 12).**

The key sentiment here is collaboration between stakeholders (see UNWTO, 2010). Saarinen (2006) draws heavily on the idea of carrying capacity for his elegantly simple definition:

> **'The scale of tourism that can occur in a spatial unit without doing any serious harm to the natural, economic and socio-cultural elements at destinations' (p. 1126).**

In the first case study for this chapter we show how the very structure of a particular type of tourism – in this case, township tourism – can undermine its sustainability.

Mini Case Study 6.1
Is Township Tourism Sustainable?

Freedom Square, Soweto.
Source: © Moment Open/George Pachantouris/Getty Images

Introduction

Tours to the townships of South Africa have been developed in recent years as a form of pro-poor tourism and to meet the demand for authenticity from the 'new tourist'. However, this type of tourism is controversial and its very configuration raises the question of sustainability, exemplified by this case of the township of Soweto.

The townships of South Africa developed in the early 1950s as a result of the planning policy of racial segregation imposed by the former apartheid system of white supremacy. This has left these communities with a legacy of poor-quality housing such as corrugated iron shacks and 'matchbox houses', unemployment, overcrowding, high crime rates and poor infrastructure caused by the lack of investment in the apartheid years.

Soweto

Soweto is the largest and most influential of the townships in terms of the arts and politics, famed for its resistance to apartheid and its association with internationally known personalities such as Nelson Mandela and Desmond Tutu.

The main attraction of the townships is the spontaneity of the everyday life and culture of the community, with its music, dancing, art, music, galleries, craft centres, sport and shops. There are also a number of dedicated tourist attractions, including museums, Archbishop Tutu's house, Freedom Square, churches and themed routes such as the 'struggle route tour'. Accommodation in Soweto is mainly in bed and breakfast guesthouses; however, despite winning tourism awards and being totally authentic, the guesthouses are struggling to remain viable, as many tourists prefer to stay in more luxury accommodation in the suburbs of Johannesburg – raising the question of the sustainability of the local enterprises. In addition, a Holiday Inn has opened in Freedom Square in Soweto, creating more competition for the indigenous accommodation owners. Authenticity can also equate to an amateur approach to hospitality. To combat this, the government is providing training courses for guesthouse owners and their staff. Transport around Soweto is mainly by guided tour, with a large number of 'local' guided tours available, many of which arrange for tourists to meet local people and to visit their homes.

Sustainability?

Of course, it is difficult to argue against the concept of 'township tourism' but it does raise a number of key issues in respect of sustainability:

● The potential social and cultural impact of township tourism is great if visitors are not well managed, especially as the volume of visitors is growing.

● The geographical configuration of the township means that there is no critical mass of attractions that cluster together and which link to support facilities. There remains a lack of infrastructure and tourists are warned not to go into Soweto alone. In addition, language barriers and differences in culture constrain the opportunity for businesses to sell art and crafts and to engage with the visitor; moreover, the townships operate on a cash economy whereas tourists often assume credit cards will be accepted.

● A particular issue related to township tourism, and one that is acute in Soweto, is the fact that the operation of tourism is both small-scale and not embedded within the tourism sector. Most of the businesses are small and find it difficult to link into the supply chain and do not have strong bargaining power. The solution here is for businesses to work together, forming cooperatives to bargain for better supply prices, market themselves and access the supply chain.

So the question is whether these structural issues threaten the sustainability of township tourism. Yet, there is no doubt that township tours do provide tourists with a genuine learning experience about the way of life of the townships. Soweto also benefits from the corporate social responsibility of large tourism companies who are re-investing profits into Soweto development schemes and assisting with training and human capacity development.

DISCUSSION QUESTIONS

1. Is township tourism sustainable?

2. Draft the key elements of a training programme to assist guesthouse owners in Soweto to develop professional hospitality skills.

3. Debate in class the pros and cons of township tours – on the one hand, they are a means of effecting pro-poor tourism, on the other hand, they exploit the culture and history of the townships.

Sources:
Binns, T. and Etienne, N. (2002) Tourism as a local development strategy in South Africa, *The Geographical Journal* **168**(3), 235–247.
George, R. and Booyens, I. (2014) Township tourism demand: tourists' perceptions of safety and security, *Urban Forum* **25**(4), 449–467.
Koens, K. and Thomas, R. (2015) Is small beautiful? Understanding the contribution of small businesses in township tourism to economic development, *Development Southern Africa* **32**(3), 320–332.
Steinbrink, M. (2012) 'We did the Slum!'– urban poverty tourism in historical perspective, *Tourism Geographies* **14**(2), 213–234.
www.soweto.co.za
www.joburg.org.za
www.gauteng.net/

Types of Tourism Sustainability

Hunter (1997) maps out four different types of tourism sustainability showing that there are different levels of both sustainable commitment and also permissible tourism development. His typology can be seen as a continuum, where tourism is strong at one end and sustainability is strong at the other (Figure 6.3):

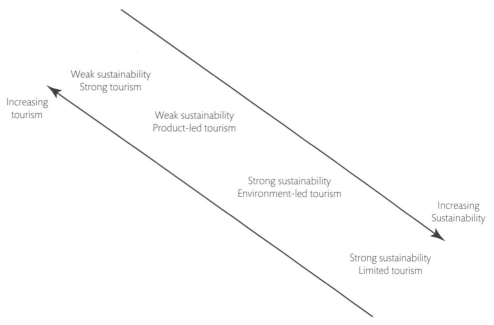

Figure 6.3 A continuum of sustainable tourism
Source: after Hunter, 1997

1. **Very weak sustainability/strong tourism imperative.** Here the emphasis is on satisfying the demands of the tourism sector and tourists, sometimes at the expense of destination resources. Often this occurs in the early stages of tourism at a destination where growth is encouraged.

2. **Weak sustainability/product-led tourism.** This scenario is where tourism remains dominant and sustainability secondary to the development of new products, although the need for resource conservation and the management of growth is recognised.

3. **Strong sustainability/environmental-led tourism.** This is a familiar type of sustainable tourism where environmental management lies at the heart of destination management and niche tourism products include ecotourism.

4. **Very strong sustainability/limited tourism.** Here, tourism activity is small in scale, and in places discouraged if it could cause environmental damage. The use of both renewable and non-renewable resources is limited through the use of environmental management techniques. The general view is against economic growth.

Clarke (1997) has classified approaches to sustainable tourism into four positions from early ideas of polar opposites, to mass tourism, moving to convergence where all tourism should be sustainable (Table 6.2). These approaches reflect the thinking of the times (Table 6.3). For example, the contemporary viewpoint is one of 'convergence' where sustainable tourism takes an interdisciplinary approach combining both natural and social science. This has replaced the earlier 'product-based' approach where sustainable tourism is seen as the polar opposite of mass tourism. The UNWTO is a strong advocate of the convergence position, stressing that sustainable development of tourism should apply to all forms of tourism, not simply special interest and nature-based forms of tourism, but also mass tourism. Here, Spanish destinations such as the Balearic Islands have led the way (see, for example, the Calvia strategy for integrated sustainable development at www.calvia.com). The Calvia example is interesting because it opens up the debate as to whether regeneration projects for 'tired' mass tourism destinations are as useful as, say, small-scale rural or green tourism projects. In the classic paper for this chapter we single out Hunter's (1997) pivotal contribution to the sustainability debate.

Table 6.2 Sustainable tourism positions

Position	Features
Polar opposite	In the early 1990s, sustainable tourism was seen as the polar opposite of mass tourism, and different forms of alternative tourism, including ecotourism, were seen as the answer to sustainability.
Continuum	During the 1990s, the polar opposite position was rejected as too simplistic and replaced by the idea of a continuum of tourism approaches from mass tourism to sustainable tourism.
Movement	Eventually, it was recognised that all forms of tourism should be sustainable, including the movement of mass tourism towards a sustainable model, rethinking scale and applying ideas to achieve this.
Convergence	All tourism should be sustainable - very much the goals of the UNWTO's sustainable tourism unit.

Source: Clarke, 1997

Table 6.3 The evolution of the sustainability concept in the tourism literature

Platform	Characteristics
Advocacy 1950s and 1960s	Tourism seen uncritically as an economic benefit and solution to growth in the developing world and encouraged by international agencies.
Cautionary 1970s and early 1980s	The negative effects of tourism development are exposed and the value of tourism begins to be questioned.
Adaptive Mid-1980s to early 1990s	Realisation that alternative forms of tourism can be developed and that sustainable tourism can be managed.
Knowledge based Mid-1990s onwards	Recognition that sustainability concepts need a factual or knowledge underpinning including the development of sustainability indicators.

Source: Jafari, 1990

Classic Paper
Hunter, C. (1997) Sustainable tourism as an adaptive paradigm,
Annals of Tourism Research **24(4), 850–867**

Hunter's paper was influential in changing the thinking on sustainability, marking the turning point from the rather narrow 'product led' approach of tourism which saw sustainable tourism simply as another form of tourism at the other end of the spectrum from mass tourism. In doing so, his intention was to open up debate as to how sustainable tourism can be seen in a different light. Hunter's paper draws the tourism debate into the mainstream of sustainable development thinking, and he is critical of previous 'tourist-centric' approaches, which fail to encompass the wider and complex systems of which destinations are a part. As a result, he states that tourism can learn much from the wider literature on sustainable development. The main lesson of Hunter's paper is that 'Sustainable tourism should not be regarded as a rigid framework, but rather as an adaptive paradigm which legitimises a variety of approaches according to specific circumstances' (p. 851).

Hunter then goes on to outline a 'theoretical array' of sustainable tourism which allows for individual circumstances of particular destinations and situations; situations which allow for differences across host communities and their desire for participation, tourism demand, tourism supply, and various environmental impacts. This allows for trade-offs between sustainability and development at different stages of destination evolution, but above all encourages informed and transparent decision-making. Hunter's array comprises four categories:

1. **Sustainable development through a tourism imperative.** This type of tourism is concerned with satisfying the needs of tourists and developers and does not prioritise environmental concerns or planning. Hunter suggests that this form of tourism could occur in three situations – (i) where tourism is a priority for poverty alleviation, (ii) where tourism replaces an environmentally degrading activity such as open cast mining, and (iii) where the development of tourism can prevent the development of other environmentally degrading activities.

2. **Sustainable tourism through product-led tourism.** Here, the development of new products and expansion of the distribution channels through the use of intermediaries takes precedence over environmental concerns except where they can be seen to sustain the development of tourism products. This situation can occur in well-developed tourism destinations where the economic benefits of tourism sustain the local community.

3. **Sustainable tourism through environment-led tourism.** Here concerns for the environment and host community move more to the centre of the stage in tourism development, often in areas where tourism is being newly introduced, or where tourism is highly dependent upon the quality of environmental resources to be successful.

4. **Sustainable development through neotenous tourism.** In this approach environmental concerns are paramount and tourism may be actively discouraged, or heavily managed through, say, the use of access permits. The exploration or involvement stage of the tourism area life-cycle would be an appropriate stage for this type of development. Hunter debates this approach at length and voices concerns that such an 'extreme' management approach is open to criticism on the basis of elitism.

These four types of sustainable tourism development illustrate Hunter's notion of an 'adaptive paradigm capable of addressing widely different situations and articulating different goals in terms of utilisation of natural resources' (p. 864). He ends with a challenging question: 'who decides on the most appropriate approach for a destination?'

Principles of Sustainable Tourism

As the tourism community has embraced the concept of sustainable tourism, it has moved along the path from concepts, definitions and typologies towards elucidating the principles of sustainability and how it can be implemented.

The UNWTO (2005, p. 18) has been influential in shaping the sustainable tourism agenda. They state that sustainable tourism comprises two elements:

1. the ability of tourism to continue as an activity in the future, ensuring that the conditions are right for this; and

2. the ability of society and the environment to absorb and benefit from the impacts of tourism in a positive way.

They go on to outline that the principles of sustainable tourism are to:

- ensure that all forms of tourism are sustainable – sustainable tourism is not a discrete type of tourism, all tourism should be sustainable;

- take a long-term view;

- take a 'whole of destination' approach – this ensures balanced development and that one element of the destination mix does not surge ahead of the others. It is important not to take a tourist-centric approach as was done in early debates on sustainable tourism;

- balance global and local impacts – for example, local initiatives to reduce carbon emissions will have a positive global impact;

- ensure tourists are aware of the issue and pursue sustainable consumption;
- make optimal use of environmental resources;
- develop cultural richness of the destination by respecting the socio-cultural integrity and authenticity of host communities;
- conserve tangible and intangible heritage;
- ensure that businesses are economically viable over the long term;
- involve all stakeholders at the destination;
- ensure community well-being such that communities benefit from tourism; and
- provide a high-quality tourist experience to maintain high levels of tourist satisfaction.

We feel that there should be two additions to this list:

1. the need for tourism to embrace the principles of the green economy and to minimise its carbon footprint; and
2. the need to incorporate values into sustainable tourism covering areas of stewardship, professionalism and ethics (see, for example, www.besteducationnetwork.org).

By adhering to these principles, the aims of sustainable tourism can be articulated as triple bottom line sustainability – environmental, social and economic (Figure 6.1). These aims are also about balancing the negative impacts of tourism with the positive benefits that it can bring, particularly to communities (through, say, poverty alleviation), economies and environmental protection. This delivers a strategy for long-term destination competitiveness along five key dimensions:

1. Influencing the location and form of tourism development through land use planning, design control, building codes and planning regulation.
2. Empowering local communities through ensuring participation in decision making, building local tourism expertise and capacity through training and ensuring the economic viability of local businesses through financial assistance where necessary.
3. Ensuring a high-quality tourist experience by managing the destination elements of safety, access, information and interpretation.
4. Conserving and managing destination heritage by site and visitor management techniques.
5. Integrating environmental management into tourism facilities including energy, water and waste management and strategies for minimising carbon emissions. This should be on the basis of 'reduce, reuse recycle'.

The importance of delivering a high-quality experience is central to any sustainable tourism strategy. This dimension of visitor fulfilment must not be neglected in any consideration of sustainable tourism. As the sector and the activity of tourism have matured, the market has become experienced and sensitised to the potential damaging effects of tourism. As a result, the tourism market now is concerned for the social and environmental well-being of destinations, and particularly where this impacts directly upon their own experience. This is compounded by the fact that tourists are increasingly attracted to unique and special places which are vulnerable to visitation and their authenticity and integrity is placed at risk. As a result of these issues, and the growing awareness of climate change, tourists are expressing concern about their own actions of, say, flying long-haul, and are prepared to pay more for the experience, whether it be through increased charges, taxes or carbon offsetting. Here, British Airways' 'One Destination' responsible air travel programme recognises that tourists need to be 'confident that together we are acting responsibly to take care of the world we live in' (http://responsibleflying.ba.com/). The issue here is one of visitor education and awareness to ensure that decisions are taken on a reasoned basis. Of course, codes of conduct for visitors and guidelines for ethical behaviour play an important role here (see, for example, the World Wild Life Fund codes of conduct for the Mediterranean and also for Arctic tourists – www.wwf.org; and guidelines for tourists to Africa at www.roveafrica.net, or the Middle East at www.kasbahdutoubkal.com). Another initiative is 'clean up tourism', based on the notion of 'enhancive sustainability' where the aim is to leave the destination in a better state than when the tourist arrived (see, for example, initiatives for the Nile and Botswana).

Implementation of Sustainability

The concept of sustainable tourism is intuitively appealing but one that is more difficult to implement in practice. In part this is because tourism is part of complex social and environmental systems. This means that any initiatives to implement sustainable tourism development have to recognise that tourism is just one part of these complex systems and so has to 'adapt' as such. The earlier approaches to address sustainable tourism through a 'tourism-centric' approach were not successful because they failed to address this issue and saw tourism as separate. One feature of the implementation of sustainability in the tourism sector has been the degree of voluntary and industry led initiatives. Here, the Tour Operators Initiative (TOI) is an excellent example of a sector of the industry getting together 'committed to operating and marketing tourism in a sustainable manner,' with a particular focus on the supply chain (www.toinitiative.org). (We provide a detailed case study of the TOI in Chapter 9.) Other examples include the concept of certification which acts to quality-assure a tourism businesses. These certification schemes audit the environmental performance of tourism organisations; assess product quality; and assess corporate social responsibility initiatives. Examples include Green Globe (www.greenglobe.com), Ecotel for accommodation operators, Caribsave (http://caribsave.org), the UNEP Green passport (www.unep.fr/greenpassport/), the Rainforest Alliance (www.rainforest-alliance.org) and Australia's Eco Certification programme (www.ecotourism.org.au/). In part, these initiatives were started to avoid strong government involvement and regulation in tourism and to some extent they have succeeded. They have also shown that a strong business case can be made for sustainability. Table 6.4 lists the main instruments that can be used to implement

Table 6.4 Instruments of tourism sustainability

Type of Instrument	Examples
Command and control	Legislation regulation and licensing Land use planning and development control
Voluntary instruments	Certification schemes and self-declarations
Private sector	Guidelines and codes of conduct Reporting and auditing Certification and ecolabels Awards Private sector policies and associations
Economic instruments	Taxes and charges – particularly through the 'polluter pays' principle Financial agreements and incentives
Supporting instruments	Infrastructure provision and management Capacity building Marketing and information services
Measurement and monitoring instruments	Indicators Benchmarking Carrying capacity

Source: UNWTO, 2005

Table 6.5 Stakeholder mapping for sustainability

Sector	Stakeholders
Public	Local authorities and officials National, regional and local agencies and officials Management agencies for cultural and natural heritage
Private sector companies – here the issues are not simply profit but also public image and corporate social responsibility and their impact upon the environment	Intermediaries Accommodation, food and beverage Transportation Producers and suppliers Trade organisation and chambers of trade
NGOs	Environmental and conservation groups Community development groups
Communities, who are concerned to protect their quality of life	Local environmental and conservation groups Property owners Consumer associations
Tourists are seeking quality experiences, but also safe environments and reassurance about destination stewardship	Tourists Tourism pressure groups

Source: UNWTO, 2005

the sustainable development of tourism. Here, there are two general principles that have to be adhered to in the implementation of sustainable tourism:

1. recognise that it is the local, or destination, level where initiatives will be the most effective; and

2. initiatives will only be effective if all destination stakeholders are involved. Table 6.5 maps the stakeholders involved in many destinations.

The Role of Government in Implementing Sustainable Tourism

Traditionally, government has taken a leading role in implementing sustainable tourism development, although of course it is the responsibility of all stakeholders to ensure sustainability. The public sector, particularly at the local level, is critical for coordination, regulation and facilitation of sustainable tourism. In tourism, the role of government is important because:

- the sector is fragmented and a coordination role is needed;
- the sector lacks leadership and this is a role that government can play;
- there is often a need for some public funding for sustainability initiatives, for example, in terms of overseeing eco labelling as with the European Commission's eco labelling scheme (www.ecolabel-tourism.eu);
- many vulnerable elements of the destination – coasts, wetlands, small islands or the built heritage are in public ownership (see, for example, the UN's COAST initiative); and
- government has the mandate to regulate, plan and legislate.

Government was slow to act in addressing sustainable development in tourism until the 1992 UN Earth Summit in Rio. A key outcome from Rio was Agenda 21, signed by over 180 governments (www.un.org/esa/sustdev/agenda21.htm). Agenda 21 was a commitment on the part of governments to address the issue of development and the environment across a range of activities. For tourism, an important feature of Agenda 21 is the focus on implementation at the local destination level, through local government, with international coordination of initiatives provided by the Earth Council Alliance (www.earthcouncilalliance.org). Although criticised for potentially curtailing individual choices, the principles of Agenda 21 were re-affirmed at Rio+20. Agenda 21 reflects contemporary thinking on sustainable development in two ways:

1. Whilst tourism is the focus of many Agenda 21 plans in, for example, resorts, small islands and in heritage towns, tourism also forms an integral part of other Agenda 21 initiatives stressing the need for 'whole of destination' management.

2. Projects involve not only government but also NGOs (such as the World Wildlife Fund) and the private sector stressing the need for all stakeholders to be involved.

More recently, the private sector, in the shape of large multinational companies has taken the lead in terms of sustainability. These companies include Accor, Tui, P&O and Whitbread, but we can also identify smaller family-run companies who are leading on sustainable initiatives. Mini Case Study 6.2 focuses on a family-run hotel in the Caribbean that has firmly embedded itself in the local destination.

Mini Case Study 6.2
Jakes Hotel, Jamaica

Introduction

Jakes Hotel in Jamaica is one of the world's leading proponents of sustainability, not simply through recycling and encouraging guests not to use all their towels, but instead is fully involved and immersed in its local community and environment. Set on Treasure Beach, on Jamaica's south coast, the hotel began as a restaurant in 1991 and now comprises a collection of 30 rooms, cottages and villas, each individually designed. Nearby, the hotel offers access to golf, fishing, caves and waterfalls, adventure tours, ecotourism and dolphins. The guests are fully involved in the hotel's sustainability mission with a $1 per night levy and the opportunity to visit the various projects.

A Sustainable Company

As a company, Jakes Hotel has a distinctive view of sustainability. According to the website:

'sustainability is not just about eco-friendly practices, it is as much about cultural preservation and maintaining what is unique about our community . . . we believe sustainability is an interactive system between our community and the environment, where each element is cared for and nurtured, so that we can continue to occupy this special place in the world with only positive impact' (www.jakeshotel.com).

The company aims to be a model for future sustainability initiatives in the Caribbean. The BREDS Treasure Beach Foundation works with the local community supporting education, sports, cultural heritage and emergency healthcare. The Foundation is led by volunteers and has completed community projects, including repairing the roof and building classrooms at local schools and building houses for the disadvantaged.

One of the Foundation's major projects is the development of the BREDS Treasure Beach Sports Park. The principle behind the Park is that sport can bind a community together. The Park was inaugurated in 2010 and when completed it will be a 15-acre park with cricket pavilion, regulation-size soccer pitch, children's playground, and sites for weddings and other functions such as retreats and workshops.

As well as working with the local community the hotel also is concerned for the local environment, funding projects to protect the local vegetation and ecology of Treasure Beach, rounding off a set of sustainable initiatives that embed the hotel within the destination.

DISCUSSION QUESTIONS

1. In class discuss whether there is a danger that the mission of the hotel may deter guests from visiting.

2. Visit the Jakes Hotel website. What is their unique selling proposition (USP) and how strongly does sustainability feature in their USP?

3. Staying on the website, how true is the hotel to sustainability principles in operating the hotel – employing local people, fair trade and local sourcing of food?

Sources:
www.breds.org
www.jakeshotel.com

Contemporary Tools of Sustainable Tourism

Visitor Management and Interpretation

Sustainable tourism demands not only that the visitor receives a satisfying and high-quality experience but also that the destination is sustainable. These twin objectives of sustainable tourism can be achieved if we utilise innovative and effective tools of sustainable tourism. One such approach is the application of visitor management techniques to tourism. Visitor management is a tool of sustainable tourism as it ensures that the increasingly experienced and discerning 'new tourist' does indeed receive a high-quality experience while also sustaining the destination for future generations (Harrison, 1994; UNWTO, 2011).

Visitor management is an approach that was developed in natural areas, particularly national parks and sensitive natural reserves, where there was a need to manage visitation. Here, the real innovation of visitor management approaches is the focus on positive planning and provision rather than negative restrictions and prohibition. In so doing, visitor management provides a true focus on the visitor and recognises that each visitor is different, bringing to a destination or site his or her own prejudices, needs, preferences and ignorances. After all, a group of teenage friends visiting a destination will be seeking very different benefits from, say, a family group.

The objectives of visitor management are therefore transparent and straightforward. On the part of the visitor, it:

- enhances the visit experience;
- increases the chances of repeat visitation;
- encourages higher spending; and
- induces greater sympathy for the cause of, say, wildlife conservation, or historic preservation, at a destination.

At the same time, visitor management provides a flow of benefits to the destination:

- it allows visits to be spread in both space and time;
- it encourages a longer length of stay (or dwell time);

- it reduces the environmental impact of visitation through effective management;
- there is increasing evidence that visitor management, and particularly interpretation techniques, foster a sense of civic pride and sense of ownership amongst the host community; and
- it creates revenue streams that can be used for conservation (The International Union for the Conservation of nature estimates that 80 per cent of national parks are under-funded worldwide – www.iucn.org/). This can be done through a variety of mechanisms:
  - government funding;
  - visitor revenue – entrance fees, parking, special events, donations and visitor payback;
  - business revenue – concession fees – accommodation, equipment rental, food and beverage, retail; and
  - other forms of revenue – licensing images, publications.

To be effective, visitor management should be integrated into the management of every destination but to date it tends to be viewed as an approach that can be added in at the end. In one sense, this recognises the lack of exposure to the technique on behalf of tourism planners and consultants. Visitor management is very much a practitioner-based approach with few manuals of good practice or well-documented case studies of its positive effects. And yet there are a number of leading attraction companies – such as the Disney Corporation – who are very skilled at the art.

Figure 6.4 shows the outline approach that may be adopted for visitor management of a site, destination or region. For a museum, for example, the critical unit will be the rooms housing the displays and the pathways between them. The technique will ensure visitors move freely between each room and get the best out of the experience. However, for a theme park it will be the themed areas and their links that form the unit of analysis; while for a region the approach will be based on sub-areas or resorts.

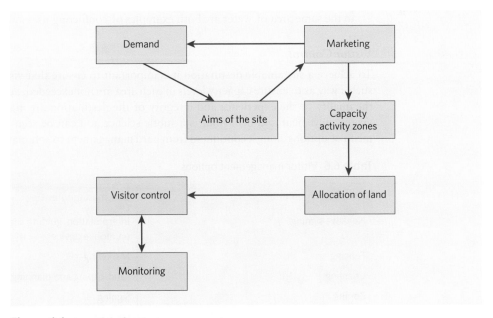

Figure 6.4 A model of visitor management

Approaching Visitor Management

Destination Objectives

Determination of objectives is critical for the sustainable management of any destination. The simple question to be asked is – why do we want to attract visitors to this destination? Of course, the obvious answer may be an economic one of profit or return on investment. Other reasons, however, are also possible including educational reasons (for a wildlife reserve, say) or propaganda (as in show sites in socialist republics). The visitor management process demands that the destination is very clear on these objectives since they drive the whole management process.

Destination Demand and Marketing

A second key variable is demand – the profile and numbers of visitors attracted to the destination. It is important that marketing communicates clearly the objectives to ensure that appropriate types of visitor are attracted. The most common management problems occur when the wrong type of visitor is attracted to a destination. If these problems do arise, then it is the role of marketing constantly to adjust the visitor profile to the objectives of the destination. This can be done in subtle ways such as through the choice of merchandising in the shops, the type and price of food and beverage in the cafés, or communication strategies adopted in the marketing campaign and social media.

Capacity and Activity Zones

At this stage of the visitor management process, decisions are taken as to the intensity of visitation at each part of the destination, and also the type of activity to be scheduled there. For green-field sites the planner has a relatively free hand, but for sites such as museums or historic houses then it is probable that the use of rooms and displays will be fixed. Nonetheless there are two important principles involved at this stage:

1. **Determination of capacity.** Here, planners have to determine the volume of visitors that can be sustained in each part of the site. The key question is then: do you manage a site for its peak capacity, or a percentage of that capacity?

2. **Avoidance of conflicting uses in the same area.** For example, the use of motorised vehicles or trail bikes where children are likely to congregate, or allowing motorboats and bathing in the same area of water are both examples of conflicting uses and should be avoided.

Visitor Control

To achieve a sustainable destination it is important to ensure that visitors are managed in such a way as to ensure capacity levels in each area are not exceeded, and therefore that both the quality of the experience and integrity of the destination are maintained. Influencing visitor movement and behaviour is a subtle science and can be seen as a selection from a menu of options along a continuum from hard management to soft management (Table 6.6):

Table 6.6 Visitor management options

Hard management	Soft management
Negative signing	Interpretation, guiding and use of information on mobile devices
Fencing	Marketing
Charging	Landscaping and planning
Zoning	Signing
Security measures	Location of facilities

- Hard visitor management can be problematic as neither destination manager nor visitor is satisfied as both recognise the severity of the measures adopted. There are occasions, however, where hard management is inevitable. Guarding valuable sites, or where there is potential danger to visitors, are cases in point.

- Soft management on the other hand, is perhaps the most effective form of visitor management. The visitor is influenced without knowing it and the manager is effective because the destination is running smoothly. There are many well-known examples of soft management. In theme parks where one area is over capacity and another is under capacity, managers assemble a cast of their characters playing in a band and walk them through the busy area. Visitors all follow and are led into the under-used area – perfect and unobtrusive visitor control. At sites where there are 'pinch points' (areas where too many visitors congregate in small areas preventing an even flow around the site) it is common to provide a taped commentary of the object or display in question. Once the tape loop is complete and begins again, visitors naturally move on to the next display. Interpretation and information are increasingly favoured approaches. Here, the destination is displayed to the visitor using a variety of techniques such as guiding, trails, apps on mobile devices and signboards.

Monitoring

There is no point in developing sophisticated visitor management approaches without a means of monitoring their success. There are a variety of options here:

- a formal questionnaire with the visitor to elicit their level of enjoyment;
- the more cost-effective approach of debriefing of destination staff on a regular basis to check all is well; or
- many of the larger theme parks have constant monitoring through devices including electronic eyes and turnstiles.

There is much to be said for the technique of visitor management as a contemporary tool of sustainable tourism to deliver many of the benefits sought by both visitor and destination alike. It neatly ties together the nature of the destination, elements of the new demand and approaches to both planning and marketing at the destination level.

However, the approach could be seen as controversial and does raise a number of important questions:

- Are we becoming too scientific and organised in our development of tourist destinations and thereby losing some of the magic?
- Are techniques such as interpretation taking away the spontaneity and moment of discovery if everything is labelled and sanitised?
- Are we simply becoming too slick in the marketing and management of destinations?
- Are some places just too 'busy' with information, signboards and hi-tech interpretive equipment?
- Who decides on the information to be given or displayed to the visitor and is this 'gatekeeper' role one that we can safely entrust to planners and interpreters, or should the local community be more involved?

Sustainable Tourism Indicators

A vital, but previously neglected, issue in terms of sustainable tourism is that of measurement and the development of indicators of sustainability. Clearly, to manage for sustainable tourism we have to be able to measure and monitor the degree of sustainability at the destination, in the enterprises and by the tourists themselves. Delivery of accurate information

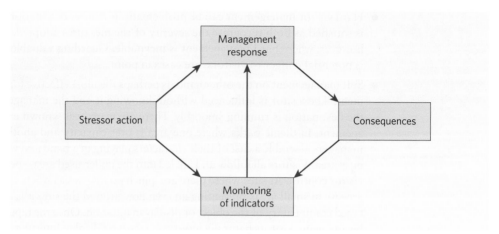

Figure 6.5 The role of indicators in monitoring sustainability
Source: Miller and Twining-Ward, 2005

for decision makers is therefore critical and the UNWTO is developing an international network of sustainable tourism observatories' to gather and report sustainability data. Indicators are the key building blocks and tools for developing sustainable tourism. Quite simply, by developing credible indicators of sustainability and monitoring them on a regular basis, destinations receive early warning of potential problems and can take remedial action (Figure 6.5). The UNWTO (2006) defines sustainability indicators as:

> **'Information sets which are formally selected for a regular use to measure changes in key assets and issues of tourism destinations and sites' (p. 5).**

Indicators can be used to measure:

- changes in tourism at the destination itself;
- changes in the external environment which impact upon the destination; and
- impacts caused by tourism at the destination.

To be effective, indicators must be readily accessible and relatively straightforward to measure; they must be relevant and responsive to changes in the tourism system and they must be credible. Table 6.7 provides a list of commonly used indicators. Here there a number of issues to be considered. Firstly, how the indicators are selected to be representative of destination sustainability – and this is not straightforward. Increasingly indicators are chosen with the agreement of the host community at the destination and rather than treating indicators as simple thresholds to trigger action, decisions are taken as to an 'acceptable

Table 6.7 Types of sustainability indicators

Type of measurement	Indicator
Quantitative	Data – number of tourists, bed nights, carbon emissions Ratios – ratio of tourists to residents Percentages – occupancy levels, trained staff, change in tourist numbers
Qualitative	Category indices – level of protection Normative indicators – existence of recycling plan, yes or no Nominal indicators – ecolabelling, certification Opinion-based indicators – level of satisfaction of tourists, residents' tolerance of tourists

Source: UNWTO, 2004

range' for each indicator and only when measurements fall outside that range is action needed. Secondly, it is important to consider how these indicators will be utilised by managers. Often a traffic light system is used: green – everything is running well; amber – the indicator is showing that intervention may be needed; and red – the indicator shows that remedial action is needed to bring the destination back on track. This 'early warning' system is effective as it allows managers to intervene before the problem has become too severe. This approach demands stability and consistency in measurement and that the results are clearly communicated to managers on a regular basis. One of the first approaches to achieve this was the TOMM planning approach for Kangaroo Island in South Australia. Here a major research exercise identified the key indicators, the community was consulted as to the levels of 'acceptable change' that they would tolerate in terms of tourism, and the indicators monitored on a regular basis and communicated to the community and managers (www.tomm.info/).

It is possible to use existing data as indicators and so reduce the cost of collecting data, but many destinations have now embarked on comprehensive research exercises for indicators (www.sectur.gob.mx). Indicators can also be envisaged at different levels and therefore will nest. For example, national levels of indicators will detect broad levels of change in, say, tourism employment; at the regional level finer grained indicators can be used for reliable planning whilst, at the local level, specific indicators can be tailored for destinations, sites, or companies.

Good tourism sustainability indicators will:

- facilitate better decision-making;
- involve the host community;
- identify emerging issues at the destination;
- identify tourism impacts;
- facilitate performance measurement of plans or strategies by providing KPIs and clarity;
- reduce the risk of poor decisions;
- allow for greater accountability;
- facilitate constant monitoring; and
- provide a catalyst for future action.

Of course, there are some problems associated with the development of indicators of sustainability. These include: lack of consistency in measurement between different destinations and poor coordination across different agencies; the fact that there may be gaps in the indicators and key elements of sustainability are missed; many destinations do not have the qualified staff – or the budget – to monitor indicators; and, finally, indicators are often not collected nor communicated to encourage effective decision making.

SUMMARY

This chapter has analysed the deceptively simple concept of sustainable tourism. We began the chapter by outlining how the idea of sustainable development has evolved and the various important milestones along the way. We saw that tourism came late to the debate, not really seen as significant until the Rio Earth Summit. The chapter then discussed the various approaches to defining sustainable development and sustainable tourism, concluding that many of the terms are used loosely and that the UNWTO has moved the debate forward with a set of statements and definitions. The tourism community has adopted a range of underpinning principles of sustainability, including the idea of triple bottom line sustainability with equal consideration the environment, the economy and the community. Here, we examined the case of township tourism and questioned whether it is truly sustainable. It has been shown that different types of sustainable tourism approaches can be identified, ranging from the early approach where sustainable tourism was seen as the polar opposite of mass tourism, to the contemporary approach of 'convergence' where all forms of tourism should be sustainable. Hunter's 'classic paper' showed how he contributed to this debate. Finally, the chapter outlined contemporary approaches to implementing sustainability, highlighting the significance of managing visitors and developing a system of indicators to warn against potential problems at the destination. Here two case studies were used as 'stand out' examples in implementation: Jakes Hotel, Jamaica; and Rios Tropicales in Costa Rica.

Discussion Questions

1. Why is sustainable tourism so difficult to define?
2. Table 6.2 provides a range of 'positions that have been taken with regards to sustainable tourism'. Do you agree that the tourism sector has now embraced the idea of the final position of 'convergence'?
3. Table 6.4 outlines the main instruments of sustainable tourism development. Match each one with an example and make a judgement as to which instruments are the most effective.
4. Taking a destination with which you are familiar, map out up to 20 indicators of sustainability that you feel would accurately reflect the character of the destination. How easy would these be to measure?
5. Take a tourist site with which you are familiar – such as a theme park or museum – and revisit it with the eyes of a visitor manager. Make your own evaluation – does the site work in terms of visitor movement and rhythms, is the experience enhanced and did you enjoy it?

Annotated Further Reading

1. Butler, R. (1999) Sustainable tourism – a state of the art review, *Tourism Geographies* **1**(1), 7–25.
    Does exactly what is says, providing an insightful and wide-ranging review.
2. Gössling, S., Hall, C.M. and Scott, D. (2015) *Tourism and Water*, Channel View, Bristol.
    The first comprehensive book on tourism and water.
3. Hall, C.M., Gössling, S. and Scott, D. (2015) *The Routledge Handbook of Tourism and Sustainability*, Routledge, London.
    An all-embracing, one-stop handbook on tourism and sustainability.
4. Krippendorf, J. (1987) *The Holidaymakers: Understanding the Impact of Leisure and Travel*, Oxford, Butterworth Heinemann.
    One of the first books to map out a sustainable tourism agenda.
5. Liburd, J. and Edwards, D. (2010) *Understanding the Sustainable Development of Tourism*, Goodfellow, Oxford.
    Thorough and accessible text.
6. Miller, G. and Twining-Ward, L. (2005) *Monitoring for a Sustainable Tourism Transition: The Challenge of Developing and Using Indicators*, CABI, Wallingford.
    A comprehensive and contemporary approach to sustainable tourism.

7. UNWTO (2004) *Indicators of Sustainable Tourism,* UNWTO, Madrid.
   A state of the art manual on sustainable tourism indicators.

8. UNWTO (2005) *Making Tourism More Sustainable: A Guide for Policy Makers,* UNWTO, Madrid.
   A comprehensive yet practical approach to sustainable tourism.

9. UNWTO (2011) *Communicating Heritage: A Handbook for the Tourism Sector,* UNWTO, Madrid.
   A useful manual of visitor management.

10. Weaver, D. (2014) The sustainable development of tourism: a state of the art perspective, Chapter 42 in Lew, A.L., Hall, C.M. and Williams, A.M. (eds) *The Wiley Blackwell Companion to Tourism,* Wiley, Chichester.
    Excellent review.

References Cited

Buckley, R. (2012) Sustainable tourism: research and reality, *Annals of Tourism Research* **39**(2), 528–546.

Clarke, J. (1997) A framework of approaches to sustainable tourism, *Journal of Sustainable Tourism* **5**(3), 224–233.

Harrison, R. (1994) *A Manual of Heritage Management,* Butterworth-Heinemann, Oxford.

Hunter, C. (1997) Sustainable tourism as an adaptive paradigm, *Annals of Tourism Research* **24**(4), 850–867.

Jafari, J. (1990) Research and scholarship: the basis of tourism education, *Journal of Tourism Studies* **1**(1), 33–41.

Krippendorf, J. (1982) Towards new tourism policies the importance of environmental and sociocultural factors, *Tourism Management,* September, 135–148.

Liburd, J. and Edwards, D. (2010) *Understanding the Sustainable Development of Tourism,* Goodfellow, Oxford.

Miller, G. and Twining-Ward, L. (2005) *Monitoring for a Sustainable Tourism Transition: The Challenge of Developing and Using Indicators,* CABI, Wallingford.

Muller, H. (1994) The thorny path to sustainable tourism development, *Journal of Sustainable Tourism* **2**(2), 131–136.

Saarinen J (2006) Traditions of sustainability in tourism studies, *Annals of Tourism Research* **33**(4), 1121–1140.

Saarinen, J., Rogerson, C.M., Manwa, H. (2012) *Tourism and the Millennium Development Goals Tourism, Local Communities and Development,* Routledge, London.

UNWTO (2004) *Indicators of Sustainable Tourism,* UNWTO, Madrid.

UNWTO (2005) *Making Tourism More Sustainable: A Guide for Policy Makers,* UNWTO, Madrid.

UNWTO (2010) *Joining Forces: Collaboration Processes for Sustainable and Competitive Tourism,* UNWTO, Madrid.

UNWTO (2011) *Communicating Heritage: A Handbook for the Tourism Sector,* UNWTO, Madrid.

World Commission on Environment and Development (1987) *Our Common Future,* Oxford University Press, Oxford.

Major Case Study 6.1
Rios Tropicales – Sustainable Adventure Tourism

Introduction

Costa Rica is globally significant for biodiversity and eco-tourism; as a result 25 per cent of the land area is protected by a national system of conservation areas. Operating in this environment, the tour operator Rios Tropicales is a beacon of sustainability good practice. Rios Tropicales was founded in 1985 with the abiding mission:

> 'To share the rivers and natural resources of Costa Rica, our culture and conservation values, always committed to professionalism, safety, high quality and extraordinary service' (www.riostropicales.com).

The company delivers their mission through the dedication of its founders to sustainable values and its daily operations and programmes which are run sustainably, conscientiously and for the benefit of its stakeholders – tourists, employees, local communities and the environment, whilst also promoting environmental conservation and stressing education.

Sustainable Tourism Operations

Rios Tropicales is active across the spectrum of sustainability from environmental conservation through education to community support. Their major initiatives are as follows.

Environmental Conservation

- In 1989, the company bought land along the Pacuare River from a local family who had deforested the area to create farmland. Rios Tropicales re-hired the family to plant trees across the land to raise awareness of environmental protection and reforestation.

Education Programmes

- The company founded the Rios Tropicales Foundation in 1994 as a not-for-profit environmental organisation to assist in the preservation, protection and restoration of the rivers, streams and watersheds of Costa Rica. The Foundation provides environmental education programmes in elementary schools in Costa Rica. The philosophy is that:

> 'By educating the children on how and why they should care for their natural resources, Rios is arming a generation of future leaders with knowledge and tools for sustainable business practices that incorporate environmental management' (www.riostropicales.com).

- The company began the Regional River Environmental Education Pilot Project in the Atlantic region of Turrialba and Siquirres, and aims to create environmental awareness in rural school children.

Community Engagement

- The Rios Tropicales Lodge was purchased from a local family and developed as an eco-lodge. The local family members now act as guides and employees in the company and a number of them have been supported through college by the company.

- Rios Tropicales has helped to build two health clinics in remote, rural areas serving over 600 residents.

- The company has always tried to protect wildlife. Through community engagement they have educated local communities on the dangers and long-term damage of illegal hunting and fishing. In the early 1990s, on land purchased by Rios Tropicales, a range of species had been wiped out, but with education of the community these species are now beginning to return.

- In the rural areas where the company operates, local community members have changed their lifestyle as a result of the impact of sustainable tourism, forming cooperatives and participating in organic farming.

Economic Benefits for Local Communities

Rios Tropicales operates in remote rural areas. This has led them to engage and collaborate with local communities as a source of employment, knowledge and expertise. This close working relationship with local communities has resulted in a unique approach to sharing the economic benefits of sustainable tourism.

The company has done this by creating 'ecopreneurs' through facilitating entrepreneurial approaches such as the creation of a Private Label Organic Coffee Market. The company uses 95 per cent local guides who earn higher wages and are exposed to more opportunity and international experience than they otherwise would. Of course, the key here is to maintain the quality of the tourist experience, and so Rios Tropicales has developed a world-class river guide-training programme drawing on international industry standards.

Rios Tropicales has taken its approach to sharing economic benefits a step further by directly facilitating the establishment of complementary 'geo-tourism companies' owned solely by the company's former top guides who have now become 'ecopreneurs'.

The company's guides not only earn a good wage but they also serve as role models for other members of their families and communities, especially young people. In these communities jobs are often limited to subsistence farming and so the company has helped to show that there are other economic opportunities available in eco and adventure tourism.

In the Santa Maria de Dota area Rios Tropicales offers tours which have now evolved into local community projects involving homestays and activities involving local families. As a result, the communities receive regular income from lodging and meals during the tourist season.

DISCUSSION QUESTIONS

1. It is clear that Rios Tropicales has had a significant impact on the lifestyle and economies of local rural communities. Are all these impacts desirable?

2. Visit the company's website and assess the potential environmental impact of their tours. Are you confident that the company's sustainable mission will minimise these impacts?

3. Rios Tropicales is to be applauded for its ecopreneurs initiative. Discuss the advantages and disadvantages of this approach for the future competitiveness of the company – does it create competing businesses for its own products?

Sources:
www.riostropicales.com
www.visitcostarica.com
www.tourism-costarica.com

PART 3
TOURISM SECTOR ESSENTIALS

In this part we consider the tourism sector, made up of both private and the public organisations. In terms of the private sector we consider attractions, hospitality, transportation and intermediaries – tour operators and travel agents. But it is important not to neglect government as they have a major stake in tourism in most destinations, not only in terms of planning and regulation, but also they often own many key attractions such as coastlines, national parks and the built heritage.

Tourism is often described as one of the world's largest industries, with large figures quoted for the value of the tourism industry and the numbers it employs. The tourism sector sprawls across many parts of the economy, and commentators agree that it does not form a coherent industry from an economic point of view. This is because many industries are involved in delivering the tourism product such that tourism is in fact only partially an industry as governments, communities and others are involved in delivering the product.

Together tourism businesses form the contemporary tourism sector, the machinery of tourism production which manipulates and permits the tourist experience to happen. As we see in the following chapters, in recent years the sector has become global in scale and restructured in response to technology, changing consumer demand, increasing concentration in the industry, and the demands of flexible specialisation which creates integrated networks of supply and destinations. Technology, in particular, has had a major impact upon tourism businesses, particularly intermediaries, whilst the carbon debate and 'wild card' events such as the 2015 Germanwings disaster have impacted upon air transport.

We also show in this part that the tourism industry is highly diverse and fragmented and made up predominantly of small businesses and entrepreneurs. This has implications for the level of management competence in tourism as well as for the ability of the sector to both innovate and invest in new products and ideas.

CHAPTER 7
ATTRACTIONS

Learning Outcomes

This chapter considers visitor attractions as the key element of the destination, motivating the visit and energising the total tourism system. The chapter outlines approaches to defining and classifying attractions before considering how visitor attractions are managed and their future. The chapter is designed to provide you with:

- an awareness of the issues surrounding definitions of attractions;
- an understanding of the various approaches available to classify attractions;
- an appreciation of the economics of attractions;
- an understanding of the key management issues and approaches for attractions; and
- insights into the future of attractions.

Photograph: Olympic stadium, London © Athol Pictures/Alamy Images

Introduction

Visitor attractions are the *raison d'être* for tourism; they generate the visit, give rise to excursion circuits and create an industry of their own. As such they are the main motivator for travel, energising the tourism system and providing tourists with the reason to visit a destination. Indeed, such is the power of attractions that they can transform a destination from the mundane to the spectacular as we have seen with Dubai. Clare Gunn (1972) puts it well, describing attractions as 'lodestones for pleasure'.

It is therefore important from the outset to understand the distinction between attractions, the *motivators* of the visit, and support services, such as accommodation, transport and retail, that *facilitate* the visit. There are, of course, exceptions to this rule in destinations such as Las Vegas where support services such as hospitality are an integral part of the attraction in their large themed casinos. Attractions appeal to different visitor audiences from international and domestic tourists, through to day visitors, local residents and those visiting friends and relatives.

Attractions have a long history, featuring strongly in Grand Tour itineraries, for example. They have developed hand-in-hand with transportation, particularly since the advent of the railway in the mid-nineteenth century and then the boom in tourism demand following the Second World War, when purpose-built attractions were further developed and grew. This long pedigree has left a heritage of custom and practice in managing attractions that has survived from the past and is still in use today.

Defining Visitor Attractions

Definitions of visitor attractions are difficult because the environment within which they operate is so dynamic – a definition today may seem dated in 10 years' time (Leask, 2010). It is nonetheless important to define attractions for statistical measurement purposes and to allow comparison of, say, performance. In part, the lack of an accepted definition is due to the fact that research into attractions and their management is not as developed as in other parts of tourism. This makes the comparison of attraction statistics difficult internationally. Effectively we can think of an attraction as:

Anything that has sufficient appeal to 'attract' a visit.

Defining attractions is made more difficult by the fact that they come in a variety of forms including fixed points such as museums, linear attractions such as heritage railways, or temporary attractions such as events – indeed one of the constant debates is whether events are, in fact, 'attractions'. They can be distinguished from the broader concept of a destination by virtue of their smaller size and the fact that they are based upon a key feature. The link between attractions and the destination is an intimate one, however. Destinations are finding it increasingly difficult to compete in the visitor economy and increasingly use attractions as one means to differentiate their appeal to the market.

Characteristics of Visitor Attractions

We can identify five main characteristics of visitor attractions:

1. **Cultural appraisals.** Attractions are a tourism resource, and this means that what is attractive to one tourist may not be to another. The sector, and indeed the tourist, therefore has to recognise that an attraction is of value before it can become an attraction and draw visits. For example, until the eighteenth century, mountains were viewed by most people in the West as places to be feared, rather than as scenic attractions. Similarly, until sunbathing became fashionable in the 1920s, the combination of sun, sand and sea was not seen as a valuable attraction, and we are now beginning to see people's perceptions of the beach holiday change again due to fears of skin cancer. In other words, the core product of the attraction has to be seen to have a utility for the tourist and so be worth the visit. An interesting example here is the concept of 'dark tourism' where sites such as battlefields or concentration camps become attractions, but only after an acceptable interval of time has passed. Attractions are therefore inherently dynamic and can pass into and out of favour. New technologies also allow attractions to come to life – wet suits, for example, have lengthened the surfing season at many coastal destinations.

2. **Multiple use.** Many visitor attractions are not used exclusively by tourists. Apart from resort areas or theme parks where tourism is the dominant use, natural and built heritage attractions are shared with other uses such as, say, agriculture, forestry, religion or residents using local services. In national parks, for example, tourism is a significant use but rarely the dominant one, and this can lead to conflict with tourism, as a latecomer, being 'fitted in' with other users. This is known as *multiple use*, and needs skilful management and coordination of users to be successful. The same is true of events such as the Australian Formula One Grand Prix, for example, which is held in a public park.

3. **Perishability.** Visitor attractions are perishable in two senses. Firstly, they can suffer from intensive use, with daily and seasonal peaking and the consequent pressure upon the attraction. This means that they need effective visitor management. Secondly, in common with many service industries, attractions are also perishable in another sense.

Visitor days or ride seats in theme parks are impossible to stock and have to be consumed when and where they exist. This has led to the development of techniques such as differential pricing and timed tickets to maximise the use of the attraction. It has also led some attractions such as museums and zoos to allow visitors to visit at night to maximise the available time for income generation (see, for example, the sleepovers now allowed at Sydney's Taronga Zoo – http://taronga.org.au).

4. **Economic significance.** Visitor attractions, including events, play an important part in the visitor economy of a destination, generating income, jobs and competitiveness for the destination. Although they motivate the visit, attractions themselves do not receive the majority of tourists' expenditure, which tends to be upon accommodation and transportation. However, attractions and events often form the centrepiece of regional development and civic regeneration schemes, providing an anchor for both tourism and residents' visits.

5. **Ownership.** Perhaps surprisingly, the attractions' sector is not dominated by large corporations such as Disney, although they do dominate in terms of good practice. Instead, the operation and ownership of attractions is fragmented across a variety of organisations including the private sector, the public sector and voluntary organisations such as charities. Indeed, one of the reasons why attractions have been a late entry into serious academic research is due to the fact that the sector is dominated by small attractions, often with limited resources and development potential. Charities include the National Trust in the UK (www.nationaltrust.org.uk) who operate a large number of properties or the National Trust for Historic Preservation in the USA (www.preservationnation.org/). The public sector is heavily involved in owning attractions because it is the guardian of the historic, cultural and natural heritage in many countries. However, in some parts of the world other agencies have had to step in as shown in the following case study on Cambodia.

Mini Case Study 7.1
Heritage Watch, Cambodia

Introduction

Cambodia and other countries of South East Asia are rich in heritage attractions. Indeed, these attractions are vital to allow South East Asian countries to differentiate themselves from other destinations based upon more ubiquitous resort tourism. Cambodia, for example, has become known worldwide for the temples at Angkor Wat. However, these very attractions have become increasingly vulnerable to theft, damage, looting and degradation from other developments. Indeed, tourism in countries such as Cambodia, Laos and Vietnam operates against a background of corruption and poverty. The temptation to exploit the rich heritage is therefore strong and many crimes, such as looting, are driven by poverty. The trade in antiquities is flourishing in South East Asia, a trade that involves theft of artefacts and sculptures and degrades not just the tourist attractions of the country, but also their historical record. This is particularly the case in poorer parts of the world where resources to research the historic record are not available. The Heritage Watch organisation in Cambodia has led the way in protecting the country's heritage attractions using a variety of approaches.

Heritage Watch

Heritage Watch was created in 2003 to combat a sharp rise in the destruction of heritage attractions and looting. It is a non-profit organisation 'dedicated to protecting Cambodia's cultural heritage' with a mission of 'Preserving the past, enriching the future'. The main goals of the organisation are to 'prevent the looting and illicit trade of antiquities in

→

Cambodia while promoting tourism and economic development that is responsible, sustainable and heritage friendly'. Heritage Watch utilises the power of tourism stakeholders to get its message across to tourists, the industry, schools, universities and the Cambodian population.

Heritage Watch has a major campaign which includes training for heritage site security guards, a confidential telephone hotline where people can safely report suspected looting and corruption, education for the tourism sector about ancient and modern Cambodia and its customs, and the urgent need to protect Cambodia's cultural heritage. Travellers learn about responsible tourism practices, unique places to visit in Cambodia, and how to support 'heritage friendly' businesses.

To quote the website, the mandate of Heritage Watch is to:

- Study threats to cultural heritage, including the illicit trade in antiquities, the looting of archaeological sites and loss of historic architecture.
- Educate the public on the importance of heritage resources.
- Increase access to, and awareness of, national and international law affecting cultural property and work with the authorities to implement, enforce and improve the law.
- Promote responsible tourism that furthers cultural and economic development and encourage the tourism industry to support the arts, culture, heritage and development.
- Foster communication between relevant governmental and intergovernmental agencies, non-governmental organisations (NGOs), academic institutions and individuals.

Heritage Watch has launched a number of initiatives to address the problem of the destruction of Cambodia's heritage attractions:

1. Reducing *demand* for antiquities through 'heritage friendly tourism' (HFT):
   - airport kiosks displaying looted items.
   - monitoring and documenting the antiquities trade with a database and understanding the complex international laws by establishing the 'database of historic and archaeological regulations for the management of antiquities' (DHARMA legal database).
   - encourage private sector philanthropy;
   - market alternative routes and destinations;
   - education and awareness campaigns for responsible tourism and the heritage.
2. Reducing the supply of antiquities through:
   - village workshops to raise awareness of the problem;
   - NGO workshops;
   - public service announcements;
   - sustainable development and heritage preservation campaigns;
   - protection of historic architecture including colonial buildings;
   - rescue excavations;
   - community stewardship programmes – for example, the Banteay Chhmar temples project;
   - involving children and schools – for example, 'heritage for kids' is a project aimed at Cambodia's children.

DISCUSSION QUESTIONS

1. Draft a marketing campaign targeted at tour operators to persuade them to support Heritage Watch and especially HFT.
2. Research tourism in Cambodia. How important is the country's heritage as an attraction compared to, say, natural attractions?
3. In class, debate whether the root cause of the problems faced by heritage attractions in South East Asia stems from poverty.

Sources:
www.heritagewatchinternational.org
www.savingantiquities.org
www.sustainablepreservation.org
www.Tourismfortomorrow.com/Case_Studies/

Classifying Visitor Attractions

There are many approaches to classifying visitor attractions, some obvious, others simplistic and some that offer real insights into the core of the attraction and its management. Leask (2008) has neatly encapsulated the many approaches into one diagram (Figure 7.1).

One of the oldest and most useful approaches is by Clawson (Clawson and Knetsch, 1966). It was designed for the broader categories of recreational resources, but it works well for attractions and provides insights into their management and operation. Clawson views attractions as forming a continuum from intensive theme park development at one extreme to wilderness attractions at the other. His scheme therefore incorporates the core of the attraction itself, the marketplace and management issues. Clawson's three basic categories are:

1. **User-oriented attractions** of highly intensive development close to population centres. This would include theme parks, zoos, museums and many events. In other words, attractions designed specifically with a particular market in mind and located strategically to attract that market. Here, management issues relate to managing large numbers of visitors.

2. **Resource-based attractions** where the core product determines the market but the location is determined by the product itself – examples here would include significant natural attractions such as the Grand Canyon or cultural icon attractions such as the Taj Mahal. Here, management issues are more concerned with managing visitation and protecting the attraction from damage.

3. **An intermediate category,** where access is the determining factor and the market is more regional or local. Examples would include local arts festivals or regional forest parks.

In Table 7.1 we relate a selection of recreation activities to Clawson's classification.

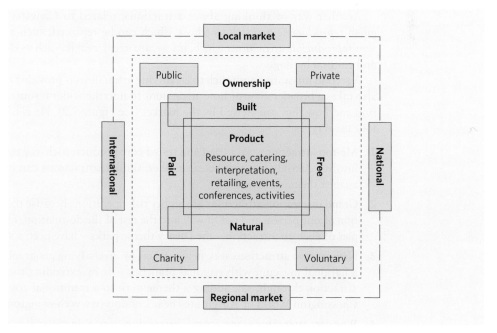

Figure 7.1 Classification of visitor attractions
Source: Leask, 2008

Table 7.1 A classification of recreational resources

Use-orientated	Intermediate	Resource-based
Based on resource close to the user. Often artificial developments (city parks, stadiums, etc.). Highly intensive developments. Activities often highly seasonal, closing in off-peak	Best resources available within accessible distance to users. Access very important. Natural resources more significant than user-orientated facilities, but these experience a high degree of visitor pressure	Outstanding resources. Based on their location, not that of the market. Primary focus is resource quality. Often distant from user, the resource determines the activity

Reproducible ◄──────────────────────────► Non-reproducible
Activity paramount ◄──────────────────────► Resource paramount
Artificiality ◄──────────────────────────► Naturalness
　　　　　◄──────── Intensity of development ────────►
Proximity ◄──────── Distance from user ────────► Remoteness

Examples of activities:	Examples of activities:	Examples of activities:
Golf Tennis Spectator sports Visits to theme parks, zoos, resorts, etc.	Yachting Windsurfing Boating Camping Hiking Angling Field sports Downhill skiing Snowboarding	Sightseeing Mountain climbing Trekking Safaris Expeditions Surfing Whitewater rafting Canoeing Potholing Scuba diving
Typical resource: Theme park	**Typical resource:** Heathland	**Typical resource:** Unique historical monument National park

Source: Boniface and Cooper, 2009

Another way of thinking about attractions, related to Clawson's ideas, is to distinguish *reproducible* attractions (those which can be replaced, such as theme parks) from *non-reproducible* attractions which, if lost, are irreplaceable, such as elements of the natural and cultural heritage.

A second innovative approach to classifying attractions is provided by Wanhill (2008). He also takes a broader view of how attractions fit into the wider resource base of the destination and how they are viewed by the market (see Figure 7.2). He classifies attractions into four main types:

1. **Me-too attractions** use a tried and tested core product, such as a museum, and therefore involve relatively low risk because other, similar, attractions can be used to benchmark against them.

2. **Grand inspiration attractions** are higher risk operations because they may be the inspiration of one person and not fit well into the rest of the destination. Here, the classic examples of such an attraction – the Disney theme parks – have been a spectacular success.

3. **New version attractions** seek new markets by diversifying geographically – for example, a national museum with regional branches – or by extending the core product of the attraction through, say, adding a theme park to a traditional zoo, as has happened at Chessington World of Adventures near London (www.chessington.com/).

4. **Wonder attractions** are iconic attractions on a large scale, often involving significant public sector support. An example here would be the Sydney Opera House (www.sydneyoperahouse.com).

Market	Image	
	Current	**New**
Current	Q I 'Me too' attraction	Q II 'Grand inspiration' attraction
New	Q III 'New version' attraction	Q IV 'Wonder' attraction

Figure 7.2 The attraction market–imagescape mix
Source: Fyall *et al.*, 2008

Other approaches to classifying attractions include:

- **By the size of the attraction.** Page and Connell (2014) quote analysts who classify attractions by visitor numbers:

  - fewer than 50,000 visitors annually counts as small attraction and would include a local museum;
  - 50,000–300,000 visitors annually, a medium-sized attraction; and
  - 300,000 visitors or more per year, a large attraction, such as The Smithsonian Museum in Washington (www.si.edu/).

- **By the 'pulling power' of the attraction or event (Figure 7.3).** Iconic attractions are few in number but act as a magnet for tourists from all over the world, due to their status as national 'icons'. Second-order attractions might be visited as part of an excursion circuit focusing on one or two major 'sights'. Then there are a host of minor attractions which draw their visitors from within the immediate region.

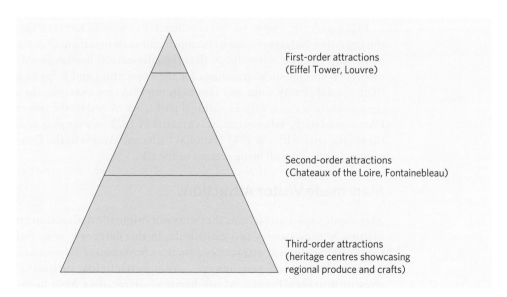

Figure 7.3 A hierarchy of tourist attractions
Source: Boniface and Cooper, 2009

- **By primary attractions**, which generate the visit, and secondary attractions, which enhance the experience but do not necessarily motivate to visit the destination.
- **By the pricing regime of the attraction** – whether it is free or charges an admission fee, or has a combination of the two with free entry but an extra charge for special exhibitions.
- **By ownership of the attraction.**

However, by far the most common approach to classifying visitor attractions is by the nature of their core product. Like Clawson's approach, this too has a long pedigree, dating from the USA's Outdoor Recreation Resources Review Commission in the early 1960s. It has since been adapted by a number of authors including Swarbrooke (2001). The basic approach takes a simple division of natural or man-made attractions:

- cultural or human-made attractions such as theme parks, townscapes, museums, national monuments; and
- natural attractions such as wilderness areas and national parks.

This division is problematic, however, given that all visitor attractions are inherently cultural appraisals. Indeed, a decision to set aside an area as national park is as much of a reflection of culture as it would be to farm the same area of land. The classification also omits attractions such as events. Clearly then, the simple two-fold classification needs to be developed further as follows (Swarbrooke, 2001):

1. natural attractions;
2. man-made visitor attractions;
3. man-made and purpose-built visitor attractions; and
4. event attractions.

Natural Attractions

Natural attractions include rivers, lakes, beaches, caves, scenic features such as the Victoria Falls, flora and fauna, national parks, wilderness areas and forests. These are often, though not exclusively, in public ownership and demand strict management regimes to protect them from tourist use. These attractions would be classified as resource-based attractions by Clawson.

Many such attractions are not commercially viable in terms of the investment costs and the operating budgets needed to establish and maintain them. They are therefore in public ownership because it is unlikely that the commercial market could sustain them. Public ownership secures such attractions for the population and helps to conserve and manage their natural beauty, flora and fauna. In the USA, for example, the vast majority of outdoor recreation areas, such as national parks, are owned by the government. Here, the first US national park, Yellowstone, was created in 1872 (www.nps.gov/yell/), whilst in the UK they came later with the 1945 National Parks and Access to the Countryside Act – indeed national parks are still being created in the UK.

Man-made Visitor Attractions

Man-made visitor attractions that were not originally designed to attract tourists include historic houses, castles and cathedrals. In this category we can place heritage attractions, archaeological attractions, such as Stonehenge (www.english-heritage.org.uk/daysout/properties/stonehenge/), and battlefields including First World War sites in northern France. Many heritage attractions have been built around existing towns, villages or settlements such as Colonial Williamsburg in the USA (www.colonialwilliamsburg.com/), or complexes of buildings in conservation areas and city centres such as the rebuilt old city of Warsaw. In Northern Europe, North America, Australia and New Zealand these heritage attractions are conserved and protected. Elsewhere in the world, however, this is not the case and many are lost to development – Singapore, for example, has lost the majority of its old buildings and in other countries historic buildings and monuments are poorly maintained. Archaeological remains are even more difficult to protect; often they are in the centre of cities and destroyed by developers, or in remoter rural areas. Equally they can be sensitive to the environment, as with the prehistoric caves at Lascaux where an artificial version has now been created to deflect visitation (www.lascaux.culture.fr/). These attractions, and others such as heritage and visitor centres, have been criticised as overly commercialising or even patronising history by turning it into a commodity to be consumed and purchased by the tourist.

We can also place industrial and transport attractions into this category. They are interesting because they exemplify the notion of resources that become attractions by virtue of the market wanting to visit. We can include here wineries, factories and industrial archaeology. The marketing of industrial heritage as an attraction is very powerful and is exemplified by the Blackstone valley in the USA (www.tourblackstone.com), or by Ironbridge Gorge in the UK (www.ironbridge.org.uk/). Some companies have leveraged from the demand to visit by creating a themed attraction alongside the factory, as has happened at Cadbury World in the UK (www.cadburyworld.co.uk/). In terms of transport, heritage railways and tramways create linear attractions, whilst iconic destinations such as the departure and arrival point of immigrants to the USA are popular. Historic ships are also being created as attractions as with the Cunard's Queen Mary moored in Long Beach California. Other attractions in this category include backstage tours, theatre tours, tours of TV and film locations and behind-the-scenes visits to famous sporting venues such as the Melbourne Cricket Ground (www.mcg.org.au).

Man-made and Purpose-built Visitor Attractions

Man-made and purpose-built visitor attractions are created with the purpose of attracting tourists. Here we can include museums, art galleries, exhibition centres, casinos, theme parks, aqua-parks, zoos and aquaria. Zoos, menageries and aquaria have a long history and are now reinventing themselves as foci of conservation to deflect the criticism of cruelty and stress to animals. Artificial environments such as the UK's Eden project in Cornwall (www.edenproject.com/), or indoor rainforests in the USA, such as the Lied Jungle in Nebraska (www.omahazoo.com), and Australia (in the Sydney Aquarium – http:///sydneyaquarium.myfun.com.au/) are now being created alongside existing attractions. Safari Parks are, of course, the staple attraction of southern African countries.

Museums and galleries are now shrugging off their old-fashioned image and developing technologically-driven displays and special exhibitions, again in a bid to reinvent themselves to appeal to new audiences. Many iconic museums such as the Guggenheim in New York (www.guggenheim.org/) and Bilbao, the Smithsonian in Washington and the British Museum in London (www.britishmuseum.org) are significant attractions in their own right.

Other attractions in this category include recreation attractions such swimming pools, golf courses and major shopping venues. Whilst we think of shopping as mainly a support facility, it can be an attraction in its own right as at Subic Bay in the Philippines, a giant duty-free centre on the old US naval base (www.visitsubic.com/). In the future, as large numbers of Asian tourists travel overseas, shopping will become an important part of the experience. Factory outlet shopping centres and large shopping malls such as the West Edmonton Mall in Canada (www.wem.ca) are attractions in their own right. Shopping, too, is a major attraction for cross border tourism and capital city tourism.

Event Attractions

Event attractions have been neglected as a category until recently. We include here the whole range of events from small community festivals to major 'hallmark' events such as pop festivals (as we saw in Mini Case Study 2.2 in Chapter 2). Event attractions differ from other attractions because they occur only periodically and in some cases change venues. Major hallmark events include sporting occasions, notably the Football World Cup, the Commonwealth Games, Formula One Grand Prix and both the Summer and Winter Olympics. Hallmark events present unique opportunities to promote the host country and have a spin-off effect encouraging other attractions nearby. They also require considerable investment in buildings and infrastructure, planning and organisation to safeguard the health, safety and security of visitors and participants as we see below. Cultural event attractions of major international significance would include Rio de Janeiro's Carnival and the Edinburgh Festival.

Of course, whilst it is useful to classify attractions, we must also recognise that it is often a combination of attractions that motivate a visit – a theme park combined with a casino as in Sun City, South Africa, for example (www.sun-city-south-africa.com/). Excursion itineraries are also important in allowing the visitor to see a number of attractions over a period of a few days – the golden triangle in India is a classic example here with Delhi, Jaipur and the Taj Mahal at Agra all on the circuit. This allows us to begin to think of a destination system of attractions with associated support facilities, signing and transport necessary to sustain tourism at the destination. Some destinations have adopted this system and cluster attractions together for marketing purposes to create critical mass and to attract visitors, including multiple pass tickets. Of course, this can be a problem where one or two attractions dominate and smaller satellite attractions suffer as in the case of Orlando, Florida (www.visitorlando.com). Clustering does assist destinations in fostering a sense of cooperation (see, for example, the case study in Chapter 11 on the Hawke's Bay Wine Country Tourism Association, New Zealand – www.hawkesbaynz.com/). As a result, forward-thinking tourism authorities have created strategies to support both fixed and event attractions in their destination.

Specific Types of Visitor Attraction

Theme Parks

Sometimes known as amusement parks, theme parks have a long history of entertaining visitors, dating back to the sixteenth century with the development of pleasure gardens in Copenhagen, and more recently iconic theme parks such as the UK's Blackpool Pleasure Beach (www.blackpoolpleasurebeach.com/) and New York's Coney Island, site of the first roller coaster, the gravity pleasure switchback in 1884 (www.coneyisland.com/). The industrial revolution saw a demand for amusement parks coincide with the development of engineering technology that enabled the rides to be constructed. The industry came of age in 1955 with the opening of Disneyland in California (http://disneyland.disney.go.com/), followed by other parks in the USA, France, Japan and Hong Kong and the extension of the concept to studios and wildlife conservation. Disney transformed the concept of the amusement park into the theme park by extending the range of activities not only to rides, but also to parades, themed restaurants and accommodation and the sheer professionalism of the corporation. Theme parks are increasingly based upon entertainment and media stars such as Elvis Presley. This is reflected in the contemporary parks of film studios, such as Universal Studios (www.universalorlando.com/), and Disney, which now dominate the industry both in terms of size and expertise. The resulting theme park industry is therefore complex. Holloway and Taylor (2006) classify theme parks into three types:

1. local parks focused on the day trip market such as Adventure Wonderland in Dorset, UK;
2. flagship attractions such as the Tivoli Gardens (www.tivoli.dk/composite-7438.htm); and
3. iconic parks which attract a worldwide market such as the Disney parks.

As the industry has grown, it has created a range of industry associations to support it. These include:

- the Association of Leading Visitor Attractions (ALVA) in the UK (www.alva.org.uk/);
- the International Association of Amusement Parks and Attractions (IAAPA), a global trade association (www.iaapa.org/); and
- the Themed Entertainment Association (TEA) in the USA (www.themeit.com).

Theme parks are classic 'user-oriented' attractions in Clawson's classification. They tend to locate close to large conurbations, as in Japan, or close to large holiday areas such as the parks on Australia's Gold Coast, or the US parks in Florida and California. Most, though not all, theme parks have a family market, appealing to children. They tend to be designed to a particular formula which includes the pay one price (POP) concept, meaning that the admission price pays for all the rides and activities. They also tend to be designed around a series of themed 'zones' or 'lands' often with a main thoroughfare, or 'main street' linking the zones with a spine of restaurants and other facilities. In recent years, hybrids of the parks have developed with water parks, safari lands, shopping and accommodation all on the site.

Theme parks are also characterised by their sophisticated marketing and use of technology. But, like all attractions, they must constantly reinvent themselves with new and refreshed rides, signature rides unique to a particular park, new products and merchandising – often based upon media celebrities or TV programmes. Here, there is a recognised

Disney theme parks are amongst the best managed in the world.
Source: © Elvele Images Ltd/Alamy Images

life-cycle of visitation with a rise in visits as the attraction becomes known, followed by a fall-off in visits after the first five years as the park reaches market saturation, as without innovation in the product, attractions are not sustainable. The industry also faces threats such as competition from destinations like Las Vegas. In response, the globally significant parks in central Florida now cooperate on marketing and other activities and are using technology to enhance the experience (as we see in Chapter 14).

Globally, the Disney theme parks and studios dominate the industry but, of course, there are other popular theme parks:

- Everland, South Korea – www.everland.com/
- Lotte World, South Korea – www.lotteworld.com/
- Yokohama Hakkeijima Sea Paradis, Japan – www.seaparadise.co.jp/english/
- Parc Asterix, France – www.parcasterix.fr/
- Legoland, Denmark – www.legoland.dk/

The following mini case study outlines the plans for an innovative, technologically-based theme park in southern England – Jurassica.

Mini Case Study 7.2
Jurassica: Bringing the Jurassic to Life

Jurassica is a proposed new attraction in the south of England, due to open in 2021. It is a unique blend of technological and nature-based attraction, using Japanese animatronics to bring back the world of the dinosaurs to a Jurassic shoreline. The concept of Jurassica is to be the 'world's most spectacular prehistoric visitor attraction' (www.jurassica. org). The park will be based in a quarry on the Jurassic coast on the Isle of Purbeck on the World Heritage listed Jurassic Coast. The quarry will be glassed over with steps leading down to a Jurassic shoreline where visitors can see the dinosaurs in their recreated environment.

Jurassica is a contemporary attraction in many ways:

- The concept is based upon state of the art technology using innovative cutting-edge virtual reality to bring the Jurassic world alive.
- Jurassica's architectural aim is to make the project carbon-neutral including a transport plan that minimises the use of cars.
- Jurassica will both entertain and yet be a serious museum showing the modern research and preparation techniques of palaeontology.
- Jurassica's mission is education for the public through the establishment of an educational and scientific resource of global significance.
- Its differentiating feature will be its scientific authenticity.

The Attraction

The total site for the attraction is around 80 acres. Jurassica will be mostly below ground level within Broadcroft Quarry, itself a site of significant industrial heritage. Jurassica will 'recreate a subterranean geological spectacle using cutting-edge visual technology and scientific expertise, all housed in a world-class architectural space' (www.jurassica.org). This will be 'Jurassic Cove', the largest immersive prehistoric exhibit in the world. The cove will be set under a translucent roof and filled with natural light, visitors will walk along 'a seashore littered with shells – not of today's limpets and cockles, but of ammonites and the large Jurassic oysters that lived in the tropical seas, lagoons and beaches . . . complete with pterosaurs perching on the rock ledges' (www.jurassica.org).

Other features include:

- galleries of fossil collections;
- an aquarium with animatronic Jurassic marine reptiles;
- a large restaurant and café;
- an education area; and
- temporary exhibitions.

Local Impact

Jurassica will be an international attraction that will complement other regional and local attractions and destinations. The project will involve locals in training, volunteering, work placements and jobs at all levels. It will also foster pride in the Jurassic heritage of the coastal and inland communities as well as boosting the local economy through local procurement plans and the attraction of tourists to the region.

DISCUSSION QUESTIONS

1. Draw up a promotional plan for Jurassica with a clear vision of target markets.

2. Jurassica is dependent upon technology to bring the Jurassic world to life. Is there a tension here between the entertainment and educational aims of the project?

3. Research the local economy of Dorset and the Isle of Purbeck in particular – how will an attention on this scale be of benefit locally?

Sources:
www.jurassica.org/
http://jurassiccoast.org/

Festivals and Event Attractions

Festival and events are attractions that are time constrained. They are rarely permanent, although they can reoccur on a regular basis on the same site. They are not only used to attract visitors to a destination, but can also be used to extend the season (as with Blackpool's illuminations) and to target particular market segments. Event attractions have become increasingly important to building destination success (as we saw in Mini Case Study 2.2 in Chapter 2).

Festivals and events have their roots in medieval travelling fairs, and more recently in the huge mega events created by sports such as the Football World Cup, the Olympics and Formula One Grand Prix, or in hallmark events such as the Calgary Stampede. These events are estimated to generate huge economic benefits for their host destinations, as well as acting to place the destination on the world map (see, for example, Ritchie's classic paper in this chapter). Hallmark events demand huge investment from the host destination (as we saw in Chapter 3), but it is not simply the benefits of the event whilst it is being held that is important. The 'legacy' effects of hallmark events are, if anything, more important. This is not only in terms of the facilities constructed, but also in terms of the social and environmental benefits. The Olympic Games in both Atlanta and Barcelona generated major urban renewal projects, for example. The London Olympics have regenerated run-down parts of London, created new green spaces, stimulated improved airport gateways and a convention centre in London (UK Government and Mayor of London, 2014). We can also think of events that have occurred in the past, such as the festival of Britain that now has the legacy of South Bank in London. In the classic paper for this chapter, Ritchie outlines a comprehensive approach to assessing the impact of hallmark events.

Classic Paper
Ritchie, J.R.B. (1984) Assessing the impact of hallmark events: conceptual and research issues, *Journal of Travel Research* 23(1), 2–11

This paper is a classic because not only was it written at least 10 years before the realisation of the significance of events for tourism and the consequent boom in event management literature, but also because it displays the author's characteristic insights into how tourism works and his thoroughness in coverage.

The paper begins with a definition and characterisation of hallmark events as:

'Major one-time or recurring events of limited duration, developed primarily to enhance the awareness, appeal and profitability of a tourism destination in the short and/or long term' (p. 2).

Such events are classified as world fairs, unique carnivals and festivals, major sporting events, significant cultural and religious events, historical milestones, classic commercial and agricultural events and major political personage events. To quote Brent Ritchie, 'previous discussions of the impact of hallmark events have tended to be largely one-dimensional . . . a broader analytical framework is both useful and necessary' (p. 4). The paper examines the consequences of these major events, not simply in terms of economic, environmental and socio/cultural, but instead Ritchie takes a broader approach including political, commercial and psychological consequences.

The paper discusses the difficulties associated with measuring each of these consequences of holding a hallmark event. Ritchie rightly views the economic dimension as the most developed in terms of practice and methodology; this is in contrast to the tourism/commercial impacts. Here we would include the impact of sponsorship which boosts the attractiveness of the destination generally and for investment purposes. Of course, these are difficult to measure in the short term and often the benefits are intangible, exemplified by the issue that has arisen in Australia with the debate over the real benefits of the State of Victoria's significant sponsorship of the Melbourne Formula One Grand Prix.

The remainder of the paper is devoted to a consideration of the research and measurement challenges of each of the six consequences of holding a hallmark event.

The paper concludes that the field is young (as indeed it was when this pioneering paper was written) and that it is hoped that the paper will stimulate further work in the field. That has certainly been the case and Brent Ritchie's paper set the research agenda for event management over the ensuing decades, hence it is a truly 'classic' paper.

Of course, not all events are on the scale of hallmark events, and worldwide there are many local-scale arts festivals, music events and sporting activities. Many smaller events in the past were targeted at local residents, but the popularity of events now means that many small festivals attract visitors from outside the area.

For the large events, government are often a major sponsor, but festivals and events also need to attract other sponsors. They are often run by volunteers, particularly community and charity-run events, with a small professional team of managers. Page and Connell (2009) distinguish between event tourism as a strategic approach to utilising events in destination management, where many destinations now have their own event strategy, and event management as the approach to designing, producing and managing events (Getz, 2012). Event management is now a popular degree programme and is leading to the professionalism of events and festivals, although many of the jobs available are simply relabelled – for example, 'hotel function managers' are now 'hotel events managers'. The events industry also has its own professional organisation – the International Festivals and Events association (IFEA – www.ifeaeurope.com/).

Iconic Attractions

As we have already seen, some attractions have come to be widely regarded as icons by virtue of the large numbers of people who visit them. As a result they are closely associated with the destination's image – think of the Eiffel Tower and Paris, for example, or Table

Mountain and Cape Town. For a destination to be competitive it is important to have an iconic focal point. These icons were often not designed with tourism in mind, however; indeed it is difficult to create such icons deliberately.

UNESCO has designated many such iconic attractions as world heritage sites on its World Heritage List (http://whc.unesco.org/en/list). The list includes 1007 properties which are part of the global cultural and natural heritage, considered by the World Heritage Committee as having outstanding universal value. The list includes:

- 779 cultural sites;
- 197 natural sites; and
- 31 sites which are 'mixed' – both natural and cultural.

However, the committee also lists 46 World Heritage Sites that are in danger.

Managing Visitor Attractions

The majority of visitor attractions operate as businesses and have a set of key performance indicators (KPIs) associated with them against which their management is measured. These KPIs include visitor numbers, visitor revenue and both gross and net profit. However, by far the most important KPI is visitor numbers. Visitor numbers drive the overall performance of the attraction and the rest of the attraction's business – catering, retail and special events. Visitor numbers can be formally recorded by ticket sales, through questionnaire surveys, automatic counters or observers. Surveys at attractions are common to determine not only numbers of visitors, but also their demographic and visit profile, their spending and their likes and dislikes. Figure 7.4 summarises the key factors involved in managing effective visitor attractions.

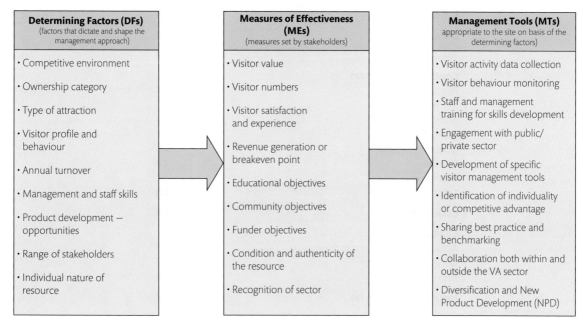

Determining Factors (DFs) (factors that dictate and shape the management approach)	Measures of Effectiveness (MEs) (measures set by stakeholders)	Management Tools (MTs) appropriate to the site on basis of the determining factors
• Competitive environment • Ownership category • Type of attraction • Visitor profile and behaviour • Annual turnover • Management and staff skills • Product development – opportunities • Range of stakeholders • Individual nature of resource	• Visitor value • Visitor numbers • Visitor satisfaction and experience • Revenue generation or breakeven point • Educational objectives • Community objectives • Funder objectives • Condition and authenticity of the resource • Recognition of sector	• Visitor activity data collection • Visitor behaviour monitoring • Staff and management training for skills development • Engagement with public/ private sector • Development of specific visitor management tools • Identification of individuality or competitive advantage • Sharing best practice and benchmarking • Collaboration both within and outside the VA sector • Diversification and New Product Development (NPD)

Figure 7.4 Key factors for effective attraction management
Source: Leask, 2010

Economics of Visitor Attractions

The economics of managing attractions are ably described by Wanhill (in Fyall *et al.*, 2008). Most attractions are characterised by a very high ratio of fixed to variable costs, simply by virtue of the considerable capital investment needed to establish an attraction. This means that attractions tend to require a relatively high number of visitors to generate revenue before they can break even and begin to make a profit. Of course, this means that the marketing of the attraction (often approaching 10 per cent of costs) and its location close to large population catchment areas is even more important.

Attractions therefore have to diversify and secure a range of income streams, from tickets, merchandise, catering, event functions to car parks if they are to be successful, There are a number of ways to achieve this including diversifying into educational or corporate markets, persuading visitors to stay longer (dwell time), and so spend more, or seek commercial sponsorship. Table 7.2 demonstrates the breakdown of costs and revenue for a 1.5 million visitor theme park. The table shows that with discounts it is usual to achieve 70–80 per cent of ticket price. Aside from investment, the highest costs are mainly for seasonal and salaried labour.

Table 7.2 Income breakdown for a 1.5 million visitor theme park

Item	Revenue percentages
Revenue	
Admissions (a)	55.6
Catering	22.2
Merchandising	16.7
Miscellaneous (b)	5.6
Total	**100.0**
Cost of sales	
Catering	8.9
Merchandise	8.3
Total	**17.2**
Gross profit	**82.8**
Other income (c)	**9.0**
Total income	**91.8**
Controllable expenses	
Payroll	32.4
Marketing	10.2
Administration	4.3
Maintenance	3.1
Operating supplies	2.5
Utilities	4.3
Insurance	3.1
Total	**60.0**
Cash flow	**34.9**
Capital expenses	
Attraction replacement and renewals	14.7
Occupation costs (d)	5.7
Total	**20.5**
Net income before tax	**11.3**

(a) Adult admission is $US45 giving an average discount (after sales tax) of 30.2%
(b) Includes rentals, arcades and vending machines
(c) Sponsorship, corporate hospitality and rental of facilities
(d) Rental provision for site and premises.

Source: Fyall *et al.*, 2008

In terms of revenue, the type of pricing policy adopted by the attraction is critical. Simply to receive the cost of the initial fixed investment in an attraction means that the price of entry has to be set well above the operational cost of supplying the facilities and labour for each visit. So critical is this decision that attractions are now adopting a yield management approach to ticketing where they achieve the best price possible for a ticket for each day and each time of day. Strategies include 'pay one price' for admission, which is good for families, can be used in marketing and is cost efficient for the attraction.

There is, of course, a fierce debate about whether the public sector should charge admission to, say, museums or galleries. It could be argued that local people have already subsidised the museum through their taxes, but of course this does not apply to tourists. As a result, some countries, such as Finland, have a differential charging policy.

Management Approach

Attractions management is focused on *positive* planning and provision rather than *negative* restrictions and prohibition. Attraction management is also very much a practitioner-based approach with few manuals of good practice or well-documented case studies. Yet, as we have already noted, there are a number of leading attractions companies – such as the Walt Disney Corporation – who are very skilled at the art.

The visitor management approach (which we introduced in Chapter 6, see Figure 6.4) is commonly used at attractions, and we can identify the following elements relating to attractions:

- **Management objectives.** Determination of management objectives is critical for the successful management of any attraction at the outset as they will determine the overall management strategy. Here, some attractions struggle to determine their true objectives – think of St Paul's Cathedral in London, for example, which is an iconic tourist attraction, but also a place of worship. For some attractions the answer is easy – an economic objective or one of profit or return on investment. Other objectives, however, are also possible. These include educational reasons (for a wildlife reserve, say) or propaganda (as in show sites in socialist republics). The management process demands that we have to be very clear on these objectives since they drive the whole process.

- **Demand.** A second key variable is demand – the profile and numbers of visitors attracted to the attraction. It is important that marketing communicates clearly the objectives of the attraction to ensure that appropriate types of visitor are attracted. The most common management problems occur when the wrong type of visitor is attracted. If these problems do arise, then it is the role of marketing to constantly adjust the visitor profile to the management objectives. A key consideration here is the determination of approaches for resource-based and user-based attractions.

- **Capacity.** At this stage of the visitor management process, decisions are taken as to the intensity of visitation at each part of the site, and also the type of activity to be scheduled there. For green field sites the planner has a relatively free hand, but for sites such as museums or historic houses than it is probable that the use of rooms and displays will be fixed. Here attraction managers have to determine the volume of visitors that can be sustained in each part of the site. This is done using the concepts of:

    - **annual physical capacity** (APC) which is the number of users that can be sustained in one year; and

    - **sustained physical capacity** (SPC) which is the maximum number of visitors that can be accommodated at any one point in time without deterioration in the condition of the site.

The calculation is then:

APC = SPC × number of periods open

This is a useful approach as it allows planners to build-in seasonality effects. Wanhill (2008), for example, suggests that industry norms for theme parks mean that the park is designed on the basis of 80–90 per cent of the peak number of visitors expected.

- **Visitor management.** Once a decision has been made for the attraction to open, it is then important to ensure that visitors are managed in such a way as to ensure capacity levels in each area are not exceeded, and therefore that the quality of experience is maintained. Influencing visitor movement and behaviour is a subtle science and can be seen as selection from a range of options along a continuum, from hard management to soft management (as we saw in Chapter 6).

- **Monitoring.** There is no point in developing sophisticated management approaches without a means of monitoring their success. This includes administering formal questionnaires, debriefing front line staff or monitoring through the use of electronic eyes, turnstiles or other technology.

Management Issues

Seasonality

A key issue for attractions is the seasonal nature of tourism. Whilst this is often put down to climate, in fact there are institutional reasons for seasonality too, such as school and other holidays from the demand side and supply-side reasons such as labour supply and transport access. Goulding (2008) identifies a range of issues for attractions stemming from the inherent seasonality of demand. These include:

- staffing, where the skills developed by seasonal workers are lost in the off season;
- poor use of the attraction's capacity with crowding at peak times, leading to congestion and poor visitor experience; and
- perishability of the unit of production such that revenue-earning opportunities are lost.

Goulding (2008) maps a range of management responses to the issue of seasonality, including developing yield management systems, prioritising staffing at peak times to ensure revenue is maximised, diversifying to less seasonally sensitive markets such as corporates, flexible pricing strategies which are sensitive to seasonal variation, and extending the attraction product to, say, events, or developing new facilities. For destinations it is important to develop a portfolio of attractions, some of which will be weather resistant. Seasonality impacts on the profitability and operation of the attraction and demands particular strategies – museums, for example, mount special exhibitions, or differential pricing to encourage local people or schools to visit in the off peak.

Marketing

Creating and managing a memorable visitor experience is the key to successful attraction marketing. This involves designing a memorable set of activities and experiences and putting in place quality assurance across the whole experience. One poor aspect of the visit – such as catering, say – can influence the whole memory and desire to return.

Attractions are competing for expenditure across the leisure sector, including entertainment and white goods as well as other attractions and destinations. Changing patterns of leisure, an increasingly competitive marketplace and technological innovation mean that consumer expectations are rising. The challenge for attractions is to create products to satisfy these new patterns of demand with their media and entertainment-driven expectations. Here, there is no doubt that smaller attractions are vulnerable as they cannot access the investment required to meet the market's expectations and, as Leask (2010) notes, it is unusual for attractions to collaborate in terms of marketing. Voase (2008) examines the needs of the 'new tourist' when it comes to attractions. He characterises the new tourist as more demanding and sophisticated, identifying two key types:

1. **the thoughtful consumer** seeking a more active involvement from the attraction and a learning experience; and

2. **the smart consumer** accepting commoditisation of attractions, and seeing the visit as more of a transaction.

It is therefore vital for attractions to understand visitor motivation in targeting their market. Quite clearly different target markets are attracted to different types of attraction. Theme parks attract the family and the younger market, whilst heritage attractions tend to attract a more mature market. The target market then determines all the aspects of the attractions marketing mix. For attractions, promotion through word of mouth is important, and the sector still uses old-fashioned promotional techniques such as leafleting.

The Future of Visitor Attractions

As the visitor attraction sector matures, a number of trends are becoming evident. We are seeing greater professionalism developing across the industry with a more strategic approach to staff and their training, as well as more professional management approaches to the attractions themselves. In part, this is driven by competition. Here, attractions are increasingly compared to the entertainment and media sector and this has led to new product development, in particular the innovative use of technology. In the future, immersive experiences, virtual reality and combined experiences with other parts of tourism such as accommodation, dining and cruising will be part of the attractions landscape. This has led one industry commentator to predict a new generation of multifaceted, all-inclusive destinations that will appeal to many markets, and provide sound return on investment (Stevens, 2000).

Attractions, and events too, will have to embrace sustainability in all its forms, from the type of transport used to reach them, through the management of local community relationships, to the notion of ethical trading in shops and restaurants. Smart tourism demands not only that the visitor receives a satisfying and high-quality experience, but also that the destination is sustainable. Innovative application of visitor management ensures that the increasingly experienced and discerning new tourist does indeed receive a high-quality experience, while also sustaining the destination for future use. Here, innovative engineering such as that used in the Grand Canyon Skywalk Lookout – a horseshoe-shaped, glass-floored walkway over the canyon – are leading the way (www.destinationgrandcanyon.com), whilst technology based upon the 'Internet of Things' is helping to 'curate' the visitor experience.

SUMMARY

This chapter has analysed visitor attractions and outlined key elements of their management. Clearly, visitor attractions motivate the visit to a tourism destination and in so doing, energise the tourism system. It is important to distinguish attractions from support facilities at the destination, although we need both for tourism to function effectively. Defining attractions is fraught with difficulty but any definition must be based on the ability of a facility to attract visitation. Classifying attractions can be done simply by listing different types – such as natural or cultural attractions – or, and more usefully, we can classify according to an approach that assists in management decisions as was done by Clawson. Specific types of attraction demand different management approaches. Events, for example, an important and recent entrant into classifications, are time-limited attractions and are often run by a core of professionals, supported by many volunteers. Theme parks on the other hand have a long history and are very professionally managed. Natural attractions are often owned by the public sector and their management is more about conservation and protection of the resource. The management of attractions also depends on a keen understanding of their economics, particularly the significant up-front investment costs, and it also demands a clear identification of management objectives which then determines the remaining management decisions. The future of attractions will be dominated by technology, a demand for sustainability and a closer linkage of attractions with other aspects of tourism in order to create multifaceted, all-inclusive destinations that will appeal to many markets, and provide sound return on investment.

Discussion Questions

1. Design a survey to assess visitor profile and visitor satisfaction for an attraction that you are familiar with. Limit your number of questions to 20 or less.

2. Take a tourist attraction with which you are familiar – such as a theme park or museum – and revisit it with the eyes of a visitor manager. Does the attraction work in terms of visitor movement and rhythms, is the experience enhanced and did you enjoy it?

3. In class, discuss the advantages and disadvantages of a city government sponsoring a hallmark event such as a Formula One Grand Prix.

4. Take the example of a local museum or religious building that attracts significant number of visitors – is it managed as a visitor 'attraction'? If not, should it be?

5. Debate whether attractions in the public domain – national parks, museums, etc. – should be free, or should charge visitors an entrance fee.

Annotated Further Reading

1. Foley, M. and Lennon, J. (2000) *Dark Tourism*, Continuum, New York.
   A useful text considering this particularly 'dark' aspect of visitor attractions.

2. Fyall, A., Garrod, B., Leask, A. and Wanhill, S. (2008) *Managing Visitor Attractions: New Directions*, Butterworth Heinemann, Oxford.
   An excellent edited text covering all aspects of visitor attractions and their management.

3. Getz, D. (2012) *Event Studies Theory, Research and Policy for Planned Events*, 2nd edn, Routledge, London.
   Contemporary and thorough review of events as attractions.

4. Gunn, C.A. (1972) *Vacationscape: Designing Tourist Regions*, Bureau of Business Research, Austin, TX.
   Classic text with a strong design flavour and an innovative way of thinking about visitor attractions.

5. Hall, C.M. (1992) *Hallmark Tourist Events: Impacts, Management and Planning*, Belhaven, London.
   Classic early text on hallmark event attractions and their characteristics and issues.

6. Leask, A. (2010) Progress in visitor attraction research: toward more effective management, *Tourism Management* **31**, 155–166.
   An excellent comprehensive review paper of tourist attractions.

7. Lew, A., Hall, C.M. and Williams, A.M. (eds) (2014) *The Wiley Blackwell Companion to Tourism*, Wiley, Chichester.
   Section 6 has a range of contemporary chapters on attractions.

8. Swarbrooke, J. (2001) *The Development and Management of Visitor Attractions*, Butterworth Heinemann, Oxford.
   User-friendly text with thorough coverage of visitor attractions

9. Timothy, D. and Boyd, S. (2003) *Heritage Tourism*, Prentice Hall, New York.
   Useful text covering the key issues relating to heritage attractions.

References Cited

Boniface, B. and Cooper, C. (2009) *Worldwide Destinations: The Geography of Travel and Tourism*, Heinemann, London.

Clawson, M. and Knetsch, J. (1966) *The Economics of Outdoor Recreation*, Johns Hopkins University Press, Baltimore, OH.

Getz, D. (2012) Event Studies Theory, Research and Policy for Planned Events, 2nd edn, Routledge, London.

Fyall, A., Garrod, B., Leask, A. and Wanhill, S. (2008) *Managing Visitor Attractions: New Directions*, Butterworth Heinemann, Oxford.

Goulding, P. (2008) Managing temporal variation in visitor attractions, pp. 197–216 in Fyall, A., Garrod, B., Leask, A. and Wanhill, S., *Managing Visitor Attractions: New Directions*, Butterworth Heinemann, Oxford.

Gunn, C.A. (1972) *Vacationscape: Designing Tourist Regions*, Bureau of Business Research, Austin, TX.

Holloway, J.C. and Taylor, N. (2006) *The Business of Tourism*, Prentice Hall, Harlow.

Leask, A. (2008) The nature and role of visitor attractions, pp. 3–15 in Fyall, A., Garrod, B., Leask, A. and Wanhill, S., *Managing Visitor Attractions: New Directions*, Butterworth Heinemann, Oxford.

Leask, A. (2010) Progress in visitor attraction research: toward more effective management, *Tourism Management* **31**, 155–166.

Page, S.J. and Connell, J. (2014) *Tourism: A Modern Synthesis*, Cengage Learning, Andover.

Stevens, T. (2000) The future of visitor attractions, *Travel and Tourism Analyst* **1**, 61–85.

Swarbrooke, J. (2001) *The Development and Management of Visitor Attractions*, Butterworth Heinemann, Oxford.

UK Government and Mayor of London (2014) *Inspired by 2012: The Legacy from the Olympics and Paralympic Games*, Cabinet Office, London.

Voase, R. (2008) Rediscovering the imagination. meeting the needs of the new visitor, pp. 148–164 in Fyall, A., Garrod, B., Leask, A. and Wanhill, S., *Managing Visitor Attractions: New Directions*, Butterworth Heinemann, Oxford.

Wanhill, S (2008) Economic aspects of developing theme parks, pp. 59–79 in Fyall, A., Garrod, B., Leask, A. and Wanhill, S., *Managing Visitor Attractions: New Directions*, Butterworth Heinemann, Oxford.

Major Case Study 7.1
The Burren and Cliffs of Moher Geopark, Ireland

Cliffs of Moher, Ireland
Source: © Patryk Kosmider/Shutterstock.com

Introduction

Geoparks are a network of parks with significant environmental value. They are managed by developing strong and sustainable relationships with all stakeholders involved. The key for this type of attraction, therefore, is to ensure that the visitor experience is enhanced whilst also conserving the environmental values of the particular location.

A recent addition to the UNESCO list of Geoparks is the Burren and Cliffs of Moher Geopark in the west of Ireland. The Burren is a complex area, with sensitive issues embracing landscape, history, geology and archaeology. Because of this complexity, the project demands a multi-organisation and partnership approach and therefore the management of stakeholders is an essential part of running the Geopark. This approach will ensure 'a cared-for landscape, a better understood heritage, more sustainable tourism, a vibrant community and strengthened livelihoods' (www.burrengeopark.ie/).

The Geopark is managed by Clare County Council and supported by a range of national bodies including the Failte Ireland (Ireland's national tourist board), Geological agencies, nature conservation and planning agencies and universities. Core funding for the Geopark comes from Clare County Council, the Geological Survey of Ireland and Failte Ireland.

As a tourist attraction, the purpose of the park is:

'To spearhead sustainable tourism that develops and promotes the area as a truly special encounter-rich destination, strengthens the local economy and improves the visitor experience' (www.burrengeopark.ie/).

The aim of the Geopark, therefore, is to become a sustainable, vibrant and world-class attraction. According to the website, the key features of the Geopark are:

- fostering collaboration between all stakeholders to collectively develop and promote the Geopark as a sustainable tourism destination;

- participating in conserving the natural and cultural heritage in accordance with the international standards;

- ensuring high standards of communication and understanding of the unique character of the locale and its stories, emphasising the particular attributes and strengths of the Geopark;

- building capacity in destination management and stewardship, focusing on enhancing the quality and standards of visitor experiences and tourism products and services;

- optimising tourism's potential as both an economic and social development tool which benefits hosts as well as visitors; and

- creating strong economic benefits through product development, marketing and promotion, cost and energy savings, local sourcing and the creation of local employment.

The Attraction

The Geopark combines two very different visitor and landscape experiences. The Cliffs of Moher is a spectacular coastal landscape, whilst the Burren is a larger landscape of limestone terrain. The Geopark encourages active visitation with a learning and experience element. The Geopark's management provides a range of educational and interpretive materials, trails which include food and cycling trails and local guides. The aim is for an immersive experience in the area's natural, cultural and local resources including surfing, kayaking, caving and experiencing local food and local music.

The Geopark is structured around nine Geosites, each with its own management plan and interpretive approach. Low-impact tourism is promoted through Leave No Trace Ireland, a not-for-profit company (www.leavenotraceireland.org/).

Integrating Tourism into a Sensitive Landscape

The Geopark is actively working with local tourism enterprises through workshops, training courses and seminars. The training is designed for the nature of tourism on the Burren and specifically aims to increase professional expertise in two specific areas:

1. Reducing environmental impacts. Whilst the aim of low-impact tourism is a laudable one, achieving this in practice is more difficult. The key to achieving the Geopark's objectives is to carefully integrate tourism activity with the natural environment, geology and archaeological features. This is done by working with tourism enterprises to reduce their potential impact and strengthen their capability to use natural resources and become resource and energy efficient by using renewable energy, waste reduction and reducing their carbon footprint. Tourism enterprises will be asked to think about their impacts on the environment and the economy, to align their products with conservation. This approach is very much along the lines of 'ecotourism', and the Geopark is hoping to 'mainstream' elements of ecotourism into more general tourism enterprises.

2. Enhancing economic impacts. The Geopark is also keen to enhance the positive economic impact of tourism enterprises for the benefit of the area. Enterprises are encouraged to cooperate and work with local suppliers and partners, so spreading economic benefit out to the community. Local sourcing can be used as a marketing advantage and builds on the immersive nature of the tourism experience in the Geopark. Here, initiatives such as the establishment of farmers' markets or working with local artists and crafts people all helps to boost the spend by tourists. The area itself is isolated and most tourism enterprises are small, but also the share of imported materials is low so most of the expenditure stays in the area.

The Burren and Cliffs of Moher Geopark is an excellent case study of how to manage multiple stakeholders to successfully operate a complex tourist attraction. It also demonstrates clearly the value of working with local tourism enterprises to integrate tourism activity into a sensitive environmental region.

DISCUSSION QUESTIONS

1. The Geopark is an area of outstanding environmental significance. Does tourism have a role in this type of region or should it be 'de-marketed'?

2. How can the local businesses boost the economy of this remote rural region?

3. What might be the challenges of operating an attraction like the Geopark with so many management interests and agencies involved?

Sources:
www.burrengeopark.ie/
www.leavenotraceireland.org/

CHAPTER 8
HOSPITALITY

Learning Outcomes

This chapter focuses upon a key industry of the tourism sector, that of hospitality. Hospitality partly defines the tourism industry as it services the overnight stay of the visitor. This chapter is designed to provide you with:

- an understanding of the scope and definitions of hospitality;

- a disciplined approach to analysing the sectors of the hospitality industry;

- an awareness of the different approaches to managing the hospitality industry;

- an understanding of the key operational aspects of hospitality units;

- clarity on the role of occupancy, pricing and yield management in the hospitality industry; and

- awareness of the environmental consequences and responses of the hospitality industry.

Photograph: Bed and Breakfast accommodation © Dmitry Naumov/Shutterstock.com

Introduction

The provision of overnight accommodation, food and beverage for tourists partly defines the tourism industry and is an integral part of Leiper's destination region. It is also the one that delivers the most significant economic benefits and spend to the destination when compared to, say, a day visitor. Hospitality comes in many different forms, ranging from condominiums through resorts and conference centres to guesthouses, homestay, visiting friends and relatives and restaurants and bars. It is the hospitality industry that provides the welcome and delivers the food, flavours and local colour at the destination. As a result, it is important that the industry has a good strategic fit with the destination providing appropriate products for the visitor – it could, for example, be argued that the Victorian accommodation buildings of many UK seaside resorts are inappropriate for twenty-first century expectations. Here, we can see that hospitality is an important part of the tourism product, but we must remember that it is unusual for hospitality to be the motivation for the visit. Of course there are exceptions here, such as a stay at a landmark hotel such as the Raffles in Singapore (www.raffles.com/) or the iconic Burj-Al-Arab Hotel in Dubai (www.jumeirah.com/en/hotels-resorts/dubai/burj-al-arab/).

Definitions and Scope

Definitions of the hospitality industry and the traditional focus of the literature have been dominated by the hotel industry, its management and business – partly because of the size and dominance of the hotel industry in tourism. Indeed, the scope of just what is meant by the hospitality industry has been at the heart of the debate about defining tourism from a supply-side perspective. In the late twentieth century, emergence of satellite account methodology clarified the debate (as we saw in Chapter 3). More recently, definitions of hospitality have broadened from the purely commercial aspect of providing accommodation, food and beverage to include the social and cultural aspects of host and guest relationships and 'gastronomy', where the geography and culture of food and wine becomes important (Lynch *et al.*, 2011). Along these lines, Lashley (2000) has broadened definitions of hospitality to:

> 'contemporaneous human exchange, which is voluntarily entered into and designed to enhance the mutual well being of the parties concerned through the provision of accommodation and/or food and drink' (p. 14).

This definition implies that hospitality is not a purely commercial transaction, but includes human interactions, cultural considerations and exchange. Lashley and Morrison (2000) have taken this further by identifying three domains of hospitality, each representing a particular aspect of hospitality. Their overlap is where hospitality management is performed (Figure 8.1). These domains are:

1. **the private domain** – relating to the host/guest relationship and fulfilling physiological and psychological needs;

2. **the commercial domain** – relating to services provided for profit, clearly linked to the economics of the marketplace – here, the host–guest relationship is commoditised; and

3. **the social domain** – providing hospitality for strangers in an act of generosity and the social space in which this occurs.

These definitions and domains are contentious, however, and authors such as Slattery and Brotherton have joined the debate, arguing that Lashley and Morrison's approach firstly

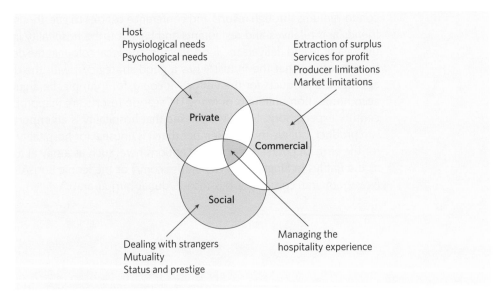

Figure 8.1 The three domains of hospitality
Source: Lashley and Morrison, 2000

overlooks the 'relationship' aspect of hospitality, that between the host and the guest, and secondly, underplays the 'corporate' element of hospitality that has emerged since industrialisation (see Jones, 2004, for a good summary of the debate).

History of the Hospitality Industry

The concept of hospitality dates back to ancient times when communities took strangers into their homes to provide food, drink and accommodation. Hospitality developed into one of the earliest forms of business with guest quarters provided in monasteries and inns, particularly as the Roman and Greek empires expanded internationally. Whilst the Grand Tour demanded that hospitality was provided for tourists throughout Europe, it was not until the nineteenth century that hotels as we know them developed. They initially grew in Europe, partly in response to travellers' needs as the railways developed. Indeed there has always been a close link between the development of hospitality and both transportation and economic growth, as Knowles (1998) observes. The nineteenth century saw changing working patterns and the growth of transport infrastructure encouraged the provision of food, drink and hospitality, particularly at the focus of new destinations such as coastal resorts. In the twentieth century, the development of the motor car and associated infrastructure led to an expansion of accommodation and hospitality, including dedicated facilities for motorists such as motels and drive-in restaurants. After the Second World War, the focus of accommodation trends moved to the USA where American-style hospitality management developed to include standardisation of provision and service, and a strong emphasis on marketing and branding – for example, like that observed in Hilton (www.Hilton.com), Hyatt (www.Hyatt.com) and Holiday Inn (www.HolidayInn.com). By the beginning of the twenty-first century the hospitality industry is estimated to comprise 300,000 hotels and 8 million restaurants, to employ 60 million people and to contribute US$950 billion annually to the global economy. The industry is concentrated in the leading destination regions of the world, particularly Europe, North America and increasingly in Asia. For the future, investment and growth is occurring in emergent destinations such as the Middle East, India and China.

Structure of the Hospitality Industry

The characteristics of supply of the hospitality industry polarises into many small businesses, which dominate in terms of numbers of establishments, and very large companies, such as, say, Hilton or Marriott (www.marriott.com/), which dominate in terms of practice and the profession. Between these two extremes lies a myriad of different businesses and hospitality concepts – so many in fact that it is difficult to generalise and encapsulate the hospitality industry. A key supply-side trend is increased concentration with a decline in small and independent hotels and an increase in franchise and chain properties. This means that medium-sized companies are vulnerable to take-over or failure as they do not have the market strength, productivity and economies of scale of the large chains, nor the identifiable niche of the small hotel.

Serviced Accommodation

Serviced accommodation comes in many forms, not only including hotels and guest houses, but also campus accommodation, medical accommodation such as the spas of the former Eastern Europe, and of course cruise ships and other forms of transport such as sleeper trains where accommodation is provided.

Hotels

Hotels are a key element of the accommodation stock of most destinations, ranging in size from the boutique hotel to the large 'bed factories' found in resorts such as Las Vegas. In fact, many commentators mistake hotels as surrogate for the whole accommodation industry, and even tourism itself, as they are such a visible and often iconic part of the destination. Of course there are many landmark properties such as the Savoy in London (www.the-savoy.com), but in fact within the hotel industry there is huge variation.

The vast majority of hotels are small family-run businesses. Here estimates vary, but a good rule of thumb is that 80 per cent of accommodation establishments have a capacity of less than 50 rooms; the accommodation stock in France, for example, predominantly comprises small hotels (Knowles, 1998). These small family-run hotels come in a number of forms – many are 'lifestyle businesses' where the owners buy a property in an attractive destination and run it as a small hotel, others are boutique hotels, seeking a niche in the market, such as spas or lifestyle retreats, to compete with the larger companies on personalised service.

The small hotels contrast with the large, professional, heavily branded style of operation demonstrated by the household names of Hilton, Marriott or Intercontinental (www.InterContinental.com). Many of these larger companies also operate hotels on management contracts whilst others operate franchises. The large chains bring the advantage of scale to their operation with their own reservations systems, marketing, training, technology expertise including the use of social media and leverage over suppliers. They are also integrated with tour operators and transport companies to provide a seamless product for the tourist.

The hotel sector is very varied. For example, hotels often form part of the national heritage as with the Palace hotels in India, and governments actively encourage conversion of heritage properties into hotels – see, for example, the 'paradores' in Spain (www.paradores-spain.com/) or the 'pousadas' in Portugal (www.pousadas.pt/). Budget hotels represent a significant growth industry with companies such as 'Travelodge' (www.travelodge.co.uk/) and 'Days Inn' (www.daysinn.com/) that are heavily branded and operate to strict standards so that the guest knows exactly what to expect in terms of the service and the room. Originally developed in North America, budget hotels are now found across Europe in major resorts, cities and also on transport routes at airports, rail stations and motorways. This sector of the hotel industry has grown at the expense of the more variable quality of bed and breakfast market.

We can also see specialist provision of serviced accommodation in the form of resorts, condominiums and holiday camps in major tourism destinations. Early examples include the Butlins holiday resorts established in the UK in the 1930s (www.Butlins.com), which morphed into the Center Parcs resort concept in the late 1960s (www.centerparcs.com/). This part of the hotel industry tends to offer accommodation 'plus' other activities. These might include organised activities as well as substantial investment in leisure facilities such as sports and swimming pools and extensive grounds. Many also provide an 'all-inclusive' tariff where food and drink is included. We look at the future of the hotel in Chapter 14.

Bed and Breakfast/Guesthouses

Long the source of many jokes as standards and quality can be variable, the guesthouse industry is comprised dominantly of small businesses which are often owner-occupied and come in many forms such as farm stay, as well as the traditional small bed and breakfast establishment. The size of establishment and the facilities on offer distinguish guesthouses from hotels, with guesthouses often having only a few bedrooms. Typically the traditional owner-occupied guesthouse may lack the management expertise and investment to compete with more professional companies. Here, the response has been the highly professional development of lifestyle and luxury guesthouses (see, for example, www.thenumberoneblackpool.com). The major advantage of guesthouses is that they provide a genuine feel and flavour of the destination in a way that the five-star chain hotels fail to do. However, it is still the case that family-run businesses often do not have the expertise to manage a property to its full potential. The following mini case study shows how smart thinking combined practical operational considerations with environmental concerns to show small business owners how to update tired accommodation infrastructure in Australia.

Mini Case Study 8.1
Motel Makeover, Australia

Introduction

The motel concept was a response to the needs of the car-borne tourist and dates from the 1950s. The motel is typically low-rise accommodation with dedicated parking outside each room.

Away from the capital cities, the majority of accommodation in Australia is still in the form of motels. These motels are found in regional centres, along the main road arteries and around major tourism attractions. The Australian government views tourism as an important part of the economy of regional Australia – indeed with drought, failing agriculture and depopulation in many parts of regional Australia, tourism is the only source of hope for the economy. However, the accommodation superstructure to support regional tourism is dated and of poor quality – dominantly motels built in the 1970s and 1980s. Add this to the fact that these motels tend to be owned by small businesses with limited management expertise or investment capability, and set it against rising expectations of the market, and we can see that there is a problem. And to make things worse there are more motel rooms available in the regions than there are tourists to fill them.

The Motel Makeover Guide

The Australian government supported a sustainable tourism cooperative research centre (STCRC) in a collaboration between universities, industry and government. One of their projects was to provide a practical guide for motel owners on how to bring their properties up to the standards of the twenty-first century consumer – the *Motel Makeover Guide*. Tackling one of the biggest practical issues facing Australian tourism, this guide is a practical and smart approach on behalf of the STCRC and one that could be replicated in many different markets – such as the small hotel market in the UK, for example.

The typical Australian motel has the following features:

- built in the 1970s or 1980s;
- constructed of brick and render;
- early motels average 36 rooms, later ones up to 60;
- one or two storeys with parking for each room; and
- dated décor, joinery and fittings.

In the 1970s, this type of accommodation matched or exceeded the average Australian home, but over the years housing standards and amenities have overtaken the motels. There is now a gap between what the market expects and what the motels can deliver. For owners looking to bring their properties up to standard, the *Motel Makeover Guide* provides an all-inclusive resource. It guides the owner into understanding markets, budgeting, estimating and other business disciplines. But more significantly, the *Guide* provides a step-by-step guide to deciding what refurbishment needs to be done, showing a thorough understanding of the economics and the design of the typical 1970s Australian motel.

The *Guide* stresses that each motel has a different location, market and budget for refurbishment, but on page 2 it provides some key questions for owners to consider:

- **Bathroom** – does it need a bath and a shower, or just a shower, should it have more mirrors?
- **Kitchenette** – should rooms have cooking facilities, if so what equipment is needed – a microwave or a hob – and how are odours extracted?
- **Furniture and fittings** – fitted or free standing furniture? Is a coat of paint enough as a refurbishment? Are fitted carpets needed?

- **Space** – how can good design create the impression of space in old rooms?
- **Seating** – how can a second bed be combined with comfortable seating in the room?
- **Lighting** – what should be provided and how can power costs be contained?

The *Guide* then goes on to outline motel consumers' wants and needs on the basis of surveys. Basically consumers are looking for 'a home away from home' with a motel that provides:

- good lighting;
- spacious rooms;
- plastered walls in light colours;
- comfortable seating;
- latest electronic equipment;
- bright bathrooms;
- well-equipped kitchenettes; and
- attractive gardens.

The *Guide* then goes on to provide detailed guidance for the motel in how to go about providing these facilities for the market. The *Guide* is insightful in its understanding of the motel issue, and the building and design challenges they face. In assisting the economy of regional Australia, this is a modest, but significant document.

DISCUSSION QUESTIONS

1. Draft an itinerary from Alice Springs to Darwin in the Northern Territory of Australia. Examining the overnight locations, assess the quality of accommodation available to you.
2. How do you think tourism can help the flagging economies of regional Australia?
3. Visit the STCRC website (www.crctourism.com.au) and download the *Motel Makeover Guide* from the bookshop. Examine the four case studies at the end of the Guide and identify the success factors across all four cases.

Source:
Beall, J., Roberts, R. and Jago, L. (2005) *Motel Makeover Guide*, Sustainable Tourism Cooperative Research Centre, Gold Coast, Australia.
www.crctourism.com.au

Homestay

Homestays, sometimes known as home hosting, are increasingly popular and are a variant on the guesthouse concept. Here tourists stay in the homes of the host community with local families. Homestays can be organised by government tourism organisations as in Malaysia, individuals as in Bali or by community organisations at the destination. Homestays are viewed as a low-impact form of tourism, allowing tourists to understand local ways of life, cuisine and culture.

Self-serviced Accommodation

Self-serviced accommodation does not provide any form of food or beverage and typically comprises rental apartments which are common across the pleasure periphery of Europe and throughout North America and includes the suites and motels found in North America and Australia. Other forms of self-catering accommodation are timeshare, which we deal with below, the use of university accommodation for tourists in vacation periods or house rental such as the 'gite' concept in France. There is no doubt that this type of accommodation has grown since 1945, and has taken market share from the serviced accommodation industry. There are also blended forms of accommodation that have taken the elements of both serviced and self-serviced accommodation, such as all-suite hotels.

Timeshare

The Organisation for Timeshare in Europe (OTE) defines timeshare as

'a form of ownership interest that may include an estate interest in immovable property and which allows use of the property on a recurring annual basis for a fixed or variable time period.'

Effectively, timeshare allows ownership of a holiday property for multiples of weeks and also the opportunity to exchange time in that property for time in another. The timeshare concept began in Europe in the 1960s as an innovative way of increasing and diversifying the tourism offer and it has developed significantly since then. It does, however, have a reputation for pressure selling and in response the European Union has implemented the timeshare directive to regulate the industry. Traditionally, timeshare properties were concentrated in North America, the Caribbean and Europe but they are growing in Asia and the former countries of Eastern Europe. It is interesting that many timeshare properties were purchased by the baby boomer generation and it is not certain that their children will want to continue with the arrangement.

Camping, Caravans and Motor Homes

Camping has a down-market image, but this contrasts with the concept of luxury campsites in, say, the safari parks of Africa or the notion of up-market camping – 'glamping'. In countries such as Australia and the USA, camping is a popular domestic holiday option, and campsites are well equipped with electricity, water, entertainment and Internet access. Caravans and motor homes provide 'mobile' accommodation for the owners, and these vehicles can also be rented – to travel across North America or Australia, for example. Caravan sites provide for both 'static' and 'mobile' caravans, but have been criticised on the basis of their impact on the landscape.

Conventions and Meetings

The conventions and meetings market is an important part of the hospitality industry. Often facilities are provided within hotels but it is also common for destinations to have their own dedicated convention centre. The conventions and meetings industry is a major generator of revenue for companies and destinations, with delegates typically spending more than the leisure tourist, although the length of stay tends to be shorter. Competition for conferences and meetings is fierce and, whilst the major international conferences attract the headlines, it is the smaller domestic meetings that are the mainstay of the industry.

Non-commercial Forms of Accommodation

This chapter is mainly concerned with the commercial side of the hospitality industry, but it must be remembered that there is a considerable non-commercial industry when it comes to tourism accommodation. The visiting friends and relatives (VFR) market, for example, is well known, but we must also consider tourists' use of their own properties such as second homes, boats for overnight accommodation or exchanging homes with tourists from another destination (Muller, 2014). Visiting friends and relatives is often overlooked as an accommodation type, and surveys of bed nights in destinations frequently undercount because they fail to survey VFR. In recent years, destination management organisations have realised the value of the VFR market for attractions and the economic benefits it delivers to the destination.

Food and Beverage

Food and beverage is essential to the tourism product, but it is also increasingly complex as new concepts emerge and traditional boundaries between product types become blurred. For example, traditionally in the UK, pubs were in the beverage industry but increasingly they are a major force in food retailing. Rather like accommodation, food and beverage is one of the earliest commercial industries with provision of food and drink for strangers. Of course (as we saw when discussing the tourism satellite account in Chapter 3), a large proportion of the food and beverage market is local residents, but many food and drink outlets also have a significant percentage of turnover from tourists. This is particularly the case in major destinations such as Orlando in Florida or Australia's Gold Coast.

Food and beverage outlets can be classified in many ways, but the most common approach is to think of them as restaurants, fast food outlets, bars, cafeterias, clubs and canteens. Here, fast food outlets have seen the most rapid growth, built upon a robust business model which delivers high levels of productivity, low costs and use of the franchise model, although concerns for healthy eating have meant that they have had to make menu adjustments. Two key issues for the food service industry are:

1. labour supply and the quality of jobs on offer (as we saw in Chapter 3); and

2. their sensitivity to economic conditions for demand. We will look at the future of the sector in Chapter 14.

Gaming

With historic roots in destinations such as Monte Carlo (www.yourmonaco.com/), gaming has now become a major economic phenomenon in destinations such as Las Vegas (www.visitlasvegas.com/) and Macau (www.macautourism.gov.mo/). Legalisation of gambling in the latter half of the twentieth century allowed companies to tap into considerable latent demand and created a sub-sector of the hospitality industry based upon casinos, often within large themed hotels. Here, resorts such as Las Vegas have cleverly integrated gaming with other attractions such as big ticket entertainment events and cabaret. Casinos are used by governments as a source of revenue; to revitalise run-down resorts (as at Scheveningen in the Netherlands); and as a means to further develop tourism. Gaming as an activity is often opposed by local residents, who link the activity with crime and the social consequences of gambling addiction. The future of gaming linked to tourism may be constrained by the increased availability of Internet gaming, and the increased legalisation of gaming means that gamblers will not need to travel to find a casino.

We close this section by looking at a company that challenges the conventional classifications of the hospitality sectors – Airbnb.

Mini Case Study 8.2
Airbnb – A Business Model for the Informal Accommodation Sector

Background

The Airbnb concept traces its roots back to 2007 when a US website offered private accommodation for conference delegates. It was launched as airbedandbreakfast.com in 2008, based on bed and breakfast in private homes using air beds in bedrooms and living rooms. By 2009 the concept was spreading across the USA and it was renamed Airbnb; by 2011 Airbnb was acquiring competitors internationally and began opening new offices – initially in Paris, Milan, Barcelona, Copenhagen, Moscow and São Paulo to add to its existing offices in San Francisco, London, Hamburg and Berlin. Expansion continued into Asia, and by 2015 Airbnb had:

- over 25 million total guests.
- presence in over 34,000 cities.
- presence in over 190 countries.
- over 1 million accommodation listings.

The Concept

Airbnb is a perfect example of innovation in the hospitality sector with a very new concept and way of doing business – effectively a technology company morphing into a hospitality company. It is also an example of the growth of the 'sharing economy'. The concept is clear:

'Airbnb is an online marketplace for vacation rentals that connects users with property to rent with users looking to rent the space' (www.airbnb.com/).

The concept is a simple one, bringing together 'hosts' who have spare rooms or space in their property – or indeed a spare property to rent; and 'guests' who are seeking accommodation in the particular location. The Airbnb website gives very clear guidance for those thinking of acting as a host:

'We encourage hosts to think carefully about their responsibilities. Hosting offers rich experiences, but it comes with a certain level of commitment' (www.airbnb.com/).

The Airbnb concept is innovative whilst being simple and clear. The following are the key features of the business model:

- Airbnb provides a secure payment method for the transaction – Airbnb's primary source of revenue comes from service fees from bookings;
- both hosts and guests must register with Airbnb;
- both hosts and guests have profiles which include features such as user reviews and shared social connections to build reputation and trust in the Airbnb marketplace.
- Airbnb provides a secure messaging system for hosts and guests to communicate;
- Airbnb provides insurance against damage, theft, etc.;
- Airbnb does not own any rooms or properties;
- Airbnb has developed a social networking system, particularly using Facebook; and
- Airbnb has developed a 'neighbourhoods' product which acts as a guide to the locality.

Issues

Airbnb is a good example of a disruptive innovation, by creating new sources of demand and supply in the accommodation market. However, this innovation has brought with it some negative issues and criticism:

- a number of US authorities do not allow this type of renting out of rooms;
- there is a quality issue in terms of the product as it is impossible for Airbnb to control the quality of the accommodation;
- hosts are exposed to risk of property damage and theft; and
- the concept is open to abuse by being used by commercial accommodation operators and property developers rather than individuals with a spare room. They use the site to avoid paying taxes and charges.

DISCUSSION QUESTIONS

1. Airbnb is growing rapidly – is there a danger that it will outgrow its roots?
2. Airbnb is an example of a 'disruptive innovation' – what other examples can you identify in the hospitality sector?
3. What are the key features of the huge success of Airbnb?

Sources:
Guttentaga, D. (2013) Airbnb: disruptive innovation and the rise of an informal tourism accommodation sector, *Current Issues in Tourism* **18**(6), 1–26.
www.airbnb.com/

Hospitality Organisations

At the international level, the 'International Hotel and Restaurant Association' (IHRA – www.ih-ra.com/) was founded in 1946 in Paris and is the peak industry body providing industry information and research for the industry as well as lobbying in bodies such as the UNWTO.

At the national level each country has its own set of organisations. The two major trade associations in North America are the 'American Hotel and Lodging Association' (www.ahla.com/) and the 'National Restaurant Association' (www.restaurant.org/). They provide a range of support for their members including publications, lobbying and advice on industry practice. In the UK, the major trade association is the 'British Hospitality Association' providing educational and information services for its members, including services for students, and it is influential in hospitality education and training (www.bha.org.uk/).

At the destination level, there are many organisations representing the hospitality industry; indeed, some argue that this has led to fragmented representation of the industry in many destinations. For example, a destination may have separate trade associations for guest houses, hotels and for restaurants.

Managing the Hospitality Industry

The hospitality industry is large and complex, demanding particular management approaches. We can think of these approaches focusing upon management, marketing and quality management.

Management Approaches

At the strategic level, there is increasing pressure upon hospitality businesses to deliver a return on investment for their owners and investors. Traditionally, the hospitality industry has been characterised by low rates of return on investment, and this explains the fact that many investors enter the hospitality industry for the long term gains of property value and business goodwill rather than short-term considerations of profitability. A strategy of growth has meant that in the hotel sector, for example, there is a trend to larger and larger hotels. With this trend, new management options have emerged as often owners of hospitality businesses are now companies such as financial institutions who do not have the expertise needed to run the business. As a result, there is a trend towards increasing concentration in the hospitality industry. This is due simply to the advantages that can be leveraged by larger organisations. Indeed, as Knowles (1998) observes, globally the hotel industry is dominated by a small group of large companies. Economies of scale for hotels are found in increased purchasing power, economies of centralising services such as laundry, reservations or marketing, the ability to raise finance and lower administration and training costs.

International strategy

These trends are set against the background of a global marketplace, the rise of e-intermediaries and the Internet which is encouraging development of consumer sites such as www.tripadvisor. com (as we will see in Chapter 13). For market and revenue growth, hospitality businesses look beyond domestic markets to international expansion. This has led to two contrasting approaches:

1. development of standardised products, operating procedures and properties across the world – here there is a danger of all destinations becoming similar with identikit Hiltons, Marriotts and fast food outlets; or

2. development of locally sensitised products and locally designed hotels and products tailored according to the destination, often by companies that specialise in particular regions of the world, such as the Taj group in India (www.tajhotels.com/) – the issue here is for companies to balance the need for international quality standards with local delivery in indigenously designed properties with local decor and culture.

Of course, the disadvantage of either approach for the destination is that profits may be repatriated back to the home country of head office. The Maldives is a good example of a destination that suffers in this way.

Management strategies

Strategic options for hospitality businesses focus upon creating market and revenue growth. These options include:

- **Management contracts.** Management contracts are common in the hospitality industry, particularly in larger properties at the upper end of the market. Here, a professional management company manages the property on behalf of the owner, bringing guaranteed operating standards and good practice. Knowles (1998) defines a management contract as:

  'a written agreement between the owner and the operator of a hotel . . . by which the owner employs the operator as an agent to assume full responsibility for operating and managing the property' (p. 73).

  Management contracts benefit owners of hotels who may not have expertise in hospitality or a desire to operate the property, and they benefit the managing company who do not have to have large capital commitments in property. In other words, the owner supplies the fixed assets including the property and grounds, whilst the operator undertakes operation of the property for an agreed management fee. Contracts vary in their arrangements, but all have up-front expectations of performance in terms of income and profitability.

- **Franchising.** Franchising is a common strategy in the hospitality industry as it avoids expensive fixed investment costs. It is found in both accommodation companies (especially in the budget market) and food service companies (such as McDonalds – www.mcdonalds.com/, and Pizza Express – www.pizzaexpress.com/). Franchising operates by the *franchisor* granting the rights to a product format – such as a fast food restaurant – to a *franchisee,* and the right to distribute its products or services (Knowles, 1998). Franchising brings significant benefits for both sides – the franchisor can grow their concept rapidly using investment from the franchisee, whilst the franchisee has access to an established product and support network such as market and product knowledge, allowing access to the industry for small businesses. Normally the franchisee pays an upfront fee and then a percentage of turnover to the franchisor. However, franchising can provide problems for the franchising group, particularly in terms of maintaining quality and standards.

- **Consortia.** One issue for small hospitality businesses is their lack of marketing and purchasing power. This has led to the development of 'consortia' of businesses where resources are pooled for purchasing and marketing. As a result, the businesses are often marketed under one brand name, even though they are each independently owned. The Best Western Group is an example of a successful consortium (www.bestwestern.com/).

- **Contract catering.** The hospitality industry has a poor image as an employer and there is a perennial shortage of skilled labour such as chefs. For the industry, use of contact caterers to provide 'cook chill' meals is a common solution as it cuts out the need for skilled functions. As a result, it has been accused of encouraging deskilling.

Fast food outlets are classic examples of franchise operations.
Source: © Hisham Ibrahim/PhotoV/Alamy Images

Marketing Approaches

Sophisticated hospitality marketing began in the USA in the post war period with the strong development of brands such as Holiday Inn. As a service, the hospitality product is produced where it is consumed. It is therefore important for hospitality managers to understand where their customers come from, and to raise awareness of their premises to boost the flow of customers. The hospitality product itself comprises both tangible elements – the bedroom or the food, and intangible elements such as the ambience of a hotel, or the service in a restaurant. For accommodation, Medlik and Ingram (2000) have developed five features which impact upon the market and the marketing of a property:

1. **Location** is a primary influence upon the market, whether by the geographical location of the hotel within the destination, or the destination itself. Resort hotels will experience annual seasonality, whilst city hotels will experience weekly peaking of demand, busier during the week and with less demand at the weekend, hence they offer cheaper leisure-based packages for Friday and Saturday night.

2. **The mix of facilities** in terms of public rooms, leisure centre, restaurants or conference halls is an important influence. The mix will depend upon the particular market served – for example, demand for accommodation itself tends to be from national and international markets, whilst demand for restaurants will be more localised.

3. **Image** in terms of formality and how it is presented to the market, particularly in terms of websites and presence on social media.

4. **The type of service** provided including the level of staffing.

5. **Price** is also influenced by the factors above – for example, location and the level of facilities and services all impact upon the price charged. Hotels will also vary their prices according to season and market segment.

The larger hospitality companies lead the way in terms of marketing thinking, especially in terms of market segmentation and distribution strategies.

Market segmentation has grown in significance in the hospitality industry, particularly in the accommodation sector. In the early years of hospitality marketing, segmentation was crudely based upon segments such as leisure, business or convention groups. However, with increased competition in the industry, segmentation has become more sophisticated and includes preferences and motivations for stay. For example, the larger chains offer different products for different segments from budget to luxury formats. As a result, many of the larger chains have diversified their branding to meet the particular needs of market segments, to develop brand loyalty (through, for example, loyalty schemes such as Intercontinental Hotels 'rewards club') and to clarify their product offering in the face of confusion over accommodation grading. Here, development of budget brands is a common response. A useful example is the Accor group which has developed luxury properties marketed as Sofitel or Novotel, whilst their budget brands are the Ibis and Formule 1 brands (www.accorhotels.com). This allows Accor to closely target the hotel product to the particular market segment through pricing, facilities and marketing.

In terms of distribution, the larger hotel chains, and consortia have access to computer reservation systems and keep in close touch with tour operators and both the airlines (and their CRS) and the coach companies. With Internet distribution many hospitality companies not only have their own website, but they also provide their room stock to last minute booking sites such as www.lastminute.com and www.wotif.com. For smaller accommodation units, public industry tourist boards also provide a source of bookings for a commission.

Managing Quality

To be a successful hospitality business it is vital to be customer-focused and to understand the needs of the guest at each 'touch point' with the unit and its personnel. Here, the concept of the 'guest cycle' is useful (Figure 8.2). The hospitality industry has embraced the concept of quality in terms of service-oriented strategies (Solnet, 2015). In other words, the heart of a hospitality business is anticipating and serving customer needs. Solnet (2015) identifies the key dimensions of this approach:

- **The service encounter** can be defined as the interaction between a guest and a hospitality operation through its frontline employees. If the encounter is successful then it builds loyalty and creates satisfaction. To quote Solnet (2008) 'At the heart of service management is the unavoidable fact that a significant proportion of tourism experiences are delivered by people (tourism employees, managers, owners). From the tourist's perspective, the most immediate evidence of service quality is the service encounter itself'. Customer contact employees are a hospitality organisation's primary interface with customers and, as such, employees are often perceived by the customer as being the product itself.

- **Customer satisfaction** is difficult to measure but generally when customers are satisfied they become loyal, often repeat visit, will recommend and become less price sensitive. Indeed so important is this concept to the service approach that many operations now aim to 'delight' rather than merely 'satisfy' the customer.

- **Service quality** has been defined as a cognitive evaluation of a performance by a service provider (Parasuraman *et al.*, 1988) and its broad dimensions include some degrees of reliability, responsiveness, tangibles, empathy and assurance (Solnet, 2015). Measuring service quality is particularly difficult, because different people rate individual dimensions of service in different ways and with different weightings of importance. There are two distinct models of service quality:

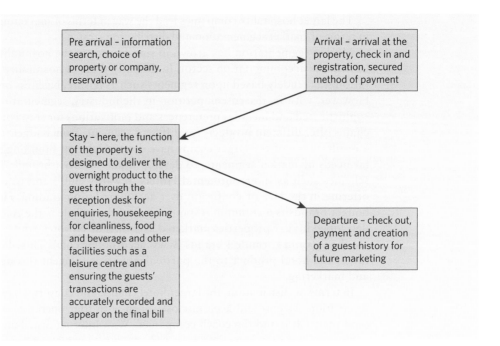

Figure 8.2 Guest cycle for an accommodation unit

- SERVQUAL, where service quality is measured using five dimensions, evaluating the guest's actual expectation with their expectations (Parasuraman *et al.*, 1988) – we have chosen this paper as the classic paper for this chapter; and

- the Nordic Model, which has two dimensions – an 'outcome' dimension, such as providing a meal; and a 'process' dimension – how the meal was prepared and served.

- **Linking service quality and business performance** has emerged as an important driver of hospitality businesses. Here, hospitality operations develop quality management programmes to overtly boost financial performance through building customer satisfaction and loyalty.

Classic Paper

Parasuraman, A., Berry, L and Zeithaml, V. (1988) SERVQUAL: a multiple-item scale for measuring consumer perceptions of service quality, *Journal of Retailing* **64(1), 12–40**

Parasuraman, Berry and Zeithaml's 1988 paper has become a classic, frequently cited and spawned set of literature of its own focusing upon their particular model of service quality. As a result, there are many interpretations, debates and controversies surrounding their 'SERVQUAL' model. Nonetheless, there is no substitute to returning to their original paper and reading it before forming a view.

The paper introduces the concept of service quality and takes the view that the consumer defines service quality, seeking certain benefits from any service that is performed on their behalf. The paper then identifies five 'gaps' that may be experienced by the consumer when the service delivered does not come up to expectations Their model has subsequently become known as the service quality 'gaps' model, labelled by the three authors as 'SERVQUAL'.

The basis of SERVQUAL is five dimensions of service:

1. reliability – accurate and dependable service;

2. responsiveness – prompt and helpful service;

3. empathy – caring and personalised attention;

4. assurance – knowledgeable and trustworthy; and

5. tangibles – appearance of physical facilities.

These dimensions are used in the pre- and post-evaluation of a service in order to compare the variance between expectation and actual performance.

The SERVQUAL model is known as a 'gaps' model because of its measurement of the variance between expectations and performance. The paper goes on to develop a measurement approach to five gaps between expectation and performance:

1. Gap between management perceptions and consumer expectations – the company does not understand its market and the service is not aligned with what the customer expects.

2. Gap between management perceptions and service specification – this may occur when the company is trying to reduce costs and so fails to deliver a service that meets expectations.

3. Gap between service quality specification and service delivery – here it is at the point of delivery where the service fails to satisfy, often due to poor training of front-line staff.

4. Gap between service delivery and external communications – effectively this means that the company has over-promised in terms of service delivery and the reality has not met the promise.

5. Gap between expectations and perceptions – the totality of the service delivery does not meet customer expectations.

As mentioned above, SERVQUAL has generated controversy, particularly in terms of its measurement approach and the difficulty of applying it across different types of service, from hospitality to banking.

Classification and grading

An important aspect of controlling the quality of hospitality businesses is classification and grading of accommodation and food service outlets. It is done for quality control purposes, legislation and consumer information. An added benefit is that it encourages owners to invest in their properties, raises standards and provides a means of comparing across properties in similar price and quality bands. It also provides properties with differentiating positioning for marketing purposes. Classification and grading is a controversial issue and competing organisations are involved in the process. These include:

● In some countries registration for classification and grading purposes is compulsory to gain a licence to operate – schemes are often run by tourism ministries or boards and some argue that this approach generates red tape and inhibits innovation.

● Private organisations are also involved and include the Automobile Association with its star rating of accommodation (www.theaa.com) or Michelin (www.michelinguide.com/).

● Public industry organisations such as tourist boards also classify and grade accommodation for legal purposes.

It is important to distinguish between 'classification' which allocates properties to a particular class on the basis of their features and services – in other words, it is a descriptive approach, and 'grading' which looks not only at the facilities but also at a range of verifiable features and services, such as the time room service is available, to deliver a 'grade' for the property. Both grading and classification schemes operate on an inspection basis.

The very many different schemes and lack of agreement means that for the consumer, classification and grading schemes can be both confusing and misleading. They have also been criticised as being too subjective, based upon an inspector's judgement, as well as only relating to the particular point in time when the inspection is done.

Hospitality Operations

At the heart of any hospitality operation are the human resources involved and their ability to deliver a high-quality service. This is essential in the concept of service marketing where the staff not only influence perception and evaluation of the hotel stay or the meal experience, but are closely involved in the 'co-creation' of the hospitality experience. Of course, this process must deliver a profitable business for the company. As a result, the role of a hospitality manager, in a pub, restaurant, hotel or resort is complex, involving a thorough understanding of all elements of the business. These elements are outlined below.

Finance

Most hospitality businesses, and particularly accommodation properties, require major investment in the fixed plant of a destination. As a result, hotel and resort financing and investment have attracted considerable literature and interest. The level of investment in accommodation at a destination can act as a major constraint upon tourism development, or as a stimulus. In Australia, for example, the opening up of new budget airline routes to regional airports prompted a considerable investment in accommodation in 'new' destinations.

Location is an important consideration for accommodation investors. This is not only due to the importance of location in relation to the market, but also because the bulk of investment in accommodation units is in the land and the buildings. In other words, the up-front investment required is considerable and this impacts upon pricing decisions as the revenue streams from the unit have to contribute to very high fixed costs, whilst the variable costs of each extra guest are low. This means that accommodation units have to achieve high levels of utilisation. Of course, here the classic dilemma of services is at play, as an unsold room can never recoup the lost revenue, hence the importance of techniques such as yield management to maximise revenue and the importance of understanding the various market segments for the accommodation unit.

The hospitality industry is characterised by a high ratio of fixed costs to operating costs – quite simply the fixed costs in developing and building an accommodation unit, for example, are very high and are therefore subject to extensive feasibility study. Figure 8.3 shows a breakdown of costs and revenue for a typical large hotel.

Figure 8.3 shows the main elements of hotel balance accounts:

- rooms revenue which depends on the rate charged and occupancy level;
- food and beverage revenue is partly dependent upon occupancy, but also upon the local market and will include revenue from functions and events; and
- other revenue.

The relative importance of each of these three sources will vary according to the size, location and market for the hotel.

The operating costs for a large hotel can be classified as:

- labour;
- marketing and administration;
- energy and maintenance; and
- food and beverage.

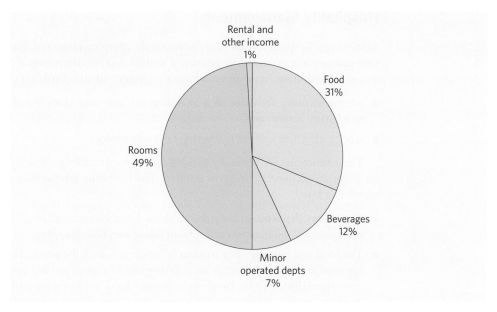

Figure 8.3 Percentage distribution of hotel revenue
Source: Knowles, 1998

Of these costs, labour is by far the highest and for five star hotels the number of employees per guest is substantially higher than for budget hotels. As a result, some companies are experimenting with using robots to provide service as in the Henna-na Hotel in Nagasaki, Japan and robot bars on cruise ships (see the Royal Caribbean Lines' *Anthem of the Seas*). The ratio of staff per guest also varies in different parts of the world where, for example, unemployment may be high and wage costs low. Both revenue and costs are captured in an accounting system that is unique to the industry, known as the 'uniform system of accounts', developed to allow comparison of the accounts of different properties.

Occupancy

The concepts of occupancy and yield management are important tools for the hospitality manager. Occupancy is a simple measure of the number of rooms or beds occupied as a percentage of the total available. It is also used in the food service industry with 'covers' as the measure. Average accommodation occupancies worldwide are around 65 per cent, but across Asia and in many world cities such as London, New York or Milan they are considerably higher. In most European capitals, the average room rates are also high. In contrast, destinations in decline, such as some cold-water resorts, experience marked seasonal peaking of occupancy that brings down the overall average.

Yield management is a technique used to maximise the revenue achieved per room by managing occupancy. Ideally, hotels will achieve the full-advertised price for the room (rack rate) but more commonly they will vary their rates in a trade-off between occupancy and yield per room. Accommodation has adapted the concept of yield from the airline industry and the larger companies have sophisticated yield (or revenue) management systems designed to cope with peaks and troughs in demand. This has given rise to the notion of late booking where consumers can book a room at the last minute for a cheaper price, as the property discounts the room to make a contribution to fixed costs. Specialist websites such as lastminute.com, laterooms.com and Wotif.com have taken advantage of this trend.

Hospitality Management

Managing a hospitality unit is an increasingly complex task, and managers in the twenty-first century are expected to possess a wide range of competencies and knowledge. For accommodation, most proprieties have a management structure that distinguishes between:

- revenue earning activities such as restaurant, accommodation and other functions such as a leisure centre; and
- service activities such as marketing or reservations.

These functions are normally divided into departments – such as front of house, to allow for accurate accounting and cost control. The following are the major operational departments in a hotel:

- **The rooms department** includes all those functions related to the overnight stay of the guest and will include reception/front office and housekeeping.
- **The food and beverage department** is concerned with the production of food and beverage service on the property from ordering and receipt of goods, menu design and kitchen operations through to managing the various food and beverage outlets in the property. In recent years, this department has become the focus of a major new branch of legislation – food safety legislation, partly in response to a rise in the number of food poisoning cases. Here, technology is increasingly used in menu design and cost control.
- **The administration department** is the main servicing area for the property's business and includes functions such as accounts, marketing and reservations, human resources, engineering and maintenance, and one function which has become increasingly important – security and risk management. This area, along with front office, has seen the greatest impact of technology. Indeed, technology has transformed the hospitality industry through online services for guests, social media and the use of software marketing, managing properties and in cost control.

Environmental Issues

Environmental issues for the hospitality industry have come to the fore since the 1990s and are of increasing concern to consumers (Hawkins and Bohdanowicz, 2011). Surprisingly, the accommodation industry is a significant source of carbon emissions, as well as being perceived as a heavy user of energy and water. Major accommodation developments have to undergo an environmental impact assessment, whilst many properties adopt environmental auditing of their operations. Of course, there is controversy over how the industry has addressed these issues, with some using 'green' initiatives as a major marketing point of differentiation. Accor, for example, has state-of-the-art environmental management systems and publish their green credentials in their annual report, as we see in the final case study of this chapter. There are a number of initiatives which have been established to promote sound environmental behaviour by hotels:

- The International Tourism Partnership (www.tourismpartnership.org) provides advice to accommodation companies on responsible business including energy consumption and greening the supply chain.
- Hotel Energy Solutions is an energy management toolkit available for accommodation properties supported by international agencies including the IHRA and the UNWTO (www.hotelenergysolutions.net). The initiative deals with energy strategies including saving energy costs and advise on installing renewable energy systems, claiming savings of 20 per cent on energy costs with simple operational changes.

- Considerate hoteliers (www.consideratehoteliers.com) is an association of independent hoteliers that encourages and supports good socially- responsible environmental policies and practices in their properties. Initiatives include publications on 'green sourcing' and saving energy costs.

SUMMARY

This chapter has analysed the hospitality industry as a key element of the tourism system as it provides the overnight stay. The industry is significant in economic terms and scale globally, though, as we saw, it comprises predominantly small businesses. In the past, it has been narrowly defined as the commercial part of the industry, but contemporary approaches now view hospitality more generally as including all transactions and the space in which they occur. We showed that the hospitality industry is complex, comprising many sectors such as serviced and self-serviced accommodation, food service outlets, non-commercial activities such as visiting friends and relatives, and new segments such as the approach of Airbnb which we provided as a case study. Managing the hospitality industry is complex, and there are a number of approaches that have been used to minimise investment, including management contracts and franchising as well as upgrading properties, as we saw in the motel makeover case. The industry has become adept at marketing too in recent years, closely matching, say, accommodation products with market segments. This is particularly true of the larger companies. Of course, the heart of hospitality is providing service, and we have seen the various approaches to service quality and its management. The chapter then considered the operational aspects of hospitality management, and closed with an overview of the environmental issues facing the sector, some of the responses to these issues and a case study of Accor's sustainability approach.

Discussion Questions

1. The dominance of small businesses in hospitality means that it will be difficult to improve environmental practice. How true is this statement?
2. Taking a large hotel chain of your choice, examine the various brands that they use to market their groups of properties and draft a customer profile for each brand.
3. As the CEO of a major restaurant chain, draft a memo to your board explaining the advantages of franchising your concept to achieve growth.
4. Examining a recent hospitality experience, how 'customer centric' was the experience?
5. Design in outline a training scheme for prospective small businesses wishing to enter the guesthouse industry.

Annotated Further Reading

1. Angelo, R.M. and Vladimir, A.N. (2011) *Hospitality Today: An Introduction,* 7th edn, American Hotel & Lodging Educational Institute, Orlando, FL.
   Good introductory text with a North American flavour.

2. Brotherton, R. and Wood, R. (2008) *The Sage Handbook of Hospitality Management,* Sage, London.
   Comprehensive handbook.

3. Hawkins, R. and Bohdanowicz, P. (2011) *Responsible Hospitality*, Goodfellow, Oxford.
   Accessible and contemporary account of sustainability and CSR.

4. Lashley, C. and Morrison, A. (eds) (2000) *In Search of Hospitality: Theoretical Perspectives and Debates*, Butterworth Heinemann, Oxford.
   Landmark volume challenging traditional thinking about hospitality as a subject and an industry.

5. Olsen, M., West, J. and Tse, E. (1998) *Strategic Management in the Hospitality Industry*, John Wiley & Sons, New York.
   Classic text focusing on hospitality strategy.

6. Parasuraman, A., Berry, L. and Zeithaml, V. (1988) SERVQUAL: a multiple-item scale for measuring consumer perceptions of service quality, *Journal of Retailing* 64(1), 12–40.
   Classic paper that paved the way for measuring service quality.

7. Singh, A.J. and Houdré, H. (2012) *Hotel Sustainable Development Principles and Practices*, American Hotel & Lodging Educational Institute, Orlando, FL.
   Thorough US text on sustainability in accommodation

8. Solnet, D. (2015) Service management and tourism, pp. 91–128 in Cooper, C. *Contemporary Tourism Reviews, Volume 1*, Goodfellow, Oxford.
   Contemporary and practitioner-based account of service management approaches.

9. www.ehotelier.com
   A well-respected website with many useful features for the student and researcher.

References Cited

Jones, P. (2004) Finding the hospitality industry or finding hospitality schools of thought, *Journal of Hospitality, Leisure, Sport and Tourism Education* 3(1), 33–45.

Hawkins, R. and Bohdanowicz, P. (2011) *Responsible Hospitality*, Goodfellow, Oxford.

Knowles, T. (1998) *Hospitality Management: An Introduction*, Longman, Harlow.

Lashley, C. (2000) Towards a theoretical understanding, pp. 1–17 in Lashley, C. and Morrison, A. (eds) *In Search of Hospitality: Theoretical Perspectives and Debates*, Butterworth Heinemann, Oxford.

Lashley, C. and Morrison, A. (eds) (2000) *In Search of Hospitality: Theoretical Perspectives and Debates*, Butterworth Heinemann, Oxford.

Lynch, P., Molz, J.G., Mcintosh, A., Lugosi, P. and Lashley, C. (2011) Theorizing hospitality, *Hospitality & Society* 1(1), 3–24.

Medlik, R. and Ingram, S. (2000) *The Business of Hotels*, Butterworth Heinemann, Oxford.

Muller, D. (2014) Progress in second home tourism research, Chapter 31 in Lew, A.L., Hall, C.M. and Williams, A.M. (eds) *The Wiley Blackwell Companion to Tourism*, Wiley, Chichester.

Parasuraman, A., Berry, L and Zeithaml, V. (1988) SERVQUAL: a multiple-item scale for measuring consumer perceptions of service quality, *Journal of Retailing* 64(1), 12–40.

Solnet, D. (2008) Supporting the contemporary tourism product: service management, pp. 307–343 in Cooper, C. and Hall, C.M. (eds) *Contemporary Tourism: An International Approach*, Elsevier Butterworth Heinemann, Oxford.

Solnet, D. (2015) Service management and tourism, pp. 91–128 in Cooper, C. *Contemporary Tourism Reviews, Volume 1*, Goodfellow, Oxford.

Major Case Study 8.1
The Accor Group – Leadership in Sustainability

Accor hotel with clear signing.
Source: © Newscast/Alamy Images

Introduction

Accor is one of the world's major international hotel chains. The company leads the sector in terms of its thinking and operations in sustainability. At Accor, sustainability is wired into key performance indicators, reporting and every aspect of the company's operation. It is not treated as an add-on or as 'greenwashing'. Accor's commitment to sustainability dates back to the mid-1990s, but it is the more recent initiatives and research which mark the company out as a leader in the field. These include a set of reports, toolkits and research which we summarise in this case study.

Accor aims to 'create a virtuous circle that benefits its ecosystem – comprising employees, customers, partners, local communities, in which hotels are implanted . . . creating value for its operations' (Accor, 2011a, p. 2). In other words, all stakeholders are involved, including hotel guests and suppliers which is essential if Accor is to reduce its environmental impact. But also, and perhaps more importantly, Accor is honest in its statement that it is involved in this field to boost its 'competitiveness'.

Accor established an Environment Department back in 1994. This is now the 'Sustainable Development Department', which:

- initiates sustainability projects for the Accor Group; and,
- assists in the implementation of sustainable development for both accommodation operations and support services (such as HR, purchasing or marketing) through communication of good practice and development of projects.

Accor has developed a coherent suite of tools for sustainability, each underpinned by research.

Charter 21 and PLANET 21 Management Tool and Reporting System

Charter 21 was introduced in 2005 when the Accor Hotels Environment Charter recommended 65 actions that Accor properties could utilise to reduce their environmental footprint. These actions included recycling glass, recovering rainwater or using eco-labelled products. The reporting side of Charter 21 was achieved by hotel managers providing an annual report of their Charter 21 actions.

As Accor's thinking developed, Charter 21 was updated in 2011 and became part of the new PLANET 21 strategy, reflecting the UN's 'Agenda 21' initiatives (see Chapter 6). This involved updating indicators for the 65 actions and the addition of items relating to social responsibility (for example, the use of fair trade products and the organisation of staff training on health and well-being). PLANET 21 is made up of seven pillars, with 21 commitments implemented by the company across 92 countries:

1. **Health**
   (a) Ensure healthy interiors
   (b) Promote responsible eating
   (c) Prevent diseases

2. **Nature**
   (a) Reduce water use
   (b) Expand waste recycling
   (c) Protect biodiversity

3. **Carbon**
   (a) Reduce energy use
   (b) Reduce CO_2 emissions
   (c) Increase use of renewable energy

4. **Innovation**
   (a) Encourage eco-design
   (b) Promote sustainable building
   (c) Introduce sustainable offers and technologies

5. **Local**
   (a) Protect children from abuse
   (b) Support responsible purchasing practices
   (c) Protect ecosystems

6. **Employment**
   (a) Support employee growth and skills
   (b) Make diversity an asset
   (c) Improve quality of work life

7. **Dialogue**
   (a) Conduct business openly and transparently
   (b) Engage franchised and managed hotels
   (c) Share commitment with suppliers

Earth Guest Research

In 2011, Accor released their ground-breaking research into the environmental footprint of its guests and the company – 'Earth Guest Research' – available for all to share. The research is the basis for communication to the rest of the industry and for training and e-learning modules, clearly demonstrating Accor's leadership in this field. Two reports were released:

1. *Sustainable Hospitality* is a study of guest attitudes to sustainability (Accor, 2011a). The key idea is to understand the impact of its guests from booking to checking out and beyond. There are four key research findings:

   (a) All hotel guests feel concerned by sustainable development.
   (b) High expectations concerning concrete actions in four areas – energy, water, waste and child protection.

   (c) Guests consider themselves an essential link in the chain of sustainable development.
   (d) Hotel guests declare they are ready to act and change their behaviour.

2. *The Accor Group's Environmental Footprint* is a multi-criteria life-cycle analysis (Accor, 2011b). The study set out to assess the impact of the Accor group on the environment and, by focusing on the total life-cycle, it looks back to the impact of suppliers – such as dairy farms – on the environment. There are three key findings:

   (a) Carbon and energy are the first pointers for progress for the group.
   (b) Food purchases account for most of the water consumed and contaminated.
   (c) Building sites are a critical link in the waste production chain.

In order to achieve and manage their environmental mission Accor have developed a suite of tools, reporting, audits and initiatives. These include the following.

The OPEN tool

The OPEN tool was released in 2005. It acts as an internal management tool for the Accor group's hotel managers allowing them steer the implementation of PLANET 21, track changes in energy and water use and manage waste production. For the Sustainable Development Department the OPEN tool allows them to have a global picture of sustainability metrics across the group.

Environmental data external audit

In 2007 Accor initiated an external audit of their environmental data and also its level of reporting to see if improvements could be made. The audit examined monitoring of Charter 21 activities and led to the integration of a sustainable development component in Accor's quality audits. From then on, the audits were expanded to cover water and energy consumption data, greenhouse gas emissions and social information.

ACT-HIV initiative

Also in 2007, Accor launched an international programme to fight HIV/AIDS, for use by hotel managers.

The Environmental Sustainable Development Reporting Protocol

Accor developed a Sustainable Development Reporting Protocol in 2008 to allow them to 'clarify and improve' the organisation of environmental and social information.

Innovation

The sustainability initiatives and research outlined above have allowed Accor to be an innovator in sustainability in many ways:

- establishing hotel refurbishment and construction standards;
- renewable energy and solar panel initiatives;

- installation of low-energy light bulbs;
- tree planting schemes;
- water flow regulators;
- fair trade practices; and
- organic waste composters.

DISCUSSION QUESTIONS

1. How would you communicate Accor's leadership in sustainability to a hotel guest in the property?

2. Why do you think Accor has invested so much in research and development for sustainability?

3. How would you communicate the environmental imperative to a small family run guest house?

Sources:
Accor (2011a) *Sustainable Hospitality: Ready to Check in*, Accor, Paris.
Accor (2011b) *The Accor Group's Environmental Footprint*, Accor, Paris.
Accor (2013) *The Planet 21 Programme*, Accor, Paris.
www.accorhotels.com/gb/sustainable-development/index.shtml

CHAPTER 9
INTERMEDIARIES

Learning Outcomes

This chapter considers intermediaries – tour operators and travel agents – as a key element of the tourism distribution channel and of the tourism sector. The chapter is designed to provide you with:

- an understanding of the role and behaviour of distribution channels in tourism;

- clarity on the role of intermediaries – tour operators and travel agents – in the distribution channel;

- an appreciation of the role and significance of integration within the distribution channel;

- an understanding of the way that technology has re-engineered the tourism distribution channel; and

- insights into the future of intermediaries.

Photograph: Singapore tourist information centre, Orchard Road, Singapore
© Maximilian Weinzierl/Alamy Images

Introduction

In the past, distribution was the unglamorous part of tourism but is now seen as critical to the profitability and competitiveness of both organisations and destinations. Distribution forms the 'place' aspect of the classic 4 Ps of the marketing mix (see Chapter 13). Yet for tourism, distribution is so critical because the consumer is physically distant from the product itself. Distribution therefore acts to link supply and demand, producer and consumer, and to allow the consumer to obtain information about a product and to book it. In other words, it provides *access* to the product and *facilitates* its purchase. The distribution process is achieved through channels – the means by which the tourism product is delivered to the customer. The distribution channel in tourism can be complex, involving a number of organisations and stages. Typically the channel will involve:

- a tourism supplier such as an airline or hotel;
- a tour operator who buys in bulk and packages together elements of supply;
- a travel agent acting as a point of sale; and
- the customer.

Here, the elements of supply represent the 'core' tourism products of transport, accommodation and attractions and these are distributed by 'intermediaries'. Intermediaries include tour operators or wholesalers, travel agents and increasingly 'eIntermediaries', as the Internet has changed the traditional supply chain pattern significantly.

Tourism Distribution Channels

Models and diagrams of tourism distribution channels tend to show single direction transactions, outward from suppliers to the consumer (see Figure 9.1). This, however, masks just how complex the relationships can be between the various players in the channel. In reality, distribution channels in tourism are complex behavioural systems with many different products and segmented markets (Pearce, 2007). This means, as Pearce and Schott (2010) stress, that we should take a broader view of tourism distribution by considering not only the needs of tourism suppliers and intermediaries, but also the needs of the tourists themselves. Li and Petrick (2008) take this further, stating that the role of distribution in the service dominant logic paradigm of marketing should focus on transactions, the consumer and the complex networks of consumers and suppliers (see Chapter 13). This is captured in Stern and El-Ansary's (1992) comprehensive view of a channel as:

'sets of interdependent organisations involved in the process of making a product or service available for use or consumption'.

They go on to say that channels both satisfy and stimulate demand:

'therefore channels should be viewed as an orchestrated network that creates value for the user or consumer through the generation of form, possession, time and place utilities' (pp. 1–2).

For tourism we can modify this definition to define a distribution channel as:

'An operating structure, system or linkages of various combinations of travel organisations through which a producer of travel products describes and confirms travel arrangements to the buyer' (Goeldner and Ritchie, 2009, p. 182).

What is clear from this discussion is that we cannot ignore the end user in the distribution process – the tourist. Indeed, technology is transforming the role of the intermediary from being an agent of the *supplier*, to being an agent of the *tourist*, as we see later in this chapter. Distribution after all is one part of the marketing mix and the starting point for the mix is to identify the target market of consumers. Ultimately, it is the consumer who determines the level of service required – for example, do they require simply a booking service, or a full travel counselling service? Understanding customer needs is therefore critical to a successful distribution strategy in a service industry such as tourism. Baby boomers, generation X and generation Y will each require a different level of service from the members of the distribution channel and channel members therefore have to design their strategy accordingly.

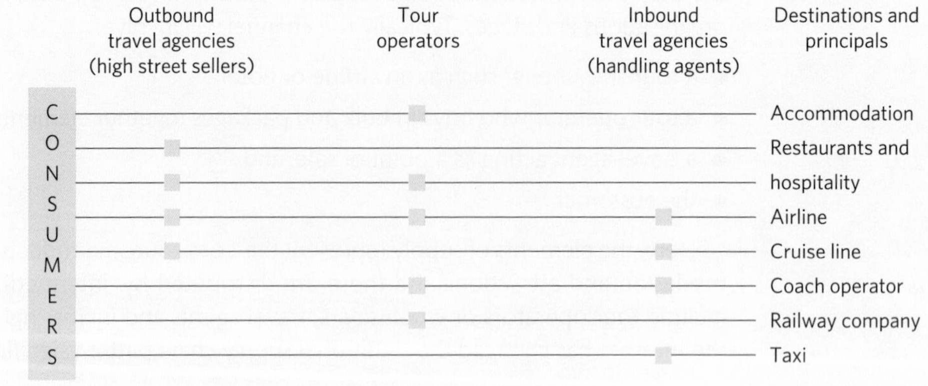

Figure 9.1 Tourism distribution mechanisms
Source: Buhalis and Laws, 2001; Page and Connell, 2009

Distribution Strategy, Power and Relationships

The fact that the tourism product is both a service and is distant from the consumer has two important implications:

1. the product is a service and cannot be stored – intermediaries such as travel agents therefore do not hold any stock; and
2. intermediaries therefore have no reason to be loyal to a particular supplier and can therefore be influential in the purchase – the intermediary is not impartial.

Tourism organisations face a number of choices in their distribution strategy. Here, it is important that distribution conforms to the overall objectives of the marketing strategy and ties in with other elements of the marketing mix. We would not, for example, expect mass-market inclusive tours to be sold through highly exclusive retail outlets. Mill and Morrison (1985) outline three basic distribution options for a supplier:

1. **intensive** – where the plan maximises exposure of the product through all available channels;
2. **exclusive** – where a limited number of channels are chosen to distribute the product, carefully mapping onto the supplier's marketing strategy; and
3. **selective** – where a combination of the two above approaches is adopted; not every channel is used but instead a wide selection of appropriate channels are chosen, often targeting particular market segments.

As we have already seen, there are a number of players in the distribution channel each of whom play a particular role, but all of whom are dependent upon each other. This has led to both conflict and cooperation in the channel. In tourism, in the past, channel relationships were adversarial, with members striving to gain market share and channel power from other members. Tour operators, for example, had an adversarial relationship with hoteliers in terms of squeezing them on price. Kotler *et al.* (2014) term this 'vertical conflict' in the channel, whilst 'horizontal conflict' occurs between channel members at the same level – for example, between travel agents vying for market share. Of course, this conflict can be viewed as healthy competition but, increasingly, channel members have realised the importance of striving towards the same objectives in the channel, as the final case study in this chapter shows. Channel members are dependent upon each other for success and any change by one reverberates through the channel; this means that the selection of partners in the channel has to be carefully done. For example, a tour operator selecting a travel agent would use a variety of criteria, including economic considerations. Equally, considerations of control are important if a franchise operation is being considered (Kotler *et al.*, 2014). Finally, channel members are dependent upon the overall health and competitiveness of their destinations. The next case study showcases an innovative organisational model to achieve both commercial success and conservation of the destination.

Mini Case Study 9.1
Red Travel Mexico

Introduction

The conflict between commercial tour operators and nature conservation is well known. The tour operator Red Travel Mexico has tackled this issue head on by combining commerce with not-for-profit conservation projects. As such, Red Travel Mexico is a contemporary tour operator, distinguished by its innovative organisational structure, and focus on sustainability and community. The organisation was founded in 2009 and set up as a hybrid social enterprise that combines a commercial tour operation company with a not-for-profit organisation providing training, small business incubation and assistance to rural communities in north-west Mexico. The website states that objectives of Red Travel Mexico are to:

- create sustainable employment alternatives;
- generate direct benefits for conservation and natural resource management; and
- drive tourism development in Mexico towards more sustainable models.

Conservation Projects

Red Travel Mexico sees 'travel as a vehicle for change' (http://redtravelmexico) and uses its projects to implement change in its destinations in north west Mexico. The company 'links community development with wildlife and habitat conservation . . . going *beyond* sustainability to regeneration of habitat, communities, traditions and culture' (http://redtravelmexico). Red Travel Mexico's projects include:

- Two projects working with Mexico's Commission for Natural Protected Areas:
  - Integrating tourism into sensitive natural areas through communication and interpretation for visitors, visitor management regimes, and increasing the awareness of natural parks and protected areas amongst other tour operators.
  - Creating tourism products and guide training in the Cabo Pulma National Park and Espiritu Santo Biosphere Reserve.
- Monitoring sea turtles and reducing impacts in Magdelena Bay by recruiting and training local fisher conservationists as an alternative employment strategy. This is funded through trip fees and donations and clearly places the stewardship of the bay with the local fishermen.
- Providing training for SMEs in conservation areas. Most tourism businesses in these areas are SMEs and lack the expertise to implement sustainable forms of tourism.
- Creating a sustainable tourism corridor along the coastal zone of the Sierra la Giganta range. This creates sustainable tourism opportunities for those whose living has depended on the land and the sea, and will attempt to stem the loss of culture and tradition caused by young people leaving the region for work.
- Training urban women to become tour guides to provide a sustainable alternative form of employment. This provides the women with skills and the opportunity to open their own guiding business.
- Developing an experiential curriculum for local youth to understand the human and nature connections in the Sierra de la Laguna biosphere reserve.

Through these projects Red Travel Mexico has trained individuals in the principles of small business management and sustainability, assisted rural communities to access government funding and raised funding from travellers for community projects.

DISCUSSION QUESTIONS

1. The hybrid of a tour operator and social enterprise organisation seems a smart solution to many issues of tourism and the environment. Do you think it would work in other destinations outside Mexico?

2. Visit Red Travel's website. Do you feel that the tourism products they offer are in harmony with their mission?

3. Red Travel's projects are based on providing sustainable alternative employment to, say, fishing or agriculture – are such alternative jobs really *sustainable*?

Source:
http://redtravelmexico

Table 9.1 The basis of power in the distribution channel

Sales and profit	Increased sales of a tour operator's products through a specific travel agent or their network means that the agent can place pressure on the operator for greater commission.
Role performance	Agents will favour those operators who regularly communicate and build a business-to-business relationship.
Specific assets	Tour operators who invest in IT systems and install them in favoured travel agents will 'lock in' those agents to their sales.
Trust	The greater the degree of trust that develops between organisations in the channel, the more likely it is that favourable financial deals will be done.

Source: Ujma, 2001

Power in the channel is exercised when the actions of one channel member leads to a change in behaviour of another. Each player in the channel has a 'base' of power that is exercised by their size, ownership of other members of the channel or contractual relationships (Ujma, 2001). Some channel members are so powerful that they are known as 'channel leaders' who formulate policy for the complete channel (Table 9.1). This has led Mill and Morrison (1985) to define three types of channel on the basis of power:

1. **consensus** – no member exercises power over another – instead they work together for common good;
2. **vertically integrated** – producers and retailers are owned by the same organisation or managed by them; and
3. **vertically coordinated** – where members are related through a contract or franchise arrangement rather than ownership.

Finally, as we will see in this chapter, there are two basic approaches to understanding distribution channels – the economic approach and the behavioural approach (Ujma, 2001). The economic approach covers transactions and the costs and benefits of distribution, whilst the behavioural approach looks at how organisations within the channel behave, their relationships and how they compete for channel power.

Intermediaries

It is important to recognise the importance of intermediaries and intermediation in the tourism distribution channel. Intermediaries include tour operators who bundle together two or more elements of supply (say an airline seat and accommodation) and sell it to the public. Suppliers and tour operators are known as 'principals'. Because it is not practical for a principal to have a sales office in every city in the world, they use a second type of 'intermediary' to access the market – travel agents. Agents are found in the high street and in cyberspace and are paid commission for sales. According to Fyall and Wanhill (2008), the roles played by intermediaries in the distribution channel include:

- making markets by matching buyers and sellers;
- transferring risk owned by a supplier, such as a hotel, say, to a tour operator who purchases their hotel bedstock in bulk;
- reduction of marketing costs for the principal by finding buyers and communicating with the marketplace;
- ability to pass on knowledge and price advantage;

- acting as a one stop shop for many products for the consumer;
- acting as a cheaper source of products because intermediaries can negotiate and purchase in bulk and pass on the savings; and
- helping improve the competitiveness of destinations who leverage from the intermediary's extensive marketing network – there is a danger here, however, as destinations can become overly dependent upon, say, tour operators to deliver tourists and so lose control of their own markets, as has been the case for some Mediterranean islands.

Intermediaries: Tour Operators

The nature of the tourism product as a fragmented set of services has created an important role for tour operators, bridging elements of supply with the consumer. Effectively, tour operators bundle together two or more elements of supply and sell them for a single price. They make contracts in bulk with hotels, airlines and ground transport companies and assemble them into 'inclusive tours' communicated to the market through print brochures or the Internet. Tour operators therefore act as 'wholesalers', as they are known in North America, passing on the savings to the traveller that they have made by contracting in bulk. Their core product is the inclusive tour, assembled by the operator, easy to purchase, competitively priced and distributed traditionally through travel agents but increasingly via the Internet.

Tour operators are historically significant to tourism and have shaped the way that the industry has developed. Most commentators agree that the historic roots of tour operation date back to Thomas Cook's UK tours in the nineteenth century, later followed by his expansion internationally. However, it was after 1945 that tour operation really came into its own, responding to pent-up demand for holidays and taking advantage of the availability of cheap air travel.

Types of Tour Operator

It is possible to classify tour operators in a number of ways, though the most basic distinction is between domestic, outbound and inbound operators:

- **Domestic operators** tend to focus on particular markets such as the youth/student market or the elderly, and upon particular tour formats such as coach holidays, city breaks and short break holidays.
- **Outbound operators** have grown substantially since 1945, taking advantage of the growth in demand for international travel. They normally package together flights, accommodation and transfers into a well-tried inclusive tour format. Initially focused on the short-haul market, outbound operators are increasingly expanding into long-haul travel. The incentive here is that long-haul tours tend to have a high yield as opposed to the low yield for short-haul.
- **Inbound operators** are often overlooked yet they play a significant role for the destination. They tend to contract transfers, accommodation and attractions/events and are normally appointed by a tour operator or organisation to handle ground-based aspects of a tour. They are often small operators with substantial destination-based expertise (Buhalis, 2001).

We can also classify operators by the type of transport they use (such as rail-based operators), by accommodation type such as, say, villa holidays, by market segment (for example, the elderly), by type of tourism such as adventure specialists, or by particular destinations. These specialist operators have more flexibility in their operations and can command higher prices. Other types of tour operator include brokers and consolidators who purchase air tickets in bulk and distribute them at a substantial discount, often working closely with airlines to sell off excess capacity.

Regulation and the Consumer

The knife-edge economics of tour operation, dealt with below, has led to a number of high-profile company failures. These failures have stranded tourists overseas and meant that many prospective travellers have lost money. In response, the tour operation sector has been the subject of significant government legislation to protect the consumer. In Europe, legislation developed in the 1960s and took the form of government bonding schemes. In the UK, this was managed by the Civil Aviation Authority (www.caa.co.uk/) and the trade association, the Association of British Travel Agents (ABTA) (www.abta.com/). This was followed by intervention by the European Commission in 1990 with an extensive piece of consumer protection legislation, the Package Travel Directive. The Package Travel Directive is not simply a response to the economics of tour operation, however. It recognises the rise of the empowered consumer and sets standards of quality and operation against which operators are measured. This recognises that relationships within the distribution channel are changing and that the consumer is gaining channel power. In the USA, tour wholesaling industry associations dealing with these issues include the National Tour Association (NTA – www.ntaonline.com/) and the US Tour Operators Association (USTOA – www.ustoa.com/).

Tour Planning and Economics

It is important to understand the economics of tour operation as this has driven developments in the industry. For all but the specialist operators, inclusive tours are sold in high volume and competitively on price. This means that the profit per passenger tends to be very small because competition keeps profit margins low, and so bearing down upon costs and efficient capacity utilisation are critical to success.

The economics of tour operation is based upon the marginal cost principle. Once the fixed costs of offering the tour are covered by revenue, then each extra passenger above this 'break even' point is almost pure profit. For any tour, fixed costs are high and will include accommodation and transport costs. Once these have been covered for the tour, then the cost to the operator of carrying an extra passenger is simply the variable cost associated with that person – say the airline meal. Clearly, the reverse applies, for every passenger below break-even the operator makes a substantial loss (Table 9.2). It is these 'knife edge' economics that have led to failures in the tour operation sector.

The economics of tour operation has a number of implications for how the industry operates. These include:

- The adoption of yield management to facilitate constant changes in pricing which allows operators to combat the trend to late booking, dump late unsold capacity and achieve the best possible price for each tour.
- Effective capacity management and utilisation of aircraft to achieve high load factors. Here, operators reserve the right to consolidate flights as the fixed capacity of planes means that demand is lumpy. The Boeing 737 is often viewed as the ideal size of aircraft to provide flexibility in tour operation.
- Tour prices are competitive and have to be set for each market, to cover costs, achieve a return on investment and match competitors. Here, the fact that some tours will be more profitable than others means that operators allocate their overheads across their whole portfolio of tours rather than by individual tours. Operators can also charge additional supplements for elements of the tour, such as single rooms. Other pricing decisions include differential pricing for the low and shoulder season as well as pricing by market segments such as for the elderly, the youth market or group travel.

Table 9.2 Mass market tour operator pricing

Mass-market operator pricing	£
Flight costs, based on 25 departures (back to back) on Boeing 737 148-seat aircraft at £14,750 per flight:	368,750
Plus one empty leg each way at beginning and end of the season: (a) out	7,375
(b) home	7,375
Total flight costs:	383,500
Cost per flight:	15,340
Cost per seat at 90% occupancy (133 seats), i.e. £15,340 ÷ 133	115.34
Plus air charges (air passenger duty, passenger service charges):	23.00
Net hotel cost per person, 14 nights half board:	225.80
Resort agent's handling fees and transfers, per person:	7.00
Gratuities, porterage:	1.00
Total cost per person:	372.14
Add mark-up of approx. 30% on cost price to cover agency commission, marketing costs (including brochure, ticket wallet etc.), head office administrative costs and profit:	111.64
Selling price: say	485.00

Source: The Business of Tourism (Holloway, J.C. and Taylor, N. 2006) © Pearson Education Limited 1983, 2002, 2006

- Use of the Internet and reservation systems means that operators can bypass traditional travel agent intermediaries, saving on commission and providing more flexibility on pricing.
- Operators can also boost their profitability by hedging on foreign exchange.

Planning an inclusive tour can take 18 months to two years (as shown in Table 9.3). Whilst the core inclusive tour product has not changed for over a hundred years, aspects of the planning process have changed substantially. This is very true for the issue of seasonality, and how operators communicate and distribute to the market.

- **Seasonality.** Given the importance of capacity utilisation, any seasonal variations in demand will damage an operator's profitability. The European market, for example, is highly seasonal compared to the long-haul market, with prices varying by up to one third between peak and low season. In the immediate post-war period operators were dominantly operating in the summer season and so created a demand for winter sun to utilise their spare capacity. This has since been supplemented by sophisticated market segmentation and product development to ensure year round operation.
- **Communication and distribution.** Until the 1980s, the norm was for tour operators to have an expensive and comprehensive brochure for their products and to distribute through the high street retail travel agent. Technology, however, has changed these practices substantially. Tour operators' brochures are usually full colour representations of their product portfolio and therefore expensive. Today, the Internet allows operators to significantly cut the costs of the printed brochure and also provides a much more flexible means of communicating with the market. It is, for example, easy to post price changes. In many ways, the operators' websites can communicate the same features as a brochure. As Holloway and Taylor (2006) demonstrate, the brochure or website must show visual

Table 9.3 Typical timescale for planning a summer tour programme

Research/ planning	Year 1	Summer	First stages of research. Look at economic factors influencing the future development of package tours. Identify likely selection of destinations.
		September/ December	Second stages of research. In-depth comparison of alternative destinations.
	Year 2	January	Determine destinations, hotels and capacity, duration of tours, departure dates. Make policy decision on size and design of brochure, number of brochures to print, date for completion of print.
Negotiation		February/March	Tenders put out for design, production and printing of brochures. Negotiate with the airlines for charter flights. Negotiate with hotels, transfer services, optional excursion operators.
		April/May	Typesetting and printing space booked with printer, copy for text commissioned. Illustrations commissioned or borrowed. Early artwork and text under development at design studio, with layout suggestions. Contracts completed with hotels and airlines, transfer services, etc.
		June	Production of brochure starts.
Administration		July	Determine exchange rates. Estimate selling prices based on inflation etc. Galley proofs from printer, corrections made. Any necessary reservations staff recruited and trained.
		August	Final tour prices to printer. Brochures printed and reservations system established.
Marketing		September/ October	Brochure on market, distribution to agents. Initial agency sales promotion, including launch. First public media advertising, and trade publicity through press, etc.
	Year 3	January/March	Peak advertising and promotion to trade and public.
		February/April	Recruitment and training of resort representatives, etc.
		May	First tour departures.

Source: The Business of Tourism (Holloway, J.C. and Taylor, N. 2006) © Pearson Education Limited 1983, 2002, 2006

images of the resort and accommodation, describe the product with dates and departures, show the prices and provide terms and conditions.

Operators are also questioning the value of the retail travel agent as we see below. This is because technology has provided an alternative. Of course, many operators still utilise retail agents as part of their distribution strategy. Here, operators are conscious to keep distribution costs down by carefully selecting their agents and rewarding the productive ones.

Intermediaries: Travel Agents

Travel agents act as a distributor of individual elements of tourism supply or inclusive tours. For principals, they act as a convenient network of sales outlets, whilst for the public they provide advice and a location for booking products, saving the consumer search time and money. As intermediaries, they do not carry stock and act for principals such as airlines or tour operators. Travel agents therefore simply make products from tourism suppliers available and so are cheap to establish and, unless they are part of a larger organisation, they carry no loyalty to any particular supplier. This is unusual in other distribution channels. Agents carry a large range of products including tours, tickets, currency, insurance, accommodation, and tickets for attractions.

Traditional high street travel agents are having to reinvent themselves.
Source: © Bigred/Alamy Images

The history of travel agents has many parallels with tour operators. They too have a long and influential pedigree, dating back to the late nineteenth century and they developed quickly following the advent of air travel: airlines needed a network of sales offices, whilst the main modes of travel before them – shipping and rail – had city centre terminals and offices and no need of travel agents.

Types of Travel Agent

Travel agents can be clearly classified into three main types:

1. Leisure travel agents tend to be located in the high street because location is critical to this very competitive market where high turnover is needed to generate profit. This sector of the agency market has been subject to substantial concentration through take-overs and mergers as we explore further below. They also demonstrate the benefits of integration in the channel with many owned outright by mass-market tour operators.

2. Business travel agents such as American Express tend to be located in cities or close to concentrations of industry such as industrial estates or universities. Some agencies also 'in-plant' themselves within large companies to provide an exclusive service. This travel agency sector tends to be specialised and demanding and is changing as e-tickets have become the norm for airlines and the traditional role of the agent is bypassed.

3. The home-based independent is a rapidly growing sector in North America where the key success factor is product knowledge. A dedicated qualification – the certified travel counselor (CTC) – is now available for this sector.

Regulation and Industry Bodies

As travel intermediaries, agents are subject to extensive government control and bonding. In many Asian countries, for example, agents have to be registered with the relevant government department. In the UK, both travel agents and tour operators have a strong industry association – ABTA. ABTA pioneered and now manages the fund established by government to protect consumers in the event of the failure of an agent or operator. In the USA, the American Society of Travel Agents (ASTA) represents the sector and is the largest industry association for travel agents in the world, promoting professional standards, acting as an information resource and lobbying on behalf of the industry (www.asta.org/).

Economics and Trends

For mass-market travel agents operating in the leisure sector, turnover has to be high because the profit margin on each transaction is very small. We show the operating costs of a typical European independent travel agency operation in Table 9.4. The table shows that, in terms of costs, staffing takes up a significant proportion, which underlines the importance of investment in good training. For business travel and the more specialist agencies, margins are higher.

Table 9.4 Hypothetical operating costs of an independent travel agency

Sales		1,500,000	
Gross profit (commission at average 9.4%)		141,000	
Expenditure			
Personnel			
Salaries, NHI, pensions	60,000		
Staff travel, training, subscriptions	3,000		
		63,000	(44.68%)
Establishment			
Rent, rates, water	22,000		
Light and heat	3,000		
Insurance	2,000		
Cleaning	1,300		
		28,300	(20.07%)
Administration			
Computers, telephone, website	10,000		
Postage	2,000		
Printing & stationery	2,000		
Hire of equipment	1,000		
Advertising and publicity	4,000		
Publications, timetables	1,000		
		20,000	(14.18%)
Financial and legal			
Credit cards	3,500		
Bank charges	1,500		
Auditing and accounting	4,000		
Legal fees	500		
Bad debts	500		
		10,000	(7.09%)
Depreciation and amortization		4,600	(3.26%)
Total operational costs		125,900	(89.29%)
Net profit before tax		15,100	(10.71%)
			100.00%
	Note: net profit as % of sales		(1.01%)

Source: The Business of Tourism (Holloway, J.C. and Taylor, N. 2006) © Pearson Education Limited 1983, 2002, 2006

Economics have driven the shape of development of the travel agency sector. The fact that the tourism distribution channel is so dependent on intermediaries such as agents has meant that it is vulnerable to external factors such as the development of the Internet. Travel agents in particular have found that many of their traditional functions are being replaced by eIntermediaries or by principals going direct to the public with their own websites. Innovations in the tourism sector such as the web-based operation of low-cost airlines (see Chapter 10) has accelerated this trend as the consumer is actively discouraged from booking in any other way than through the airline's own website. It is also true that principals are constantly seeking ways to reduce their costs, and cutting out intermediaries and either reducing or capping their commission is one way to do this. It also allows principals to control their communication with their customers.

As a result, travel agents have had to reinvent their role in the channel. This is happening in a number of ways. For example, the home-based independent role in North America is based upon specialist advice to the consumer, advice that is difficult to extract from the chaos of the Internet. At the same time, traditional agents are establishing their own eIntermediary operations and with the concept of 'dynamic packaging' (dealt with below) they can also become tour operators and develop a new income stream. Agents are also re-engineering their processes in order to update their offering, improve customer satisfaction and remain competitive. This re-engineering will involve consideration of customer relationship management and their gradual integration with loyalty schemes (Buhalis, 2003). Of course, reinventing travel agencies may require new staff skills and competencies, and as the role becomes more demanding, pay and training will have to be enhanced. At the end of the day, travel agencies will have to provide added value to the consumer to survive.

Integration in the Distribution Channel

The difficult economics of intermediaries, allied to the fact that the distribution channel comprises many different organisations, has led channel members to forge close alliances. These alliances allow organisations to control the costs of distribution as, typically, distribution is an activity external to the organisation, performed by intermediaries for a fee. By integrating with other organisations in the channel through ownership or contracting, these costs can be minimised. Effectively, this internalises the otherwise 'external' distribution cost to the organisation.

This process is known as 'integration', an economic concept to describe formal linking arrangements between one organisation and another. Not only does integration reduce distribution costs, but it also allows enterprises to be in control of how their product is represented and to more closely match distribution channels to particular market segments. In an increasingly competitive marketplace, integration has become one way to be more efficient and to compete. We are also beginning to see integration across international boundaries, particularly as trading blocs such as the European Union harmonise regulations. The Internet is, however, reducing some advantages of integration because it has reduced the number of links in the channel and so the cost saving is lower. We can think of integration as either horizontal or vertical within the channel.

Horizontal Integration

Horizontal integration occurs when alliances are forged between enterprises of similar type in the channel, for example a tour operator links with another tour operator. This has been common in both the tour operator and travel agency sector for the simple reason of gaining economies of scale through increasing size. This creates large organisations within the channel who command channel power, buying power and deliver cost efficiencies because they can (i) sell more units and (ii) the fixed costs of each unit are correspondingly lower. A further benefit can be to extend the geographical reach of, say, a travel agency chain by merging with one in another region or country, developing powerful branding to gain market profile and deliver quality assurance. There are clear benefits of increased size for organisations within the channel:

- securing supplies and increasing buying power – for example, larger retail agency chains can leverage better commission from principals, and principals, too, often prefer to deal with larger organisations;
- increased market profile and presence;
- increased geographical representation;
- assured consumer confidence through quality control of processes;
- greater investment capability and revenue streams;
- higher Internet traffic and lower customer acquisition costs; and
- improved yield per transaction.

Vertical (Diagonal) Integration

Vertical integration occurs when an enterprise within the channel links along the production process with an enterprise closer to suppliers (backward integration), or closer to the market (forward integration). For example, a tour operator may purchase a hotel chain or an airline in an example of backward integration in a bid to secure supply and reduce contracting costs. On the other hand, a tour operator may purchase a travel agency chain to secure sales as an example of forward integration to the market. These linkages can take place in the form of ownership, contracts, alliances or franchising. The benefits of vertical integration are similar to those of horizontal integration – economies of scale, securing supply and internalising costs that would otherwise go to an external organisation. There are also benefits through enhanced channel power. Holloway and Taylor (2006), for example, speak of 'directional selling' where travel agents give preference to the sale of products of their parent tour operator.

Reactionary Strategies

Of course, because of the creation of larger organisations within the channel through integration, other channel members become vulnerable and have to devise defensive strategies. There are a number of strategies that have been devised to counter the threat of large organisations exercising channel power:

- The small size of independent travel agencies means that they risk loss of market share and so, in response, have grouped together to form consortia in order to strengthen their negotiation power in the distribution channel. This is often facilitated by trade associations such as ASTA and ABTA.
- Independent agents can also adopt strategies of differentiation through niche marketing and specialising in particular markets or destinations, enhancing service to consumers through, say, travel counselling and an ability to deal with barriers that increase with consolidation, most notably in the form of price wars.
- 'Dynamic packaging' is an option for smaller agents and operators, where they allow consumers to assemble their own packages using flexible elements of supply.

- Destinations, too, are concerned about the domination of the channel by large organisations, not only because it gives them enhanced bargaining power with, say, a destination's hotels, but also because it removes control of marketing from the destination.

Whilst the consumer will benefit from the trend to integration within the channel, there is no doubt that it is impacting upon industry structure. Buhalis (2003), for example, suggests that the result will be a future where tour operators will fall into two distinct groups:

1. multinational, large and vertically integrated operators with economies of scale, wide distribution and a global network, taking a high-volume, low-profit approach; and

2. small, niche, differentiated operators focusing on particular destinations or products, taking a low-volume, high-profit approach.

And, of course, it will be technology that drives the future of intermediaries. Before turning to consider the impact of technology, the classic paper for this chapter by Dimitrios Buhalis provides a useful introduction.

Classic Paper
Buhalis, D. and Licata, M.C. (2002) The future of eTourism intermediaries, *Tourism Management* **23(3), 207–220**

This classic paper tackles one of the key issues facing the tourism sector in the first two decades of the twenty-first century, namely how information communication technologies impact upon the distribution process. We have already seen in this chapter that technology has initially led to a process of 'disintermediation' as the Internet has replaced the traditional functions of tour operators and travel agents. However, this classic paper examines the next stage of the process, the 're-intermediation' process as operators and agents reinvent themselves and define their core competencies.

The paper surveys expert opinion leaders in the UK about the future of etourism intermediaries, the new breed of companies that have moved into the tourism distribution channel. The survey found that 'the use of new distribution channels and the launch of value added services features across all ePlatforms and distribution channels [are] . . . the main factors affecting the competitiveness of all tourism intermediaries' (p. 218). In other words, the intermediaries have acted as an innovation that has impacted upon the total distribution channel and all its members. Even here, there are new eIntermediaries developing which are challenging the older model of eIntermediaries, particularly through the use of mobile commerce and interactive television and the convergence of these technologies with the Internet.

However, the survey did identify the fact that many of these newer eIntermediaries lack experience in tourism, do not have a robust business model and their links with suppliers are not secure. An issue here is that the investment needed is considerable and many do not expect to break even for four or five years, and as a result they need to quickly establish themselves and their brands in the marketplace and secure a significant level of bookings. Of course, building relationships with suppliers will be important, as many suppliers, such as the airlines, already have done. Finally, of course, it will be vital to deliver a personalised service and value to the customer, through building relationships online.

In terms of global distribution systems (GDS), the survey found that experts felt that they could become sophisticated hosts for inventory and connections between suppliers, and so will be enablers rather than intermediaries, supporting eIntermediaries rather than actually doing the booking. Other experts felt that a GDS also had the potential to serve the business market.

The paper concludes that 'flexible and dynamic eIntermediaries will use both old and new ePlatforms to survive and expand in the future . . . the only winner in the future will be the consumer' (p. 219).

Technology

The Internet influences every aspect of the contemporary tourism business and has changed the culture and behaviour of how people purchase, search and communicate (Buhalis and Soo, 2011). It connects companies, customers and governments at low cost and without constraints of time or space and as such is a paradigm-breaking marketing tool and a 'disruptive innovation'. This is because it has significant advantages over traditional communication media, such as reach, low cost, richness, speed of communication and interactivity. Significantly, technology has shifted power from suppliers and intermediaries to the tourist, facilitating access to information and the ability to manage reservations and itineraries.

As technology develops, it is having a profound impact upon how distribution channels operate in tourism, and how other elements of the marketing mix such as promotion and pricing are done. For the tourism sector, technology provides the opportunity for direct communication with customers and other channel members, as well as interactivity, massive data storage, processing power, speed of communication and the ability to build, track and maintain relationships. Technology also provides a medium for consumers to gather information, communicate with each other through social media and to make purchasing decisions.

Through technology, a new branch of tourism marketing has developed – E-marketing. E-marketing is ideally suited to tourism and has allowed the emergence and rapid development of electronic intermediaries. Specifically, technology has brought the following innovations to the channel:

- Information communication technologies (ICTs) facilitate the exchange of information that is critical in the distribution channel.

- For tour operators and suppliers, technology allows the development of online brochures that can deliver rich multimedia content, which blends text, images, sound and video into multimedia documents which deliver the ability to 'test drive' the product and overcomes its intangible nature.

- It allows suppliers to instantly change dates, prices and availability online so saving expensive brochure reprints.

- It delivers significant cost savings through the electronic processing of bookings (such as e-tickets and electronic confirmations) and other transactions, reducing labour costs and office space. This encourages suppliers and intermediaries to go 'paperless' and allows customised messages to facilitate relationship building with suppliers and customers.

- Electronic distribution works well for tourism where the product is fragmented and web portals allow companies to provide and deliver a dynamic assembly of all of the elements of the product (Expedia – www.expedia.com – is good example here).

- The Internet gives smaller suppliers such as independent hotels a degree of global market reach previously unheard of, and allows them to bypass the marketing muscle of intermediaries.

- It provides a powerful tool for an increasingly computer-literate consumer to search for and book tourism products. It also makes direct sales possible and gives power to the consumer to manipulate their own travel.

- It encourages customer-driven distribution through blogs and websites (www.tripadvisor.co.uk).

Buhalis (2003) confirms that a major impact of technology has been upon the tourism distribution channel:

> **'As a result of developing information marketplace and electronic commerce, new opportunities and challenges emerge. Although it is not clear who will be the final winners and losers of this process, it is quite apparent that the internet bridges the gap between consumers and suppliers and provides opportunities for dis-intermediation and re-intermediation' (p. 39).**

There is no doubt that electronic distribution has decimated traditional intermediaries such as 'bricks and mortar travel agents'. By 're-engineering' the channel, traditional power relationships are changing, with the role of intermediaries weakening and that of suppliers and the consumer strengthening. As a result, distribution channels have changed significantly since the 1990s with the growth of 'eTailing' and 'eIntermediaries' leading to 'dis-intermediation' (Buhalis 2003). In other words, technology has replaced the old way of distributing the tourism product with a 'merchant model' of suppliers, who can sell direct to the customer and control suppliers' inventory (Page and Connell, 2009). eIntermediaries do their business through powerful websites – Orbitz (www.orbitz.com), Expedia and Travelocity are examples here. The airlines soon followed this trend once the benefits became clear – low-cost airlines, for example, financially penalise customers who do not book on-line. The US airline Southwest Airlines was the first to develop a fully functioning website and e-tickets in the mid-1990s (www.southwest.com/).

However, as we saw above, tour operators and other intermediaries are responding to this threat by reinventing themselves. All members of the channel have had to redefine and evaluate their core competencies – tour operators, for example, now have the ability to 'dynamically package' the product and to deal directly with their customers, whilst travel agents increasingly act as travel counsellors or develop their own electronic presence (cyber-mediation).

Global Distribution Systems

An early development of technology in the channel was the 'global distribution system' – 'large and sophisticated travel reservation systems in use throughout the world' (Goeldner and Ritchie, 2009, p. 194). Global distribution systems (GDS) were the forerunner of Internet-based reservations and e-ticketing and have been hugely influential in the distribution channel. They were created in the post-war period when the major airlines developed their own automated 'computer reservation systems' (CRS), facilitated by the growth of the processing power of computing and transmission speed of communication technology. By the late 1970s, airlines began to share their systems with other suppliers offering a comprehensive range of services and products, and today airlines such as Air Canada are leaders in the field (www.aircanada.com/). They also installed terminals in travel agents' offices to ensure that their system was used. This saw the gradual shift from CRS to GDS and, as the systems have matured and merged, three major GDS have resulted – Amadeus (www.amadeus.com), Sabre (www.sabre.com/) and Travelport (www.travelport.com). These GDS have almost become markets in their own right and deliver significant benefits to suppliers and consumers (Buhalis, 2003):

- they provide easy access to products and information for consumers;
- they allow suppliers to manage their capacity and yield;
- they provide instant interactivity for intermediaries and suppliers; and
- they can be expanded into other services such as baggage handling and in-flight catering and entertainment.

For the future it will be interesting to see how the much more 'open' nature of the Internet relates to the 'closed' system of a GDS.

Constraints

Despite the obvious advantages of its use, technology does bring with it certain constraints when used in the distribution channel. For example, for the tourist trying to book a vacation, consumer technology skills are highly variable and many have concerns over the sheer chaos of and lack of quality standards on the Internet with doubts over the security of financial information and personal identity as well as question marks over the credibility of some websites such as those promoting individuals' second homes for rent. In addition, most websites are in English so creating a barrier to access, and in some countries access to the Internet comes at a high cost.

Yet, despite these issues, intermediaries have to embrace technology. The following case study showcases an innovative approach that also acts as a good link to the future of intermediaries.

Mini Case Study 9.2
Adventure Engine – an Innovative Web-based Intermediary

Introduction

Adventure Engine represents the future of intermediaries on the Internet. It has won many travel awards for its innovative approach to international travel technology and specialises in adventure and experiential travel. Adventure Engine is a sophisticated reservations system that offers a variety of products to both operators and travel agents. In so doing it provides the 'missing link' between adventure tourism industry providers and the market.

Adventure Engine

Adventure Engine runs a web-based system, which means that clients do not need new software or complicated systems. It is a good example of a company that has leveraged from contemporary approaches including networking across the industry and building strong relationships with both its industry and consumer clients. The company makes its industry knowledge as an adventure travel specialist available to clients through advice, training and planning. Its clients fall into three groups – tour operators, travel agents and communities.

Tour Operator Products

Adventure Engine offers reservation and booking engine solutions for all sizes of tour operator. The strength of the system is that it manages all aspects of the travel activity, saving staff time for the tour operator. This is especially valuable for small, niche operators.

The system works by loading trips and tours as basic packages. These tours range from simple day visits to complex multi-destination itineraries:

- The basic operation offers packages with set start and end times, a set minimum/maximum number of tourists per trip and a range of options to add to the base package. These include rentals, photo packages or extra hotel nights. Trips can have different prices by date and client type.

- The complex inventory operation is for more complicated trips which may include vehicles, a range of accommodation and rental equipment as might be used by adventure operators offering eco lodges, rafting or shipping trips.

Adventure Engine is also customised by size of tour operator with manual loading of the system for small operators or, for a larger company, the Adventure Engine system can interface directly with existing systems.

Each package includes reservation system, supplier accounts (including credit cards), shopping carts and unlimited distribution to agents and resellers. The system allows adventure tour operators to:

- grow their range of products without incurring high expenses;
- improve customer service through the range of services in the packages; and
- save administration time by cutting out multiple offices, dealing with enquiries and entering bookings.

Travel Agent Products

Adventure Engine allows agents to access its 'commission-ready adventure tours' and can install its own booking portal onto agents' websites.

Community Products

Adventure Engine also works with communities 'to maximize the potential of their tourism product and provide technology to members'. It offers consultation, strategic planning, industry knowledge presentations and well as technology and system implementation.

DISCUSSION QUESTIONS

1. Adventure Engine specialises in a niche product – adventure tourism. Do you think their approach is applicable more broadly across tourism?

2. Operating in the adventure travel market, Adventure Engine's market will be mainly small business. Does the reputation of SMEs as reluctant innovators pose a risk to Adventure Engine's future success?

3. Much of innovation in tourism – such as Adventure Engine – comes from outside of tourism, in this case from technology. Why do you think the tourism sector itself is slow to innovate?

Source:
www.adventureengine.com

Future Trends

The very nature of the distribution process in tourism means that it will always be under threat from somewhere. For example, the fact that enterprises are increasingly trying to control their distribution costs through, say, cuts in commission threatens agents, whilst innovation from outside the system – from the Internet or new forms of travel – stimulates change in the channel. Nonetheless, intermediaries have proved resilient as they reinvent themselves in the twenty-first century to cope with new trends. These trends include:

- Trends in tourism such as the development of the low-cost airline model where Internet bookings cut out intermediaries. We are also seeing an increase in independent travel and demand from the 'new tourist', which means that intermediaries have to be more responsive to customer needs and creative with their products.

- Trends in technology as eIntermediaries begin to outperform the overall market, threatening the more traditional intermediaries who have not kept ahead of technology. For example, the product planning cycle of traditional tour operators means that they cannot compete with the flexible and responsive model used by online operators. The trend towards eIntermediaries will also be reinforced as broadband expands across the world and other technologies such as mobile are adopted. Digital convergence will lead to overlapping and all-pervasive use of computer systems with other devices such as entertainment systems, tablets and mobile phones.

- Trends in consumer behaviour mean that intermediaries will need to be much more aware of different tourist segments and their needs, catering, for example, to the 'new tourist' who seeks a more individualised experience, flexibility and choice, and will opt for companies that behave in a sustainable and ethical way. Here, intermediaries will be able to create opportunities for added value, such as high levels of customer service by resort representatives. Of course, dynamic packaging also provides a tool to allow intermediaries to cater for and focus upon satisfying needs of the new tourist using sophisticated segmentation and tight quality control.

● Trends in corporate social responsibility will see intermediaries changing their behaviours to embrace sustainability, act responsibly towards destination communities and lock-in ethical behaviour and environmental audits with other suppliers in the distribution channel. Here, research has uncovered the 'hidden' greenhouse gas emissions of a standard European inclusive tour (Filimonau *et al.*, 2013). The end of chapter case study goes into this issue in more detail.

SUMMARY

Distribution is critical to the profitability and competitiveness of both tourism organisations and destinations. It forms the 'place' aspect of the classic 4 Ps of the marketing mix and for tourism is critical because the consumer is physically distant from the product itself. Distribution therefore acts to link supply and demand, producer and consumer, and to allow the consumer to obtain information about a product and to book it. The channel is a complex behavioural system with various players who vie for power. In tourism, distribution is performed dominantly by intermediaries. These are tour operators, who bundle the various parts of the tourism product together for sale to the consumer, and travel agents who provide points of sale in convenient locations for tour operators, airlines and other 'principals'. However, power in the tourism distribution channel has been redistributed by two developments: (i) integration within the channel which has created large powerful intermediaries; and (ii) the innovation of the Internet. The Internet provides a means for consumers to seek out tourism products and to make a reservation. As a result, traditional intermediaries have had to reinvent themselves as we saw with the case study on 'Adventure Engine'. Technology will drive the future of the travel distribution channel and intermediaries. They will need to be more consumer focused, demonstrate concern for destinations, as is shown by the case study on 'Red Travel Mexico', and adopt principles of corporate social responsibility, as we see in the end case study for this chapter, redefining their core competencies and function.

Discussion Questions

1. This chapter has stressed the significance of technology, and particularly the Internet. In class, draw up a checklist of the advantages and disadvantages that this brings to the tourism consumer.

2. Draft an Internet strategy for consideration by the board of a traditional 'bricks and mortar' travel agent.

3. Explain why integration in the distribution channel is a good thing for intermediaries, destinations and the tourism consumer.

4. Explain what is meant by 'dynamic packaging' and identify the main beneficiaries of the approach.

5. Write a newspaper article on 'the tour operator of 2020'.

Annotated Further Reading

1. Buhalis, D. and Soo, H.J. (2011) *Tourism and Technology,* Contemporary Tourism Reviews, Goodfellow, Oxford.
   A thorough and enlightening review of IT and tourism.

2. Buhalis, D. and Laws, E. (eds) (2001) *Tourism Distribution Channels: Practices, Issues and Transformations,* Continuum, London.
   A thorough edited volume covering the main aspects of tourism distribution.

3. Buhalis, D. (2003) *eTourism: Information Technology for Strategic Tourism Management,* Pearson Education, Harlow.
   A must-have book that provides thorough coverage of the development of E-intermediaries.

4. Fyall, A. and Wanhill, S. (2008) Intermediaries, pp. 372–403 in Cooper, C., Fletcher, J., Fyall, A. Gilbert, D. and Wanhill, S. (eds) *Tourism Principles and Practice,* Prentice Hall, Harlow.
   Solid coverage of tourism distribution channels.

5. Kotler, P., Bowen, J. and Makens, J. (2014) *Marketing for Hospitality and Tourism,* 6th edn, Pearson, Harlow.
   Classic text with excellent coverage of the principles and practice of tourism distribution.

6. Mill, R.C. and Morrison, A.M. (1985) *The Tourism System: An Introductory Text,* Prentice Hall, Englewood Cliffs, NJ.
   Early text with insightful analysis of distribution channels for tourism and how they operate.

7. Pearce, D. (2007) A needs-functions model of tourism distribution, *Annals of Tourism Research* **35**(1), 148–168.
   Excellent paper showing how channels can incorporate the needs of the consumer.

8. Pro-Poor Tourism (2004) International tour operators: roles, practices and implications for developing countries, Information sheet number 10, available at: www.propoortourism.org.uk/info-sheets.
   Paper analysing how developing countries can benefit from the actions of tour operators.

9. Stern, L.W. and El-Ansary, A. (1992) *Marketing Channels,* Prentice Hall, Englewood Cliffs, NJ.
   Classic and insightful text covering the generic aspects of distribution channels.

References Cited

Buhalis, D (2001) Tourism distribution channels: practices and processes, pp. 7–32 in Buhalis, D. and Laws, E. (eds) *Tourism Distribution Channels: Practices Issues and Transformations,* Continuum, London.

Buhalis, D. (2003) *eTourism: Information Technology for Strategic Tourism Management,* Pearson Education, Harlow.

Buhalis, D. and Laws, E. (eds) (2001) *Tourism Distribution Channels: Practices, Issues and Transformations,* Continuum, London.

Buhalis, D., and Soo, H.J. (2011) *Tourism and Technology,* Contemporary Tourism Reviews, Goodfellow, Oxford.

Filimonau, V., Dickinson, J., Robbins, D. and Reddy, V.M. (2013) The role of 'indirect' greenhouse gas emissions in tourism: assessing the hidden carbon impacts from a holiday package tour, *Transportation Research Part A: Policy and Practice* **54,** 78–91.

Fyall, A. and Wanhill, S. (2008) Intermediaries, pp. 372–403 in Cooper, C., Fletcher, J., Fyall, A. Gilbert, D. and Wanhill, S. (eds) *Tourism Principles and Practice,* Prentice Hall, Harlow.

Goeldner, C.R. and Brent Ritchie, J.R. (2009) *Tourism: Principles, Practices, Philosophies,* 11th edn, John Wiley & Sons, Hoboken, NJ.

Holloway, J.C. and Taylor, N. (2006) *The Business of Tourism,* Prentice Hall, Harlow.

Kotler, P., Bowen, J. and Makens, J. (2014) *Marketing for Hospitality and Tourism,* 6th edn, Pearson, Harlow.

Li, X. and Petrick, J.F. (2008) Tourism marketing in an era of paradigm shift, *Journal of Travel Research* **46,** 236–244.

Mill, R.C. and Morrison, A.M. (1985) *The Tourism System: An Introductory Text,* Prentice Hall, Englewood Cliffs, NJ.

Page, S. and Connell, J (2009) *Tourism: A Modern Synthesis,* Cengage, Andover.

Pearce, D. (2007) A needs-functions model of tourism distribution, *Annals of Tourism Research* **35**(1), 148–168.

Pearce, D. and Schott, C. (2010) Tourism distribution channels: the visitor's perspective, *Journal of Travel Research* **44,** 50–63.

Stern, L.W. and El-Ansary, A. (1992) *Marketing Channels,* Prentice Hall, Englewood Cliffs, NJ.

Ujma, D (2001) Distribution channels for tourism: theory and issues, pp. 33–52 in Buhalis, D. and Laws, E. (eds) *Tourism Distribution Channels: Practices Issues and Transformations,* Continuum, London.

Major Case Study 9.1
The Tour Operators' Initiative

Palma de Majorca sea front.
Source: © holbox/Shutterstock.com

Introduction

For intermediaries, corporate social responsibility (CSR) has added a new layer to their bottom line. Intermediaries, and particularly tour operators, recognise that they must be accountable for their impacts upon society, the environment and the economy. Corporate social responsibility is about customer satisfaction, looking after the workforce and environmental protection. Intermediaries are in a strong position to implement these concepts, as they are pivotal in the supply chain.

Until recently, however, the tourism supply chain was a combat zone with members vying for dominance. Not only was this an issue between companies, such as, say, accommodation providers and tour operators, but it was also an issue between tour operators and destinations themselves, with operators often seeing destinations as an asset to strip. Times are changing, however, with important initiatives to secure CSR, ethical behaviour and sustainable principles throughout the distribution channel. Indeed, it can be argued that the distribution channel is the perfect medium to communicate these messages to suppliers and integrate them into contracting practices. This case study outlines one such initiative.

Most tour operators recognise that a clean and safe environment is critical to their success. Fewer have the management tools or experience to design and conduct tours that minimise their negative environmental, social

and economic impacts while optimising their benefits. To develop and implement these tools in their own operations, and encourage other tour operators to do the same, a group of tour operators from different parts of the world have joined forces to create the *Tour Operators' Initiative for Sustainable Tourism Development*.

The Tour Operator's Initiative

Established in 2000, the Tour Operator's Initiative (TOI) is a voluntary, non-profit organisation open to all tour operators. In 2015 it merged with the Global Sustainable Tourism Council, representing the tour operator sector on the Council.

To quote their website:

> **'With this initiative, tour operators are moving towards sustainable tourism by committing themselves to the concepts of sustainable development as the core of their business activity and to work together through common activities to promote and disseminate methods and practices compatible with sustainable development'.**

The TOI has the support of the United Nations Environment Programme (UNEP), the United Nations Educational, Scientific and Cultural Organization (UNESCO) and the UNWTO, where the initiative is now based. It recognises that tour operators touch all parts of the value chain and that suppliers and destinations are the core of a tour opera-tor's product and that if those elements of the product are sustainable, then consumers will respond positively to their product. The approach has led to a range of benefits:

- cost savings through efficient and reduced consumption of water and power;
- increased revenues and shareholder value;
- repeat custom and new business from clients who value a responsible tourism approach;
- closer community relationships;
- a better image and reputation for tour operators;
- enhanced brand values; and
- reduced risk of conflict with destinations, governments and pressure groups.

As intermediaries, tour operators are unusual because unlike many other economic sectors, they directly influence the consumer's purchasing decision. They also have a major impact in the distribution channel through supplier con-tracting (of, say, airline seats or hotel beds). It is this unique nature of tourism distribution that allows it to be such an important medium for the dissemination of good practice.

The TOI Approach

TOI's mission is:

'To advance the sustainable development and manage-ment of tourism and to encourage tour operators to make a corporate commitment to sustainable development'.

Following the merger with the Global Sustainable Tourism Council and the Council's overt focus on destinations, the TOI has set out its next steps as:

1. establish and strengthen links with destination stakeholders;
2. engage in a transparent dialogue over the futures of their destinations with these stakeholders; and
3. establish a destination steering group to achieve the first two steps above.

The TOI's core programmes of activity include:

- **Promotion of socially responsible tourism develop-ment** through implementation of the Code of Conduct for the Protection of Children from Sexual Exploitation in Travel and Tourism.
- **Promotion of sustainable tourism development** by operating and marketing tourism in a sustainable manner to anticipate and prevent economic, environ-mental, social and cultural degradation of destinations. The TOI recognises that tourism can contribute to the viability of local economies and communities. Effectively integrating sustainability into the tour operators' busi-ness means considering environmental, social and eco-nomic aspects throughout the process of developing a holiday package. This is done through:
  - internal management;
  - product development and management;

- contracting with suppliers, by integrating sustaina-bility principles into the selection criteria and service agreements of suppliers;
  - customer relations, providing customers with infor-mation on responsible behaviour and sustainability issues at their destinations;
  - relationships with destinations; and
  - integrating sustainability principles into corporate policy and management systems, and monitoring and reporting on performance.
- **Public awareness and communication** among custom-ers towards the natural, social and cultural environment of the places they visit and encouragement for other intermediaries to adopt these values.
- **Sharing good practices** through publicising examples and cases of good practice to spread awareness of the role of tour operators towards sustainability.
- **Integrating sustainability into the supply chain** by influ-encing suppliers of tourism products to develop sustainable practices. The benefits of this are substantial and include:
  - lower costs through increased operating efficiency and reduced waste generation;
  - increased revenue and shareholder value by gener-ating more repeat business;
  - a strong positive reputation as a company results in increased customer satisfaction and loyalty, strengthened brand value, and enhanced publicity and marketing opportunities; and
  - reduced conflict with government and regulatory bodies.
- **Cooperation with destinations** that are, after all, the tour operators' core product. TOI recognises the need to work in partnership with all stakeholders at the destination and to agree a common way forward to promote sustainability.
- **Cooperation with the World Wide Fund for Nature (WWF)** to improve the management of protected areas, raise awareness about biodiversity and create a network of exemplary destinations.

DISCUSSION QUESTIONS

1. Why has this change in thinking amongst tour operators taken so long to emerge?
2. Draft the elements of sustainable practices that you might expect to see in a contract between a tour opera-tor and a hotel supplier.
3. Do you think that the 2015 merger of the TOI with the Global Sustainable Tourism Council will weaken the operation of the TOI?

Sources:
Tour Operators' Initiative (2003) *Sustainable Tourism: The Tour Operators' Contribution*, TOI, Paris.
www.toinitiative.org/
www.gstcouncil.org

CHAPTER 10
TRANSPORT

Learning Outcomes

This chapter considers transport for tourism as the element of the tourism system that links the market with the destination. The chapter outlines the general principles of transport before considering the various modes available to the tourist. The chapter is designed to provide you with:

- an understanding of the principles of transport for tourism;

- an awareness of the role of network analysis in transport for tourism;

- an appreciation of the public and private sector management principles of transport for tourism;

- an understanding of the components of a transport system for tourism; and

- an understanding of the various modes of transport available to the tourist.

Introduction

Tourism and transport are inseparable. Tourism is about being elsewhere and, in Leiper's tourism system, we can see that transport bridges the gap between origin and destination. As a result, tourism cannot happen without transportation, although there are many forms of transport that do not involve tourism – such as cargo operations, whilst others, such as, say, ferries in the Greek islands, are used by residents and local businesses as well as by tourists. When studying tourism, we need to consider transport for these reasons:

● In a historic sense, transport has developed hand-in-hand with tourism. Improvements in transport have stimulated tourism and, in turn, tourism demand has prompted transport developments such as the growth of low-cost carriers to serve the leisure market.

● Transport can be a tourism attraction in its own right, as, for example, with heritage railways or cruising, where two of the elements of Leiper's tourism system are combined and transport becomes the attraction. This illustrates that whilst transport is sometimes seen as secondary to tourism, in fact it should be integrated into the product – as, for example, with heritage railways.

● New transport provision can create new tourism demand as well as diverting demand from other modes or routes. Transport facilitates tourism and we can see that innovations have made tourism accessible to new markets. Here too, the falling real cost of transport has lowered the cost of the tourist product and widened the market.

● Transport and tourism companies are increasingly combining their resources through 'integration' to deliver a seamless tourist experience.

→

- Transport renders tourist destinations accessible to their markets in the tourist-generating areas. All tourism depends on access: indeed accessibility, or the lack of it, can make or break a destination – islands are particularly vulnerable here.

- Transport is a major sector of the tourism industry in terms of employment, investment and revenue generation: accessibility underpins inward investment and business productivity for destinations.

- Transport has significant environmental implications – particularly in terms of carbon emissions – and it is important that tourists understand the consequences of their transport choices.

Transport Networks

Transport networks play a key role in the development of destinations, especially through accessibility and connectivity to markets (Lohmann and Duval, 2015). Each transport network is made up of a series of links (along which flows take place) and nodes (terminals and interchanges). Ullman (1980) states that three factors are necessary for flows to take place between nodes in a transport system:

1. **Complementarity** means that places differ from each other and that in one place there is the desire to travel and in the other the ability to satisfy that desire.

2. **Intervening opportunities** means that there may be other destinations (nodes) in between a tourist's origin and intended destination.

3. **Friction of distance** refers to the cost (in time and money) of overcoming the distance between two places.

Duval (2007) demonstrates how the study of networks is fundamental to tourism transport:

- Networks determine flows, as the configuration of a network will affect the operation, pricing and demand for transport. It will also place some destinations in a better competitive position to receive tourists.

- Patterns and intensities of flows determine the viability of networks: 'thick' routes between, say, Washington and New York are more viable than 'thin' routes across New Zealand's South Island.

- Regulations govern network operations because governments can influence the operating characteristics of a route through pricing and demand for frequency of the service (the public sector obligation clause).

Elements of a Transport System

For flows to take place within a transport network a transport system will be needed. Faulks (1990) identifies the key elements in any transport system, each of which are found in different combinations to create a transport 'mode':

- the way;
- the terminal;
- the carrying unit;
- motive power.

The Way

The way is the medium of travel along which transport vehicles travel. A way can be artificial, including roads, railways, tramways and cableways; natural, including airspace or water; or it can be a combination of the two, such as inland waterways. The way has a number of important features:

- A natural way is effectively free, whilst if the way has to be provided artificially – roads, for example – a cost is incurred.

- If the user shares the way with others (for example, inland waterways) costs are shared, whereas if the carrier is the only user, then they bear all the costs of the way.

- Vehicles on roads and boats on inland waterways are controlled almost exclusively by their drivers or operators. In contrast, the movement of aircraft, trains and to some extent shipping is subject to traffic control, signalling or other navigational aids.

- Organisations independent of the carriers usually manage the way.

- Transport routes do not occur in isolation from the physical and economic conditions prevailing in different parts of the world. For example, mountains, the locations of major cities and political boundaries influence the way, although not all modes of transport are equally affected by these factors.

- Some modes of transport have a restricted 'way' which automatically channels movement. For natural ways, movement is also channelled, and movement does not take place across the whole available surface of, say, the sea.

Terminals

Terminals, hubs and gateways are important for access to destinations. A terminal gives access to the way for the users and acts to limit the capacity of routes through, for example, airport 'slot' control. Terminals can also act as interchanges between different transport modes allowing travellers to transfer. Terminals vary considerably in size, layout and the amenities they provide, as these are determined by the length and complexity of the journey, and the expectations of passengers. Airports are increasingly showpieces of contemporary architecture, often privatised as, for example, at Brisbane in Australia, and offer a wide range of services including accommodation, food & beverage and retail.

The Carrying Unit

Each type of way demands a particular type of carrying unit – aircraft for the air; boats for waterways; cars, buses/coaches and other vehicles for the roads; and rolling stock for the railways. Each carrying unit has distinctive costs and specifications – aircraft, for example, have to be designed to particularly high specifications to ensure safety, and are therefore costly. Aircraft, ships and road vehicles are flexible to operate compared to trains, monorails and trams, where breakdowns on the track cause extensive delays.

Motive Power

The historical development of motive power technology is closely linked to tourism development. Motive power combines with the way and the carrying unit to determine the speed, range and capacity of the transport mode in question.

Through the twentieth century, motive power for most transport modes was dependent on either coal or oil as the energy source. However, in this century, realisation of the consequences of carbon emissions has led to the search for alternative sources of motive power such as hydrogen, bio-fuels and electricity.

A key consideration for the economics of any transport system is 'capacity'. Here, the trick is to find the optimum combination of carrying unit and motive power that can hold the maximum number of passengers whilst still allowing sufficient utilisation of the transport system. Here, size is not always the most efficient option – for example, large aircraft such as the Airbus A380 require reconfigured airport access and large numbers of passengers to break-even economically. This highlights the two very different approaches taken by Airbus and Boeing: (i) Airbus see the future as long-haul travel using large aircraft; whilst (ii) Boeing instead see the future as one of shorter, point-to-point journeys.

Transport Modes

Boniface *et al.* (2012) state that each transport mode has different operational characteristics, based on the different ways in which technology is applied to the four elements of a transport system. Technology determines the appropriateness of the mode for a particular type of journey. Of course, some modes overlap in their suitability for the needs of travellers, and this may lead to competition between, say, airlines and surface transport operators on some routes, such as London to Paris. In other cases, transport modes are complementary, for example, the road or rail links between airports and city centres.

Transport Integration

An important issue for transport planners is to provide smooth transfers between transport modes. It is more common to find a lack of integration between modes in terms of poor coordination between operators, timetables and the physical siting of terminals. Integrated transport systems are therefore an ideal solution, though in practice they are expensive to deliver.

Managing Transport Systems: Demand

Demand for transport is *derived demand*, created for the transport operator because a tourist desires to get to the destination. In most cases, transport *per se* is not the tourist's real motivation for the trip. Incomes are the principal driver of travel demand, but are moderated by the cost of travel, the time taken, the distance travelled, and the characteristics of the tourist. Of course, different purposes of visit demand different levels of transport provision:

- Business travellers demand instant and flexible availability and can command a premium price.
- Leisure travellers are able to book further ahead and are often flexible in terms of dates. They therefore seek the lowest price and their demand is highly price elastic.
- Common interest travellers lie somewhere between the two – a student has to travel for the beginning of semester but has a degree of flexibility in how and when they travel.

The trend in all transport modes is for fares to match distinctive market segments, each of which have their own travel requirements. Here too, fares can be manipulated to increase traffic in the off-peak; indeed managing seasonality of demand is an important part of transport planning.

Lumsdon and Page (2004) provide a continuum of tourist transport using the type of experience sought – with at one extreme taxis or city buses which have a low intrinsic value as an experience, to the other extreme of, say, steam railways or ballooning which have a high intrinsic value as a tourist experience. Here, transport can deliver both the utilitarian aspect of tourism by getting the visitor from point A to B, as well as delivering additional motivations such as, say, romance on the Orient Express.

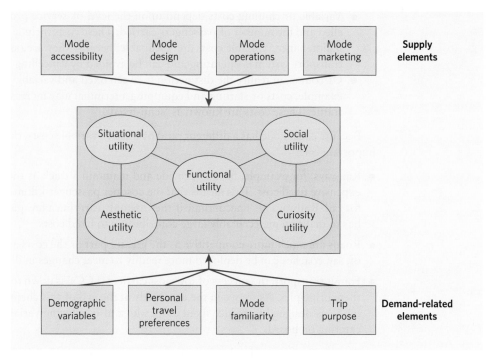

Figure 10.1 Transport mode selection model
Source: Mill and Morrison, 1985

It would be expected that particular tourism trips, and particular tourism products, will influence modal choice. This involves considering the tourist's original motivation for travel. For some trips the tourist has no choice but to travel on, say, a scheduled airline, but this can then be fine-tuned in terms of the tourist's ability to pay and their desire for different levels of ticket flexibility and comfort. In terms of their choice of transport mode, the tourist will be influenced by a variety of factors including distance and time, status and comfort, services offered, speed, competition, frequency and convenience, reliability, comfort and safety. Mill and Morrison (1985) summarise this process of decision making clearly (Figure 10.1).

Managing Transport Systems: Transport Costs and Pricing

Transport costs and pricing are fundamental to the successful operation of a transport system. The elements of each transport mode deliver a distinctive cost structure which both influences consumer choice and determines the volume of traffic on a route. Boniface *et al.* (2012) identify two types of transport cost:

1. **Social and environmental costs.** These costs are not paid for by the transport operator or user but are borne by the community. An example would be the environmental cost of aircraft carbon emissions.

2. **Private costs.** Transport operators pay private costs which are then passed on to the customer as fares. Here it is important to understand the distinction between fixed and variable costs:
   - Fixed costs, also known as overheads, are incurred before any passengers are carried or indeed before a carrying unit moves along the way. These costs are 'inescapable' and include items such as interest on capital invested in the system and depreciation of assets. The most important feature of fixed costs is that they do not vary in proportion to the number of passengers carried or the distance travelled.

- Variable or running costs depend upon the level of service provided, distance travelled and the number of passengers carried. These costs include fuel, crew wages and maintenance. Variable costs are 'escapable' because they are only incurred when the transport system is operating and can be avoided by cancelling services.
- Of course, in reality the distinction between fixed and variable costs is blurred – for example, costs of staffing and equipping a terminal may increase with the volume of traffic. These costs are known as 'semi-fixed'.

Because each mode has a different ratio of fixed to variable costs, the distinction is a very important one:

- Railways, for example, have to provide and maintain a track as the 'way' and this is an expensive fixed cost. This means that the cost per passenger-kilometre decreases rapidly for rail. Railways are uneconomic if they are only carrying a few passengers, as each one has to make an unacceptably large contribution to fixed costs.

- Roads are much more competitive as the greater part of the costs are variable, and fleets of, say, coaches can be deployed more readily to meet changes in demand.

- For air transport, the success of low-cost carriers (LCCs) is down to an understanding of these principles. As we see in the case study at the end of this chapter, the LCC business model is designed to reduce fixed costs whilst also reducing variable costs such as free catering on board.

We can identify five further key issues related to transport pricing. Firstly, compared to many activities, transport has a *high proportion of fixed costs*. The product is also perishable, because if a seat is not sold on a flight it cannot be stored to be sold later. This means that operators must achieve a high utilisation of their systems, as idle carrying units do not make a contribution to fixed costs. Finally, it is important to achieve a high *load factor* (the number of seats sold compared to the number available).

Secondly, the link between load factor and pricing is clearly illustrated by the *marginal cost principle*. For an LCC, marginal cost is the additional cost incurred by carrying one extra passenger. The carrier determines a load factor that covers the fixed costs of the journey and the variable cost of each passenger carried. If the flight is budgeted to break even at a load factor of 80 per cent, then every passenger carried over this level will incur a small marginal cost, but because variable costs are low this represents a substantial profit for the LCC. Of course, exactly the opposite also applies – for every passenger below the 80 per cent level a loss will be incurred.

Thirdly, a related problem is the fact that tourism demand tends to be *highly peaked* on a daily, weekly and annual basis. This means that airline fleets may only be fully utilised at certain times of the year. Both in Europe and North America one solution to this was the creation of the winter holiday market in the late 1960s to utilise idle aircraft and make a contribution to fixed costs. Another solution is to use *differential pricing*, offering low fares for travel in the off-peak period to increase traffic.

Fourthly, *yield management* is now universally used to optimise the profitability of transport systems. Effectively these are sophisticated computer models that match market demand in real time for a service with availability and fares. They optimise profitability because the passenger pays the maximum price achievable on a route at a particular point in time.

Finally, transport operators are not immune to the external economic environment. For example, they respond in a variety of ways to the economic downturns. In 2008, for example, airlines saw their passenger numbers fall, particularly in the premium sector as businesses cut back on costs. Resultant strategies were a combination of business and marketing approaches and included:

- closely managing capacity on routes with some cut backs;
- reducing fares;

- pursuing premium passengers;
- mergers and alliances;
- hedging fuel and currency; and
- seeking new markets.

Managing Transport Systems: The Public Sector

The transport sector is one part of the tourism system where the public sector is heavily involved. This is not only for passenger safety and security reasons, but also because governments are involved in international negotiations over routes. The public sector also has a role in protecting the public, and other operators, against unfair business practices and monopolies. Of course, some transport modes are more heavily controlled by government than others – air transport, for example, is heavily regulated whilst cruising has to date escaped significant government control. Governments, too, provide the funding for transport infrastructure development and national transport planning. This implies that transport planning cannot be achieved in isolation of other economic sectors, including tourism, whilst at the destination scale transport should be 'designed in' as part of the leisure environment – the monorail serving Darling Harbour in Sydney is a good example here. Nonetheless, high quality transport infrastructure is a key driver of destination competitiveness – compare, for example, the relatively poor infrastructure in Africa with that of the Asia/Pacific region.

Regulation

Duval (2007) identifies a range of reasons why regulation of transport is important:

1. markets are not perfect and intervention is sometimes required in the public interest;
2. regulation can prevent monopoly situations on routes;
3. regulation is necessary to ensure safety and security standards;
4. regulation is necessary to maintain a particular level of service on an otherwise unprofitable route;
5. regulation can deal with externalities such as noise or carbon emissions through legislation and taxation; and
6. regulation assists in national transport planning.

Economic Regulation

Economic regulation of transport is where government controls pricing and competition through market access to routes. Since the 1960s, the trend has been towards deregulation of transport, which we see in the airline sector as 'open skies' policies. This was led by the USA and followed by the European Union before spreading to other regions of the world – including Asia. However, with the turbulent environment of the twenty-first century's economic crises and terrorism, deregulation has not progressed as far as some countries and regions (such as the EU) intended.

Whilst other transport modes, such as shipping and coaching, are also closely regulated, it is the air transport sector where we have seen the greatest activity. Back in 1944, the Chicago Convention defined five freedoms of the air that are put into practice by bilateral agreements between pairs of countries (Figure 10.2). These freedoms are:

- the privilege of using another country's airspace;
- to land in another country for 'technical' reasons;

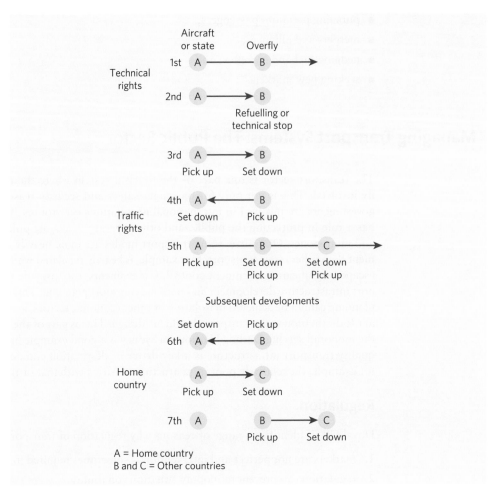

Figure 10.2 The five freedoms of the air
Source: Boniface and Cooper, 2009

- the third and fourth freedoms relate to commercial point-to-point traffic between two countries by their respective airlines; and
- the fifth freedom allows an airline to pick up and set down passengers in the territory of a country other than its destination.

As the sector has developed, these freedoms have been extended, partly as commercial considerations such as hub and spoke operations have become more important. The sixth and seventh freedoms allow an airline to pick up in a country other than the country of origin, take passengers back to its home base or 'hub' and then take them on to another destination. This 'hub and spoke' operation has encouraged the development of hub airports at a regional and intercontinental scale.

International agreements are becoming less important with the deregulation of the air transport system. This means that it is more difficult for governments to control routes, fares and volumes of traffic on flights within and across their borders. Boniface *et al.* (2012) summarise the features of deregulation as:

- encouraging competition among airlines;
- leading to the building of strategic alliances between airlines;
- encouraging the growth of regional airlines and regional airports; and

- favouring the development of LCCs on busy routes because it not only allows competition on the routes, but also opens up the possibility of using smaller regional airports.

However, many countries have yet to agree to an 'open skies' policy for reasons of military security, or to protect the national 'flag-carrier' – usually state-owned and heavily subsidised – from foreign competition.

Non-economic Regulation

- **Safety and security.** Any form of passenger transportation carries a risk of injury or death, whether through accident or malicious intent. Since '9/11' and the railway bombings in London and Madrid, safety and security have become paramount in transport operations and government have had to take a lead on this. You will all be aware of the restrictions now placed on airline passengers as they pass through the airport. The key here is to ensure that these procedures are done with a 'human touch'. Security has required major reconfiguration of the layout and operation of airports as well as innovations in aircraft design.

- For surface transport these types of checks are much more challenging and the networks are more reliant upon passenger vigilance. Of course, safety and security are now an important part of the tourists' decision process for transport – in the wake of the London underground bombings many people decided against travelling on the underground and of course we saw a huge fall in air traffic post '9/11'. Marine transport, too, is now vulnerable given attacks on cruise liners by pirates and hijackers, as well as the publicised incidents of food poisoning on cruise ships.

- **Taxation.** Air passenger taxes are added to fares to offset the externalities of travel. They have become a source of competition, with the Netherlands, for example, abolishing them in an attempt to divert passengers from other airports.

- **Infrastructure.** It is important for governments to provide high-quality transport infrastructure. Infrastructure is an important determinant of destination competitiveness, connecting destinations to markets across the world. This is particularly the case for less developed countries such as those in Africa, although there are also severe capacity constraints on the air transport network of Europe due to inadequate airport development.

- **Environment.** Governments and international agencies are pressing to make transport more sustainable. It is now recognised that tourism transport accounts for around 5 per cent of the world's carbon emissions. However, it is estimated that around 80 per cent of these emissions are caused by around 20 per cent of all trips, and that these are long-haul trips (Peeters *et al.*, 2007). Government response is through legislation to encourage cleaner technologies, particularly hydrogen-based transport, in the face of dwindling oil reserves. Passengers using the bullet train in Japan, for example, receive a note of their carbon emissions comparing it to less environmentally-friendly forms of transport such as flying.

Transport Modes for Tourism

Air Transport

Whilst surface modes of transport carry much greater volumes of traffic than the airlines, air transport has had the most impact upon the nature of international tourism and the structure of the travel industry since 1950. Few parts of the world are now more than 24 hours flying time from any other part, and it is estimated by the UN World Tourism Organization that around 20 per cent of international tourists use air transport.

Air transport took off in the early 1920s with aircraft that were noisy, unpressurised – and without toilets! At this time flying was an expensive pursuit for the elite and it was not until the 1950s that pressurised aircraft could cross the Atlantic. Even so, air travel remained for the privileged. Tourist fares were only introduced in 1952 and economy class in 1958. The real revolution in air transport came with the jet engine giving aircraft speed and range, as well as allowing more passengers to be carried, opening up the skies, and destinations, to mass tourism.

More recently, LCCs have opened up new routes and made air travel accessible to many more people than would otherwise be able to afford to fly. We deal with LCCs in the case study at the end of this chapter. Nonetheless, despite the apparent success of LCCs, the economics of air transport are precarious, characterised by a transport mode that demands high levels of capital investment in a volatile market with low returns (Graham, 2009).

The traditional distinction between air carriers has been between *scheduled airlines* operating to a timetable and flying whatever the number of passengers, and *chartered* airlines who operate on behalf of a third party such as a tour operator. However, with the rise of the LCCs, this distinction has become blurred and Duval (2007) provides a more contemporary classification:

- **Network carriers** have extensive route coverage, regular schedules and are often part of international alliances and code shares.
- **Regional airlines** ply geographical niche markets such as India and are smaller carriers with route networks that feed the network carriers' routes.
- **LCCs** serve niche markets in geographic regions (e.g. VirginAustralia in Australia and the Pacific).
- **Charter carriers** serve pre-booked tours.

The traditional network carriers are now facing fierce competition for their routes and they have responded by forming alliances. The three major alliances are the 'One World Alliance' (www.oneworld.com/), 'Skyteam' (www.skyteam.com/) and the 'Star Alliance' (www.staralliance.com/). This allows a passenger to book with, say, British Airways to Singapore and, using a codeshare with Qantas, travel on to Brisbane. Alliances bring efficiencies in operation, reduce costs, give passengers a greater choice and, above all, allow an airline access to an expanded route network.

Boniface *et al.* (2012) identify the main advantages of the air transport mode as:

- The way allows the aircraft a direct line of flight unimpeded by natural barriers such as mountain ranges, oceans, deserts or jungles.
- Superior speeds can be reached in everyday service giving aircraft both range and reach for tourism destinations.
- Air transport has a high passenger capacity and is ideally suited to journeys of over 500 kilometres, travel over difficult, roadless terrain, and journeys between groups of islands.

However, air transport does have disadvantages:

- It needs a large terminal area that may be some distance from the destination it serves and increasingly there is local opposition to new airports.
- It is relatively expensive due to the large amounts of power expended and the high safety standards demanded.
- It has significant negative environmental impacts. The true cost of air travel for the airlines and their passengers has been masked by the fact that the airlines, unlike other business enterprises, have been exempt from certain taxes, although as we have seen this situation is changing with the onset of passenger and environmental taxes. The continued growth of air traffic, particularly long-haul, may not be sustainable, given aircraft emissions. In response, companies such as Boeing are designing greener aircraft – the Boeing 787 'Dreamliner', for example, has been designed to have a much smaller carbon footprint than traditional aircraft (www.boeing.com/commercial/787/).
- As we have seen, air transport is particularly vulnerable to terrorism and to fluctuating oil prices.

Air Routes

The nature of the way has a significant impact upon global air routes. For example, air routes can utilise the shortest distance between origin and destination, with the improvements in range and technical performance that have been achieved since 1950. Aircraft can also fly 'above the weather' in extremely thin air, uniformly cold temperatures and cloudless conditions of the stratosphere. In middle latitudes routes take advantage of jet streams in the stratosphere that attain high speeds, reducing the flying time from California to Europe by over an hour compared to the journey in the opposite direction.

Despite the apparent freedom of the way, air routes are influenced by a number of factors:

- operational characteristics of aircraft;
- safety and security factors which mean that routes are channelled to avoid, say, city centres;
- the level of demand for the route;
- the extent of infrastructure on the ground for passenger handling; and
- international agreements.

As a result of these factors, most of the world's air traffic is concentrated in the three regions of Eastern USA, Western Europe and East Asia. This is due partly to market forces and partly because of the strategic location of these areas. The 'air bridge' between Europe and North America across the North Atlantic is the busiest intercontinental route, linking the two largest generators of international tourism and significant international destinations globally. On this route, the capacity provided by wide-bodied jets and vigorous competition between the airlines has brought fares within reach of many tourists.

Air routes, too, have been influential in opening up tourism regions and are utilised by governments to stimulate tourism development. This has been especially the case since the development of the jet engine brought the developing world within range of the Western traveller. In turn, establishment of international routes into a region then stimulates the development of domestic air services and inward investment into the tourism sector.

Of course, not all air routes are long-haul and for short sightseeing trips, heli-hiking and heli-skiing helicopters are used, whilst for novelty short trips tourists can also go ballooning (for, say, game watching), or take trips in a glider or micro-light.

Airports

Although the aircraft is the real star of air transport, we must not underestimate the importance of airports. Airports act as the primary gateway to a destination for tourists. As the volume of air traffic has grown, so has the size and complexity of airports, particularly given the twenty-first century demands of security checks. Airports not only have passenger terminals, but also hotels with conference facilities, transport interchanges and large car parks. Major airports such as Heathrow are akin to small cities, sustaining thousands of jobs and taking up large land areas.

The accessibility of the airport to the tourism destination is critical. Many are within a transfer distance of 20 to 30 kilometres but newer airports, as in Milan or Kuala Lumpur are much further away, necessitating dedicated train connections. Whilst these are examples of newer airports, in many parts of the world airports and the air traffic control systems are reaching capacity. Yet, despite their importance for tourism and the national economy, proposals for new airports, or for airport expansion, are fiercely opposed due to concerns about noise and land-use.

Land Transport

The nature of the way for land transport immediately places a number of constraints on routes and access. Land transport is by far the most common form of tourism transport for domestic travel and for short international trips and the forms of transport available can be viewed as:

1. **personal** – such as the car or private pleasure boats; or

2. **supplied** – services provided by rail or coach operators, for example.

From a security point of view, land transport was perceived as safe following '9/11', but this changed with the bombings of the rail networks in Madrid and London, and marine piracy, as we have seen around the horn of Africa.

Road Transport

As the most important form of tourism transport, the car has been neglected by tourism transport experts. Yet, the car has many advantages for tourism. It can provide comfort, privacy, flexibility in timing, choice of itineraries and door-to-door service – travel by other transport modes almost invariably begins and ends with a road journey. This, combined with the fact that road vehicles can only carry a small number of passengers and have a relatively low speed, makes them particularly suitable for short to medium distance journeys. Also, the development of recreational vehicles (RVs) such as campervans and caravans allows a form of motorised accommodation. Finally, the car rental sector is a major part of the tourism sector generating significant revenues.

The main disadvantage of road transport is that many users share the way and this can lead to congestion at periods of peak demand, such as in France during school holiday periods, or China during the peak annual holidays. In some destinations such as Florida or Queensland, the demands of the private car have resulted in a tourism landscape of motels and other drive-in facilities dedicated to personal mobility. The classic paper for this chapter is an early recognition of the significance of the car for tourism travel.

Classic Paper

Wall, G. (1972) The socio-economic variations in pleasure trip patterns: the case of Hull Car owners, *Transactions of the Institute of British Geographers* 57, 45–58

Geoff Wall's paper on pleasure trips taken by car owners in the city of Hull is one of the first to analyse this activity. It is classic because, despite the fact that it was based on 1969 data, many of the findings would hold true today. It is also a classic paper because it is evidence that recreation and tourism was beginning to be seen as a serious source of academic study by the late 1960s.

The paper is based upon a survey of a random sample of 500 Hull car-owners. The car owners were interviewed between August and October 1969, and asked for details of the last pleasure trip that they had taken by car. They were also asked a range of profile questions designed to see if the pattern of their trips could be linked to their demographics or family structure. The findings can be summarised as follows:

● Almost all Hull car-owners take pleasure trips by car.

● More than half of the trips had been taken in the two weeks prior to the interview.

● Many car-owners set off on their pleasure trips with no particular destination in mind, suggesting that the act of 'getting away' is just as important as the places visited.

● There are identifiable seasonal and daily rhythms to the trips.

● The car is used as the base for a trip at the destination – for picnics or games – with the party not straying far from the car itself.

● The car is used to transport large amounts of recreational equipment.

● Most journeys are less than 100 kilometres from home and most journeys lie between 20 and 40 kilometres.

● The journeys were designed to maximise variety rather than to efficiently get from Hull to the destination and back – in other words, pleasure driving is different to other forms of driving.

- As might be expected, recreation sites closer to Hull received more visits.
- A large percentage of pleasure trip takers are families, with a tiny minority of people travelling alone.

These findings would be similar if a survey was done in the twenty-first century. Of course, in the late 1960s, access to a car was less common than it is today and facilities for motorists, the sophistication of the car and the quality of the roads were all poorer. Nonetheless, the findings show the importance of the car as a recreational tool, not only used as means to reach a destination, but also for carrying recreational equipment and as a base for activities such as picnicking. As Wall observes, this means that whilst the car has spread the impact of tourism more widely, the actual impact itself is localised around the car at car parks, picnic sites and lay-bys. Interestingly, too, Wall found that these trip takers enjoyed driving and would be reluctant to use other forms of transport – an interesting observation for park and ride schemes!

As Wall's paper hints, since the 1950s, the car has become the dominant transport mode for most types of tourism, while coach travel accounts for a much smaller share of the holiday market. Coach operations differ from scheduled bus services in that they are very much part of the tourism industry and provide higher standards of comfort and service. Coach travel not only provides a transfer service at airports and other terminals, but is also used for excursions from resorts, and for touring holidays as a product in its own right. The coach has undergone a resurgence in popularity with increased levels of quality and service and a perception that it is a more sustainable form of transport than the car.

Innovations in road transport for tourism include specialised touring services and innovative park and ride schemes – the US national scenic byways program is an example here. Roads designed especially for sightseeing have been built in scenically attractive coastal and mountain areas as we see in the next case study.

Mini Case Study 10.1
The Great Tropical Drive, Australia

Introduction

As we have seen, the car is a great recreational tool, allowing space for carrying all the needs of the tourist, a base for picnics and recreation and an all-round viewing facility. As a result, the car is by far the most common form of transport for tourism. Yet surprisingly, the management of car-borne tourism has been neglected despite the fact that the car can create problems at the destination in terms of safety as well as congestion. Tourists' driving tends to be slower than that of residents and of course whilst touring they are not in a rush to get from A to B. In other words, whilst the car has brought great flexibility of access for tourists, its impact upon destinations has been problematic.

One solution to this is the creation and development of scenic drives which separate touring traffic from local traffic. Scenic drives are designed primarily to provide a distinctive driving experience for pleasure travel and have facilities such as interpretation and information; frequent stopping places for views, picnics and barbecues; and landscaped and purpose-designed driving experiences to maximise the impact of the scenery.

The Great Tropical Drive

Scenic drives are found mainly in North America but an Australian initiative has extended the concept of scenic drives. Tourism in regional Australia is an important source of revenue and jobs and significant government resources have been devoted to developing regional tourism products to tempt tourists away from the state capitals such as Sydney and Melbourne. These also have the added advantages of supporting indigenous tourism.

The Great Tropical Drive is a self-drive route in the north of Australia (Figure 10.3). The drive extends from Cairns to Townsville, and can take up to 12 days to cover the 2079 kilometres. The drive has been designed to take in some of Australia's best-known attractions including the Great Barrier Reef, the Daintree Rainforest, Hinchinbrook Island

Figure 10.3   Great Tropical Drive

Source: www.greattropicaldrive.com.au

and the Undara Lava Tubes. However, where this drive extends the concept is through the design of the experiences and products along the way.

The drive has been designed to incorporate 14 discovery trails, each of which is:

- suited to particular vehicles from four-wheel drives to campervans; and
- linked to a set of six groups of experiences including aborigine, adventure, heritage, food and wine, wildlife and nature.

For example:

- Trail 14 'Liquid Gold' is a loop of the drive in the south of the region that takes two days to cover. Along the way are three sets of experiences – aborigine, nature and heritage.
- Trail 5 'Reef to Rain Forest' is an ocean drive from Cairns, one of the major international tourism destinations in northern Australia, that takes on food and wine and nature experiences.

The design of the drive therefore fulfils the key objectives of a contemporary tourism destination – delivering an excellent tourism experience, utilising cutting-edge product development and providing a sound management framework.

DISCUSSION QUESTIONS

1. Draft a press release explaining the concept of the drive to the international travel media.
2. Create a balance sheet of the advantages and disadvantages of the car at the tourist destination.
3. Visit www.australia.com/en/itineraries/qld-tropical-drive.html and study the discovery trails. How effective do you think these trails will be in delivering the benefits of tourism to regional Queensland?

Source:
www.australia.com/en/itineraries/qld-tropical-drive.html

Whilst car *ownership* is unlikely to decline in the near future, car *use* can be reduced at destinations in a number of ways (for example, 'park and ride) or by improving access to bus and train services. In some cities measures to limit car use include road pricing or congestion charges. The environmental cost of road transport is increasingly understood and governments in some countries are taxing cars according to their carbon emissions whilst manufacturers now offer 'zero' emission and hybrid cars.

Of course, the most sustainable forms of land transport are walking, cycling and horse riding and, for niche products such as ecotourism, these forms of transport are increasingly popular with dedicated suppliers.

Rail Transport

In contrast to the road, the way used by rail – the railway track – is not shared and extra carriages can be added or removed to cope with demand. In the past this was useful at peak times in holiday areas where special trains could be run. In addition, specialised carrying units such as dining cars or viewing cars can be provided on scenic routes. The railway's main disadvantage is that the track, signalling and other equipment have to be maintained and paid for by the single user of the way. Providing railway track is particularly expensive as the motive power can only negotiate gentle gradients. This means that engineering work for cuttings, viaducts and tunnels is a major cost consideration, especially on long routes and in mountain regions. Railways are therefore characterised by high fixed costs and a need to utilise the track and rolling stock very efficiently to meet these high costs. The fact that terminals are relatively limited in numbers combined with the railway's speed and capacity to move large numbers of passengers make it suitable for journeys of 200–500 kilometres between major cities.

The steam engine was vital in the development of the railways in the nineteenth century, revolutionising transport and allowing cheap mass travel for domestic tourism. In the UK, the first railway was in 1830 and from the 1840s onwards, railway companies grew rapidly, encouraging entrepreneurs such as Thomas Cook to develop excursions. As the great trans-continental railways were built before 1914, when there was no serious competition from other modes of transport, the train was the mode that people used to travel long distances across continents. Iconic trains, such as the Orient Express, date from this period (www.orient-express.com/).

From the 1950s onwards, rail travel went into decline facing competition from airlines for long-distance traffic and from the private car for short journeys. New railway construction virtually ceased in most countries, but improvements were made to tracks and steam was replaced as motive power by diesel fuel or electricity. The decline in passenger rail transport has been greatest in the Americas.

Environmental pressures, combined with technological innovations such as high-speed trains are allowing rail to compete with air on short- to medium-haul routes. Eurostar, for example, is marketed as the 'green' alternative to flying (www.eurostar.com/), whilst in France, China and Japan there has been considerable government investment in applying new technology to the development of high-speed trains and upgrading the trunk lines between major cities. In Western Europe, the Channel Tunnel between England and France has encouraged the development of rail-based tourism products such as the 'Eurostar' service between London and Paris/Brussels, in response the European Union's development of an integrated rail network.

There is also a niche market for nostalgia-based rail travel. This includes luxury travel on, say, the 'Blue Train' (www.bluetrain.co.za/) or the 'Ghan' (www.The-Ghan.com.au) as well as the proliferation of private steam railways as in the UK.

Water-borne Transport

It was water transport rather than rail that was the first to use steam power. Water-borne transport is slow compared to air travel and by the late 1960s most of the long-haul market on the North Atlantic routes had been lost to the airlines. Boniface *et al.* (2012) identify the main advantages of the mode as:

- Ships expend relatively little power.
- Ships can be built to much larger specifications than vehicles or aircraft – they can also provide a high degree of comfort, the basis of the cruise market.
- Ships can be designed as roll-on roll-off ferries accommodating large numbers of motor vehicles – in effect 'floating bridges'. This has led to marketing directed at motorists using the short sea routes, such as those crossing the English Channel.

Technological innovations are overcoming some of the natural disadvantages of sea transport. These include hydrofoils where the hull is lifted out of the water allowing much higher speeds to be attained. Hydrofoils, however, are dependent on good weather and have relatively small capacity. Wave-piercing catamarans have proven to be more versatile than hydrofoils on some routes.

Sea Routes

There is a clear distinction between long-haul shipping routes, the short sea routes served by ferries, and cruising.

Short sea routes

Passenger traffic on the short sea routes is increasing rapidly around the world. The Indonesian and Ionian archipelagos, for example, host many ferry services, whilst in Western Europe the popularity of motoring holidays and the growth of trade between the countries of the European Union has boosted ferry traffic. The introduction of roll-on roll-off facilities has enabled ports on these routes to handle a much greater volume of cars, coaches

Aquaduck – novel forms of transport attract visitors.
Source: © dov makabaw sundry/Alamy Images

and trucks, and most ferries now operate throughout the year with greatly improved standards of comfort and service. In Scandinavia, the large ferries plying between Finland and Sweden, for example, are now equivalent to cruise liners with the associated amenities as we see the two product offerings beginning to merge. There are, however, increased safety concerns for ferry services following major accidents.

Long-haul routes

By 1890 iron ships with steam turbines were crossing the Atlantic, heralding the era of the ocean liner on long-haul routes. This era lasted from 1900 to the late 1950s as ocean liners had no competition on long distance voyages until the jet engine appeared.

Cruising

In the 1920s, cruising was for the elite, with voyages lasting for several months. The sea voyage, often undertaken for health reasons, was more important than the places visited. Faced with increasing competition from the airlines in the 1950s, ship owners diversified from operating passenger liners into cruising, although this was not an easy transition as the ships were often unsuitable. The introduction of *fly-cruising* in the 1960s was important as it allowed the cruise ship to be based at a port in the destination region, so that clients no longer had to make a long, possibly stormy, voyage from a port in their home country.

Since 1980, the cruise market has undergone a renaissance, with massive investment in large purpose-built cruise ships, with over 250 purpose-built vessels now on the seas and waterways. As well as a high standard of service and accommodation, a variety of sports, activities and entertainment, including gambling, are available. At the same time, prices have fallen and new markets have begun to cruise – there are more passengers in the younger age groups, so that cruising is less of a 'grey market' than in the past. Themed and special interest cruises are increasingly promoted as the ship provides an ideal viewing platform. For example, there is a growing number of cruises to Antarctica and the Arctic Ocean.

The majority of cruise ships are based in the USA, and around 50 per cent of cruise tourists are American, although the European market is growing. The Caribbean is the most popular cruising destination, due to its location close to the North American market, the warm climate and the wide variety of scenery offered by the islands. The two other main cruising destinations are the Mediterranean and the Far East/Pacific.

In the future larger ships will be built to benefit from economies of scale, there will be greater differentiation in the cruise offerings and new itineraries will be developed to avoid crowded routes such as the Caribbean. Cruising, too, will take its environmental responsibility more seriously – P&O, for example, have launched 'fathom' where passengers work alongside NGOs and locals on environmental and social projects (Fathom.org), whilst the Holland America Line has been a pioneer of sustainable cruising as we see in the next case.

Mini Case Study 10.2
Environmental and Socially Sustainable Cruising – The Holland America Line

Holland America Cruise ship.
Source: © Leon Werdinger/Alamy Images

Introduction

Cruise tourism has shown remarkable growth since the 1990s. Whilst Johnson (2002) clearly states that the health of the world's oceans is critical to the future of the world, we are seeing an increase in forms of tourism that utilise the oceans as a resource. Here, cruising has become the target of environmentalists; although in the twenty-first century there have been substantial improvements in their environmental practices. Johnson outlines the environmental consequences of cruising as:

- coastal infrastructure needs of cruising;
- cruise operations in terms of waste disposal, energy and water consumption, and carbon emissions;

- impacts of transferring tourists to the cruise liners, often by air; and
- social, cultural and economic consequences of cruise visitors at the destination.

Johnson (2002) concludes that whilst cruising allows large numbers of visitors to enjoy the ocean as a resource, if cruising is to be sustainable it needs to:

- implement long-term integrated planning at the international level;
- invest and promote environmental good practice;
- ensure that destinations are protected from 'mobile' cruise tourism;
- consider profit sharing between cruise line shareholders and host destinations; and
- raise cruise tourists' environmental awareness.

Holland America Line

Holland America Line is a cruise company at the forefront of implementing environmentally and socially sustainable cruise tourism, conscious of the need for stewardship of the oceans. The company is continuing to reduce its environmental footprint through a number of innovative practices. These include:

- Implementing an environmental management and reporting system to integrate sustainability into all aspects of the company's operations. Here, goals are to reduce fuel consumption, water use and refrigerant releases and implement more recycling. The management system ensures that the company adheres to international regulations for the environment.
- Including environmental duties into on board employees' work plans.
- Energy and emissions management to ensure the ships are as efficient as possible, including efforts to reduce fuel consumption by optimising speed and sharing best practice.
- Almost three quarters of on-board water used is produced on-board from seawater and condensation.
- Solid waste is managed carefully and the majority is not hazardous. It is recycled or disposed of on shore, incinerated on board or discharged to sea. Recyclable materials are separated and collected.

The company is conscious of the need to safeguard biodiversity and so manages discharges from the ships. Other approaches include:

- ensuring that ballast water, which could introduce invasive species to the ocean, is disposed of onshore;
- only using sustainable seafood on-board;
- monitor the paths of marine mammals to minimise striking them; and
- limit the time in Antarctica for each voyage.

DISCUSSION QUESTIONS

1. Given the fragile nature of the oceans, can cruise tourism ever be environmentally sustainable?
2. Draft a press release to the international travel media explaining Holland America Line's sustainability plans.
3. One of the major issues with cruise tourism is the small economic benefit gained by destinations that are swamped by cruise tourists for a few hours. Draft a plan to try to maximise the economic benefits of cruise tourism to the Caribbean islands.

Sources:
Dowling, R.K. (ed.) (2006) *Cruise Tourism: Issues, Impacts, Cases*, CABI Publishing, Wallingford.
Johnson, D. (2002) Environmentally sustainable cruise tourism: a reality check, *Marine Policy* **26,** 261–270,
Klein, R.A. (2011) Responsible cruise tourism: issues of cruise tourism and sustainability, *Journal of Hospitality and Tourism Management* **18**(1), 107–116.
Lamers, M., Eijgelaar, E. and Amelung, B. (2015) The environmental challenges of cruise tourism, p. 430 in Hall, C.M., Gössling, S. and Scott, D. (eds) *The Routledge Handbook of Tourism and Sustainability*, Routledge, London.
Peisley, T. (2006) *The Future of Cruising*, Pearson, Harlow. www.hollandamerica.com

Inland waterways

Natural waterways and artificially constructed canals provide linear tourist attractions as well as a recreational transport system. Tourists can hire boats for touring and waterbuses are used in destinations with an extensive river or canal system such as Amsterdam. Cruises on major rivers such as the Rhine, the Nile, the Danube, the Volga and the Yangtze are important tourism products. Personal craft are common on inland waters as well as inshore around coasts.

SUMMARY

This chapter has introduced the transport sector as an essential part of the tourism system, linking tourism markets and destinations. Tourism and transport have developed hand-in-hand, and breakthroughs in transport have tended to benefit tourism. We can think of transport as forming transport networks with nodes as terminals and links as routes. This allows us to analyse the efficiencies and compare the development of transport systems. These systems are comprised of four main elements – the way, the terminal, the carrying unit and motive power. A distinctive mix of each of these elements is found in each of the major modes of transport – air, land and sea. The chapter went on to analyse demand for transport and, in particular, how tourists make the choice between transport modes. An analysis of transport pricing showed the importance of distinguishing between the fixed and variable costs of transport and that the ratio of the two varies by transport mode. The public sector is intimately involved in transport systems through planning and regulation, as well as in environmental and security initiatives. A major issue is that of deregulation of transport systems, a trend we have seen over the last three decades. The chapter then considered each of the major transport modes for tourism beginning with air transport and a major case study on low-cost carriers. For surface transport we saw that, whilst the car is the major mode used for tourism, it is neglected, despite the great potential for developing tourism route as demonstrated by the Great Tropical Drive case. Rail travel is undergoing a renaissance fuelled by environmental concerns and technological innovations that have allowed development of high-speed trains. Finally, water-borne transport is also seeing a resurgence through cruise tourism and we saw how the Holland America Line is re-engineering its operations to take account of environmental considerations.

Discussion Questions

1. Draw up a balance sheet for the environmental consequences of air travel versus rail travel.
2. Draft a briefing note to your transport minister outlining the benefits of deregulating your national air transport system.
3. Create a short PowerPoint presentation for training purposes explaining the marginal cost principle.
4. Using a timeline, explore the link between transport developments and tourism.
5. Draft a checklist of the key benefits of the car for tourism.

Annotated Further Reading

1. Boniface, B., Cooper, C and Cooper, R. (2012) *Worldwide Destinations: The Geography of Travel and Tourism,* 6th edn, Routledge, London.
    Comprehensive text covering tourism transport development in every country in the world, now in its 6th edition.

2. Doganis, R (2006) *The Airline Business,* Routledge, London.
    One of the best sources around for air transport.

3. Duval, D. (2007) *Tourism and Transport: Modes, Networks and Flows,* Channel View, Clevedon.
    Contemporary and thorough text on tourism transport.

4. Graham, A. (2009) *Managing Airports,* Elsevier Butterworth Heinemann, Oxford.
    Excellent review of airports and their management.

5. Gross, S. and Klemmer, L. (2014) *Introduction to Tourism Transport,* CABI, Wallingford.
    Good introductory text.

6. Lohmann, G. and Duval, D.T. (2015) Tourism and transport, pp. 129–182 in Cooper, C. (ed.) *Contemporary Tourism Reviews, Volume 1,* Goodfellow, Oxford.
    A contemporary and thorough review of transport for tourism.

7. Page, S. and Connell, J. (2014) Transportation and tourism, Chapter 12 in Lew A.L, Hall, C.M. and Williams, A.M. (eds) *The Wiley Blackwell Companion to Tourism,* Wiley, Chichester.
    A useful overview of the field.

8. Peisley, T. (2006) *The Future of Cruising,* Pearson, Harlow.
    Excellent source for students of cruising.

References Cited

Boniface, B. and Cooper, C. (2009) *Worldwide Destinations: The Geography of Travel and Tourism,* 5th edn, Heinemann, London.

Boniface, B., Cooper, C and Cooper, R. (2012) *Worldwide Destinations: The Geography of Travel and Tourism,* 6th edn, Routledge, London.

Duval, D. (2007) *Tourism and Transport: Modes, Networks and Flows,* Channel View, Clevedon.

Faulks, R.W. (1990) *The Principles of Transport,* 4th edn, McGraw Hill, New York.

Graham, A. (2009) *Managing Airports,* Elsevier Butterworth Heinemann, Oxford.

Lohmann, G. and Duval, D.T. (2015) Tourism and transport, pp. 129–182 in Cooper, C. (ed.) *Contemporary Tourism Reviews, Volume 1,* Goodfellow, Oxford.

Lumsdon, L. and Page, S.J. (eds) (2004) *Tourism and Transport: Issues and Agendas of the New Millennium,* Amsterdam, Elsevier.

Mill, R.C. and Morrison, A. (1985) *The Tourism System: An Introductory Text,* Prentice Hall, Englewood Cliffs, NJ.

Peeters, P., Szimba, E. and Duijinisveld, D. (2007) Major environmental impacts of European tourism transport, *Journal of Transport Geography* **15**(1), 83–93.

Ullman, E. (1980) *Geography as Spatial Interaction,* University of Washington Press, Washington DC.

Major Case Study 10.1
Low-Cost Carriers: AirAsia

Introduction

Low-cost carriers (LCCs) are one of the most significant developments in air transport in recent years, although some argue that they should be called low *fare* rather than low *cost* carriers. With their innovative business model they have reduced both the fares and levels of service on routes. Yet the jury is out as to whether low-cost carriers are a true revolutionary concept or simply an evolutionary development in air transport. As air travel continues to expand across the world, there is no doubt that LCCs have fuelled this growth by creating a more competitive environment for air travel. In the future, as the model matures, there will be more LCCs on long-haul routes and variants on the model are emerging such as 'business only' carriers operating a 'less frills' rather than a 'no frills' service and LCCs adopting features such as seat reservations and frequent flier schemes. This case study examines AirAsia, one of the first Asian LCCs and one of the first to attempt a long-haul service with AirAsiaX.

The Low-cost Carrier Concept

Low-cost carriers are airlines that work to a business model of low fares and few extra services for the passenger. They are sometimes known as 'no frills' or discount airlines. LCCs have a business model that delivers much lower operating costs and a different debt structure to network carriers (Table 10.1). This is because network carriers trade on their convenience and levels of service to passengers, both of which imply higher operating costs. A range of innovations characterise the LCC business model:

- paperless ticketing;
- Internet-based bookings;
- minimising staffing levels and encouraging the multi-skilling of staff, so they can take on a variety of roles in the organisation;
- using only one type of aircraft to reduce training costs;
- one class for passengers;
- unbundling fares so that extra charges apply for, say, checking in luggage or printing boarding cards;
- earning income from services that are provided free on network carriers – such as catering, headphones and pillows;
- flights to regional airports that charge lower landing fees and often have spare capacity. this reduces congestion at the busier airports;
- flying point-to-point without the need to set up a feeder network for their airports; and
- operating a yield management system by selling seats at different prices according to supply and demand – on any one flight there may be many different fares, allowing loss-leading (and headline-grabbing) fares to be charged.

This business model allows LCCs to charge significantly lower prices than the network carriers. In turn, this increases

Table 10.1 Comparison of strategies of LCCs and network carriers

	Network Carriers	LCCs
Business model	Global strategy and high cost	Niche strategy and low cost
Network	Hub band spoke Global alliance	Point to point Regional airports
Fleet	Different types of aircraft Moderate aircraft utilisation	One type of aircraft High aircraft utilisation
Product	Full-service Branding supports full-service concept Complex fare structure	Self-service Branding emphasises price Simple fare structure
Sales policy/distribution	Sales departments Global distribution system	Direct sales Internet-based
Operations	Traditional check-in procedures Multiple classes In-flight service	eTicketing and self-service check-in One class In-flight extras available for purchase

Source: based on Duval, 2007; Boniface and Cooper, 2009

load factors and allows LCCs to make a profit on smaller operating margins. As a result, LCCs pose a significant threat to the network carriers on many routes.

AirAsia

AirAsia has enthusiastically adopted the principles of a LCC. As one of the first Asian LCCs, it was formed in 2001 and by 2014 flew to over 88 destinations and carried over 220 million passengers. The airline's mission is:

'To attain the lowest cost so that everyone can fly with AirAsia and maintain the highest quality product, embracing technology to reduce cost and enhance service levels' (www.airasia.com).

According to the AirAsia annual reports this mission is underpinned by a strategy comprising six key business principles:

1. A lean cost structure with efficient point-to-point operations, attracting the right people and continuously reducing costs and so delivering low fares. For example, AirAsia has a 25-minute turnaround on the ground to achieve high aircraft utilisation and deliver greater productivity. It also adopts the classic LCC model through self-automation, no frills, and cost-saving innovation which includes a lean distribution system offering a wide and innovative range of distribution channels, including AirAsia Expedia.

2. Maximise shareholders' value by growing profit through low costs, expanding the network sustainably and investing in the brand.

3. Ensure safety by complying with International Aviation Safety Standards and practices, keeping operations simple and transparent and ensuring the security of staff and passengers. However, in January 2015 the airline suffered its first major accident when Indonesia AirAsia Flight 8501 was lost off the coast of Indonesia.

4. Passion for guest satisfaction by keeping things simple and delivering a friendly and unique service.

5. Transparency in decision-making, information sharing and timely disclosure.

6. Human capital development by investing in skills, recognising that people contribute to success, rewarding excellence and individual contributions and maintaining one brand across the Group.

The airline is growing its route network in a sustainable way, and in 2007 entered the long-haul market with AirAsia X, launched as a low-cost, long-haul carrier. AirAsiaX is based on the same principles as its parent – high-frequency, point-to-point networks to long-haul destinations between four and eight hours in flight duration from Kuala Lumpur (including Australia, China, India, Korea, Japan, Middle East and Europe). AirAsiaX complements AirAsia's current extensive route network and is an interesting example of extending the LCC concept to long-haul. AirAsia also has associate companies to increase its geographical range. These are:

- AirAsia Berhad
- AirAsia Indonesia
- Thai AirAsia
- Philippines' AirAsia
- AirAsia India
- AirAsia Zest
- AirAsia X
- Thai AirAsia X
- Indonesia AirAsia X

In addition, AirAsia has a Foundation to support ASEAN countries to develop entrepreneurship, equal opportunities and innovation. It also has a centre of excellence for aviation and is active on social media.

DISCUSSION QUESTIONS

1. Given the threat of climate change, draw up a balance sheet of the positive and negative sides of the environmental debate surrounding LCCs.

2. Draw up a list of the key elements of the business model of AirAsia. Rank the list in order of significance and annotate the table with the elements of the business model that have been adopted by network carriers.

3. In class debate the likely success of 'stretching' the LCC model from short-haul flights to long-haul.

Sources:

Boniface, B., Cooper, C and Cooper, R. (2012) *Worldwide Destinations: The Geography of Travel and Tourism*, 6th edn, Routledge, London.

British Airports Authority (2006) *Issue Brief: Low-Cost Airlines*, BAA, London.

Civil Aviation Authority (2006) *No Frills Carriers: Revolution or Evolution?* CAA, London.

Frances, G., Dennis, N., Ison, S. and Humphreys, I. (2007) The transferability of the low cost model to long haul airline operations, *Tourism Management* **28**, 391–398.

Gross, S. and Schroeder, A. (2007) *Handbook of Low Cost Airlines – Strategies, Business Processes and Market Environment*, Kluwer, Berlin.

Klophaus, R., Conrady, R. and Fichert, F. (2012) Low cost carriers going hybrid: evidence from Europe, *Journal of Air Transport Management* **23**, 54–58.

de Wit, J.G. and Zuidberg, J. (2012) The growth limits of the low cost carrier model, *Journal of Air Transport Management* **21**, 17–23.

www.airasia.com

CHAPTER 11
GOVERNMENT AND TOURISM

Learning Outcomes

This chapter focuses upon the role of government in tourism, outlining the key reasons for government involvement in tourism and the roles played by government. The chapter is designed to provide you with:

- an understanding of why government is involved in tourism;

- an awareness of the tourism policy-making process;

- a comprehensive view of public sector tourism organisations;

- an appreciation of contemporary tourism governance;

- an overview of why tourism planning is important; and

- an outline of the tourism planning process.

Introduction

This chapter is concerned with the role of government in tourism. Some argue that tourism is a private sector activity and that government has no legitimate reason for being involved. However, we argue that exactly the opposite is true – government plays a central role in organising, managing, regulating and governing the tourism sector; indeed, following 9/11 government stepped in to keep many airlines afloat. In addition, government owns and manages many iconic tourism attractions including national parks, coastlines and heritage attractions such as museums, art galleries and historic monuments.

Of course, government has its own reasons for intervening in tourism. Tourism plays a leading economic development role in many countries, and for the developed world in countries such as Greece or Spain tourism represents a significant proportion of the economy. As a result, government cannot afford to leave such an important economic sector to the whim of the market and the private sector. Remember, too, that tourism is produced where it is consumed, creating many consequences for the environment and host communities (as we saw in Chapters 4 and 5). It is government's role to alleviate the negative consequences of tourism and to ensure that the sector is regulated and planned effectively. As a result, all levels of government play an active role in tourism although as we will see later in this chapter, the trend is to devolve government responsibility for tourism to the regional and local level.

The Role of Government in Tourism

Considering the role of government in tourism raises three key issues – firstly, why should government be involved; secondly, there is an observable shift of the government role towards *governance* rather than *regulation and control*; and, finally, the complex nature of tourism demands government coordination of activity and policies as we see in the classic paper by Scott chosen for this chapter.

Government has to be involved in tourism for a range of reasons:

- **Authority.** Government is the only body that has the authority to legislate and determine policy for tourism and is therefore able to coordinate the sector at national, regional and local level.

- **Economics.** As noted above, tourism plays an important role in many national economies, not only in terms of contributing foreign exchange, but also as an economic development tool and a generator of employment.

- **Education and training.** Government has overall control of national education and training systems including for tourism. These systems have an important role in supplying trained manpower to the tourism sector. With the human resources crisis in tourism (which we consider in Chapter 14), government plays an important role in boosting the image of tourism as a rewarding sector to work in.

- **Statistics and information.** As the private sector is reluctant to pay for large-scale tourism surveys, such as, say, international arrivals and departures or surveys of domestic travel, government has to step in to supply this service.

- **Planning and control to ensure that tourism delivers benefits and outweighs the costs.** We have seen the potential negative consequences of tourism for both natural and man-made resources and for host communities. It is the role of government to ensure that the benefits of tourism are maximised and the negative consequences managed to a minimum. Some governments, for example, view tourism as social benefit for their populations and subsidise holidays through 'social tourism schemes' for the disadvantaged.

- **Market regulation and promotion.** Government has the authority to regulate and intervene in markets, particularly in a fragmented sector such as tourism where quality control and management may need to be imposed. Increasingly this is done in cooperation with the sector through 'public private partnerships' (PPPs). Government also has the resources to promote destinations and ensure that a positive image is projected.

- **The nature of destinations.** We saw in Chapter 2 that destinations can be viewed as loosely articulated amalgams of organisations and communities, so it commonly falls to government to provide the coordination and leadership needed for destinations to function. This includes destination marketing, visitor information provision, research, and planning and management.

From Government to Governance: The Changing Role of Government

Traditionally, the role of government in tourism has been policy setting, regulation and planning. However, as the importance of tourism has grown and government's role has matured, the public sector is expected to provide a wider range of functions including marketing and promotion, destination management, strategy and sector coordination. Government agencies have struggled to deliver all of these roles alone and so they have sought out partnerships with 'non-state actors' such as the industry and communities – to deliver these functions. This approach recognises the importance of market forces and reflects a more fundamental trend in government to more collaborative ways of working. As a result, government agencies now act to coordinate the activities of tourism through 'integrated tourism governance' rather than 'regulation'. Here, we can think of tourism governance as:

Representing the whole system of rights, processes, and controls established internally and externally over the management of a destination with the objective of protecting the interests of all stakeholders.

Coordination across government

Tourism is a complex sector and, as we have seen, it impacts upon other sectors such as transport, labour and the environment. Equally, tourism interests range from the international and national level to the regional and local. As a result, it is important for government agencies to coordinate their actions and policies with respect to tourism. This is done in two ways (Scott, 2015):

1. **Horizontal coordination of tourism policy and actions.** Effective tourism governance demands that activities and policies are coordinated horizontally across the relevant government departments and ministries. For example air transport policy has a fundamental impact upon the tourism sector yet is normally not part of the tourism portfolio. In many countries, such as Australia, a cross-departmental committee has been formed to ensure that the interests of tourism are heard in relevant government ministries and departments.

2. **Vertical coordination of tourism policy and actions.** Vertical coordination in tourism governance ensures that national, regional and local activities and policies are linked and reinforcing. In addition, with the trend to devolution of tourism powers to regional and local levels, new mechanisms are being designed to ensure that vertical coordination takes place and that the regional and local authorities do not act independently of national policies and plans.

Tourism Policy

A key role of government is the determination of tourism policy. Tourism policy is a macro-level instrument that looks to the long term and, by showing the intention of government, it provides a clear sense of direction for the tourism sector. The key aims of tourism policy are to create competitive destinations, to ensure that the tourism sector functions efficiently and to deliver benefits, including income and employment to the government's stakeholders (Scott, 2015). Tourism policy also sets the administrative framework for tourism as we see below. Finally, as we noted above, given the nature of tourism, policy also has to interact with other policy areas such as, say, transport or the environment.

The UNWTO defines tourism policy as:

'All the actions carried out under the coordination of public administrations with the objectives of achieving previously defined aims in the processes of analysis, attraction, reception and evaluation of the impacts of tourism flows in a tourism system or destination.'

The process of determining tourism policy is a continuous one with constant revisions and iterations. Table 11.1 shows the policy cycle for tourism.

Wanhill (2008) classifies the main policy instruments that governments use to manage tourism into two basic types:

1. **Managing tourism demand.** The policy instruments available here include:
   - Marketing and promotion, where government funds and coordinates destination marketing activities, particularly international promotion.
   - Information provision and network development for incoming tourists.

Table 11.1 The tourism policy cycle

Stage of the cycle	Activity
Define the scope and philosophy of the policy	A period of reflection, consultation and debate to define the parameters of the policy and a framework for action, including roles and responsibilities
Analyse the existing policy framework, identify issues	An analytical and diagnostic stage scoping the internal and external factors that will influence the policy
Determine the policy objectives	Objectives are developed on the basis of the analysis above and set the framework for the policy action programmes
Develop the tourism policy plan	The tourism policy plan develops a set of coherent programmes and actions that have been agreed by consensus. These programmes and actions will relate to the competitive positioning of the destination or system
Policy implementation and outcome	Policy will be implemented by the public sector institutions, increasingly in partnership with other stakeholders. This stage will determine the relative roles, funding, timing and monitoring

- Pricing intervention to control competition and regulate the tourism market.
- Controlling access through, say, visas and immigration policy. Here, this is often not part of tourism policy but lies in the domain of immigration policy. China's tourism policy, for example, has used the control of entry and exit to the country strategically to develop its international tourism sector.
- Security and safety is another area which impacts upon tourism but often it is implemented by another public sector agency as in the USA.

2. **Managing tourism supply.** The policy instruments available here include:

- Land-use planning, building regulations and environmental control which allows government to control the location and scale of tourism development.
- Market regulation is used to govern how firms behave in the marketplace and to prevent, say, mergers which may act against the public interest – examples would include mergers of airlines which may create monopolies on certain routes.
- Market research and planning is an important aspect of government policy for tourism as government is seen as the candidate to fund large-scale surveys.
- Taxation – here tourism taxes, as in, say, Bermuda, are levied as well as other taxes which can be levied on tourism.
- Education and training is a critical area for tourism manpower development, although it is often implemented by other ministries than tourism.
- Ownership of tourism plant is more unusual but in the past has been part of government policy as in some African countries and also New Zealand.
- Investment incentives are used to influence the actions of investors in tourism.

From a public sector perspective, however, tourism is a relatively new focus for policy. Stevenson *et al.* (2008) state that this has a number of implications for the process of tourism policy making:

- it takes place in a rapidly changing environment;
- it is essentially about communication with other stakeholders;
- it takes place on the margins of political activity; and
- it is closely linked to other policy areas.

Classic Paper

Scott, N. (2015) Tourism policy, pp. 57–90 in Cooper, C. (ed.)
Contemporary Tourism Reviews, Volume 1, **Goodfellow, Oxford**

Noel Scott has written a comprehensive, deep and wide-ranging review of tourism policy. The review delivers an extensive list of the policy literature, not just in tourism, but also the core literature of political science. This paper is a classic simply because of the synoptic approach of the author, reviewing over 250 pieces of policy-related literature – a literature that Scott admits is diverse and fragmented – indeed the value of this review is in drawing together this disparate literature. The second distinguishing mark of the paper is the intellectual structure used – that of the policy cycle as a narrative for the paper.

The paper opens with an introduction outlining the purpose of the review as 'the study of government policy seek[ing] to understand how policy decisions are created, the information, interests and values involved in policy processes and what their impact are' (p. 58). The paper goes on to explain that tourism policy is important because it has a practical impact on the sector, indeed we can think of the literature splitting into both practical and academic approaches. Here, the academic approaches examine definitions of policy and different types and levels of tourism policy.

Scott then spends some time on examining the policy-creation process itself and how policy is evaluated. The review begins with policy aims, objectives and ideologies before moving on to the different geographic levels of policy. The policy-making process is examined in detail and the role of stakeholders and interested parties clearly outlined through the 'relational approach'.

The review concludes, rightly, with the fact that the policy literature is a vibrant and active field – much aided by this excellent classic paper by Noel Scott.

Government Tourism Organisations

There is a large variety of government agencies that have responsibility for tourism. These range from inter-governmental organisations such as the UNWTO to local authority tourism offices. As these agencies mature in their roles, structure and funding are changing as we explore later in this chapter.

International Organisations

At the international level, it is notoriously difficult for the public sector to design and implement tourism policy simply because it requires agreement of all the nation states involved. The European Union, for example, has limited tourism powers; instead, tourism policy and decisions are taken at the national level. Whilst there are a number of inter-governmental agencies working in tourism, there are two that stand out for their contribution:

1. **The UN World Tourism Organization (UNWTO) (www.unwto.org).** The UNWTO is the peak public sector body for tourism based in Madrid. It is a specialised agency of the United Nations and serves as a global forum for tourism policy issues and a repository of tourism expertise. The agency is committed to the development of responsible, sustainable and universally accessible tourism and to promoting the role of tourism in achieving the United Nations Sustainable Development Goals. Its major contribution, however, has been the development of statistical measurement systems for both tourism demand and supply.

2. **The Organisation for Economic Cooperation and Development (OECD) Tourism Committee (www.oecd.org).** Based in Paris, the OECD represents the governments of the world's leading economies. The OECD has an active tourism committee, formed shortly after World War Two to advise countries on how tourism could be used to rebuild

shattered economies. The committee is in a unique position to serve as an international forum for coordinating tourism policies and actions and it acts as a global forum for discussions of tourism policies.

National Organisations

In contrast to the international level, it is at the national scale that government has real powers for tourism. Government intervention at the national level is achieved through ministries of tourism or national tourism organisations (NTOs). Wanhill (2008) states that the way that these agencies for tourism are organised differs significantly across the world, but that they can but summarised into five types:

1. A Ministry of Tourism is common where tourism represents a significant proportion of the economy. Mauritius is an example (www.mauritius.net/).

2. An NTO located within the Ministry is another variant where the NTO delivers the marketing and planning functions of tourism and the Ministry takes care of policy and international relations as in Greece (www.gnto.co.uk/).

3. An NTO located outside the Ministry is increasingly common as the specialist technical functions demanded by today's tourism requires specialist staff and terms of reference. In this model, the majority of funding still comes from government although the agency may be called upon to meet some costs from entrepreneurial activities. Tourism Australia is an example here (www.australia.com/).

4. A semi-governmental agency with its own board and constitution is a more unusual approach although, again, the majority of funding comes from government. An example here is the Canadian Tourism Commission (www.canada.travel/).

5. A Convention and Visitor Bureau (CVB) may be established which is independent of government and often formed by the private sector. This type of organisation can be based upon membership with member's fees forming a significant part of the CVB's funding.

For all NTOs the source and scale of their funding is an important issue. In part it is determined by the importance of tourism to the national economy – for example, the Spanish government is generous with its funding to support tourism, but of course politics also plays a part in the level of funding. Where government provides the significant funding to tourism agencies, there is an increasing trend to attempt to assess the effectiveness of that funding through, for example, calculating the return on investment (ROI) of marketing campaigns or development funding. More controversially, governments may also choose to fund their agencies through a tourism tax. This can be on bed nights or, more commonly, on passenger movements into and out of the country, or on spending through a value added tax. Other sources of funding available to governments include:

● levies upon tourism businesses, normally based upon turnover. Investment and foreign exchange levies are also used, as are levies on tourism businesses to fund tourism training as in Kenya (http://tourismfund.co.ke/); and

● the user pays approach where organisations pay the NTO for services rendered, such as promotion or booking services.

The Role of NTOs

The effectiveness and scope of the roles that an NTO plays is obviously dependent upon the funding issue discussed above. Whilst the roles of NTOs do vary globally, there is a set of core competencies common to most NTOs. These focus around the complementary roles of 'planning and development' and 'marketing and promotion' that are particularly suited to the coordinating role that government can play, and to the fact that government has a mandate for planning.

Planning and Development

In terms of planning and development, it falls to government to plan and manage tourism at all scales, from the national to the local, and including thematic planning such as for eco-tourism or heritage-based tourism. We discuss the planning and development role in more detail later in this chapter. As part of the planning role, NTOs are often given responsibility for managing the quality of the tourism product through the issuing of licences for accommodation and food and beverage outlets to operate, as well as inspecting, registering and grading accommodation. In many countries, such as Saudi Arabia, this is a major activity of the NTO and a legal framework has been developed to support them in this role. NTOs also use their development role to influence investors and the types of tourism facilities that are encouraged. This is done through tax and investment incentives and, along with re-investing tourism taxes, is a powerful tool to shape destinations. NTOs also tend to be responsible for the collection of tourism statistics and research, both internationally and domestically. Education and training for tourism is also an area of competence for NTOs, although this is often shared with education and manpower ministries and agencies. In particular, NTOs commonly are responsible for specialist tourism training such as for guides, as in Malaysia.

Marketing and promotion

Whilst you may expect the marketing and promotion of destinations to be the preserve of the private sector, in fact it is an important part of the work of NTOs. This is for three reasons:

1. NTOs act in a coordination role for destination marketing, providing an 'umbrella' marketing function for the destination, under which individual organisations then market their own products.
2. Destination marketing and promotion is expensive, particularly at the international level – it therefore falls to government to provide this role for destinations.
3. It should also be said that government is involved in the marketing of destinations because the spin off in-terms of attracting inward investment and features such as mega-events can be considerable. In the twenty-first century, for example, there have been a number of new entrants to staging the Formula One motor racing Grand Prix, which can be overtly linked to the ambitions of those countries in the tourism marketplace.

As a result, the public sector tends to provide leadership and coordination in destination branding, promotion and in the provision of visitor information. Many NTOs, for example, have extensive networks of visitor information centres and other means of delivering information to visitors, particularly at gateways and popular tourism spots. They are also active in developing new markets, as in Singapore where the education market is seen as an important part of tourism, and they nurture high-yield markets such as the business market.

The public sector's marketing role is not an easy one, however. It could be argued that the public sector is ill-equipped to perform a professional marketing role, although as agencies have matured this criticism is less valid. Public sector budgets are set on an annual basis and this hampers long-term market planning, and the very nature of destinations, with their many stakeholders and interest groups, makes even the coordination role of the public sector difficult at times. But perhaps the most challenging aspect of the role is the fact that they have no control over the product that they are promoting. In some countries, this can be partly overcome when the prices of products are regulated and, as mentioned above, development incentives can be used as a lever to influence a particular destination, but for the most part the public sector marketing role is dependent upon the good will and involvement of the private sector stakeholders at the destination.

Contemporary Approaches to Integrated Tourism Governance

The pivotal role that government plays in tourism means that tourism cannot escape from the changes in how government operates, and from the pressures that are placed upon government. These include the impact of globalisation and changing global politics which have combined to flatten administrative structures and to demand that governments are networked into a wider world. As a result, government is becoming more accountable, more participative and more responsive to community activism. In tourism this is compounded by changing industry structures, in part driven by technology and globalisation, but also by the impact of the knowledge economy. This demands that the tourism sector in general leverages from the knowledge, competencies and skills of its employees and wider stakeholders. In other words, contemporary governments are actively encouraging the involvement of 'non-state actors' in tourism decision making.

In many respects, government tourism agencies have been leaders in responding to these challenges and we are seeing the emergence of a new style of public sector involvement in tourism which we can think of as 'contemporary integrated tourism governance'. Two key features characterise this new approach:

1. devolution of government power and responsibility away from the national level to the regional and local – in other words, closer to where the tourism product is actually delivered; and

2. the development of policy and governance networks which manage the relationship between the public sector and destination stakeholders at the local and regional level.

This new approach is designed to be more effective and efficient, to encourage partnerships and, above all, to deliver a more competitive destination. The following case study shows how destination stakeholders can be closely involved in determining the destiny of a destination and reflects the new approach of integrated tourism governance.

Mini Case Study 11.1
The Hawke's Bay Wine Country Tourism Association, New Zealand

Introduction

Traditionally, the wine and tourism industry have had little cooperation. However, since 2000, and with government encouragement, a number of wine and tourism clusters have developed in New Zealand. One of the first was in the Hawke's Bay wine region – a world famous wine region. Yet, in the past the area suffered from a proliferation of small and ineffective brands. This has meant that Hawke's Bay has not been as competitive a destination as it could be in attracting the growing wine and food tourism market. In response, Hawke's Bay Wine Country Tourism Association (HBWCTA) was established in 2000 as a membership association. It is currently creating a strong market presence for the region and its growth prompted a merger with the Hawke's Bay Tourism Association. It is now recognised as one of the more mature clusters in New Zealand (Mitchell and Schreiber, 2007).

The Roles of the Association

The Association has built its success upon three pillars:

1. creating a coherent brand for Hawke's Bay Wine Tourism – Hawkes Bay Inc.;
2. ensuring competitiveness of the local SMEs; and
3. fostering a sense of ownership for tourism

The association's varied roles contribute to the prosperity and marketability of the region.

Hawke's Bay wine.
Source: © Pete Titmuss/Alamy Images

Marketing is a key activity and this enables the area's SMEs to benefit from the organisation as participants of a larger brand presence. The HBWCTA undertakes promotional activities including exposure for its brand on television and in other media, as well as participation in trade fairs designed for both consumers and the traders. All this works to attract visitors and the area is now a successful wine tourism destination built upon a coherent brand encompassing art deco, food, wine and relaxing lifestyles, largely made possible by the unifying presence of the HBWCTA. Although Hawke's Bay has become much more than a wine region, the centrality of wine as a component of its image as a tourist attraction has become clear.

In addition to marketing, the Association is keen to enhance the competitiveness of tourism businesses within its area. Consequently, it organises business development programmes to help professionalise smaller operations and these activities are generally free to association members.

Membership of the HBWCTA is drawn from any business that sees itself part of the wine tourism sector or sees the importance of this type of tourism to the regional economy. This has helped to build a strong sense of identity for tourism in the area, not only in the creation of a business association but also an active lobby group that can be involved in commenting directly to policy-makers about what they consider to be appropriate means of supporting tourism development and the consequences of potential political measures.

The role of the public sector has been to provide support that ensures that the Association is able to develop its capability and capacity in a manner that might otherwise have taken longer to occur or, indeed, may not have developed as effectively.

This case shows clearly how the public sector facilitates and supports associations such as the one in Hawke's Bay, and in so doing works in partnership to involve civil society and the tourism sector to achieve its aims.

DISCUSSION QUESTIONS

1. Establishing the Association required foresight and local leadership. Thinking of a tourism-based initiative in your area, using local press sources, can you identify the key individuals who initiated the process?

2. Contemporary destination governance has seen a blurring of the roles of the public and private sector. Using a Venn diagram, identify the key roles of the two groups and show where they overlap.

3. Visit websites related to tourism in the Hawkes Bay area and list the number of different stakeholders involved in tourism. Do you think that the Association is an effective way to harness the energies of these stakeholders in the area?

Sources:
Mitchell, R. and Schreiber, C. (2007) Wine tourism networks and clusters: operation and barriers in New Zealand, pp. 80–106 in Michael, E. (ed) *Micro Clusters and Networks: The Growth of Tourism*, Elsevier, Oxford.
www.hawkesbaynz.com

The Anatomy of Integrated Tourism Governance

This integrated approach to tourism governance is a quantum leap from past approaches. The contemporary approach of forging partnerships between the public sector and other destination stakeholders creates a more holistic approach to governing the destination, effectively leading to more 'joined up' tourism administration as we saw with the Hawkes Bay example. Because decisions are being taken closer to the public sector's clients – the industry, other public sector organisations, and the host community – the approach integrates public sector services closer to the point of delivery. For example, local and regional tourism stakeholders are encouraged to be involved in marketing and planning decisions in the spirit of true partnership.

The integrated approach to tourism governance is a trend that can be seen across the world, from Canada, to Scotland and New Zealand. The approach is based upon the concept of destinations being made up of a relatively stable set of public and private sector actors who are linked to each other and defined by their relevant administrative boundaries. The linkages allow communication for information, communication, expertise, trust and other policy resources. Of course, in the past, stakeholders were in touch with other, but the difference here is the involvement of the public sector who pump resources into the network and make it a more formal arrangement. Above all though, the involvement of the government makes the networks more democratic and all stakeholders are given the opportunity to engage and participate in decisions.

Integrated Tourism Governance Structures

The detailed structures and operation of these new public sector arrangements for tourism vary across the world but we can discern the emergence of some common features as the approach gains momentum:

- a disciplined approach to identifying the types, roles and functions of all destination stakeholders and their relationships;
- strong public sector leadership backed by political commitment;
- technology is used to deliver a single point of access for all stakeholders – destination web portals are increasingly used;
- flexible funding arrangements are essential to respond to differing local and regional tourism contexts; and
- performance measures have been factored in.

This approach to governance is a clear departure from past approaches but is proving to be highly effective in engaging the tourism sector at the local and regional level in decision making and policy formation. Of course, there are tensions and strains as systems change and power shifts from the national level to a more dispersed regional and local level, but the successful approaches are ones where resistance to change has been anticipated and planned for. The very fact that the public sector is being taken closer to the point of delivery of the tourism product means that every context is different and so there is no 'one size fits all' model of integrated tourism governance, rather it tends to be destination specific. The potential of the approach is clear and can lead to genuine 'learning destinations' as tourism slowly comes to terms with the knowledge economy. It is interesting though that the approach is also dependent upon intangible elements such as personalities, trust, leadership and a cohesive vision.

Tourism Planning

We have noted above that an important reason for public sector involvement in tourism is their mandate from the public to plan and manage. In the case of tourism, the public sector acts as the lead planning agency ensuring that tourism is beneficial for the economy, environment and society (Morpeth and Yan, 2015). This is essential as tourism occurs in many diverse settings and is attracted to fragile resources, such as the natural heritage and cultural attractions that are both unique and special – but this also makes them vulnerable to the inseparable nature of tourism – the fact that the tourist has to be physically present to consume. In other words, there is a pressure on the resource, often focused in both space and time, that has to be planned and managed to minimise the costs and maximise the benefits of tourism to that resource.

The Anatomy of Tourism Planning

Planning is about taking a disciplined and ordered approach to organising the future – and tourism is no exception here. Effectively, tourism planning is one part of the implementation of tourism policy. We can define tourism planning as:

> **'Anticipating and regulating change in a [tourism] system to promote orderly develop-ment so as to increase social, economic and environmental benefits of the development process' (Murphy, 1985, p. 156).**

Table 11.2 catalogues why this is important in tourism in particular.

As we noted earlier in this chapter, government's approach to tourism is changing with the active involvement of 'civil society'. As a result, tourism planning now closely involves both the private sector and the host community at the destination (Sharpley and Telfer, 2014). In the section on contemporary approaches to integrated tourism governance we showed how tourism agencies are devising mechanisms and formalising networks to involve destination stakeholders in tourism decisions, including planning. Of course, this is just yet one further evolution of the 'public participation' debate, where there has long been concern that the loudest voices would be heard at a destination rather than a balanced representative view.

Table 11.2 The imperative for tourism planning

Tourism is not well understood	The lack of expertise in tourism means that planning is essential to put in place guidelines and codes of practice and to ensure a holistic view of the destination.
Complexity of tourism	The multifaceted nature of tourism demands that planners coordinate and organise all of the destination elements.
The destination is where tourism is delivered	The destination is the focus of tourism, and the inseparable nature of tourism means that benefits must be maximised and costs minimised.
Establish objectives	Planning allows the establishment of destination objectives which help to unite stakeholders.
Work together as a destination	Plans provide a rallying call for the destination with allocated roles and responsibilities to bring all stakeholders together behind one purpose.
Guidelines and standards	Plans put in place for guidelines and standards which raise the quality of the destination offering and ensure that new developments comply.
Sustainable development	Planning ensures sustainable development of all the destination elements through integrated planning approaches.
Baseline and monitoring process	Plans allow for disciplined monitoring of destination elements to observe the success, or otherwise, of the plan.
Place-making and differentiation	Competitive destinations are those that emphasise local features and design to deliver the tourist experience.

The contemporary approach to integrated tourism governance delivers a 'whole of destination approach' to tourism planning. This reflects the realities of tourism, which demand collaboration and partnerships reflecting the many stakeholders involved in delivering the product to the tourist. To reach this point, tourism planning has gone through a series of stages, beginning with plans that prioritised economic goals and moving towards contemporary plans where sustainability is the key. The evolution of tourism planning is as shown in Table 11.3.

We can identify five traditions that have characterised tourism planning (Getz, 1986; Hall, 2007):

1. **boosterism** where tourism is viewed uncritically as a means to 'boost' the profile of the destination;

2. **economic planning** based on economic and regional development where the state is involved in managing the economy and economic analysis is used to make and evaluate planning decisions;

3. **physical planning** where land use zoning and the use of geographical information systems (GIS) is dominant and based upon concepts from regional and land use planning;

4. **community-based planning** where tourism plans take account of the views of the host community, often being developed from the community upwards – there are a variety of approaches here, ranging from 'token' participation to full control by the host community (Figure 11.1); and

5. **sustainable planning** where the plans are increasingly concerned with the long-term viability of the destination and encompass issues such as environmental sustainability, carbon footprints and climate change.

Finally, tourism planning operates at a range of geographical scales:

- **International planning** is unusual, mainly for the reasons identified above when considering international government operations in tourism. Simply, it is difficult to get agreement across borders and national planning systems differ substantially. Nonetheless, an

Table 11.3 The evolution of tourism planning

Physical-based plans	These were site-specific plans, emphasising economic development with no consideration of the wider impact of the development.
Strategic-based plans	Plans began to take into account the wider regional impacts of tourism developments and were more integrated, including environmental considerations – early tourism master plans took this form.
Master plans	Tourism master plans took all the destination elements, including transport, marketing, human resources and the impacts of development into one overarching plan. These tended to be 'one off' plans that were updated every few years.
Integrated and rolling plans	The next evolution of tourism plans was away from the 'one off' plan towards a more continuous planning process with monitoring and adjustments made over the plan period.
Whole of destination approach	Contemporary approaches to tourism planning take a 'whole of destination approach' including the host community and all legitimate stakeholders to deliver competitiveness and sustainability.

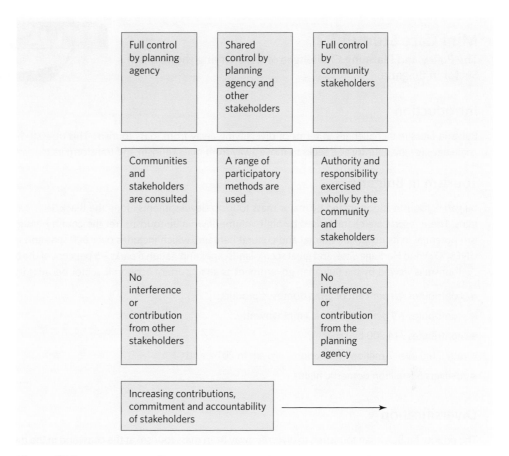

Figure 11.1 A continuum of host community involvement in tourism planning
Source: based on Selman, 2004

increasing number of international planning initiatives are being launched – particularly across borders, such as the tourism strategy for the Greater Mekong Delta Region or the Danube Regional Strategy. There is also no doubt that new destinations such as Antarctica will require an international approach to tourism planning.

- **National planning** in tourism is common and sets the framework for regional and local plans. In the past this has been the scale for master plans, as for example in former Eastern European states such as Romania and Bulgaria, although as we have seen above, the trend is now to focus more at the regional and local level.

- **Regional plans** allow for detailed tourism plans within the national framework. They will focus more closely on access, development, infrastructure and policy.

- **Development planning** is where specific areas have been zoned for tourism. These plans deal with site and facility layout, zoning and design issues as well as infrastructure and investment planning and tend to be the most common type of tourism plan.

- **Special plans** cut across geographical scales; instead they focus on tourism themes such as the Australian State of Victoria's Aboriginal Tourism Development Plan (Tourism Victoria, 2006) (www.tourism.vic.gov.au/aboriginaltourism/).

Of course, the pace of change in new thinking and approaches to planning and policy creates its own challenges and not all countries are equipped to embrace these changes quickly. In the case study below we show how tourism planning and policy in Bulgaria is struggling to embrace these contemporary ideas as the country clings to older ways of planning and managing tourism.

Mini Case Study 11.2
The Policy and Planning Challenges of Diversifying the Tourism Sector in Bulgaria

Introduction

Bulgaria faces real challenges in terms of diversifying away from mass tourism. This case study outlines the policy challenges for the country as it seeks to move away from mass tourism and transform its tourism sector.

Tourism in Bulgaria

Bulgaria's tourism is dominated by major mass tourism developments along the Black Sea Coast and in the mountains. These resorts are characterised by high-volume/low-value tourism. Yet the country has great untapped tourism potential in its unspoiled natural and cultural heritage, which includes over 600 spas and mineral springs, nine UNESCO World Heritage Sites, and great scenic landscapes and national parks – 5 per cent of the territory is protected.

Tourism is viewed by the Bulgarian government as an important economic sector because it:

- contributes 4.5 per cent of gross domestic product;
- contributes 3.9 per cent of total employment;
- contributes 314,200 bed spaces;
- attracted over 7 million international arrivals in 2014; and
- delivers 5.5 million domestic nights.

Diversification

The priority for Bulgarian tourism is to diversify away from mass tourism at the coast and in the mountains. Mass tourism brings a range of problems including dependence on a few markets, geographical concentration, high seasonality, low occupancy, acute price competition and a dependence upon overseas tour operators. By diversifying its products to include heritage and cultural tourism, nature-based tourism, and food and wine tourism, Bulgaria would be able to solve many of these problems. It would also encourage the development of high-quality products, disperse the benefits of tourism to rural and remote areas and attract high-yield visitors.

The Tourism Policy Challenges

For Bulgaria to achieve the imperative of diversification, the OECD (2007) has made a series of policy recommendations to address the challenges faced by the country in embracing contemporary approaches to policy and planning. Diversification must be part of an overall policy and strategies directing the future of Bulgarian tourism – indeed, the country's alternative varieties of tourism are a perfect complement for mass tourism. According to the OECD, policy and planning initiatives will be required to achieve diversification:

Policy Recommendations

Due to the nature of the Bulgarian political system, tourism power is concentrated at the local level with the regions particularly poorly funded and ill equipped to coordinate tourism. Strengthening of regional powers is therefore needed, reflecting current thinking on tourism policy. There is also a need for government agencies to coordinate their activities with each other as has not happened to date. In other words, structural changes in the Bulgarian political system are needed to create a transparent and inclusive policy formation process; and, finally, there is a need to develop the technical capacity of public sector personnel in tourism.

Secondly, SMEs will be the main medium for diversification. Policy should therefore be designed to support SMEs to innovate and encourage product development in such a way that tourism spend and employment can be captured locally. Policy support for SMEs must therefore be broadly based and multi-layered to include financial incentives, entrepreneurship development, and a training of the workforce.

Planning Recommendations

Away from the mass tourism resorts, there is the need to develop tourism hubs with product clusters, led by large anchor attractions where alternative forms of tourism play a key role. In addition there is the need to encourage 'coopetition' (cooperation and competition) amongst businesses in these tourism product clusters and the hubs should be linked by touring corridors and routes.

This case shows how the public sector can intervene strategically to reposition the tourism sector of a country. The challenge for Bulgaria will be to implement these ideas using contemporary approaches of integrated governance and policy development.

DISCUSSION QUESTIONS

1. Do you believe that diversification of tourism in Bulgaria should be led by policy intervention or should it be left to the private sector and market forces?

2. Draft a table of the disadvantages and advantages of mass tourism to Bulgaria. How many of these are susceptible to being influenced by public sector policy?

3. SMEs are seen as the solution to diversification in Bulgaria but many of them lack the right business background for tourism. Design a training programme for SMEs to bring them up to date with current developments in tourism management.

Sources:
Bulgarian State Tourism Agency (2006) *Strategic Plan for the Strategy for the Development of Bulgarian Tourism for the Period 2006–2009*, BSTA, Sofia.
OECD (2007) *Fostering SME and Entrepreneurship Development in the Tourism Sector in Bulgaria*, OECD, Paris.
www.tourism.government.bg/en

The Tourism Planning Process

The Bulgaria case study highlights the importance of both scale and approach to tourism planning. As we have seen, tourism planning takes many forms and acts at a variety of scales. However, we can discern a number of common threads running through contemporary approaches to the planning process.

At the beginning of any tourism planning exercise, a number of key questions have to be asked including:

- What type of tourist do we want to attract?
- What is the scale of tourism we want to develop?
- Where and how will tourism take place?
- Who will finance development?
- What is the government's view about tourism?
- Where will the manpower and infrastructure come from?

The answer to these questions will depend upon how important tourism is to the destination and the role that government plays in the planning process.

The Stages of Planning

There are many accounts of the various stages of tourism planning but the one presented by Mill and Morrison (1985) is both comprehensive and logical. Table 11.4 outlines the various stages and the tasks involved.

Tourism planning has created 'instant resorts' such as Cancun.
Source: © Dan Talson/Fotolia.com

The stages of tourism planning outlined in Table 11.4 cover the key functions of a tourism plan, although the sequencing and the details will vary according to the goals and objectives, and the scale of the plan.

Table 11.4 Stages of the tourism planning process

Stage of planning	The tasks involved
Background analysis	Desk research to set the context for the plan and identify information gaps
Situation analysis	Review current and past plans and policies, including the needs of the plan sponsors
Resource analysis	Inventory of tourism resources
Demand analysis	Market demand for the destination - volume, value, trends and characteristics
Tourism sector analysis	SWOT analysis of the tourism sector
Research	This stage plugs the gaps identified in background analysis and will involve visiting the destination
Resource research	A detailed review of the tourism resources through field visits to determine locations, types and capacities of the resources
Activities research	Identification of potential products available at the destination using the resource base
Market and competition analysis	Market research to expand on the background analysis and will include a competitor analysis
Synthesis	Here, the information from the first two stages is drawn together to inform the plan's development
Position statements	A series of reports for stakeholders to review the current situation and design the way forward. These reports will be focused on development, marketing and the sector

Table 11.4 (*continued*)

Stage of planning	The tasks involved
Goals and objectives	Based upon the research stages, plan goals and objectives are designed. They can be varied (for example, they may be economic or environmental), but they must be achievable, quantifiable and give the plan direction
Plan development	The plan is then developed into a series of actions that will deliver the goals and objectives. This may take the form of a draft plan which is then approved or modified
Programmes and actions	This is the 'engine room' of the plan, with detailed approaches for each of the plan's goals – they identify roles and responsibilities, timing, funding and monitoring
Plan monitoring	This final stage is vital. The quantified goals and objectives will be monitored on a regular basis and adjustments made to the plan if any are not being achieved. An excellent example of contemporary tourism planning using a monitoring approach is the Tourism Optimisation Management Model for Kangaroo Island in Australia (http.//www.tomm.info)

Source: Mill and Morrison, 1985

Plan Failure

A major issue for tourism planners is the fact that many plans are never implemented, or worse, they go wrong, or even fail. Consultants often tell of their expensive and detailed master plans that lie unopened on Ministry shelves. This may be because the plan could not be resourced or because the political will to implement the plan was lacking. The response to this issue by funding agencies has been to place more emphasis on the implementation and monitoring of tourism plans. Nonetheless, despite the fact that this chapter has shown the importance of public sector involvement in tourism – and of tourism planning – there are those who oppose this approach on the grounds that planning exercises are expensive, that tourism is a complex sector where planning is inappropriate and, in particular, view tourism as a private sector activity where public sector intervention is unwelcome.

Plans may also fail for a variety of reasons:

- public policy towards tourism may change and make the plan redundant;
- tourism demand may have been poorly estimated by the plan and the expected visitors do not materialise;
- expected developments such as, say, access and transportation fail to materialise;
- the competitor analysis may have underestimated particular competitors who surge ahead;
- the plan was badly conceived and out of scale with the destination and its own vision;
- the plan failed to convince key stakeholders to be involved; or
- the plan was drawn up by planners without a clear understanding of how tourism operates or the needs of the market.

When plans do fail, or are not implemented, then the destination will suffer. Firstly, there will be no disciplined allocation of resources across the destination, not simply within the tourism sector, but tourism may also lose out to other economic sectors such as, say, power generation at the coast. Secondly, failure will result in undisciplined competition between resources within tourism – for example, the clash between nature conservation and tourism access to national parks will not be resolved – and, finally, the very integrity of tourism resources at the destination will be threatened without a tourism planning framework.

SUMMARY

This chapter has demonstrated why government is so important for the tourism sector and outlined the agencies and mechanisms that deliver tourism policy, planning and marketing. Fundamentally the contribution of tourism to economies and societies is too valuable to leave it to the private sector and so governments legislate and provide a policy framework for tourism. This policy is delivered through a wide range of tourism public sector organisations and, whilst their roles vary, they can be summarised as policy, planning and marketing. To show how the approach has changed we presented a case study on Bulgaria where old-fashioned approaches still prevail. With increased pressure on the public sector, a new type of tourism governance is emerging where the organisations closest to the delivery of tourism are being empowered and networks of tourism stakeholders have developed to assist these organisations to deliver their tasks. This was illustrated by the case study on Hawkes Bay.

One of these tasks is tourism planning and we detail why it is so vital for tourism, an activity which is potentially very damaging to the destinations. The chapter outlines the tourism planning process and the fact that other destination stakeholders are increasingly involved in planning as the 'whole of destination approach' to planning becomes more widespread, as shown in the end of chapter case study on Vienna's 'crowd sourced' tourism strategy. Finally, the chapter identifies the reasons for plan failure and its consequences.

Discussion Questions

1. Draft a briefing paper for a councillor explaining why their local authority should be involved in tourism.

2. Taking a public sector tourist organisation for a destination that you know, visit their website and map their key functions.

3. For a destination that you are familiar with, create a list of the stakeholders who you would like to be involved in a policy network to assist in government decision making for tourism.

4. Justify why tourism planning is important.

5. Taking a destination that you are familiar with, design a strategy for the fair involvement of the host community in the tourism planning process.

Annotated Further Reading

1. Gunn, C.A. and Var, T. (2002) *Tourism Planning, Basics, Concepts, Cases*, 4th edn, Routledge, London.
   A tourism planning classic by Clare Gunn, a well-known practitioner in the field. It has a design bias and the cases are excellent.

2. Hall, C.M. and Jenkins, J.M. (1995) *Tourism and Public Policy*, 4th edn, Routledge, London.
   The classic text on tourism and public policy that covers all the ground in a clear and structured way.

3. Hall, C.M. (2000) *Tourism Planning*, Prentice-Hall, Harlow.
   An excellent early book providing an account of tourism planning at different scales and the influence of the different traditions of tourism planning.

4. Inskeep, E. (1997) *Tourism Planning: An Integrated and Sustainable Development Approach*, Chichester, Wiley.
   A volume by a well-known practitioner, with very much the nuts and bolts of tourism planning and essential reading for anyone interested in this topic.

5. Jenkins, J., Hall, C.M. and Mkono, M. (2014) Tourism and public policy: contemporary debates and future directions, Chapter 43 in Lew A.L., Hall, C.M. and Williams, A.M. (eds) *The Wiley Blackwell Companion to Tourism*, Wiley, Chichester.
   A thorough and contemporary review of tourism policy and governance.

6. Jeffries, D. (2001) *Governments and Tourism*, Butterworth Heinemann, Oxford.
   Another experienced practitioner providing a comprehensive and insightful book on governments and tourism.

7. Morpeth, N.D. and Yan, H. (2015) *Planning for Tourism: Towards a Sustainable Future*, CABI, Wallingford.
   Contemporary tourism planning text

8. Murphy, P.E. and Murphy, A.E. (2004). *Strategic Management for Tourism Communities*, Channel View, Clevedon.
   A thorough and expanded update on Peter Murphy's work on community tourism and the role of the hosts community in the contemporary planning process.

9. Pearce, D.G. (1992) *Tourist Organizations*, Longman, Harlow.
   A classic book that delivers a complete account of tourist organizations and their roles.

10. Sharpley, R. and Telfer, D.J. (2014) *Tourism and Development: Concepts and Issues*, 2nd edn, Channel View, Bristol.
    An excellent account of the different approaches to development that underpin tourism planning.

References Cited

Getz, D. (1986) Models in tourism planning towards integration of theory and practice, *Tourism Management* 7(1), 21–32.

Hall, C.M. (2007) Planning and managing the contemporary destination, Chapter 8 in Cooper C. and Hall, C.M. (eds) *Contemporary Tourism,* Butterworth Heinemann Elsevier, Oxford.

Mill, R.C. and Morrison, A.M. (1985) *The Tourism System: An Introductory Text,* Prentice Hall, Englewood Cliffs, NJ.

Morpeth, N.D. and Yan, H. (2015) *Planning for Tourism: Towards a Sustainable Future,* CABI, Wallingford.

Murphy, P. (1985) *Tourism: A Community Approach*, Methuen, London.

Tourism Victoria (2006) *Aboriginal Tourism Development Plan,* Tourism Victoria, Melbourne.

Scott, N. (2015) Tourism policy, pp. 57–90 in Cooper, C. (ed.) *Contemporary Tourism Reviews, Volume 1,* Goodfellow, Oxford.

Selman, P. (2004) Community participation in the planning of management of cultural landscapes, *Journal of Environmental Planning and Management* 47(3), 365–392.

Sharpley, R. and Telfer, D.J. (2014) *Tourism and Development: Concepts and Issues,* 2nd edn, Channel View, Bristol.

Stevenson, N., Airey, D. and Miller, G. (2008) Tourism policy making: the policymakers' perspectives, *Annals of Tourism Research* 35(3), 732–750.

Wanhill, S. (2008) Public sector and policy, Chapter 15 in Cooper, C., Fletcher, J., Fyall, A. Gilbert, D. and Wanhill, S. (eds) *Tourism Principles and Practice,* Prentice Hall, Harlow.

Major Case Study 11.1
Using Open Innovation to Create the Tourism Strategy for Vienna: An Inclusive Model of Tourism Governance

Introduction

Tourism is an important economic sector in Vienna, the capital of Austria. The sector contributes 4.1 per cent of GDP (direct and indirect effects, 2011) and 11 new full-time jobs are created for every million euros spent by tourists (2013). The tourism and hospitality sector is the city's fastest growing sector in terms of employment, representing almost 15 per cent of the job market (VTB, 2014). A tourism strategy, led by the public sector, is therefore an essential part of managing tourism in Vienna and the city was keen that the strategy would draw together all stakeholders in the future development of tourism in Vienna.

Tourism Strategy 2020 is a joint strategy document of the city of Vienna, the Vienna Tourist Board and the tourism industry. The strategy is the first to use the concept of 'open innovation', and in so doing the Vienna Tourist Board (VTB) has succeeded in 'co-creating' a shared and mutually accepted tourism strategy for the city of Vienna in 2020 ('Vienna 2020'), which takes into account the agendas of the various stakeholder groups (VTB, 2014). This was achieved using technology-driven empowerment of local stakeholders to facilitate collaboration and active participation in the implementation process. The technology was used to:

'facilitate a process of consultation, discussion, and eventually co-creation with a global audience of tourists and tourism stakeholders at various levels who were able to contribute their views on the opportunities and challenges for Vienna up to 2020' (VTB, 2014).

The term 'open innovation' can be defined as:

The use of purposive inflows and outflows of knowledge to accelerate internal innovation, and expand the markets for external use of innovation, respectively.

Objectives and Key Elements

VTB's vision was to co-create a shared and mutually accepted tourism strategy for Vienna based on input from the tourism industry and all its stakeholders at a local and international level. This shared vision embraced the agendas of the various stakeholder groups as well as facilitating their active participation in the implementation process and ensuring mutual acceptance of the overall vision for Vienna 2020 (VTB, 2014).

Implementation Process

There were three key stages in the open innovation process, a process that took place over four months:

1. **SWOT analysis.** In 2013 the process began with a SWOT analysis of the current situation of tourism in Vienna. This involved 50 experts in an Open Strategy Conference, identifying and weighting the key future challenges, discussing the initial strategic orientations for the strategy.

2. **Open innovation: first stage.** In the first stage, stakeholders were invited to participate in an online ideas contest to share their ideas on how to increase Vienna's attractiveness to 2020 (www.2020.vienna.info). These stakeholders were:

   - 650,000 guests (actual and potential);
   - city residents;
   - tour operators and travel agents abroad; and
   - employees in the tourism industry in Vienna.

   This first stage of the open innovation process reached more than 650,000 individuals through direct mailings, social media and PR activities. A total of about 800 users in 43 different countries registered, contributing 546 ideas (VTB, 2014).

3. **Open innovation: second stage.** In the second stage, over 2,500 local stakeholders were invited to take part in an online discussion to identify threats and opportunities based on the contributions received during the online idea contest, as well as strategic input from the VTB. Stakeholders contributed ideas, indicated priorities and became actively involved, collaborating and developing new partnerships with a clear long-term vision for growth (VTB, 2014). These stakeholders were:

   - politicians and policymakers;
   - public organisations;
   - decision makers and gatekeepers;
   - residents;
   - students; and
   - employees of Vienna's tourism industry.

   This third stage of the open innovation process resulted in some 260 registered local stakeholders, who discussed over 550 ideas and potential strategic orientations.

   The open innovation process is unique in tourism and facilitated stakeholder collaboration. The technology used, allowed for a mediated online process to facilitate the generation, discussion, development and evaluation of ideas. This meant that the VTB could be transparent in its strategy-setting process to design an 'inclusive model of tourism governance' (VTB, 2014). The resulting tourism strategy for Vienna 2020 provides:

'a clear, shared and mutually accepted vision for Vienna 2020 that not only takes into account the agendas of the various stakeholder groups, but also encourages active participation and engagement in the implementation process' (VTB, 2014).

International Advisory Panel

An international advisory panel was created to provide a global perspective and international best practice.

Although design, implementation, collaboration and analysis only took four months to complete, the results of the initiative will have a major impact upon Vienna's destination management agenda to 2020. As a result of this process, the use of open innovation has become an integral element and guiding principle of Vienna's strategy development process. As a direct consequence of this process, a vital and highly committed community has been established that has also made it possible to set up new partnerships and networks (VTB, 2014).

The VTB's open innovation approach has established new standards in the development process of tourism strategies. No previous tourism strategy has ever been derived from such a broad-based and participatory approach. The technology-enabled approach of consulting the 'wisdom of the crowds' was deployed at a strategic level for the first time in tourism. The open innovation approach served to facilitate local stakeholder collaboration. It also enabled the VTB to design a transparent and open process of stakeholder involvement aimed at creating an inclusive model of tourism governance.

DISCUSSION QUESTIONS

1. Debate in class the statement that using a 'crowd sourcing' model to develop strategy exposes the organisation to the risk of 'strategic drift'.

2. This is the first example of a crowd-sourced tourism strategy – how difficult is it to ensure that all voices are heard and not just the most influential?

3. Do you think that visitors to the city should have a legitimate stake in the strategy?

Source:
Vienna Tourist Board (VTB) (2014) *Vienna Tourism Strategy 2020*, VTB, Vienna.

PART 4

TOURISM DEMAND AND MARKETING ESSENTIALS

In this part, we focus upon the tourist, analysing how they demand tourism and are the focus of tourism marketing. Here, the emphasis is upon the 'generating region' of Leiper's tourism system. By focusing upon the tourist, this part demonstrates the influences upon their decision making process and how we can conceptualise tourism demand. Of course, we must also consider those who do not travel, but wish to, perhaps due to particular constraints such as illness. In other words, we must recognise that every tourist is an individual with particular motivations, wants and needs. This allows us to devise effective consumer decision making models although, as we show, the current models for tourism do not take into account contemporary methods of information search using the Internet and fail to factor in the 'wild card' events that are so influential on demand.

In Chapter 12 we analyse the personal influences upon tourist demand and show how these can be drawn together into models of consumer decision making for tourism. Here, we use two cases to illustrate contemporary trends – the example of the 'creative class' shows how our thinking about these personal factors is evolving and the TripAdvisor case shows how information used for decisions is changing with use of the Internet. The final, major case study in the chapter shows how demand trends for long-haul travel are changing. These personal determinants and influences of demand can be aggregated to provide a worldview of tourism demand, a picture that is influenced by factors such as economic development and demographics. In the twenty-first century, the global pattern of tourism demand has been impacted by 'wild card' events, of which 11 September 2001 was the defining one. These events have had a significant impact on demand patterns and decision making.

A thorough understanding of the influences upon tourism demand is essential for effective tourism marketing. Current thinking in terms of the scope and definition of marketing has identified a shift in focus from goods to a 'service-dominant' logic of marketing. This new approach recognises that tourism marketing thinks of the product as a bundle of both tangible and intangible elements as well as focusing on consumer needs and their involvement in the co-creation of the tourism experience. The service-dominant logic is presented in the classic paper for Chapter 13. This paper by Vargo and Lush pervades the chapter and our thinking on tourism marketing.

Chapter 13 shows how technology, and particularly the Internet, has transformed the business of tourism marketing and introduces the dimensions of e-marketing, and in a case study we show how technology has revolutionised market research. It then goes on to discuss the nature of tourism market planning and strategy and the elements of the marketing mix, and especially the implications of the nature of tourism, for the mix. We close the chapter with a review of the concept of 'tourism product markets' which draw together the market and the product in a neat framework that explains the various sub-products of tourism such as heritage or special interest tourism. The chapter also introduces the notion of destination marketing with the challenging case study of Greenland, and, in the final case study, questions whether the unchallenged migration of marketing concepts to destinations is valid.

CHAPTER 12
DEMAND

Learning Outcomes

This chapter focuses upon the tourist and their demand for travel. It outlines the reasons for tourism travel and the various influences that shape travel behaviour. The chapter is designed to provide you with:

- an awareness of the concepts and definitions of tourism demand;

- an understanding of the tourist consumer decision making process;

- an appreciation of the factors that determine tourism tourist demand;

- an ability to identify the constraints on travel; and

- an understanding of the issues surrounding forecasting of tourist demand.

Introduction

In the first chapter of this book we identified Leiper's tourism system as an effective organising concept for tourism and in this chapter we focus upon the generating region of the system. In order to manage tourism demand, it is important to understand the nature of demand in terms of definitions, the various components of demand, the consumer decision making process in tourism and how we forecast demand, as well as some of the more fundamental aspects of demand such as motivation, chosen as the focus of the classic paper for this chapter.

There is no doubt that managing tourism demand is one of the challenges for tourism in the twenty-first century as the volume of tourists grows and the remotest corners of the world are visited. In fact, we can chart how the perceptions of demand have changed over the years with early pronouncements such as the UN's Universal Declaration of Human Rights encouraging everyone to travel as a 'right' (www.un.org/en/documents/udhr/), to the present day when the tourist is urged to travel 'responsibly' and to offset their carbon emissions generated from flying.

Uysal (1998) lists three compelling reasons why we should have a thorough understanding of tourism demand:

1. it is an essential underpinning for policy and forecasting;
2. it provides critical information to allow the balancing of provision of supply and demand at destinations; and
3. it allows the tourism industry to better understand consumer behaviour and the tourism marketplace.

Definitions and Concepts

Definitions

Of course, definitions of demand vary according to the perspective of the author. The differing perspectives of various disciplines help us to fully understand tourism demand. For example, economists consider demand to be the schedule of the amount of any product or service that people are willing and able to buy at each specific price in a set of possible prices during a specified period of time. This introduces the idea of elasticity – which describes the relationship between demand and price or other variables. In contrast, psychologists view demand from the perspective of motivation and behaviour, scratching beneath the skin of the tourist to examine the interaction of personality, environment and demand for tourism. Finally, the geographers' definition encompasses a wide range of influences, in addition to price, and includes not only those who actually participate in tourism, but also those who wish to, but for some reason do not. For the purposes of this chapter we adopt this approach and use Mathieson and Wall's (1982) definition of demand:

> **'The total number of persons who travel, or wish to travel, to use tourist facilities and services at places away from their places of work and residence'.**

Concepts

The fact that some individuals may harbour a demand for tourism but are unable to realise that demand suggests that demand for tourism consists of a number of components. We can identify three basic components that make up the total demand for tourism:

1. **Effective or actual demand** is the actual number of participants in tourism or those who are travelling, i.e. de facto tourists. This is the component of demand most commonly and easily measured and the bulk of tourism statistics refer to effective demand.

2. **Suppressed demand** is made up of that section of the population who do not travel for some reason. Despite burgeoning demand for tourism across the world, only a very small percentage of the world's total population engages in international tourism. Of course, a considerably greater number participate in domestic travel, but in many parts of the world tourism remains an unobtainable luxury.

   Two elements of suppressed demand can be distinguished. First, *potential demand* refers to those who will travel at some future date if they experience a change in their circumstances – such as, say, an increase in their purchasing power. Second, *deferred demand* is a demand postponed because of a problem in the supply environment, such as a lack of capacity in accommodation, weather conditions or, perhaps, a natural disaster such as a hurricane. When the supply conditions are more favourable, those in the deferred demand category will convert to effective demand at some future date.

3. **No demand.** Finally, there will always be those who simply do not wish to travel or are unable to travel, constituting a category of *no demand*. Increasingly people are in this category because they choose to spend their discretionary income on goods other than tourism.

We can also consider other ways in which demand for tourism may be viewed and influenced. For example, *substitution of demand* refers to the case when demand for one activity (say a self-catering holiday) is substituted for another (staying in serviced accommodation). A similar concept is *redirection of demand* where the geographical location of demand is changed – say, a trip to Spain is redirected to Italy because of over-booking of accommodation. Finally, the opening of new tourism supply – say a resort, attraction or accommodation – will:

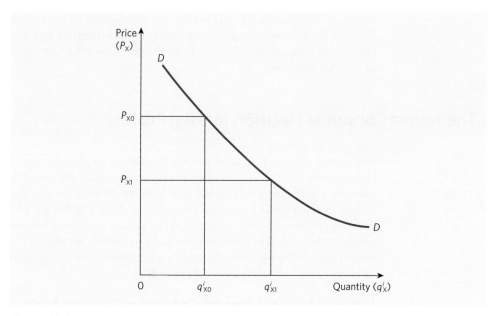

Figure 12.1 Individual's demand for product X
Source: Wanhill and Airey, 1980

- redirect demand from similar facilities in the area;
- substitute demand from other facilities; and
- generate new demand.

Economists refer to the first two of these as the *displacement effect* – in other words, demand from other facilities is displaced to the new one and no extra demand is generated.

Leiper's model of tourism makes it clear that tourism demand results in *flows* between the generating region and the destination region. These flows are complex and determined by a wide variety of factors including geographical proximity, historical trade and cultural ties, and, of course, the notion of contrasting environments, exemplified by the flow of tourists from northern Europe to the warmer countries of the Mediterranean.

In economic terms, a *demand schedule* refers to the quantities of a product that an individual wishes to purchase at different prices at a given point in time. Generally, the higher the price of the product, the lower is the demand; the lower the price, the greater is the demand. This is shown in Figure 12.1. It is normal to characterise the demand curve DD in Figure 12.1 by an appropriate measure that expresses the responsiveness of quantity to changes in price. Such a measure is termed the *elasticity of demand*.

Finally, a key concept to consider is *seasonality*. Most patterns of tourism demand demonstrate regular fluctuations due solely to the time of year known as seasonality. Although this is often the result of changes in climate over the calendar year, there are other influencing factors, such as the timing of school and work holidays, or regular special events. The perishable nature of the tourism product means that seasonality can cause major problems and is a major influence upon both employment and capital investment. It can result in seasonal employment, and the under-use or even closing down of facilities at certain times of the year. It can also result in an over-stretching by some destinations and businesses at times of peak activity, to compensate for low demand off-season. This leads to over-crowding, over-bookings, high prices and ultimately to customer dissatisfaction and a worsening reputation. Strategies to reduce seasonality vary. Typically they involve attempts to create or shift demand to the shoulder or trough months, either through setting price differentials or through the introduction or enhancement of all-year facilities. Marketing may be targeted at groups that have the time and resources to travel at any time of the year, notably the elderly, or the development of products that are less climate or weather sensitive.

The Tourist Consumer Decision Making Process

The tourist consumer decision making process is complex, not only is it influenced by the characteristics of the tourists themselves, but also their images of the many destinations available and the fact that tourism is a 'high involvement' purchase and increasingly 'technology enabled'. It is important to understand the psychology of the tourist consumer decision process, not only so that marketers know when, and how, to intervene in order to influence the process in terms of price and promotion, but also so that we understand how best to educate the tourist in their buying behaviour – for example, in their choice of travel mode *vis-à-vis* carbon emissions (Pearce, 2011).

Influences on the Tourist Consumer Decision Making Process

Kotler *et al.* (2014) view the consumer decision making process as a response to a set of marketing stimuli. For tourism these marketing stimuli will include price, promotion and distribution as well as the 'product'. Here, an important part of the product is the destination itself and the image that the potential tourist holds of a destination. Destination image can be defined as:

> **'The attitude, perception, beliefs and ideas one holds about a particular geographic area formed by the cognitive mage of a particular destination' (Gartner, 2000, p. 295).**

Effectively, an image is a simplified version of reality, a way of making sense of the many stimuli received and processed by an individual. In tourism, the image of a destination is critical as it affects both an individual's perception of a destination and their decision whether to visit. The generation of the image is different for destinations when compared to other consumer goods. Two factors make the image particularly critical for tourist decision making:

1. The intangible nature of tourism means the image is the only evidence that a visitor has of the destination before they visit.
2. The inseparable nature of the production and consumption process of tourism means that once they visit, the tourist's image of the destination is immediately changed by the experience.

The theories of image are divided into two camps. The first suggests that images can be disaggregated into many attributes and elements that can be measured. The second, 'gestalt approach', views the image as a whole, or holistic concept that cannot be disaggregated.

The formation of a destination image is based upon information acquired by the tourist from three sources (Gartner, 1993):

1. **Induced agents** controlled by sources external to the individual, such as advertisements and websites.
2. **Organic agents** acquired through personal experience. These are normally the most trusted sources of information and include social media and e-word of mouth.
3. **Autonomous agents** are media sources or popular culture. They are powerful because they can quickly alter a tourist's image of a destination.

A second set of influential variables relate to the characteristics of the tourists themselves. Kotler *et al*. (2014) have developed a four-fold classification of these characteristics:

1. Cultural characteristics are an important determinant of purchasing behaviour and include elements such as social class. An important aspect of marketing is to closely follow changes in culture in society.

2. Social characteristics refer to how tourists make purchasing decisions as part of a group, whether it is within a family or amongst peers. Here, we are seeing substantial shifts in how we view our peers and reference groups – particularly with respect to membership of online communities and social media.

3. Personal characteristics are the lifestyle and life-cycle factors that we deal with later in this chapter.

4. Psychological factors relate to the personality of the tourist and how they view themselves and the world. This is influenced by four key psychological concepts – motivation, perception, learning and attitude.

For tourism decisions, 'perception' of the destination is critical as we noted above. A second key concept that has received much attention is 'motivation'. Of course, the most well-known theory of motivations is Maslow's (1970) hierarchy of needs, reproduced in Figure 12.2.

However, the tourism literature has developed its own approach to motivation as it applies to tourist decision making. For example, in the classic paper for this chapter we present a contemporary view of tourist motivation. Other approaches include the traditional focus on:

● Physical motivators which focus around 'recreation' and refreshment' of body and spirit through physical activity or soaking in the essence of a destination through sun or sea bathing.

● Cultural motivators focused around curiosity to see new places and to scratch under the skin of destinations to understand the people, their cultures and cuisine – this is how many tourists now justify their travel and characterises the 'new tourist'.

● Interpersonal motivators focus around people, whether it is meeting new people, visiting friends or relatives, or indeed escaping from the people we interact with on a daily basis.

● Status and prestige motivators focus around the need for recognition through travel whether it be a trip for culinary education, or a culture tour of Europe.

Gray's (1970) classification of travel motivators shows how the market has evolved:

● **Wanderlust** is simply curiosity to experience the strange and unfamiliar. It refers to the basic trait in human nature to see, at first hand, different places, cultures and peoples. Status and prestige motivators would be included under this heading.

● **Sunlust** can be literally translated as the desire for sunshine and a better climate, but in fact it is broader than this and refers to the search for a better set of amenities for recreation than are available at home.

Figure 12.2 Maslow's hierarchy of needs

Source: Tourism: Principles and Practice, 4ed. (Cooper, C., Fletcher, J., Fyall, A., Gilbert, D. and Wanhill, S. 2008) p.45, Pearson Education Ltd, Harlow © Chris Cooper, John Fletcher, Alan Fyall, David Gilbert and Stephen Wanhill, 2005

Here we can identify a change in tourist consumer behaviour with a shift away from 'sunlust' to 'wanderlust' motivators, partly driven by fears of the effects of the sun, but also by the desire to fully experience the culture as well as the physical attractions of the destination.

Classic Paper

Pearce, P.L. and Lee, U. (2005) Developing a travel career approach to tourist motivation, *Journal of Travel Research* **43, 226–237**

This classic paper provides a fresh way of viewing motivation in a tourism setting. Philip Pearce is well known for his work on tourist psychology and behaviour and here he writes with Lee to develop the idea of how tourist motivation can be linked to the idea of a 'travel career'.

Motivation is the driving force of tourism and the place to start when trying to understand tourist demand and behaviour but, as we have seen, there are many conflicting theories and ways of viewing motivation in tourism studies. This paper makes a major contribution by outlining the 'travel career ladder' (TCL) theory of motivation and then further developing the concept. The TCL is similar to Maslow's hierarchy of needs and is described by Pearce and Lee as having five levels of need:

1. relaxation needs;
2. safety/security needs;
3. relationship needs;
4. self-esteem and development needs; and
5. fulfilment needs.

One or more of these needs motivates each trip, but one need will dominate. The TCL then links this idea to the fact that traveller's needs would be expected to change with experience, equating to a 'travel career'. In other words, the mix of 'needs' will change over the course of a person's life and their travel experiences. Whilst it is difficult to generalise, the TCL theory suggests that people ascend the TCL over their life, often moving from *level 1, relaxation needs* to *level 5, fulfilment needs*. Alternatively, some people may remain at one particular level of the TCL.

The paper by Pearce and Lee takes the idea of the TCL theory of motivation one stage further. The authors test the theory on travellers and conclude that the original theory is perhaps too simplistic. They find that the idea of a simple 'one direction' movement up the 'ladder' over a person's travel career is misleading. Instead the paper's findings lead to the idea of travel career patterns (TCPs) of multiple motivations rather than a simple travel career ladder. These TCPs are influenced by previous travel experience and age.

Pearce and Lee's paper therefore makes a major contribution to our understanding of tourist behaviour with a clear and intuitively appealing set of findings.

Models of Consumer Behaviour in Tourism

There are a number of traditions of modelling consumer behaviour dating back to the 1960s with each best suited to particular situations:

- **cognitive approaches,** where the purchase is the outcome of problem solving behaviour and the consumer is credited with rational behaviour;
- **the habitual approach,** where brand loyalty and inertia mean that few alternatives are considered; and
- **the reinforcement approach,** where the purchase is based upon learned past behaviour.

Each of these approaches view buying behaviour as sequential, triggered by recognition of a need from when the individual begins the decision making process. The main advantage of these models is that they force marketers to understand the whole process, rather than simply the end point – the purchase decision. For a tourism purchase, Sirakaya and Woodside (2005) structure this behaviour into a series of eight well-defined stages. Whilst the assumption is that purchasers will pass through all stages, in reality some stages may be skipped. The stages are as follows (Figure 12.3):

1. Need arousal and recognition that there is a decision to be made. Here, there is a discrepancy between a consumer's 'actual state' and their 'ideal' state.
2. Formulation of goals and objectives for the purchase.
3. Identification of alternatives for the purchase.
4. Generation of an alternative set of products from which to choose.
5. Search for information about the properties of the alternatives under consideration, using information from a variety of sources, although research shows that information from personal networks and 'e-word of mouth' are the most influential.
6. Decision made – ultimate judgement or choice among the alternatives.
7. Acting upon the decision – purchasing travel and tourism.
8. Post-purchase behaviour and feedback – the feelings experienced after the purchase, which may involve 'cognitive dissonance' – a feeling that an alternative may have been better, and sharing memories such as photographs and videos on social media.

Sirakaya and Woodside's (2005) approach is based upon generic models of consumer behaviour, but it also recognises that a tourism purchase is different to many others. For a tourism purchase:

● the consumer is highly involved;
● the purchase represents a major outlay of resources;

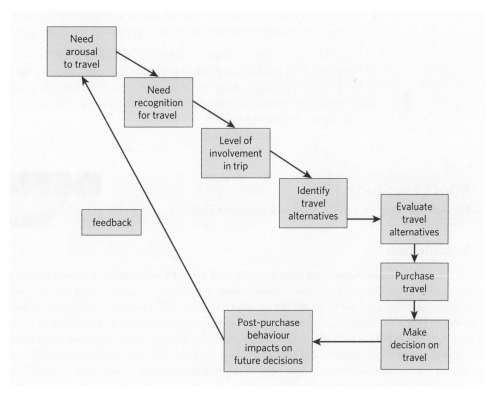

Figure 12.3 Model of consumer behaviour

- the purchase is high risk as, firstly, the tourist may have little experience of the product and, secondly, the purchase is for a service and the product is intangible;
- it takes time and effort to choose so there is a considerable investment in information search; and
- technology increasingly makes it possible to co-create the product with the supplier.

An Evaluation of Consumer Behaviour Models in Tourism

Despite a considerable literature, models of consumer decision making in tourism have been criticised on a number of grounds (Decrop, 2000; Swarbrooke and Horner, 2007):

- They are too theoretical and not grounded in any empirical testing.
- They are beginning to date and no new models have been developed since the mid-1990s, yet the travel sector has changed considerably – what, for example, is the impact of Internet bookings, Internet information sources or social media on such models (see Mills and Law, 2015; Serra Cantallops and Salvi, 2014)? And how do they factor in new patterns of behaviour such as 'ethical decision making', or the importance of experiences as opposed to destinations in the decision to travel?
- They do not help in understanding how the market would react to 'shocks' to the system such as 9/11.
- They fail to take into account the differing purchasing situations a tourist may experience – for example, a repeat versus a first-time trip.
- They view tourism from a Western developed-country perspective, yet we know that China and India will be major generators of international travel in the future.
- They fail to predict or identify the behaviour of tourists or markets and do not assist the manager in when to intervene in the buying process to secure a purchase.

It is this last point that is critical. If models of consumer behaviour in tourism cannot be used by marketers to fit products to particular market segments, then we have to question their use.

In the following case study we show how the Internet has changed the information sources used by tourists to make purchasing decisions, a change that is not reflected in current consumer behaviour models.

Mini Case Study 12.1
TripAdvisor.com – A Celebration of Consumer Power

Introduction

Star ratings and recommendations in guidebooks were once the information cues used by tourists to make purchasing decisions. With the advent of the Internet, however, it is *user-generated reviews* that have revolutionised the way tourists make the decision to travel. The Internet has drastically altered people's information search patterns and decision processes when it comes to travel, allowing everyone's opinions and thoughts to be instantly accessible to others. In travel this has led to a number of *user-generated content sites* which review travel products (Gretzel, 2007). These user-generated opinions and reviews are hugely influential in travel information search and decision making, and carry considerable credibility, with users saying that they are more up-to-date, enjoyable and reliable than, say, a company or tourist board website.

TripAdvisor.com

One of the first and most successful of these websites is TripAdvisor.com, representing the largest online network of travel consumers. The mission of TripAdvisor is to 'help people around the world plan and have the perfect trip'. The website was founded in 2000, originally as a means to link to official guides or other media but it soon evolved into a social media site and is now owned by the major online travel provider Expedia (www.expedia.com/). In 2009 a Chinese site was launched and, in 2011, TripAdvisor was floated on the stock exchange. The statistics are impressive and testament to the power of this new medium:

- Estimates suggest that 10 per cent of all trips worldwide are planned using TripAdvisor.
- It has 60 million members.
- TripAdvisor-branded sites attract more than 300 million monthly visitors.
- More than 225 million travel reviews and opinions are posted on the site.
- TripAdvisor reviews cover more than 4.9 million accommodation units, attractions and restaurants in 45 countries.
- TripAdvisor manages and operates 25 travel websites.

The website features:

- online reviews for accommodation, restaurants and attractions;
- traveller articles where users can add information on destinations;
- third-party social networking applications through applications on sites, including Facebook, which is seen by TripAdvisor as a way to personalise the site;
- photographs – over 6 million to support reviews;
- Green Leaders to encourage sustainability in accommodation providers;
- a range of apps and planning features for booking;
- Just For You – tailored recommendations;
- holiday ideas; and
- 'Best of' reviews.

Clearly TripAdvisor has evolved from a small website serving the needs of a group of travellers to a major commercial empire with 'white branding' and syndicating of review sites meaning that existing reviews occur on other seemingly independent sites. The success and development of TripAdvisor raises some important issues for tourist consumer decision making and marketing:

1. Its users are affluent, well-educated and frequent travellers making them an ideal target demographic for travel companies. As a result, TripAdvisor has become an important advertising medium as more and more reviews are posted and they become more timely and accurate – the more so as mobile technology allows for 'instant posting'.

2. A second commercial application of TripAdvisor is to extend recommendation and reviews to bookings and referrals. TripAdvisor provides easy access to online travel agencies including Expedia. Also, such is the power of the site that tour operators and tourist boards are adding TripAdvisor's reviews to their websites as this transparency fosters trust in their brands. The site also allows others to utilise its benefits – for example, the US site Raveable (www.raveable.com) now trawls reviews from sites to provide aggregated ratings for US hotels.

3. Of course, this approach may be compromised by false reviews posted to enhance a company's reputation or tarnish that of competitors. This has arisen because TripAdvisor allows reviews to be posted by anyone. However, the site clearly states that their staff moderate all reviews and that they have algorithms and filters to detect and block abuse and suppliers have the opportunity to respond to every review. This will be solved somewhat as, under EU legislation, it is illegal for hotels to represent themselves falsely as consumers on review websites, although this will not be easy to enforce.

→

4. Other issues include the fact that sites such as TripAdvisor are vulnerable to being copied and their content used by other providers such as Google. There is also suspicion amongst potential partners that Expedia could use their intelligence to compete with them. The site is also concerned at the shift to smartphone use and away from tablets and screens because the screens are less suitable to the type of content that TripAdvisor uses. Finally, it has been suggested that sites such as TripAdvisor have made travellers less adventurous and more risk averse.

DISCUSSION QUESTIONS

1. Taking a destination with which you are familiar, visit TripAdvisor.com and look up hotel reviews for the destination. Do they match with your own local knowledge of the hotels?

2. Why do you think user-generated content sites have become so powerful in influencing travel decision making?

3. Draft an advertisement for an attraction or hotel to be placed on TripAdvisor.com. What distinct features would you use given the mission and nature of the site?

Sources:
Gretzel, U. (2007) *Online Travel Review Study: Role & Impact of Online Travel Reviews,* Laboratory for Intelligent Systems in Tourism, Texas A&M University, Austin, TX.
www.tripadvisor.com/
www.expedia.com/

Determinants of Demand for Tourism

This section focuses upon the key determinants of demand for tourism and goes on to show how an understanding of these underlying influences allows us to forecast tourism demand.

Determinants at the Individual Scale

Although an individual may be motivated to travel, their ability to do so will depend on a number of factors related to both the individual themselves and the supply environment. These factors can be termed *determinants of demand* and represent the 'parameters of possibility' for the individual – even within the developed world, many are unable to participate in tourism for some reason. For example, a certain level of discretionary income is required to allow participation in tourism, and this income, and indeed the type of participation, will be influenced by such factors as job type, life-cycle stage, mobility, level of educational attainment and personality.

Once a decision to travel has been taken, the ability to undertake the trip, and the nature of that trip, will be determined by a wide range of interrelated factors. These can be broadly divided into two groups:

1. The first group of factors can be termed *lifestyle,* and includes income, employment, holiday entitlement, educational attainment and mobility.

2. The second group can be termed *life-cycle* where the age and domestic circumstances of an individual affect both the amount and type of tourism demanded.

Naturally, these factors are interrelated and complementary. In a Western society, a high-status job is normally associated with an individual in middle age with a high-income, above-average holiday entitlement, education and mobility.

Lifestyle Determinants of Demand for Tourism

Income and Employment

Income and employment are closely linked and exert important influences upon both the level and the nature of tourist demand. Tourism is an expensive activity that demands a certain threshold of income before participation is possible. Gross income gives little indication of the money available to spend on tourism – rather, it is discretionary income that provides the best indicator; that is, the income left over when tax, housing and the basics of life have been accounted for.

The relationship between income and tourism is a complex one. For example, certain tourism activities are highly sensitive to income – additional holidays and expensive pursuits such as skiing holidays are a particular case in point. The relationship is also characterised by the fact that, at the extremes of the income spectrum, tourism demand is strongly affected, whereas in the middle of the spectrum it is much more difficult to discern a clear relationship.

A fundamental distinction is between those in employment and those unemployed. The impact of unemployment on the volume of tourism demand is obvious, but the nature of demand is also changed by employment uncertainty, particularly in times of economic recession. This encourages later booking of trips, more domestic holidays and shorter lengths of stay, and switches demand away from commercial accommodation to VFR, therefore leading to lower spending levels.

Paid Holiday Entitlement

The increase in leisure time experienced by most individuals in the developed world since 1950 is well documented. However, the relationship between an individual's total time budget, leisure time and paid holiday entitlement is complex. A number of surveys suggest that, in a developed Western economy, individuals have anything from 35 to 50 hours free time a week at their disposal. This free time is greater for males, the young and single adults. However, to enable tourism, leisure time has to be blocked into two or more days to allow a stay away from home. While this obviously is the case with paid holiday entitlement, patterns of leisure time have changed to allow three-day weekends, flexi-time and longer periods of absence for those in employment.

Individual levels of paid holiday entitlement would seem to be an obvious determinant of travel demand, but again the relationship is not straightforward and, rather like the income variable, it is clearer at the extremes. Paid holiday entitlement tends to be more generous in developed economies and less so in the developing world. The pattern of entitlement is also responsible in part for the seasonality of tourism in some destinations simply because some of the entitlement has to be taken in the summer months. To an extent, this is historical and is rooted in the holiday patterns of manufacturing industries. It does, however, have an impact upon the nature of demand for tourism. In some countries, notably France, staggering of holiday entitlement has been attempted to alleviate seasonality.

Education and Mobility

Level of educational attainment is an important determinant of travel demand as education broadens horizons and stimulates the desire to travel. Also, the better educated the individual, the higher the awareness of travel opportunities, and exposure to technology, information, media and promotion.

Personal mobility also has an important influence on travel demand. The car is the dominant recreational tool for both international and domestic tourism (as we saw in Chapter 10). It provides door-to-door freedom, can carry tourism equipment (such as tents or boats) and has all-round vision for viewing. Ownership of a car stimulates travel for pleasure in all but recessionary times.

Race and Gender

Race and gender are two critical determinants of tourist demand, but the relationships are not clearly understood. Most surveys of participation in tourism suggest that whites and males have the highest levels of effective demand for tourism. However, changes in society are acting to complicate this rather simplistic view.

Clearly, for the purposes of analysing each variable, we have to separate them but it must be remembered that they all are complementary and interrelated. Indeed this is such that some writers have attempted to analyse tourism or leisure lifestyles by performing multivariate analysis on the determinants of tourism demand and then trying to group individuals into particular categories. To date these analyses have met with limited success. Even where they have been commercially adopted as market segments it is difficult to correlate them with other variables such as media habits. The following case study on the creative class shows how evolving groups in society are changing the way that we think about the influence of different segments of society.

Mini Case Study 12.2
The Creative Class

Introduction

Richard Florida's theory of *the creative class* not only identifies a newly emergent socio-economic group in society but also shows how this group influences economic development and creates successful, competitive places. The theory states simply that places with high concentrations of this new socio-economic class of creative people will be more successful in economic development and in 'place-making' – both prerequisites of successful destinations.

Florida argues that the creative class is growing in influence, representing a major societal and economic shift away from traditional and industry-based economies; indeed it can be seen as the symptom of the emergence of the knowledge economy. The creative class encompasses those working in IT, artists, musicians, the gay community, academics and knowledge workers. Florida's view is that this group creates the driving force for the economic development of post-industrial cities.

Florida estimates that in the US alone the creative class numbers 40 million workers (30 per cent of the workforce) and in the future will generate a further 10 million jobs. The creative class can be classified into two main sections:

1. **The super-creative core.** This group 'fully engage in the creative process' (Florida, 2002, p. 69) and are both innovative and creative. They include scientists and academics.

2. **Creative professionals.** This group represents highly-qualified, problem-solving knowledge workers in healthcare, business and finance, the legal sector, and education.

The Creativity Index

Florida characterises the creative class as interested in travel, outdoor recreation and active sports and leisure. But, for this concept to be used to predict travel consumer behaviour, or to be used by marketers for segmentation, it has to be measurable as we noted above – and there is no doubt that the concept of the creative class is 'fuzzy'. Here, Florida has devised the *creativity index* based upon four indicators:

1. the creative class share of the workforce;

2. innovation, measured as patents per capita;

3. the scale of the IT industry; and

4. diversity, measured by the gay index as an indicator of openness and diversity.

The Creative Class and Tourism

Here the question is how can this relate to tourism and to destinations? Florida's idea is that the creative class creates an open, diverse, tolerant and professional community which surrounds itself with an attractive environment and lifestyle. This in turn, attracts investment in such things as events, sports and entertainment centres, retailing and iconic buildings, creating a blend of café culture, bistros, galleries and entertainment – a 'Soho-isation' of a district, often focused around a waterfront, university or heritage area. Creation of attractive districts can act as a hub for tourism which in turn can attract new residents (Thulemark and Hauge, 2014).

Criticism

Florida's theory has created debate, controversy and criticism. These criticisms lie in three main areas:

1. Researchers have tested Florida's creative index but failed to find correlation with successful economic growth.

2. The argument may be circular as it is the *places* that attract the creative class who in turn entrench the character of the place with street culture and café societies.

3. Finally, he has been criticised as being elitist.

DISCUSSION QUESTIONS

1. Identify an area of your local town or city that you think is inhabited by the creative class – describe the key features of the area. Does it also act to attract tourists and day visitors?

2. Draft a marketing plan for a tour operator to target the creative class for its tours.

3. Make a list of the type of tourism products that the creative class might purchase.

Sources:
Florida, R.L. (2002) *The Rise of the Creative Class: And How it's Transforming Work, Leisure, Community and Everyday Life*, Basic Books, New York.
Florida, R.L. (2004) *The Flight of the Creative Class*, Harper Business, New York.
Florida, R.L. (2005) *Cities and the Creative Class*, Routledge, New York.
Florida, R.L. (2008) *Who's Your City?* Random House, Toronto.
Florida, R.L. (2014) *The Rise of the Creative Class – Revisited: Revised and Expanded*, Basic Books, New York.
Thulemark, M. and Hauge, A. (2014) Creativity in the recreational industry: re-conceptualisation of the creative class theory in a tourism dominated area, *Scandinavian Journal of Public Administration* **18**(1), 87–105.
www.creativeclass.com/

Life-cycle Determinants of Demand for Tourism

The demand to travel, and indeed the type of tourism experience demanded, is closely related to an individual's age. Although the conventional measurement is chronological age, *domestic age* better discriminates between types of tourist demand and levels of travel demand. Considering an individual's domestic age – or position on the *family life-cycle* (childhood, young adult, married, etc.) – is an effective explanatory variable of travel behaviour with a distinctive pattern of demand found at each stage in the cycle. Table 12.1 outlines the stages of the family life-cycle (FLC) and the type of tourism demanded.

The explanatory framework provided by the FLC approach is a powerful one. It has implications for the supply of facilities, for the analysis of market needs of particular groups and is used as a basis for market segmentation by the tourism sector. However, the FLC as outlined is only appropriate for developed Western economies and even here it is a generalisation as it does not consider, for example, one-parent families, divorcees or other ethnic groups living within Western economies.

Table 12.1 Family life-cycle stage and tourism characteristics

Family life-cycle stage	Tourism characteristics
Childhood	At this stage, decisions are taken for the individual in terms of holiday taking. However, children do have a significant influence upon both their parents' decisions. By the age of 10 or 11 years, some children take organised holidays with school or youth groups and day trips are common. These are usually domestic with self-catering arrangements.
Adolescence/young adult	At this stage, young single people not living at home have a preoccupation for independence, socialising and a search for identity. Typically, holidays independent of parents begin at around 15 years, constrained by finances but compensated by having few other commitments, no shortage of free time and a curiosity for new places and experiences. This group has a high demand to travel, mainly on budget holidays using surface transport and self-catering accommodation. Here the preoccupation is simply to 'get away' – the destination is unimportant, and is often associated with rites of passage such as the American 'Spring Break'.
Married	In married adulthood, the preoccupations are more with establishment, lifetime investments and social institutions. This FLC stage can have a number of options. For example, newly married couples who are young and with no children may have few constraints on travel, a high income and few other ties, giving them a high travel demand, frequently overseas. The arrival of children totally changes influences upon tourism demand as holidays become more organisational and less geographical and constraints of time and finance may depress travel demand. Holiday preferences switch to domestic destinations, self-catering accommodation and VFR. This is known as the full nest stage and constraints on travel will depend on the age of the children.
Empty nest	As children grow up, reach the adolescence stage and begin to travel independently, constraints of time and finance are lifted from parents and their travel demand increases. This is often a time for long-haul travel – the cruise market typically comprises this group.
Old age	The emergence of early retirement at 50 or 55 years is creating an active and mobile group in the population of many countries who will demand both domestic and international travel. However, it is too simplistic to view senior travellers as homogeneous, and there are many different categories – partly defined by the tension between physical health and financial resources In later retirement, lack of finance, infirmity and often the loss of a partner act to offset the increase in free time experienced by this group. Holidays become more hotel-based and travel demand decreases.

Suppressed Demand for Tourism

Despite a seminal paper by Haukeland in 1990, non-travellers receive short shrift in the study of tourism demand. There are two main reasons why people do not travel: firstly, they exert a preference not to travel and, secondly, they are unable to participate in travel for some reason. Nyaupane and Andereck (2008) have taken the well-known model of leisure constraints and adapted it for tourism. They structure constraints on travel into three types:

1. **Interpersonal constraints.** Lack of interest, peer group pressure and/or fear are real constraints on travel for some individuals. Physical limitations (such as ill health) are a significant reason for many people not travelling. In particular, heart disease and mental/physical handicap act as a major constraint on travel.

2. **Intrapersonal constraints.** Lack of companions to travel with acts as a constraint for some, as do family circumstances of, say, single parents or those who have to care for elderly relatives.

3. **Structural constraints.** These tend to be the most significant constraints. Travel is expensive and demands a certain threshold of income before people can enter the market. It also competes with other products for available funds. A second structural constraint

is lack of time which may be for business or family reasons. Finally, government restrictions such as currency controls and visas may act as a real barrier to travel (both inbound and outbound) for some countries.

It is common for people to experience a combination of two or more of these constraints. For example, a one-parent family may find lack of income and time will combine with family circumstances to prevent tourism travel. Obviously it is just these groups who would most benefit from a holiday and research has shown the significant impact upon families when they cannot afford a holiday (Sedgley *et al.*, 2012). As a result, tourism planners are increasingly concerned to identify these barriers and devise programmes to encourage non-participants to travel. Perhaps the best-known examples of this are: (i) the 'social tourism movement', which is concerned with facilitating the participation in travel by people with some form of handicap or disadvantage, and the measures used to encourage this participation; and (ii) increasing numbers of destinations and facilities that provide specifically for travellers with some form of handicap.

Macro Determinants of Tourism Demand

In order to demonstrate how these individual influences upon demand can be aggregated to explain patterns and rhythms of tourist demand globally we have to consider different geographical scales. For example, from what we already know, we would expect that countries with a high level of economic development and a stable, urbanised population will be major generators of tourism demand.

At the aggregate level the relationship between tourist demand and the characteristics of a population is not straightforward. In particular, we must remember that the variables which determine tourist demand are all related. A high travel demand would be expected for a developed Western economy with a high degree of urbanisation, high incomes, small household sizes and high levels of mobility. Conversely, low travel demand would be expected for rural societies with large family sizes and low incomes.

When individual purchasing patterns and the influences upon them are aggregated to the national level it is possible to gain a clearer view as to the influences upon global patterns of demand for tourism. This is known as performing a STEP analysis (sometimes known as PEST if the acronym is changed). It analyses the impact of:

S   social factors;

T   technological factors;

E   economic factors; and

P   political factors.

Social Factors

Levels of population growth, its development, distribution and density affect travel demand. Population growth and development can be closely linked to the stages of economic growth of a society by considering the demographic transition where population growth and development are seen in terms of four connected phases (Table 12.2). However, some criticise the demographic transition on the basis that it does not include migration and is less applicable to very advanced economies.

Population density has a less important influence on tourist demand than has the distribution of population between urban and rural areas. Densely populated rural nations may have low travel demand owing to the level of economic development and the simple fact that the population is mainly dependent upon subsistence agriculture and has neither the time nor the income to devote to tourism. In contrast, densely populated urban areas normally indicate a developed economy with consumer purchasing power, giving rise to high travel demand and the urge to escape from the urban environment.

Table 12.2 The demographic transition and tourism

Stage of the demographic transition	Tourism characteristics
High stationary phase	This corresponds to many undeveloped countries with high birth and death rates, keeping the population at a fluctuating, but low, level. Here, many forms of tourism are impossible.
Early expanding phase	High birth rates continue, but death rates fall due to improved health, sanitation and social stability. The population expands, characterised by young, large families. Tourism is a luxury that cannot be afforded by many.
Late expanding phase	Here, birth rates fall with the growth of an industrial society and birth control technology and both outbound and domestic tourism begin to develop.
Low stationary phase	Here, birth and death rates have stabilised at a low level and some countries are not replacing their population, leading to an ageing market.

The distribution of population within a nation also affects patterns, rather than strict levels, of tourist demand. Where population is concentrated into one part of the country, tourism demand is distorted. This asymmetrical distribution of population is well illustrated by the USA where two-thirds of the population live in the eastern third of the country. The consequent east to west pattern of tourist flows (and permanent migrants) has placed pressure on the recreation and tourist resources of the Western states.

Technological Factors

There is no doubt that technology has been a major enabling factor in terms of converting suppressed demand into effective demand. This is particularly the case in terms of transport technology where the development of the jet engine in the late 1950s gave aircraft both speed and range and stimulated the variety of tourism products available in the international market to meet pent-up demand for international travel. Developments in aircraft technology have continued but so has the level of refinement and access to the motor car. Similarly, the development of information technology, and, in particular, the Internet and mobile technology, is a critical enabling factor in terms of tourism demand. Generally, technology acts to increase access to tourism by lowering the cost or by making the product more accessible. Examples here include access to travel information and booking on the Internet, and developments in 'recreational technology' such as off-road recreational vehicles.

Economic Factors

A society's level of economic development is a major determinant of tourist demand because the economy influences so many critical, and interrelated, factors. One approach is to consider a simple division of world economies used by the International Monetary Fund (IMF, 2012). The IMF classifies countries into 'advanced economies' and 'developing economies'. Their classification has evolved over time and is based on many variables including gross domestic product, source of exports, net debt or credit and population. Advanced economies are further divided into major advanced economies (the USA, Japan, Germany, France, Italy, the UK and Canada); members of the euro area; and newly industrialised Asian economies.

As a society moves towards the advanced economy classification, a number of important processes occur. The balance of employment changes from work in the primary sector (agriculture, fishing, forestry) to work in the secondary sector (manufacturing goods) and the tertiary sector (services such as tourism). As this process unfolds, an affluent society usually emerges and the percentage of the population who are economically active increases from less than a third in the developing economies to half or more in the advanced economies. Similarly, discretionary incomes increase and create demand for consumer goods and leisure pursuits such as tourism.

Other developments are closely linked to the changing nature of employment. The population is healthier and has time for recreation and tourism (and has paid holiday entitlement). Improving educational standards and media channels boost awareness of tourism opportunities, and transportation and mobility rise in line with these changes. Institutions respond to this increased demand by developing a range of leisure products and services. These developments occur in conjunction with each other until, as a country reaches the advanced economy classification, all the economic indicators encourage high levels of travel demand. Clearly, tourism is a result of industrialisation and, quite simply, the more highly developed an economy, the greater the levels of tourist demand.

As more countries enter the advanced economy classification, so the volume of trade and foreign investment increases and business travel develops. Business travel is sensitive to economic activity, and although it could be argued that increasingly sophisticated communication systems may render business travel unnecessary, there is no evidence of this to date. Indeed, the very development of global markets and the constant need for face-to-face contact should ensure a continuing demand for business travel.

Political Factors

Politics affects tourist demand in a variety of ways. For example, the degree of government involvement in promoting and providing facilities for tourism depends upon the political complexion of the government. Governments that support the free market try to create an environment in which the tourism industries can flourish, rather than the administration being directly involved in tourism itself. Socialist administrations, on the other hand, encourage the involvement of the government in tourism and, through 'social tourism', often provide opportunities for the 'disadvantaged' to participate in tourism. Governments in times of economic problems may control levels of demand for travel overseas by limiting the amount of foreign currency that can be taken out of a country. Government restrictions on travel also include visa and passport controls as well as taxes on travel. Generally, however, these controls are not totally effective and, of course, they can be evaded.

We can also identify inadvertent political influences – for example, a government with an economy suffering high inflation may find that inbound travel is discouraged. In a more general sense, unstable political regimes or regions (where civil disorder or war is prevalent) may forbid non-essential travel, and inbound tourism will be adversely affected. In more extreme cases inbound travel becomes impossible, such as with the ISIS (Islamic State of Iraq and Syria) controlled areas of Syria, Libya, Iraq and Nigeria.

Other Factors

Finally, there are a number of further factors that will determine the demand of a population to travel to particular destinations. Destination image, for example, will strongly influence demand and would be expected to be related to promotional spend, but this relationship is notoriously difficult to measure. Other factors include:

● economic distance – the time and cost of reaching a destination; and

● cultural distance – the difference in culture between the origin area and the destination – for more adventurous travellers this acts to attract rather than to deter a visit.

Costs at a destination are not an absolute quantity but have to be considered relative to the value of the traveller's own currency. This is graphically demonstrated by the ebb and flow of traffic across the Atlantic dependent upon whether the dollar or the euro is the stronger.

Forecasting Tourism Demand

An understanding of demand determinants is fundamental to forecasting future demand (Song and Li, 2008). For example, from the discussion above, we can predict that effective demand for tourism will be highly concentrated among the affluent, industrialised nations. This information is important for managers and accurate forecasts in tourism are essential to inform decision making in both governments and the industry. Frechtling (2001) identifies why tourism demand forecasting is important:

- The tourism product is perishable and assets such as beds cannot be stored.
- In an industry as volatile as tourism and in times of rapid and unexpected change, it is important for both governments and the tourism industry to have reliable and accurate forecasts to allow them to plan and make decisions.
- The inseparability of the production and consumption of tourism means that enterprises have to be aware in advance of the level of demand for their product.
- The tourism product comprises a range of complementary providers – forecasts ensure that these are available when they are needed.
- The tourism product needs large investment in fixed costs meaning that accurate forecasts of demand are essential.

As a result, failure to forecast tourism demand accurately can have devastating consequences, as supply and demand will be unbalanced. Indeed, forecasting is difficult in tourism due to the lack of good statistical information from the past, the complex and volatile nature of tourism demand, seasonality and the occurrence of one-off 'wild card' events that gave a major influence on demand (Song and Li, 2008).

Forecasting methods

There is a wide variety of methods available for forecasting tourism demand (UNWTO, 2008). Archer (1994) lists the factors that determine the choice of method to use:

1. purpose of the forecast – this relates to the level of detail required and the scope of the forecast;
2. time period required;
3. level of accuracy required;
4. availability of information – there is no point in recommending a complex quantitative approach if the information is not available to support it; and
5. cost of the forecast and the available budget.

Choice of forecasting method basically comes down to two options: (i) quantitative approaches and (ii) qualitative approaches. However, in practice, the most successful forecasts are those that use a combination of these two methods, utilising the relative strengths of each.

Quantitative Forecasting Approaches

There are numerous quantitative approaches to forecasting demand, ranging from the simplistic to the highly technical.

- **Causative models.** At the complex end of the spectrum are causative models. These models attempt to predict changes in the variables that cause tourist demand and to analyse the relationship between those variables and the demand for tourism. The most well-known of these approaches is econometric modelling, commonly using multiple regression. A mathematical relationship is sought that establishes demand as a function of influencing variables (such as income levels and price). The advantage of this approach is that it allows us to understand the underlying causes of tourist demand and to forecast how these will change in the future. It also allows us to ask 'what if' questions to see how demand will change under a certain set of circumstances.

● **Non-causative models.** These models are often known as time series models. Essentially they rely on extrapolating future trends from the past and use techniques such as moving average, exponential smoothing and trend curve analysis. While these models can be criticised as inappropriate for a volatile industry such as tourism where past situations may not carry forward into the future, they do deliver surprisingly accurate forecasts.

Qualitative Forecasting Approaches

Qualitative approaches to forecasting demand are mainly used to predict long-term trends, or to examine specific scenarios in the future such as climate change or technological influences. The most common techniques are the Delphi technique and scenario writing.

● **The Delphi technique.** The Delphi technique relies upon a panel of experts to deliver a consensus view of the future. The panel is selected according to their expertise and a questionnaire is compiled relating to the particular future trend or forecast required. Once the panel members have completed the questionnaire, results are combined and circulated to the panel to give them chance to change their views, once they see the forecasts of other panel members. This process then goes through a number of iterations, often three or four, before a consensus forecast is reached.

There are significant advantages to this approach, as it does not rely on one individual view and can be tailored to particular needs. However, the Delphi technique can be expensive to implement and may be subject to the influence of a strong panel member; and its effectiveness depends on both the choice of questions and the selection of panel members.

● **Scenario writing.** Scenario writing is not only a technique to forecast future tourism demand, but also an approach that clarifies the issues involved. It relies upon creating alternative hypothetical futures relating to particular 'states' or sets of circumstances that will impact upon demand in the future. It involves assessing the variables that we examined in the section on STEP analysis and then creating long-term scenarios of how they may change, based upon the current situation as a baseline. (We deal with scenario writing in a detailed case study in Chapter 14.)

In a world of rapid and unexpected change, it could be argued that forecasts are irrelevant. However, the changing nature of the environment within which tourism occurs makes it all the more important to forecast future patterns of tourist demand in order to anticipate and manage them.

SUMMARY

This chapter has focused upon demand for tourism. We began by clearly identifying definitions and concepts of demand, including the notion that many people cannot travel due to particular constraints such as illness. The chapter then focused on the personal influences upon tourist demand and showed how these can be drawn together into models of consumer decision making for tourism with a classic paper re-examining the concept of 'motivation'. Here, the example of the 'creative class' shows how our thinking about these personal factors is evolving and the TripAdvisor case shows how information used for decisions is changing. We then went on to show how these personal determinants and influences of demand can be aggregated to provide a worldview of tourism demand, a picture that is influenced by factors such as economic development and demographics. The end of chapter case study demonstrates how patterns and influences of demand are changing in the long-haul travel segment.

Discussion Questions

1. Compare the advantages and disadvantages of the main techniques of forecasting tourist demand.

2. Review the relevance of the life-cycle and lifestyle determinants of tourist demand for the developing world.

3. Taking a country of your choice identify the main determinants of tourist demand and evaluate their importance.

4. Why is domestic tourism demand difficult to measure?

5. When planning their marketing campaigns, does the tourism industry take full advantage of what is known about the buying decision in tourism?

Annotated Further Reading

1. Decrop, A. (2006) *Vacation Decision Making*, CABI Publishing, Wallingford.
   An excellent text covering leisure and vacation decision making processes.

2. Pearce, P.L. (2011) *Tourist Behaviour and the Contemporary World*, Channel View, Bristol.
   An excellent research-based text reviewing the major theories and concepts of tourist behaviour.

3. Ryan, C. (2003) *Recreational Tourism Demand and Impacts*, Channel View, Clevedon.
   An excellent, thorough overview of tourism demand.

4. Smith, S.L. (1996) *Tourism Analysis*, 2nd edn, Longman, Harlow.
   A comprehensive handbook of analytical approaches, including demand estimation, various indices of demand and the models such as the gravity model.

5. Song, H. and Li, G. (2008) Tourism demand modelling and forecasting – a review of recent research, *Tourism Management* **29**, 203–220.
   A thorough and technical review of tourism demand forecasting.

6. Swarbrooke, J. and Horner, S. (2007) *Consumer Behaviour in Tourism*, 2nd edn, Routledge, Oxford.
   A thorough textbook reviewing all aspects of consumer behaviour and broader elements of tourism demand.

7. Uysal, M. (1998) The determinants of tourism demand: a theoretical perspective, pp. 79–95 in Ioannides, D. and Debbage, K. G. (eds) *The Economic Geography of the Tourist Industry: A Supply Side Analysis,* Routledge, London.
   One of the clearest and most comprehensive reviews of travel determinants.

8. World Tourism Organization (2001) *Tourism 2020 Vision – Global Forecasts and Profiles of Market Segments,* WTO, Madrid.
   An excellent and comprehensive review of future patterns of tourism demand and the key changes in determinants across the world.

9. www.world-tourism.org
   The WTO's site is an excellent source statistics of demand, definition and measurement issues.

References Cited

Archer, B.H. (1994) Demand forecasting and estimation, pp. 86–92 in Ritchie, J.R.B. and Goeldner, C.R. (eds), *Handbook of Travel, Tourism and Hospitality Research*, Wiley, New York.

Cooper, C., Fletcher., J, Fyall, A., Gilbert, D. and Wanhill (2008) *Tourism: Principles and Practice*, 4th edn, Pearson, Harlow.

Decrop, A. (2000) Tourists' decision-making and behaviour processes, pp. 103–133 in Pizam, A. and Mansfield, Y. (eds) *Consumer Behaviour in Travel and Tourism*, Haworth, New York.

Frechtling, D. (2001) *Forecasting Tourism Demand: Methods and Strategies*, Butterworth Heinemann, Oxford.

Gartner, W.C. (1993) Image formation process, pp. 191–215 in Fessenmaier, D.R. and Uysal, M. (eds) *Communication and Channel Systems in Tourism Marketing*, Horwath Press, New York.

Gartner, W.C. (2000) Image, pp. 295–296 in Jafari, J. (ed) *Encyclopedia of Tourism*, Routledge, London.

Gray, H.P. (1970) *International Travel – International Trade*, Lexington Books, MA.

Haukeland, V.J. (1990) Non-travellers: the flip side of motivation, *Annals of Tourism Research* **17**(2), 172–184.

International Monetary Fund (2012) *World Economic Outlook 2012*, IMF, Washington.

Kotler, P., Bowen, J. and Makens, J. (2014) *Marketing for Hospitality and Tourism*, 6th edn, Pearson, Harlow.

Maslow, A.H. (1970) *Motivation and Personality*, 2nd edn, Harper and Row, New York.

Mathieson, A. and Wall, G. (1982) *Tourism: Economic Physical and Social Impacts*, Longman, London.

Mills, J., and Law, R (2015) *Handbook of Consumer Behavior, Tourism, and the Internet*, Routledge, London.

Nyaupane, G.P. and Andereck, K.L. (2008) Understanding travel constraints: application and extension of a leisure constraints model, *Journal of Travel Research* **46**, 433–439.

Pearce, P.L. (2011) *Tourist Behaviour and the Contemporary World*, Channel View, Bristol.

Sedgley, D., Pritchard, A. and Morgan, N. (2012) 'Tourism poverty' in affluent societies: voices from inner-city London, *Tourism Management* **33**, 951–960.

Serra Cantallops, S. and Salvi, F. 2014) New consumer behaviour: a review of research on eWOM and hotels, *International Journal of Hospitality Management* **36**(0), 41–51.

Sirakaya, E. and Woodside, A.G. (2005) Building and testing theories of decision making by travellers, *Tourism Management* **26**, 815–832.

Song, H., and Li, G. (2008) Tourism demand modelling and forecasting – a review of recent research, *Tourism Management* **29**, 203–220.

Swarbrooke, J. and Horner, S. (2007) *Consumer Behaviour in Tourism*, 2nd edn, Routledge, Oxford.

UNWTO (2008) *Handbook on Tourism Forecasting Methodologies*, UNWTO, Madrid.

Uysal, M. (1998) The determinants of tourism demand: a theoretical perspective, pp. 79–95 in Ioannides, D. and Debbage, K. G. (eds) *The Economic Geography of the Tourist Industry: A Supply Side Analysis*, Routledge, London.

Wanhill, S.R.C. and Airey, D. (1980) Demand for accommodation, pp. 23–44 in Kotas, R. (ed.) *Managerial Economics for Hotel Operation*, Surrey University Press, Guildford.

Major Case Study 12.1
Changing Long-haul Demand: The Case of Barbados

The tourist experience in Barbados is changing to requiring participation, involvement and immersion in culture and the local environment.
Source: © Gavin Hellier/Alamy Images

Introduction

The tropical islands of the Caribbean are undergoing a major change in demand from their long-haul markets. This case study looks at the changing demands of long-haul tourism to Barbados from the UK and from Germany.

Barbados is losing market share to its competitors – both old and new. In the growing international tourism market, competition and expertise are heightening. If Barbados is to take advantage of this growth and continue to utilise tourism as a driver of the economy, then it is critical to understand its generating markets, their characteristics, determinants of demand, and preferences.

The UK and German long-haul markets have become sophisticated, experienced and discerning and some argue that Barbados has failed to keep up with their demands. The island's product is one of sea, sun and sand and its markets are highly dependent on the USA and the UK. Yet, as we have seen in this chapter, the needs and expectations of tourists have been changing, evolving from rest and relaxation to a new generation of tourists searching for new experiences that are not available at home. Seeking

experiences focuses on authenticity, education and learning through direct experience, and requires active participation, involvement and even immersion in culture and the local environment.

The UK Long-haul Market: Background

The UK has emerged as one of the largest outbound travel markets in the world in the new Millennium. The UK market is significantly larger than the German market for Barbados but is more volatile due to the economic situation in the UK since 2007. Top long-haul destinations for the UK market are the United States, Thailand, India, Canada, Australia, Africa, New Zealand, the Middle East and other South Asian countries.

Affordability remains a major consideration for UK long-haul travellers despite a slow economic rebound. The driving motivation for value across all market segments means that once a destination has been reached, often involving a high airfare component, then length of stay is increased to take advantage of competitively priced accommodation. The financial barrier to entry for long-haul tourism is closely linked to airfares. Increased penetration by low-cost, no-frills airlines will help in this regard. The literature suggests that higher fares out of the UK are linked to the UK's Air Passenger Duty (APD). However, for 2015 the banding has been reformed to the significant advantage of Caribbean destinations.

Information sources for trip planning include past visitors along with a mix of traditional media, online sources and the travel trade. Post-trip sharing of destination information in the UK long-haul market is heavily focused on in-person interactions, both conversational and photo-sharing. The UK market has traditionally had long booking lead times due to the perceived complexity of a long-haul purchase. In terms of booking channels, the UK long-haul market still relies on retail agents as British consumers look for travel protection and security. Booking through an 'online travel agent' is the second most popular booking method, closely followed by booking directly with an airline. Tour operators have a great influence over the tourism supply chain since they direct and influence the volume of tourism, the tourist destinations and facilities that are used. They play a significant role in providing advice to their clients about local products and services. They are important in promoting sustainability in the supply chain for instance, by selecting suppliers that are environmentally responsible, informing their clients about their environmental policies and advising on how to behave responsibly at the destination, offsetting carbon emissions and in some cases funding projects that improve local quality of life.

Research shows that, to be successful in the UK long-haul market, a destination must be perceived as offering value for money, relevant and multiple experiences, and unique tourism products to travellers. In general, the strongest attraction of long-haul holidays to the UK market is the opportunity to combine multiple experiences to provide variety and/or 'beach plus'. In terms of seeking value for money and controlling expenditure, demand for all-inclusive resorts in the long-haul market will continue to drive demand. Long-haul wedding/honeymoons will also continue to grow, offering a value alternative to increasingly expensive UK weddings.

The German Long-haul Market: Background

For Barbados, the German market has experienced sustained growth in arrivals since 2007. It is one of the biggest spenders on the island and one of the most significant and most sustainable globally. Growing confidence in the economy is set to show modest year-on-year increases in outbound volume until 2017. As with the UK, long-haul markets have become much more attractive to German travellers in recent years. Improved transportation links have made international destinations more accessible alongside more competitive airfares and frequency of flights.

In 2012, the Caribbean had a share of 8 per cent of the German long-haul market. In terms of volume, the major competing destinations are the USA, China, Brazil and Thailand. In addition to the main holiday, long-haul

second holidays are increasingly popular, though shorter and with a lower spend. Affordability is a key issue for the German long-haul market. As a result, Germans are good at searching for value for money and this has led to rising demand for package deals and all-inclusive holidays.

All German long-haul travellers invest heavily in searching information for their travel. They are careful planners, seeking detailed information from a range of sources prior to departure. Online travel sites and high-street travel agencies are both important. Although each channel has its merits, German travellers use a multi-channel approach when researching and booking trips. For long-haul trips, Germans commonly research information online but then make a booking with a travel agent. This mirrors the pattern for the UK market. In terms of sharing information about the destinations, Germans use postcards, talk to friends, send email, and increasingly use Facebook and other social media. The majority of travellers start planning their trip within three months of travelling.

In terms of product considerations for the German long-haul market, economic considerations mean that all-inclusive resorts have become much more appealing (as with the UK); for a country with a very short Baltic coastline, beach holidays are important; they are keen on authentic ways of life; they seek quality, comfort and luxury which often necessitate an element of city life; and seek opportunities to experience the culture and the local lifestyle unique to the destination.

DISCUSSION QUESTIONS

1. Based on the above case study, and looking at the Barbados Tourism Authority website (www.barbados.org), how can Barbados develop products to attract the UK market?

2. Based on the above case study, and looking at the Barbados Tourism Authority website (www.barbados.org), how can Barbados develop products to attract the German market?

3. Visit the Barbados Tourism Authority website (www.barbados.org). How geared up is the website to the savvy online long-haul traveller?

Sources:
Association of British Travel Agents (2013) *The Consumer Holiday Trends Report*, ABTA, London.
Canadian Tourism Commission (2013) *UK Market Profile – February 2013*, Canadian Tourism Commission, Ottawa.
Canadian Tourism Commission (2013) *Germany Market Profile – February 2013*, Canadian Tourism Commission, Ottawa.
Craigwell, R., and Worrell, D. (2008) The competitiveness of selected Caribbean tourism markets, *Social and Economic Studies* **57**(1), 72–107.
Euromonitor International (2013) *Travel and Tourism in Barbados (July 2013)*, Euromonitor International, London.
Hayes and Jarvis (2013) *Long Haul Trends Report*, Hayes and Jarvis, London.
Mintel Group Ltd (2011) *Germany Outbound 2011*, Mintel Group Ltd, London.
Mintel Group Ltd (2014) *UK Long Haul 2014*, Mintel Group Ltd, London.
Shore, S. (2011) Germany outbound, *Travel & Tourism Analyst*, **14**, 1–48.
UNWTO (2006) *Market Trends Europe*, UNWTO, Madrid.
UNWTO (2011) *Tourism Towards 2050: Global Overview*, UNWTO, Madrid.
www.barbados.org

CHAPTER 13
TOURISM MARKETING

Learning Outcomes

This chapter considers tourism marketing as a key component of any tourism organisation. It outlines the meaning of a marketing approach, how marketing is undertaken in tourism and, finally, the chapter discusses market planning and the marketing mix. The chapter is designed to provide you with:

- an understanding of what marketing means in tourism;

- an awareness of the service-dominant logic approach;

- an appreciation of the role of technology in tourism marketing;

- an understanding of market strategy and planning and the elements of the marketing mix; and

- an awareness of the concept of tourism product markets and how they give rise to different types of tourism.

Photograph: Summer holiday photos © viperagp/Fotolia.com

Introduction

This chapter introduces the dimensions of tourism marketing. It outlines current thinking in terms of the scope and definition of marketing and, in particular, charts the shift in focus from goods to a service-dominant logic of marketing. This new approach recognises that tourism marketing thinks of the product as a bundle of both tangible and intangible elements as well as focusing on consumer needs and their involvement in the co-creation of the tourism experience. The chapter shows how technology, and particularly the Internet, has transformed the business of tourism marketing. It then goes on to discuss the nature of tourism market planning and strategy and the elements of the marketing mix, and especially the implications of the nature of tourism, for the mix. The chapter closes with a review of the concept of tourism product markets.

The Concept of Marketing

Marketing takes a particular approach and is a distinctive way of thinking about the world. Effectively, it is a management philosophy that prioritises a focus on the consumer. Marketing as a concept is evolving quickly and, interestingly for tourism, there is a growing trend to conceptualise marketing based upon services rather than physical goods. Whilst there are many definitions of marketing, they all focus around the need to identify and supply customer needs and the contemporary approach is to go beyond *satisfying* those needs to *delighting* the customer. Contemporary definitions of marketing reflect this thinking with a focus upon the many actors in the marketplace. Kotler *et al.*'s (2003) definitions are the most commonly used:

- A market is:

    'A set of actual and potential buyers who might transact with a seller. This market can be a physical or virtual space' (Kotler et al., 2003, p. 20).

- Marketing is:

    'A social and managerial process by which individuals and groups obtain what they need and want through creating and exchanging products and value with others' (Kotler et al., 2003, p.12).

These definitions work well for tourism as they include the non-profit sector (such as destination marketing organisations – DMOs), but do not lose sight of the two central concepts of marketing – the concept of exchange and relationships and the imperative to supply consumer needs:

1. The concept of exchange states that exchange takes place when parties agree about a transaction and will be worse off without the exchange – it therefore creates 'value'. Relationships in the tourism marketplace lead to exchanges and naturally have led to the concept of relationship marketing where the nurturing of the relationship is more important than single exchanges. Given the nature of tourism as a high-involvement product, relationship marketing plays an important role.

2. The process of identifying and supplying consumer needs lies at the heart of tourism marketing. The marketing concept is tightly focused on delivering value to the consumer, where value is viewed as the difference in the benefits that consumer receives from the product and the costs of obtaining the product. There is an important difference here between tourism marketing and that of physical goods.

Evolution of Marketing Approaches

We can identify the key stages of the evolution of marketing in terms of the orientation of production. These stages are:

1. **Production orientation.** Here the dominant preoccupation is to produce as many goods as possible to meet strong demand. In tourism, this can be likened to the industrialisation of tourism in the 1960s and 1970s when many products were made available (beds and airline seats).

2. **Sales orientation.** Once more product was available, the emphasis switched to securing sales. Major tour operators in the 1970s and 1980s had huge sales teams and developed computer reservations systems (CRS) to boost sales. Here the focus was on exchange rather than building a longer-term relationship, simply persuading consumers to buy rather than understanding their decision-making process.

Table 13.1 Translating marketing orientation into action

Task	Marketing function
Identifying consumer needs	Marketing research
Analysing marketing opportunities	Market segmentation and understanding relationships
Translating needs into products	Product planning and formulation
Determining product value in different seasons	Pricing policy and creation of value delivery
Making the product available	Distribution policy
Informing and motivating the customer	Promotion strategy and tactics

Source: Cooper *et al.*, 2006, p. 583

3. **Marketing orientation.** The next logical stage of evolution is to focus on consumer needs and to re-orientate thinking to ensure that products are formulated and marketing processes designed, to meet the needs of the tourist. This has not happened quickly in tourism. Initially, the trend to marketing simply meant taking down the 'sales department' sign and replacing it with a 'marketing department' sign, but gradually a shift in thinking took place such that the whole company was encouraged to think about meeting customer needs and delivering high-quality service. For tourism, a marketing orientation implies that an organisation displays four characteristics:

(a) a dominant marketing philosophy which demonstrates an unwavering focus on the consumer and which is underpinned by research;

(b) it encourages exchange and strengthens both its networks and loyalty through recognising the importance of developing long-term relationships with customers;

(c) a thought process accepting that strategic and tactical planning goes hand-in-hand and includes constant evaluation and review of activities; and

(d) it demonstrates an integrated organisational structure geared to the organisation's goals of delivering value to the consumer through business-to-customer and business-to-business activities.

The road to achieving these characteristics is shown in Table 13.1.

4. **Societal marketing** More recently, as the negative impacts of tourism have come to the fore, and issues such as climate change have emerged, marketing has evolved further to embrace concepts of corporate social responsibility and ethical behaviour – in tourism these initiatives have focused upon stewardship of the destination and actions to mitigate climate change (Goodwin, and Font, 2011). In other words, marketing takes into account the broader needs of society rather than just the consumer. Of course, a CSR or an ethical approach to the tourism marketplace may be cynically used to pre-empt the development of legislation applying to, say, the greening of hotels as noted by Font *et al.* (2012). However, there is no doubt that the ethical tourism marketplace also attracts particular groups of consumers. Goodwin (2003), for example, notes the growth of the ethical purchasing of tourism with an ethical purchasing index which calibrates the ethical marketplace.

An Alternative View: From Goods-Dominant Logic to Service-Dominant Logic

The classic paper in this chapter is by Vargo and Lusch (2004), two authors who have had a major impact on recent marketing thought and who see marketing as a having a 'service-dominant logic' (S-D logic) rather than the traditional 'goods-dominant logic' (G-D logic).

In their paper they chart the evolution of marketing thought and show how it has swung from one extreme to the other:

1. Nineteenth-century thinking viewed marketing as based upon the exchange principle inherited from economics. This focuses on the unit of output and places the 'good' in the centre of the stage. When marketing is based upon goods, it focuses on tangibility, embedded value and transactions.

2. A new paradigm emerged in the 1970s and 1980s that viewed services as different from goods. This contemporary thinking shifted marketing thought to a service-oriented view where the key drivers are intangibility, co-creation of value and relationship marketing.

Vargo and Lusch (Vargo and Lusch, 2004; Lusch and Vargo, 2014) have articulated this second approach as the contemporary logic of marketing, and it is now informing the way that tourism marketers approach their craft (Shaw *et al.*, 2011). Vargo and Lusch state that whilst the 4 Ps are a handy framework, they are in fact meaningless in an age where marketing is seen as an innovating and adaptive force and where the focus is on the continuous nature of relationships between all market actors. Their view is shared by Lovelock and Gummesson (2004), who agree that the dominant logic of marketing is reflected in an emphasis on provision of service. For tourism marketing, the implications are fundamental as it means that organisations must reposition themselves to get closer to their consumers (Li and Petrick, 2008). For example, intermediaries must recognise that (i) consumers can easily access information on products; (ii) consumers have transparent price comparisons such that the traditional 'one-to-one' distribution channels are now many-to-many; and (iii) intermediaries themselves have the choice of going electronic, being replaced or repositioning themselves (as we saw in Chapter 9).

Of course, the true situation often lies between the two extremes and there is an increasing view that goods and services are both part of the marketing offering and in fact what has occurred is more of a shift away from manufacturing to a customer-centred approach. This approach to the product as a mix of both services and goods has been termed 'the molecular approach' by Shostack (1977). He views products as made up of many parts, some tangible, some intangible – in other words, an amalgam that is exemplified by the fragmented nature of the tourism product. This 'molecular' approach allows managers to manage the total product and to realise the synergies between parts of the amalgam.

Classic Paper
Vargo, S.L. and Lusch, R.F. (2004) Evolving to a new dominant logic for marketing, *Journal of Marketing* 68 (January), 1–17

This paper by Vargo and Lusch represents a significant milestone in marketing thought and it has been hugely influential in setting research agendas and the way that marketers view the world. Basically, Vargo and Lusch argue that marketing has viewed the world from an economics perspective where the currency is one of 'exchange' and products are manufactured. The thrust of the Vargo and Lusch paper is that since the closing decades of the twentieth century 'new perspectives have emerged that have a revised logic focused on intangible resources, the co-creation of value and relationships' (p. 1). For tourism this is significant development as it heralds a new era of marketing thought where service provision and their characteristics, rather than goods, have become the 'dominant logic' of marketing.

The paper begins with a thorough and insightful review of how marketing thinking has evolved and, in particular, details the new approaches, often based on services, that allowed thinking to break away from the 4 Ps concept. Vargo and Lusch conceptualise a timeline of marketing thought as follows:

1800–1920	Classical and neo-classical economics
1900–1950	Early/formative marketing
1950–1980	Marketing management
1980–2000 and beyond	Marketing as a social and economic process

However, as we stress in this chapter, the paper is not a plea for a separate field of services marketing, but instead that a 'service-dominant logic' should be applied across the whole field of marketing, including goods. Indeed it is rare to think of a marketing offering that is not a bundle of both goods and services as we saw above. Yet it is the services aspect that has been long neglected. The paper then goes on to outline the key features of the new 'service-dominant logic' (p. 5):

1. The core competencies of an organisation are the fundamental knowledge and skills and this represents potential competitive advantage. This recognises the importance of knowledge management, the importance of the 'learning organisation' and how the skills and competitions of the work force provide a competitive edge.

2. Organisations identify other entities (potential customers) that could benefit from these competencies. This recognises the imperative to develop relationships with customers to allow co-creation – an increasingly important aspect of marketing facilitated by the Internet and networked on line communities, as we have seen elsewhere in this book.

3. Organisations cultivate relationships that involve the customers developing customised, competitively compelling value propositions to meet specific needs. This means developing networked organisations that allow enterprises to leverage from others in the network.

4. Organisations gauge marketplace feedback to learn how to improve the firm's offering to customers and improve firm performance. In other words, the enterprise continually improves.

Throughout the paper, Vargo and Lusch weave contemporary approaches of relationship building, networked organisations and knowledge management into the paper and show how these approaches support the 'service-dominant logic'. This tripartite approach is supported by a further paper by Li and Petrick (2008) and a later book by Lusch and Vargo (2014). To conclude with the words of Vargo and Lusch (2004):

'the focus is shifting away from tangibles towards intangibles, such as skills, information and knowledge, and toward interactivity and connectivity and ongoing relationships. The orientation has shifted from the producer to the consumer' (p. 15).

A Tourism Marketing Gap?

So far we have dealt with generic concepts of marketing. When we consider tourism marketing, however, there is a question as to whether many of these ideas have been accepted. In tourism, the very strong traditions of custom and practice, reflected in the conservative nature of the industry, mean that organisations are often a number of years behind other economic sectors in terms of adoption of new ideas such as the service-dominant logic. In part, this is due to the tradition of promoting managers up through the ranks rather than educating them, the view that tourism products somehow need a different approach, and the later adoption of technology in the sector. However, as the tourism market matures, there will be less of a place for the amateur entrepreneur and professional marketing managers will be more in demand. The question is then whether the tourism sector has the professional and technical capacity to cope with the contemporary marketing environment.

Marketing Approaches for Tourism Organisations

There are two considerations to take into account in order to understand how best to approach tourism marketing:

*   firstly, technology and, in particular, the Internet, has transformed the way that tourism marketing is done; and
*   secondly, it is vital to understand the nature of the tourism product itself, and the nature of the purchasing process (Table 13.2).

Table 13.2 Distinguishing features of tourism purchasing

Distinguishing features of a tourism purchase	Distinguishing features of tourism products
A tourism purchase is highly involving of the customer	Tourism products comprise a bundle of tangible and intangible (experiential) goods
A tourism purchase offers great ability to develop relationships with the customer	Tourism products are characterised by unstable demand which is not only highly elastic but also tends not to be loyal
A tourism purchase offers the ability for co-creation of the tourism product with the customer	Tourism products are distributed by intermediaries (traditional or electronic) who can influence the purchase decision
A tourism purchase is high risk as it is difficult to predetermine value and the intangible elements of the product	There is considerable regulation and consumer legislation of tourism products On purchase, the consumer does not own the tourism product The tourism product is fragmented and delivered by many different suppliers

The Role of Technology

The Internet influences every aspect of tourism and has changed the culture and behaviour of how people purchase, search and communicate (Benckendorff *et al.*, 2014). It connects companies, customers and governments at low cost and without constraints of time or space and as such is a transformative marketing tool. This is because it has significant advantages over traditional communication media; advantages such as reach, low cost, richness, speed of communication and interactivity. Indeed, technology facilitates many of the processes that are needed in the new marketing paradigm of relationship building and co-creation (UNWTO, 2014). These include communication with customers, interactivity, tools for research, massive data storage and the ability to build, track and maintain relationships.

Technology has created a whole new marketing industry – eMarketing – which can be defined as the promotion of a tourism product, company service or website online and can include a variety of activities from online advertising to search engine optimisation. It is also provides a medium and delivery mechanism for consumers to gather information and to make purchasing decisions.

eMarketing is ideally suited to tourism. It allows the development of online brochures that can deliver rich multimedia content, blending text, images, sound and video into multimedia documents to overcome the intangible nature of the product. Through video and interactivity it delivers the ability to 'test drive' the product. It also gives tourism organisations the ability to instantly change dates, prices and availability online, saving expensive brochure reprints. Technology also allows organisations to individually target customers through 'narrow casting' to customise messages, utilise email and web links to engage in 'viral marketing' and, of course, the Internet gives small businesses and destinations a degree of global market reach previously unheard of.

eMarketing in tourism aims to generate traffic to an organisation's website, to engage the customer and to convert that traffic into sales. There is a range of mechanisms for closely engaging with the consumer through eMarketing, social media and tracking use of the website. This includes how often they visit, for how long and which pages are browsed.

Despite the obvious advantages of its use, technology does bring with it certain constraints when used in marketing. For example, there are concerns over the security of financial information and personal identity (Mills and Law, 2015). Most websites are in English so creating a barrier to access, and in some countries access to the Internet comes at a high cost. In the future the limits to this technology will be economic, in terms of investment; human, in terms of attitude and habits; and technological, in terms of computing power, storage and bandwidth.

In the future, digital convergence will provide overlapping and ubiquitous use of computer systems with devices such as entertainment systems, smart phones, tablets and other devices. For tourism, one of the most exciting of the potential marketing applications is the use of mobile devices to deliver marketing messages and information. Technology has also empowered the consumer. Social media and the Internet have revolutionised information search for products and increasingly appear in search engines (Xiang and Gretzel, 2010).

In the next mini case study we show how researching social media can uncover new segments and has revolutionised market research.

Mini Case Study 13.1
Researching Social Media – Turning Market Research on its Head

Introduction

Social media provide a rich source of data for market research and for segmenting tourism markets. No longer does the researcher have to question the consumer in the high street or in their home, instead the consumer is constantly posting their thoughts and opinions online for all to access. Traditional market research can be costly and time-intensive; as a result, many organisations have begun to turn to social media as a cost-effective and in-depth tool for gaining real-time insights into their customers, market, brand appearance and other important market research aspects. This is leading to new ways to segment markets based on social media behaviour and habits.

The flow of information available from social media has been termed 'big data'. The trick for organisations is to:

● extract this data using mining tools;

● model and analyse the data – distinguishing the 'signal' from the 'noise'; and

● use knowledge management to communicate the findings for use by marketing managers.

This is the approach that is emerging, but with a commercial edge – the sale and analysis of real-time social media data. Companies such as 'DataSift' and 'Gnip' analyse tweets and blogs to track opinions of products and service in real time, whilst other research companies such as 'klout' analyse the influence of those who post opinions online. These companies are 'data platforms', collecting and standardising information from social media sites such as Twitter, Facebook, YouTube and others. The companies can do this by enforcing the licensing rules for social media which state that a tweet can be 'analysed' but not 'republished'. The sophistication of the approach allows data from different companies to be combined to create powerful analytics. This is a new departure for market research and one that has moved rapidly from a cottage industry to the mainstream as the sophistication of the technology has improved.

The significance of this development should not be underestimated – it turns market research on its head, no longer do researchers need to wait on the high street with clipboards. However, there is a cloud on the horizon – the companies do not simply analyse a tweet but will also know everything about the poster from their information on their profile page. There is a danger therefore that the tweets become less revealing as on-line users become more cautious.

This social media research allows tourism organisations to

● track trends with social media for real-time insights into online habits, opinions of products and views of service;

● learn the language that the audience uses;

● uncover trends by engaging with the audience so that, for example, brands can be co-created; and

● re-segment markets by online habits which can be linked to other profile variables for individual tourists.

DISCUSSION QUESTIONS

1. How can social media habits be used in market segmentation?

2. The approach described in this case study is revolutionising market research. How would you use this approach to research service perceptions of a large fast food restaurant chain?

3. Co-creation of brands and even destination images can be conceived in the future using this approach. Which social media would be best suited to do this – and why?

Sources:
www.attensity.com/home
http://datasift.com
http://gnip.com
http://klout.com
www.lexalytics.com
http://sysomos.com

The Nature of Tourism

We argue that tourism is simply a particular type of offering to the marketplace that demands a differentiated approach from other products. This approach includes the following approaches:

- Wherever possible the product should be made tangible, for example, through the use of staff uniforms and the careful design of the environment – or service-scape – where the product is delivered.

- Employees become an additional part of the marketing mix and therefore need to be well trained. The tourism product is produced where it is consumed and this means that employees can influence not only the successful delivery of the product, but also the tourist's evaluation of the service during the short time that they are exposed to it.

- Perceived risk should be managed through strong quality assurance, to ensure consistent and standardised service delivery. This consistency should be communicated to the customer through strong branding of the product which itself acts to reassure the customer about the service.

- Other elements of the mix should be carefully aligned with tourism, with promotion stressing emotive aspects and relationship building with intermediaries.

- The nature of services as perishable mean that it is essential to manage both capacity and demand through yield management which adjusts pricing to demand, and so smooths out the demand curve.

These points can be summarised into two key approaches that characterise tourism marketing and are designed to help retain and build relationships with customers, avoid price competition, retain employees and reduce costs:

1. Relationship marketing has evolved to embrace the use of social media where the power has shifted to the customer as they engage with products and services in real time. Organisations therefore link with the customer base through social media to secure a loyalty and commitment, allowing for co-creation of the product and so creating, maintaining and enhancing strong relationships with consumers.

2. Service quality management is designed to 'industrialise' service delivery by guaranteeing standardised and consistent services.

Market Planning in Tourism and Hospitality

It is essential for tourism organisations to plan their marketing strategically as well as tactically. Tourism market planning provides a common point of reference for the organisation acting as a coordination mechanism – particularly important for destination marketing. It is also encourages a disciplined approach to marketing by ensuring that objectives are set for markets and products, that each market has activities and resources allocated and, of course, the planning process itself sets key performance indicators (KPIs) against which the success – or otherwise – of the plan can be monitored. Market planning takes both strategic, long-term and tactical, short-term approaches. Increasingly these plans are flexible and subject to constant revision. The process is summarised in Figure 13.1.

Strategic Approaches

There are a number of approaches to determining market strategy in tourism. These include:

- product market portfolios;
- growth and development strategies;
- positioning; and
- branding.

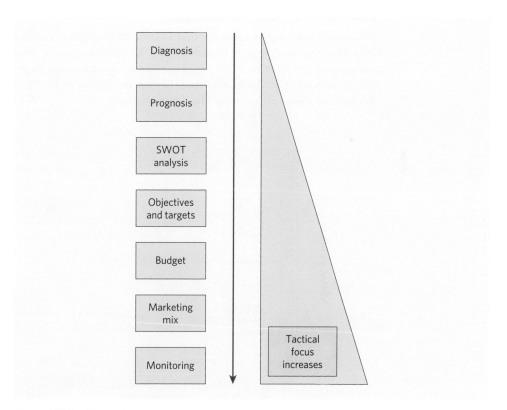

Figure 13.1 The marketing planning process
Source: Kotler *et al.,* 2003

Product Market Portfolios

The product market portfolio approach lends itself well to tourism and the most well-known is the Boston Consulting Group Growth Share Matrix (BCG matrix). The BCG matrix is a management tool that allows an organisation to classify its products and then apply particular strategies to them. The matrix has two dimensions and four cells (Figure 13.2). The two dimensions are relative market share and market growth:

1. the market share dimension is a measure of the health of the product relative to its competitors; and
2. the market growth dimension is a measure of the product life-cycle and can be used to estimate the level of resources needed.

This creates four cells in the matrix:

1. Cash cows are highly profitable and do not need significant investment.
2. Stars are product leaders in high-growth markets.
3. Question marks have not achieved a dominant market position, and hence do not generate much cash.
4. Dogs are a drain on the organisation's resources with low market share in a low-growth market.

According to where a product lies within the matrix, particular marketing strategy is appropriate. The BCG matrix is not perfect as it is subjective and requires substantial amounts of data; however, it is widely used due to its intuitive appeal.

Growth and Development Strategies

Also using a matrix approach, the best-known tool for growth and development strategies is the Ansoff product market growth matrix. Ansoff's matrix is a simple tool that combines markets and products to allow organisations to consider how to grow and develop their business according to the market that they are in (Figure 13.3). There are two dimensions which create a four-cell matrix. The dimensions are:

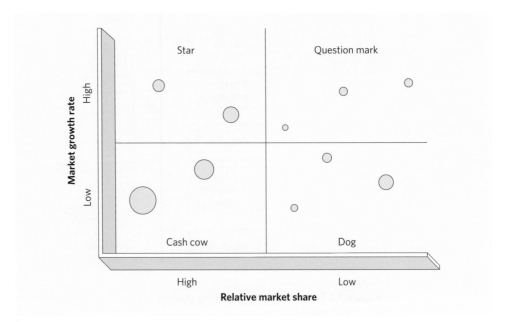

Figure 13.2 Market growth – market share portfolio analysis matrix
Source: Kotler *et al.,* 2003

	Existing product	**New product**
Existing market	Ski tours in Europe	Lakes and mountains walking tours
New market	Ski tours in southern hemisphere to give 12 month sales	Ski clothing and accessories

Figure 13.3 Ansoff product market growth matrix for a British ski tour operator
Source: based on Ansoff, 1957

1. existing and/or new products; and
2. existing and/or new markets.

   The cells then provide strategy options:

- Market penetration, which involves increasing market share at the expense of competitors.
- Product development, which involves developing new products to server existing markets.
- Market development, which involves seeking new markets for existing products.
- Diversification, which involves entering new markets with new products.

Positioning

A key component of a destination or product strategy is the positioning of the destination or product against the competition. This ensures that the destination or product delivers a unique position in relation to its competitors and occupies a particular place in the minds of potential tourists. Positioning is based upon differentiation, cost and developing a unique focus. Positioning must be consistent with cost and value for money, market trends and consumer preferences, convenience of purchase, technology and demographic trends. Finally, positioning must take into account the capability and resources of the destination or product to deliver the promise.

Branding

Branding is an important strategic tool in the tourism marketing process – to quote Kotler *et al*. (2003) 'branding is the art and cornerstone of marketing' (p. 418). A brand can be defined as:

> 'A name, term, sign, symbol or design or combination of them, intended to identify the goods or services of one seller or group of sellers and to differentiate them from those of competitors' (Kotler 2000, p. 404).

Brands can be approached from two viewpoints:

1. **The product plus approach** views the brand as an addition to the product (along with, say, price) and is concerned with communication and differentiation.
2. **The holistic approach** views the brand as greater than the sum of its parts such that brands reside in the minds of consumers. This approach is common in destination marketing.

Brands signify identity and originated as a means of ownership and identification by farmers or craftsmen. Brands became important as mass markets developed for products in the twentieth century. This was for two reasons: firstly, consumers became more sophisticated and were faced with greater product choice; and, secondly, branding was developed for 'fast moving consumer goods' (FMCG) as they are characterised by low-involvement products with the need for branding to build loyalty and communicate benefits over competitors.

Nonetheless, whilst it may appear that brands are fabricated, they are real entities, based upon products, resistant to change and dependent upon occupying defensible niches within product categories. Developing and managing tourism brands is therefore as much a strategic operation as it is tactical.

Tactical Level

For most organisations, the tactical level of tourism marketing is focused upon marketing campaigns. Here, the starting point is to identify the target market and then to use elements of the marketing mix to approach that market. We can think of the marketing mix as the set of marketing tools that the firm uses to pursue its marketing objectives in the target market, where each element of the mix supports the others and none stand alone. Also, as we noted above, with the move to a service-dominant logic, the marketing mix can be expanded from the traditional 4 Ps to include other influencing variables such as the people involved in delivering the service, the physical setting – or service-scape – where the service is delivered and the actual process of delivering the service.

Target Market

Defining the target market is an essential first step in the market planning process. Here, the technique of market segmentation allows marketers to tightly define subsets of the market and allows those grouped to be targeted in terms of formulating products and devising marketing campaigns. Despite the obvious importance of market segmentation, tourism has been slow to adopt a sophisticated approach with some arguing that it is a rather arid and academic approach to marketing with little real life relevance. Nonetheless, market segmentation has much to offer the tourism marketer. To be successful market segments must have a number of key features. They must be:

- **Measurable.** There is no point in creating a sophisticated approach to segmentation if the group cannot be measured on variables that allow them to be identified and reached by the marketer.
- **Substantial.** Segments must be substantial enough to be worth devising campaigns or products to meet their needs.
- **Durable.** The segments must be durable in terms of time. If a company is targeting a particular segment it needs to be confident that the segment will remain stable for a number of years.
- **Competitive.** The company must be confident that it has a competitive offering to attract purchasers from the particular segment.

Segmentation in tourism has taken a traditional 'common sense' approach in the past, for example segmenting by demographics or by geography. In part, this is because tourism statistics are organised in this way making it relatively easy to identify these segments. However, in the twenty-first century, and with the support of sophisticated market research and technology, it is possible to be much more creative in segmentation. This involves adopting a 'data-driven' approach including variables such as use of technology, preference for adventure and overall leisure lifestyles. It is also possible to apply social technographics which segments consumers according to their behaviour on social networking sites. These contemporary approaches to market segmentation demand sophisticated research techniques including qualitative market research and multivariate analysis. Deep and meaningful research underpins new approaches to segmentation that can deliver detailed customer profiles and identify elements of consumer behaviour. The following are common segmentation approaches used in tourism:

- Demographic, using standard census-based data to segment the market by gender or age.
- Socio-demographic, which combines demographic data with social variables such as family size.

- Geographic, using standard geographic data such as address or country of residence.
- Geo-demographic, which is a more sophisticated approach combining demographics with data such as post or zip codes to map where particular segments live.
- Buyer behaviour is where particular purchasing groups, such as business or leisure tourists are grouped together. This can be more sophisticated, however, using segments of late bookers, or of adventure travellers.
- Psychographics is a more sophisticated approach, reliant on qualitative market research and multivariate analysis to segment the market by psychological profiles.
- Increasingly, segmentation based upon experiences will be developed, as we can see in the next case study which focuses on marketing Greenland.

Mini Case Study 13.2
Branding Challenging Destinations – Greenland

Greenland's spectacular landscape.
Source: © sorincolac/Fotolia.com

Introduction

Greenland is a challenging destination to market. It is perceived as a vast, isolated and remote destination that is difficult to get to. And, whilst Greenland is clearly visible on world maps, its representation and exposure in the world's media is low. For destination marketers these are difficult perceptions to overcome.

Visit Greenland

In 1992 Greenland Tourism was created to develop a viable tourism industry. In 2012 the organisation was renamed Visit Greenland with the overall objective to improve and streamline the tourism sector. The organisation has three key aims:

1. to create a unique Greenlandic image based on the country's strengths, values, culture and regional diversity;
2. to facilitate strong regional networks of knowledge sharing; and
3. to guide decision makers to develop the best possible legislative framework for tourism.

In addition to the geographical challenges of access and remoteness, Visit Greenland is faced with a number of structural challenges in the tourism sector, each of which impacts upon their ability to market the destination. These challenges can be summarised as a lack of statistics, accessibility in terms of air access and harbour berthing, seasonality, and the need for market development using both segmentation and product development.

Markets, Products and a Digital Strategy

In terms of the latter challenge faced by the organisation, Greenland has researched its market segments and is looking to develop new products. This is particularly important given that new air access routes are opening up and new types of tourist will begin to visit. Greenland needs to be prepared to receive them. The island's market segments have been structured on two dimensions:

- experiences classified as culture, culture & nature, nature, and special interest; and
- interaction – visitors who observe, interact or immerse themselves in the experience.

Product development is focused around high-end experiences such as trophy hunting, heli-skiing, adventure camps and sport fishing as well as dual destination products with Iceland.

A major plank of Visit Greenland's approach has been the development of a digital marketing strategy strongly based upon digital images and video of Greenland – in other words, the use of visual presentations and strong imagery to evoke an emotional response, create interaction with potential visitors and thus create a desire to visit. A new website was launched in 2012 and Greenland's attractions of silence, vastness and solitude are represented through rich and immersive videos. As part of the digital approach, Visit Greenland decided upon a 100 per cent online marketing strategy. The strategy stayed true to Greenland's over-arching brand – 'Be a Pioneer' – interpreting the brand into the 'Big Artic 5', which draw together the winter and spring seasons with:

- ice and snow;
- northern lights;
- dog sledding;
- whales; and
- pioneering people.

DISCUSSION QUESTIONS

1. Taking a destination of your choice, examine how many brand messages are involved and debate which is the most effective.
2. Thinking of the challenges of marketing Greenland as a destination, how effective is the Visit Greenland website?
3. Greenland exposes the classic debate about whether visitors choose a destination or an experience – what are your views on this question?

Source:
www.greenland.com

The Tourism Product

The tourism product represents the utilities and benefits offered to the marketplace. Kotler *et al.* (2014) view the product as comprising three parts:

1. **The core product** is the essence of the offering. In tourism this may be the core idea of a holiday on a tropical island.

2. **The tangible product** is the offering itself and, for the holiday to the tropical island, will be made up of the actual elements (tickets, accommodation) of the holiday. These elements of the product must all be present for the tourist to use the services.

3. **The augmented product** is where the supplier of the product adds extra features to be competitive. These may include additional free nights, transfers at no extra cost, or a free champagne breakfast on arrival.

Tourism products are complex and multifaceted and, as a result, there is a number of ways of viewing the product:

- **The product as a bundle of tangible and intangible elements** . It is a myth that the tourism product is entirely intangible, although of course elements of it are. Instead, we can think of the tourism product as a bundle of tangible elements (such as hotel rooms and the destination environment) and intangibles (the experience of travelling). This reflects the service-dominant logic view incorporating notions of relationships, the co-creation of value, the recognition of intangible products and the consideration of all market actors.

- **The product as a destination amalgam.** A second approach is to view the product as synonymous with the destination, such that the tourism product is an 'amalgam' of destination elements including attractions; supporting services including accommodation and food & beverage; and transportation. There are significant implications of this 'amalgam' for tourism marketing, particularly the challenge of managing quality across the various elements, each of which is often supplied by a different organisation. Because each of these elements is normally supplied by a different organisation, this creates real challenges for the tourism marketer – especially, say, a destination manager who attempts to coordinate the delivery of the tourism product. The challenge is simple – any element of the product that is of poor quality compromises the rest of the product bundle and means that the tourist will leave with a negative impression of the destination and may not return.

- **The product as a series of stages**. The tourism product can be disaggregated into stages of the vacation from anticipation and planning, to booking, travel and evaluation. This stresses the importance of the consumer focus and of service delivery. Indeed some companies have successfully integrated these stages into their products by, for example, keeping in touch with the customer during the run up to the trip and providing free transfers from home to the transport terminal, as well as providing welcome home packs and reunion parties. Finally, tourists increasingly share memories and photographs of their trip through social media sites. Product life-cycles are a further important consideration for tourism. Here the analogy is that products are developed, launched, grow and develop, eventually move into decline and, finally, are taken off the market. (We deal with this aspect of tourism destination in detail in Chapter 2.)

- **The product as experience.** Gilbert (1990) takes the idea further, arguing that the tourism product is in fact the total experience. He defines the tourism product as:

'an amalgam of different goods and services offered as an activity experience to the tourist' (Gilbert, 1990, p. 20).

Gilbert's idea can be extended to consider the tourism product as developed and engineered as an experience; indeed many tourism products are staged experiences, recognising that meaningful experiences cannot be guaranteed but that they can be managed.

Here, the trend to combining tourism with the creative industries will see exciting new experience-based products develop. As tourism markets mature they seek authentic tourism products. Suppliers and destinations are responding to this challenge by delivering experience-based products (Frochot and Batat, 2013). Pine and Gilmore (1999) have termed this trend the 'experience economy'. In the experience economy, changing values from older to younger generations mean that consumers are seeking new meaning and self-actualisation in their tourism consumption patterns as they move beyond material possessions and services to experiences. Tourism products are increasingly being formulated to serve this demand by engineering experiences to match the expectations of the marketplace, not only in tourism but also across the services sector (Morgan *et al.*, 2010). Here, Pine and Gilmore (1999) see experiences along two dimensions: passive to active; and absorption to immersion, with the ability of a good experience to 'transform' the visitor. Experiences are therefore personal, memorable, evoking an emotional response as the tourist enters into a multifaceted relationship with both the actors and destination setting of the experience. They cannot be guaranteed, but they can be managed (Kuiper and Smith, 2014).

Finally, an imperative for tourism marketing is innovation through new product development (NPD). Changing tastes, technology and heightened competition mean that new product development in tourism is vital. As products and destinations progress through the life-cycle, they need to be continuously refreshed and revitalised. Moutinho (1994) states that new products are the lifeblood of tourism organisations, delivering increased revenue, competitiveness and facilitating market positioning, diversification and growth. Failure to innovate risks failing to meet consumer demands, engage with new technology and keep up with the competition. New service development is also important for tourism but here the process is less well understood and it is important to recognise the pre-conditions for delivering the service are unlikely to change.

Price

Tourism is both perishable and highly price elastic, which means that consumers will switch products on the basis of price. As a result, pricing is a critical element of the marketing mix, yet it is also one that is subject to government regulation (for example, air fares) reducing the options of the marketing manager. There are both strategic and tactical approaches to pricing. Tactical approaches can be clearly seen in the windows of travel agents and on airline websites where prices are reduced to offload excess capacity close to the date of departure. Strategic approaches to pricing include:

- **Cost-oriented pricing** – where the price is determined by the cost of providing the product, not always easy to do in tourism.

- **Rate of return pricing** – where the price is determined to deliver a set rate of return for the company.

- **Demand oriented pricing** – where the price is set according to what the market as prepared to pay.

- **Discrimination pricing** – where prices differ according to different market sectors (students, for example) or time of the year (high and low season).

- **Backward pricing** – where the price is decided upon and then the product 'reverse engineered' to deliver that price. For example, using hotels a few blocks from the beach or flying at night can achieve a low price.

- **Penetration pricing** – where a low price is set in the early stages of the life-cycle in order to build market share.

- **Skimming pricing** – with this strategy the company often has a monopoly on a shortage product and can charge a premium price.

Promotion

The nature of tourism as an experience product, albeit with many tangible elements, means that it particularly lends itself to promotion. Remember, too, that the tourism market tends not to be loyal and so demand for tourism products is unstable, as well as seasonal and price sensitive. This means that promotion can play a powerful role in influencing demand, reducing seasonality and creating loyalty. Promotion is about persuading, informing, reminding and communicating benefits to the potential consumer. Promotion in tourism marketing does not stand alone and is used to support other elements of the mix; for example, it can communicate pricing strategy. Smart tourism promotion intervenes in the tourism purchasing process to influence behaviour. (We examined the purchasing process in detail in Chapter 12.) Here the key decisions for the marketer are what type of message to promote and when to send the message to ensure maximum impact. Of course, the media used are also critical and increasingly promotion is done using electronic media, social media and 'viral campaigns' on websites such as YouTube (www.YouTube.com). These decisions are part of the promotion planning process which is outlined in Figure 13.4.

Distribution

In tourism marketing a distribution channel is (Goeldner and Ritchie, 2009):

> 'an operating structure, system or linkages of various combinations of travel organisations through which a producer of travel products describes and confirms travel arrangements to the buyer' (p. 182).

Sometimes known as intermediation, distribution is an important element of the tourism industry (as we saw in Chapter 9). Distribution of the product is carried out by intermediaries – travel agents and tour operators/wholesalers – who have increasingly been impacted upon by newcomers in the market in the form of e-distribution companies such as Expedia (www.expedia.com). Indeed, the nature of tourism distribution has been transformed by the Internet and its use by both new style e-intermediaries and tourists themselves, seeking to bypass intermediaries.

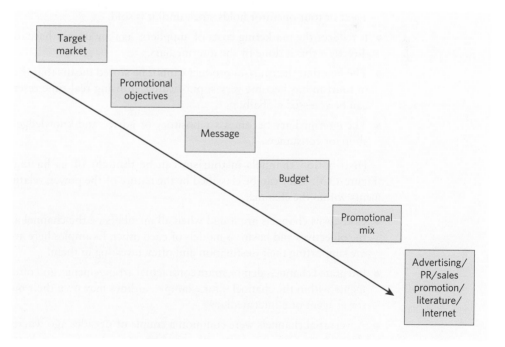

Figure 13.4 Promotion planning

Festivals and events have become a key strategy for many destinations to extend their season.
Source: © The Photolibrary Wales/Alamy Images

In tourism, distribution channels link suppliers with the customer. Distribution in tourism has particular characteristics that are not shared by other products:

- The nature of intermediaries means that they can influence the purchasing decision through advice and selective offerings. This is because intermediaries provide access to a range of products and can facilitate their purchase.
- The distribution process transfers risk from the supplier to the intermediary as a travel agent or tour operator holds stock until it is sold.
- It reduces the marketing costs of suppliers, as they do not have to reach the consumer directly – this is done by the intermediary.
- The fact that the tourism product cannot be stored means that the distribution process in tourism has become very sophisticated, utilising real-time reservations systems that can be accessed globally.
- The intermediary becomes a repository of advice and knowledge acting as a one-stop shop for consumers.

Distribution channels in tourism can be thought of as having a number of steps (Figure 13.5). They can be classified by the nature of the power, relationships and arrangements within the channel:

- Consensus channels are found when all members of the channel are in agreement with the objectives and business models of each other. Examples here are tour operators who are supporting their destination and often investing in them.
- Integrated channels demonstrate contractual arrangements, and often ownership arrangements within the channel – for example, airlines may own their own tour operator and travel agent or e-intermediary
- Adversarial channels were common a couple of decades ago where each member of the channel was jockeying for position and intent on a competitive battle with the rest of the channel.

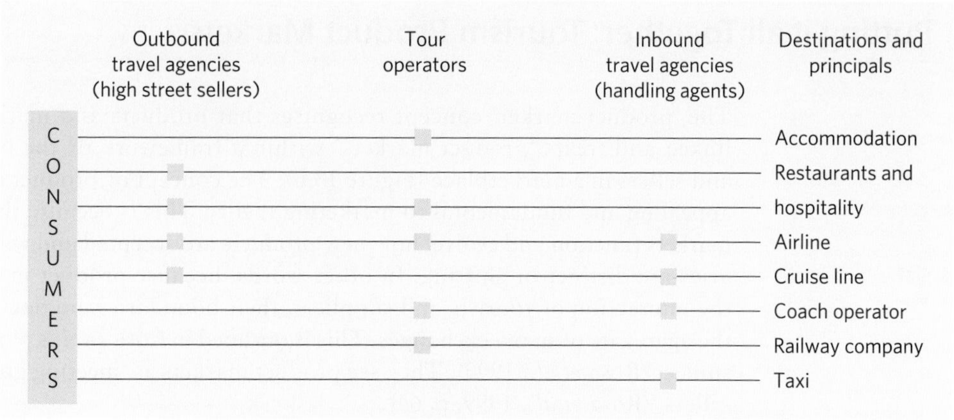

	Outbound travel agencies (high street sellers)	Tour operators	Inbound travel agencies (handling agents)	Destinations and principals
C O N S U M E R S				Accommodation
				Restaurants and
				hospitality
				Airline
				Cruise line
				Coach operator
				Railway company
				Taxi

Figure 13.5 Tourism distribution mechanisms
Source: Buhalis and Laws, 2001; Page and Connell, 2009

As with other elements of the marketing mix, it is important for organisations to take a disciplined and planned approach to distribution. This will ensure that the type of channel used will conform to the product's promotion and design, as well as supporting the pricing strategy. It also ensures that management can control distribution costs and the strategy adopted. Here distribution strategy options include:

- intensive distribution where the product is sold through every available channel;
- exclusive distribution where the product where the product is sold through a small number of highly appropriate channels which meet the product's image; and
- selective distribution, which is a combination of the above two approaches – the product is sold through a wide number of channels but these channels closely meet the product's image and campaign objectives.

Distribution is one of the elements of the marketing mix that has been transformed by technology. Liu (2000) notes that electronic distribution has a number of advantages:

- drastic cost reduction achieved through the electronic processing of bookings (such as e-tickets and electronic confirmations) and other transactions;
- automation reducing labour costs and office space;
- direct and personal links to the customer; and
- it encourages customer-driven distribution through social media and websites (such as www.tripadvisor.com).

Of course, electronic distribution has decimated traditional intermediaries such as 'bricks and mortar' travel agents. Tour operators, on the other hand, are reinventing themselves with the ability to flexibly package the product (dynamic packaging) and deal directly with their customers (as we saw in Chapter 9). This shows that electronic distribution works well for tourism where the product is fragmented and web portals allow companies to provide and deliver a dynamic assembly of all of the elements of the product (Expedia is a good example here). Buhalis (2003) suggests that in the future tour operators will fall into two distinct groups:

1. multinational, large and vertically integrated operators with economies of scale, wide distribution and a global network, taking a high-volume, low-profit approach; and
2. small, niche differentiated operators focusing on particular destinations or products, taking a low-volume, high-profit approach.

Putting it all Together: Tourism Product Markets

The 'product market' concept recognises that products and markets are inextricably linked and treats 'product markets' within a framework of the interaction of buyers and sellers in a marketplace (Figure 13.6). The concept of product markets is intuitively appealing and fundamental to marketing theory. This is because they help explain how markets function and evolve, how new products are accepted and whether market boundaries are distinct or shifting. In other words, because product markets are formed by the interaction of tourists and suppliers, their boundaries are flexible as they represent the aggregate of many exchanges. This is outlined in Rosa *et al.*'s pioneering paper on the subject (Rosa *et al.*, 1999). They see product markets as 'meeting grounds for buyers and sellers' (Rosa *et al.*, 1999, p. 64).

Product markets are very helpful in understanding different types of tourism and how they can be classified. In tourism, each exchange between a tourist and a supplier is unique, simply because of the nature of tourism supply as highly heterogeneous, and the many different levels of involvement by the tourist. There are two processes at work here:

1. exchanges can be grouped and aggregated into a product market; and

2. the product market concept shows that both the supplier and the tourist can influence these exchanges.

In other words, different tourism product markets are defined by the interaction between suppliers and tourists and include ecotourism, dark tourism, adventure tourism, heritage tourism or cultural tourism. In each product market, tourists can be classified by their behaviour and involvement, as their 'wants' will tend to cluster, whilst suppliers will tend to specialise in particular product markets. It must be remembered, however, that product markets are not destinations. Destinations are bounded geographical entities which act as the 'setting' for product markets, and therefore different 'types of tourism' (as we saw in

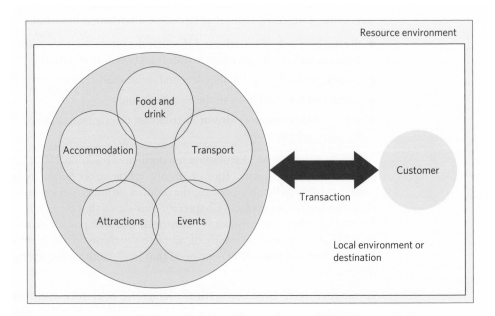

Figure 13.6 The tourism product market
Source: Cooper *et al.*, 2006

Chapter 2). Destinations can therefore be the stage for many product markets – each with its group of own group of customers and suppliers. An example here is volunteer tourism – or 'volun-tourism' – a contemporary and growing 'type' of tourism which is beginning to attract its own set of suppliers, which include charitable bodies. Volunteer tourism is characterised by:

● a market that is somewhat altruistic, often seeking self-development and offering their time for free; and

● a product that is based upon environmental or social improvement at the destination – for example, cleaning up Everest, or helping rural villages to develop their education.

Putting these together into a product market for the type of tourism known as volunteer tourism results in a 'conscious, seamlessly integrated combination of voluntary service to a destination' (www.voluntourism.org/).

SUMMARY

This chapter has introduced the nature and scope of tourism marketing. In particular, it has charted the evolution of the marketing concept and shown how the service-dominant logic is now replacing the previous goods-dominant logic of marketing. We presented the ground-breaking paper by Vargo and Lusch on the service-dominant logic as our classic paper for the chapter. The particular nature of tourism as a fragmented product has a number of implications for tourism marketers and may have led to a 'marketing gap'. We also showed how the creative use of technology has transformed the business of tourism marketing and in a case study showed how social media has 'turned market research on its head'. We then presented the process of tourism market planning and strategy, and showed its uses in tourism. The chapter went on to consider the marketing mix, focused as it is upon a target market, and showed the challenges of destination branding with a case study on Greenland. We discussed each element of the mix, and the implications of the nature of tourism for how these elements of the mix can be applied in marketing. Finally, the chapter outlined the very useful concept of the tourism product market as a way of thinking about tourism marketing and types of tourism, and closed with a case study questioning the easy translation of destinations into products.

Discussion Questions

1. Taking a tourism company of your choice, discuss to what extent it displays the characteristics of a societal marketing approach, or whether it is in an earlier stage of evolution (marketing, production or sales).

2. Discuss the advantages and disadvantages that the Internet has brought to tourism marketers.

3. Taking a tourism product of your choice, dissect the dimensions of the product and chart the various companies and organisations responsible for their delivery.

4. Construct a table of the four traditional elements of the marketing mix in one column. In the second column list the considerations the mix should take into account when focusing on tourism markets.

5. Using the Internet and library sources, research Porter's classic model of competitiveness. How appropriate is this model for tourism?

Annotated Further Reading

1. Fyall, A. and Garrod, B. (2005) *Tourism Marketing. A Collaborative Approach*, Channel View, Clevedon.
   Edited volume thoroughly reviewing the use and role of collaboration and partnership in tourism marketing.

2. Kotler, P., Bowen, J. and Makens, J. (2014) *Marketing for Hospitality and Tourism*, 6th edn, Pearson, Harlow.
   Classic marketing text re-oriented with a tourism flavour.

3. Lovelock, C. and Gummesson, E. (2004) Whither services marketing? In search of new paradigm and fresh perspectives, *Journal of Service Research* 7(1), 20–41.
   Classic paper on services marketing.

4. Lusch, R.F. and Vargo, S.L. (2014) *The Service-dominant Logic of Marketing: Dialog, Debate, and Directions,* Routledge, London.
   Contemporary debate on their approach.

5. McCabe, S (2013) *The Routledge Handbook of Tourism Marketing,* Routledge, London.
   Comprehensive overview of current tourism marketing themes.

6. Pearce, P. (2014) Tourism motivations and decision making, Chapter 3 in Lew A.L., Hall, C.M. and Williams, A.M. (eds) *The Wiley Blackwell Companion to Tourism*, Wiley, Chichester.
   An excellent and contemporary account of tourism consumer decision making.

7. Pine, J. and Gilmore, J. (1999) *The Experience Economy,* University of Harvard Press, Harvard.
   A ground-breaking book reconceptualising the way we think about experiences as products.

8. Scott, N., Laws, E. and Boksberger, P. (eds) (2010) *The Marketing of Tourism and Leisure Experiences,* Routledge, Abingdon.
   A comprehensive consideration of how tourism and leisure have adopted the experience marketing approach.

9. Shaw, G., Bailey, A. and Williams, A. (2011) Aspects of service-dominant logic and its implications for tourism management: examples from the hotel industry, *Tourism Management* **32**, 207–214.
   Useful consideration of the Vargo and Lusch approach to tourism.

10. Tressider, R., and Hirst, C. (2015) *Marketing in Tourism Events and Food,* Goodfellow, Oxford.
    Accessible current text on tourism marketing.

References Cited

Ansoff, I. (1957) Strategies of diversification, *Harvard Business Review* **25**(5), 113–125.

Benckendorff, P.J., Sheldon, P. and Fessenmaier, D. (2014) *Tourism Information Technology,* 2nd edn, CABI, Wallingford.

Buhalis, D. (2003) *eTourism: Information Technology for Strategic Tourism Management,* Pearson Education, Harlow.

Buhalis, D. and Laws, E. (eds) (2001) *Tourism Distribution Channels: Practices Issues and Transformations,* Continuum, London.

Cooper, C., Scott, N. and Kester, J. (2006) New and emerging markets, pp. 19–29 in Buhalis, D. and Costa, C. (eds) *Tourism Business Frontiers: Consumers, Products and Industry,* Elsevier Butterworth Heinemann, London.

Font, X., Walmsley, A., Cogotti, S., McCombes, L. and Häusler, N. (2012) Corporate social responsibility: the disclosure performance gap, *Tourism Management* 33, 1544–1553.

Frochot, I. and Batat, W. (2013) *Marketing and Designing the Tourist Experience,* Goodfellow, Oxford.

Gilbert, D. (1990) Conceptual issues in the meaning of tourism, pp. 4–27 in Cooper, C. (ed.), *Progress in Tourism, Recreation and Hospitality Management*, Belhaven Press, London.

Goeldner, C.R. and Ritchie, J.R.B. (2009) *Tourism Principles, Practices, Philosophies,* Wiley, Hoboken, NJ.

Goodwin, H. (2003) Ethical and responsible tourism: consumer trends in the UK, *Journal of Vacation Marketing* 9(3), 271–283.

Goodwin, H. and Font, X. (2011) *Taking Responsibility for Tourism,* Goodfellow, Oxford.

Kotler, P. (2000) *Marketing Management: The Millennium Edition,* Prentice Hall, Englewood Cliffs, NJ.

Kotler, P., Bowen, J. and Makens, J. (2003) *Marketing for Hospitality and Tourism,* 3rd edn, Prentice Hall, Englewood Cliffs, NJ.

Kotler, P., Bowen, J. and Makens, J. (2014) *Marketing for Hospitality and Tourism,* 6th edn, Pearson, Harlow.

Kuiper, G. and Smith, B. (2014) *Imagineering Innovation in the Experience Economy,* CABI, Wallingford.

Li, X. and Petrick, J.F. (2008) Tourism marketing in an era of paradigm shift, *Journal of Travel Research* 46, 235–244.

Liu, Z. (2000) *Internet Tourism Marketing: Potential and Constraints,* paper presented at the Fourth International Conference, Tourism in South East Asia and Indo China: Development, Marketing and Sustainability.

Lovelock, C. and Gummesson, E. (2004) Whither services marketing? In search of new paradigm and fresh perspectives, *Journal of Service Research* 7(1), 20–41.

Lusch, R.F. and Vargo, S.L. (2014) The *Service-dominant Logic of Marketing: Dialog, Debate, and Directions,* Routledge, London.

Mills, J. and Law, R (2015) *Handbook of Consumer Behavior, Tourism, and the Internet,* Routledge, London.

Morgan, M., Lugosi, P. and Brent Ritchie, J.R. (2010) *The Tourism and Leisure Experience: Consumer and Leisure Perspectives,* Channel View, Bristol.

Moutinho, L. (1994) New product development, pp. 350–353 in Witt, S.F. and Moutinho, L. (eds) *Tourism Marketing and Management Handbook,* Prentice Hall, Hemel Hempstead.

Page, S.J. and Connell, J. (2009) *Tourism: A Modern Synthesis,* Cengage Learning, Andover.

Pine, J. and Gilmore, J. (1999) *The Experience Economy,* University of Harvard Press, Harvard.

Rosa, J.A., Porac, J.F., Spanjol, J.R. and Saxon, M.S. (1999) Sociocognitive dynamics in a product market, *Journal of Marketing* 63(4), 64–77.

Shostack, G.L. (1977) Breaking free from product marketing, *Journal of Marketing* 41, 73–80.

Shaw, G., Bailey, A. and Williams, A. (2011) Aspects of service-dominant logic and its implications for tourism management: examples from the hotel industry, *Tourism Management* 32, 207–214.

UNWTO (2014) *Handbook on E-marketing for Tourism Destinations,* UNWTO, Madrid.

Vargo, S.L. and Lusch, R.F. (2004) Evolving to a new dominant logic for marketing, *Journal of Marketing* 68(January), 1–17.

Xiang, Z. and Gretzel, U. (2010) Role of social media in online travel information search, *Tourism Management* 31(2), 179–188.

Major Case Study 13.1
Should Destinations be Marketed?

This case study debates whether marketers should treat destinations as products to be marketed and branded, indeed there is a view that destinations do not readily lend themselves to traditional marketing approaches. The case first provides a brief outline of destination marketing.

Destination Marketing

The *process* of destination marketing involves dealing with the complexities of destinations and their many stakeholders, whilst the *outcome* is a brand or the image of the destination. In other words, a good destination marketer will focus upon two key operations:

1. managing the destination's many stakeholders and networks; and

2. formulating and managing the destination brand.

The idea of destination marketing continues to evolve and a view is emerging that it is 'branding' that is the glue that holds the marketing of the destination together. The two key components of destination marketing are image and brand:

1. **Destination image.** Understanding the formation and characteristics of the destination image is critical for destination marketing. A destination's image is a simplified version of reality, a way of making sense of the many destination stimuli received and processed by the visitor or potential visitor. The image of a destination is critical to marketing as it affects an individual's perception and choice of a destination. The generation of the image is different for destinations to many other products, because it is the tourists themselves who generate a destination image by selecting different sources of information. As a result, destination marketeers have much less influence on images, despite their critical importance to destination choice. Whilst image formation is not the same as branding, it is closely related. This is because the choice of branding and brand attributes of a destination reinforce the destination image.

2. **Destination branding.** To quote Kotler (2003) 'branding is the art and cornerstone of marketing' (p. 418) and can be defined as:

    'A name, term, sign, symbol or design or combination of them, intended to identify the goods or services of one seller or group of sellers and to differentiate them from those of competitors' (Kotler, 2003, p. 404).

Branding tends to be undertaken by public sector led destination management organisations (DMOs), in consultation with destination stakeholders. Branding is a complex and controversial issue for destinations and is surrounded by a range of issues focused upon how appropriate it is to market destinations as products.

Should Destinations be Marketed?

We can identify three key areas of controversy in regards to destination marketing:

1 The Role of the Public Sector

The public sector tends to take the lead in destination marketing, coordinating other inputs and stakeholders. However, we have to question whether government is the most appropriate agency to deliver destination marketing. Government does not control destination product quality or private sector suppliers and so cannot address deficiencies in the product mix. It also has to be even-handed in its dealings with stakeholders and cannot be seen to 'back winners'. Traditionally, government tends not to be entrepreneurial, lacking in both marketing and technological expertise and commonly can only facilitate bookings and often cannot close a sale. Finally, the nature of the public sector means that budgets may be inadequate for significant promotion and market research. Government does, however, have the ability to act in a leadership and coordination role when it comes to destination marketing.

2 The Role of Destination Stakeholders

A second key issue for destination marketing is to ensure involvement and commitment by all stakeholders in the destination marketing process. Here, destination politics are notoriously destructive and it is therefore vital to be inclusive from the outset. The key here is to manage the relationship between collaboration and power and to recognise that the views of the local community must be included in destination marketing as destinations are also places where people live, work and play. Collaboration can be seen to encompass three key issues:

*   **Creation of a shared brand.** Creation of a shared brand ensures that the destination brand image is built on shared destination attributes. This allows citizens to be brand champions (but also enemies if they do not subscribe to the brand).

*   **Collaboration and inclusiveness.** It is essential that the destination brand is the positive outcome of the achievement of unity and collaboration amongst stakeholders; indeed it could be argued that effective destination marketing hinges on relationship building with stakeholders. Yet collaboration across destination stakeholders is a complex and politicised process. The danger is that larger

stakeholders will take their own brands to market, which damages the smaller players and the overall destination brand. In other words, support offered by stakeholders makes or breaks the destination marketing process.

● **Destinations as loosely articulated networks.** Collaboration recognises that destination stakeholders are critically dependent upon each other. This involves joint decision-making with individuals and interest groups operating at different levels of the destination.

3 The Nature of the Tourist Destination

Should the places where people live, work and play be transformed into brands and products? The development of destination brands may conflict with a community's perception and feelings for the place where they live, work and play. This can be exacerbated by the delivery of the brand on the ground through the use of signage, street furniture and landscaping. Destinations are contested spaces and the various users of this space each hold their own images, identities and interests.

Does the very nature of the tourist destination run counter to the ability to transform it into a brand? The theory on branding is built largely upon the experience of manufactured products. It could be argued that this theory cannot be simply transferred to the marketing of destinations. The nature of the destination as a fragmented and complex amalgam of attractions and support facilities, delivered by many different providers, means that the definition and formulation of the destination product is problematic. If it is to succeed, destination marketing must recognise that it is a more collective activity than is normally found in marketing.

DISCUSSION QUESTIONS

1. What are the benefits of destination marketing?

2. Debate whether the public sector is the appropriate agency for destination marketing and, if not, who should assume this role.

3. Is marketing theory overstretched when applied to destinations?

Sources:

Buhalis, D. (2000) Marketing the competitive destination of the future, *Tourism Management* **21**, 97–116.

Heath, E. and Wall, G. (1992) *Marketing Tourism Destinations*, Wiley, Chichester.

Kotler, P. (2003) *Principles of Marketing*, 2nd edn, Prentice Hall, Frenchs Forest, New South Wales.

Morgan, N., Pritchard, A. and Pride, R. (2004) *Destination Branding: Creating the Unique Destination Proposition*, 2nd edn, Elsevier, Oxford.

Pike, S. (2004) *Destination Marketing Organizations*, Elsevier, Amsterdam.

Pike, S. and Page, S (2014) Destination marketing organizations and destination marketing: a narrative analysis of the literature, *Tourism Management* **41**, 202–227.

PART 5
TOURISM FUTURES: THE ESSENTIALS

In the final part of this book we turn to the futures of tourism. Here, we move into uncharted territory where few authors dare to tread – though there are notable exceptions such as the *Journal of Tourism Futures*. The future is unknown. Therefore everything is possible. That is why this chapter talks of *tourism futures*, rather than a *tourism future*, because there are an infinite number of futures for us to consider. Predicting tourism futures is not an easy task. Since the first edition of this book, for example, social media, smartphones and texting have grown exponentially, the 'Twittersphere' is highly influential and everything and everyone is connected – leading us to a world of driverless cars, smart cities and cashless payments with digital wallets. The United Nations World Tourism Organization (UNWTO) has termed the uncertainty caused by the radical change experienced in the twenty-first century as the 'new normal', suggesting that tourism will never return to the relatively stable conditions of the twentieth century. Indeed, tourism is inextricably integrated with society and other economic sectors and so is exposed to their changes and influences.

Whilst it is easy to 'hype up' the future of tourism and provide a sensationalist account of flying cars and virtual reality theme parks, the future is indeed an exciting one; one where we can envisage bio fuels and carbon sinks, transformational travel to move people rapidly between continents, personal translators to remove any language barrier for travellers, and China, South Asia and Latin America becoming global super powers. Kaku, for example, in his 2008 book *Physics of the Impossible*, actually speaks of flying cars, nanorobotics, biochips and teleportation. Nonetheless, it is important to take a disciplined and structured approach to the issue, indeed despite pessimistic accounts of the human race being wiped out by disease, meteorites or aliens, it is likely that we will be around for some time to come. It is also possible that with gloomy scenarios of energy shortages, we may come to see the early years of this century as one of privileged travel. We provide two frameworks within which to consider and analyse tourism futures:

1. We analyse the drivers of the future and then consider how tourism might respond in the future. Here, we can see that these drivers, such as demographics or technology, will have a fundamental influence upon tourism futures, but it is misleading to treat each one in isolation. For example, social and economic drivers will encourage the growth of tourism, but they will also determine social attitudes to processes such as climate change and, as a consequence, we will see the very nature of tourism operations begin to change. Underpinning these drivers will be cross-cutting variables such as technology that will pervade every aspect of tourism in the future.

→

Photograph: Old town Dubrovnik, Croatia © Inu/Shutterstock.com

2. Secondly, we analyse this response of tourism to these drivers by using Leiper's tourism system (introduced in Chapter 1) as a way of thinking. The reason that we like Leiper's framework is that it is an all-encompassing approach to studying tourism. Tourism futurists commonly focus only on the tourism destination part of the system. But this fails to recognise the complexity of the tourism sector and the need to match up trends both on the demand and supply side. To consider any one of these in isolation would provide an unbalanced assessment of the futures of tourism. A good example here is the concept of product markets (which we introduced in Chapter 13). Here, drivers of future market trends will combine with technology and destination management to create the products of the future, whether they are in space or deep under the sea.

All of this means that tourism futures are an exciting and stimulating area of study. What is clear is that the tourism of the future will have to embrace the principles of the green economy to deliver 'smart tourism': characterised by a clean, green, ethical, and quality tourism; underpinned by a concern for the environment, for the destination, for local communities and particularly the poor. Above all it will use technology and networked enterprises to deliver a high-quality experience to the discerning tourists of the future.

And so let's take a shot at a prediction . . .

Imagine it is the year 2030, and you are booking a holiday. You want to recreate your honeymoon but the news last night confirmed that this is now impossible: the last inch of the Maldives has just disappeared under the Indian Ocean. You have saved hard for this trip – not financially, as all flights are incredibly cheap, but in terms of your rationed air miles. For two solid years you have saved your carbon allowances so that you will be able to fly almost anywhere in the world without paying hefty premiums on what is not covered by your ration cards. Going on to the web you enter a virtual travel office, and walk around the badly deteriorated ruins of Angkor Wat for a while, before clicking through onto a virtual reality beach on the east coast of Australia. Here, other visitors have left virtual versions of themselves, who tell you about the facilities, what to do, where to stay and what to avoid. Australia is attractive now that the flight goes into space and only takes 6 hours, but the carbon rations needed make you feel that it may be a waste, now that all the coral of the Great Barrier Reef has been bleached . . .

CHAPTER 14

TOURISM FUTURES

Learning Outcomes

This chapter focuses upon the futures of tourism, outlining the key drivers of the future and possible scenarios for both the tourist and the tourism sector itself. The chapter is designed to provide you with:

- a disciplined approach to analysing and anticipating the futures of the tourism system;

- an understanding of the key drivers of tourism futures;

- an awareness of the way that tourism markets will evolve in the future;

- an approach to understanding how both destinations and the tourism sector, including transport, will be shaped in the future; and

- an awareness of the cross-cutting issues that will impact upon tourism futures.

Photograph: Virgin Galactic SpaceShip2 © HO/Reuters/Corbis

Introduction

The future is as yet unknown and there are therefore many possibilities. This is why we speak of *tourism futures*. This chapter introduces you to a disciplined approach to studying tourism futures, beginning by examining the leading reports on tourism futures and going on to examine the key drivers of tourism futures. It will then move its focus to the response of markets, destinations and the sector itself to these drivers before closing with an examination of cross-cutting issues.

There are a number of important reports that examine tourism futures. On the demand side, the UNWTO's forecasts of international tourism are essential reading for anyone interested in global trends to 2030 (UNWTO, 2001; 2007; 2011a). These forecasts show that, despite the setbacks of the early twenty-first century, tourism has grown from 434 million international arrivals in 1990 to 1,133 million in 2014 and will approach two billion by 2030. This continuous growth is unusual for any economic sector. Demand for domestic tourism will expand at a slower rate and some countries will reach demand-side ceilings of capacity and available leisure time which will constrain further growth. International arrivals will continue to be concentrated in Europe, East Asia and the Pacific and the Americas and the major growth areas will be long-haul travel and newer destinations such as those in East Asia and the Pacific.

On the supply side it is more difficult to identify one single influential source. The British travel sector, for example, has developed a collaborative vision of how tourism will look in 2023 to guide the sector into the future (Forum for the Future, 2009). A report on 'Tourism for Tomorrow' by the world's peak tourism industry body, the World Travel and Tourism

→

Council (WTTC), is concerned for the future sustainability of tourism and provides a set of recommendations to ensure that tourism growth does not compromise resources, people or businesses (WTTC, 2013). The main recommendations are for businesses to provide leadership, investment and be accountable.

In addition to the focused reports on the demand and supply side of tourism futures, there are a number of influential synoptic reviews. Yeoman (2012) has written a synoptic view of tourism in 2050, whilst in Europe reports by the European Tourism Futures Institute (2014) and the European Tourism Research Institute on the Future of Tourism in Europe and 'Tourism of Tomorrow' utilise techniques from futures research to analyse the driving forces of change for tourism (Nordin, 2005). The report is noteworthy for the adaptation of the STEEP methodology to understanding the environment within which tourism operates. STEEP can be characterised as comprising social, technological, environmental, economic and political forces, all of which work together. The report then draws in the idea of 'wild cards' – events that have a low probability of occurring, but which are devastating when they do so. Of course, 11 September 2001 is the defining 'wild card' for contemporary tourism but events such as the financial crisis of 2008/09 also impact severely upon tourism.

Still in Europe, the European Travel Commission (2006) has written a tight and comprehensive analysis of European tourism futures scanning both demand- and supply-side trends, whilst the Scottish Tourism Alliance (2013) has examined the future of tourism in Scotland in 2020.

In Australia, the Sustainable Tourism Cooperative Research Centre (STCRC) (Dwyer *et al.*, 2007) has published an influential report on tourism megatrends to 2020, with the aim of alerting the tourism sector to upcoming trends and mapping their implications for tourism.

This chapter adopts a similar approach to the STCRC by analysing the drivers of tourism futures and then outlining possible scenarios for both the tourist and the sector itself. The classic paper for this chapter is, however, cautious about predictions and observes that few have the courage to write about tourism futures.

Classic Paper

Special Issue of the journal *Futures* (2009). Cole, S. and Razak, V. (2009) 'Tourism as future', *Futures* 41(6), 335–345

This issue of *Futures* focuses exclusively on the futures of tourism and features papers by leading tourism scholars, overall evidencing the case that:

'futurists should address the topic of tourism, and that tourism specialists and policy-makers should use futures thinking to better address their concerns and explore wider perspectives'.

The introduction by Coles and Razak is particularly useful, synoptically mapping the scope of tourism and its futures. But it also, perhaps surprisingly, speaks of the 'missing futures' of tourism, pointing out that papers on tourism futures are hard to find. It is interesting to speculate as to why this is so; certainly it may be explained by the fact that tourism is comprised of so many component parts and has a fickle market.

As the exception to the rule, this volume provides a range of excellent papers on tourism futures. To quote the editors:

'Papers in this special issue elaborate the issues involved both through historic review and theoretical analysis, and by providing case studies that demonstrate possible directions for international tourism analysis and policy. Collectively, the papers explore the relationships between destination countries and their markets, and the extent to which tourism might fulfil its promise to promote economic development and stability, peace, poverty reduction, and sustainable development'.

The Future Drivers of Tourism

This section examines the major drivers of tourism futures. In reality, most of these trends and variables are interlinked and mutually reinforcing. For example, the very economic development that has fuelled tourism growth is contributing to climate change, which threatens to alter the nature of many destinations. There is no doubt that these trends, when combined, will have a fundamental impact upon future tourism scenarios and as a consequence cannot be ignored. Yet, no single trend will dominate and each will impact upon tourism futures in a different way, but at key times some trends will tip and become significant – and irreversible; the adoption of the Internet in the 1990s is an obvious example here – the possible futures of tourism are many and varied (Buckley *et al.*, 2015).

Social Drivers of Change

Demographic Drivers

Despite the fact that the world will be home to 9.6 billion people in 2050, for most of the traditional generators of domestic and international tourism, population growth is either static or even negative, with populations ageing as people live longer in North America, Europe and Japan (UNWTO, 2010). By 2020 one in eight people will be aged 60 years or more as average life expectancy lengthens. Ageing populations tend to be associated with urbanisation and conservative politics, and markets for their goods and services have clear implications for the tourism sector – the ageing baby boomer generations of the developed world are currently one of the most influential market segments, fitter, healthier and more demanding than previous generations, but in the future their influence will wane. Instead it is the younger generations who will shape tourism futures. Generations X, Y and Z will remain in the youth market longer as they marry later and continue with their youth lifestyle, so changing the nature of the traditional nuclear family household. Generation Y, roughly speaking those born between 1978 and 2000, is the largest population bulge since the babyboomers and will therefore influence future consumer behaviour as technologically adept and more savvy consumers, sceptical about marketing messages, seeking networked and virtual communities. However, this is not the case for emerging generators of international tourism such as China and India where populations continue to grow apace. In fact in the future the majority of population growth will take place in the developing world with Africa set to grow the most creating a new middle class and young workforce that will benefit tourism.

Social Drivers

Throughout much of society there is a move to more flexible working practices and a fluid balance between work and leisure. The knowledge economy places a premium on education creating a 'creative class' of educated, networked and self-motivated individuals where English is the dominant language (see case study in Chapter 12). With education comes an increasing concern for ethical consumption, environmental concerns which will change attitudes to mobility in general, and a conflicting emphasis on pleasure-seeking conspicuous consumption. Family structures in the developed world are changing with a trend to later marriage, more one-parent families and having children at a later age. Here, there are three key social trends that have specific implications for tourism:

1. Worldwide, more people will choose to live in cities such that by 2020 more than 60 per cent of the world's population will live in urban areas. Urbanisation has important policy implications in terms of the growth of city-states; the use of tourism to market cities; and the fact that tourist resources will be increasingly located adjacent to the urban market, favouring artificial types of development such as theme parks, as has occurred in Japan.

2. In many countries, both the status and influence of women are on the increase. Women will have an increasing say not only in purchasing decisions, but also in the types of products offered by the tourism sector. This is leading to provision of women-only hotels and excursions such as the 'women only' luxury spa retreat in Marrakech, Morocco offered by responsibletravel.com.

3. Populations are becoming more culturally diverse as improved communications, increasing wealth and mobility stimulate people to try to understand other cultures. Tourism products and their marketing will increasingly have to embrace cultural diversity, and niche products – such as gay tourism – are emerging as a consequence.

Political and Economic Drivers of Change

Tourism futures are intricately linked to politics and economies at all levels. Initiatives at different geographical scales are changing the world order as we witness the rising economic power of newly emerging economies such as Brazil, Russia, India and China (the BRIC economies) and the new group of strong economies of Mexico, Indonesia, Nigeria and Turkey (MINT), all reducing the influence of the USA on the world stage. At the international level, tourism futures will be influenced by four key trends – the forging of international trading blocs; globalisation; religion; and economic growth.

Trade Blocs and Regionalism

Opportunities for tourism will be enhanced by the formation of a number of trading blocs across the globe as country groupings come together in deregulated economic alliances. Notable here are the North American Free Trade Agreement (NAFTA) and the creation and expansion of the European Union (EU). In the EU, adoption of the euro has demonstrated the power of these blocs, as the currency encourages tourism across Europe; while the expansion of the EU itself will begin to change the balance of tourism flows within Europe.

A contradictory trend at the regional level is the rise of regionalism and a search for cultural identity. Here, 'city states' are emerging as major visitor destinations where tourism plays a key role in 'boosting' their reputations, lifestyle and economies. Cities can significantly leverage their image by staging a major event; for example, Sydney benefited from hosting the Olympic Games, as did Singapore from the first night-time Formula One Grand Prix. Similarly, regionalism is growing with the pressure for independence of regions such as Scotland and Catalonia creating tensions within the large mega trading blocs. However, there is a darker side to regionalism exemplified by the growth of extremist groups such as ISIS (Islamic State of Iraq and Syria) creating no-go areas for travel.

Globalisation

Underlying the changing world order is the globalisation of tourism businesses – a powerful force shaping national and regional economies, which are linked and interdependent as never before. Globalisation is the combination of the revolution in information technology, telecommunications and transport; a consensus among governments for free trade; and the democratisation of financial markets. Globalisation results in the increasing interdependence of markets and production in different countries creating a 'borderless world' (Dwyer, 2014). Key drivers of globalisation in tourism are:

- decreasing costs of international travel allowing access to most markets in the world;
- increasing income and wealth in the generating countries;
- newly emerging destinations and the increased demand for international travel;
- adoption of free trade agreements, removing barriers to international transactions;
- computer and communications technology encouraging 'ebusiness'; and
- worldwide acting suppliers.

Some of the consequences of globalisation for the tourism sector will include:

- increasingly standardised products, procedures and global brands such as Disney;
- pressure for alliances and mergers;
- increased concentration in the marketplace; and
- pressure on vulnerable businesses such as local SMEs.

Indeed, it is the larger, international companies that can take advantage of these consequences as globalisation encourages increased concentration in the tourism industry as major companies gain market share and market influence. At the same time, we are seeing the concentration of capital in a few tourism companies; a trend that also drives tourism towards the key performance indicators (KPIs), return on investment measures (ROI) and business practices demanded by the finance industry.

A particular problem associated with this trend is that most of the larger corporations do not have a relationship with a specific destination. They may therefore be less sensitive to the impact of their operations on that destination. In addition, SMEs and local destinations fear the 'neo-colonial' relationship which can emerge from dealing with large companies. This is an important consideration for tourism where, at the end of the day, the product is delivered locally; hence the conundrum of balancing the global forces upon an essentially 'local' product.

Economic Drivers

In the long term, the economies of most generating countries will grow leading to higher per capita incomes. Not only will the world economy be up to 80 per cent larger in 2020 compared to 2005, but also per capita incomes will grow by up to 50 per cent. This enhances the ability to consume tourism products as discretionary income rises proportionately, which will be particularly the case in the emergent economies of China and India. However, environmental concerns may check growing levels of consumption. The STCRC's report (Dwyer *et al.*, 2007) identifies seven drivers of economic growth:

1. political pressures for higher living standards;
2. improved macroeconomic policies;
3. deregulation/liberalisation;
4. rising trade and investment;
5. diffusion of information technology;
6. an increasingly dynamic private sector; and
7. evolving global financial markets.

Science and the Environmental Drivers of Change

Science allows more creative media for tourism and entertainment and resources for recreation. Science, too, helps us to understand environmental change and its potential impact upon tourism futures as the sector continues its imperative for sustainable development. One of the major factors here that will impact upon tourism futures is the concern for the environment. And as the STCRC's (Dwyer *et al.*, 2007) report so clearly states, environmental change will be with us for the remainder of the century, whereas most of the other drivers of the futures identified here have a much shorter time horizon.

The United Nations Environment Program (UNEP 2002) has identified three environmental concerns for the future:

1. climate change;
2. depletion of natural resources (energy, water and land-use); and
3. loss of biodiversity.

Of these, climate change has become the major issue for tourism (as we saw in Chapter 4). This is because not only is the scientific evidence compelling, but also tourism is a climate-sensitive sector. Climate determines tourism seasons, determines destination choice and impacts upon tourism product development. Concern for the impact of human activity upon the climate is altering consumer behaviour and has increasingly become a focus for tourism policy and management initiatives. There is also no doubt that tourism is both a vector and a victim of climate change, with estimates suggesting that the tourism sector contributes 5 per cent of global greenhouse gas emissions.

Fortunately, our understanding of the science of climate change is increasing, as is the world's awareness of the seriousness of the issue. Global climate change includes long-term factors such as global warming and the erosion of the ozone layer. In order to analyse the impact of climate change on tourism we need to consider the total tourism system, including transport. On the supply side, there is no doubt that the raising of the earth's temperature and the consequent rise in sea level will affect tourism destinations such as wetlands, deserts, islands, mountains and coastal areas. Much of tourism investment is found in locations that fringe the coast, and global warming will irrevocably alter vital tourism resources. These include the disappearance of iconic destinations such as the Maldives, the deterioration of coral reefs through coral bleaching and the loss of snow in winter resorts. On the demand side, fear of skin cancer and eye cataracts may reduce the demand for products such as beach tourism which, in turn, will impact upon destination and product development. Finally, we have to recognise that some transport modes used for tourism contribute to climate change and will need to change.

The other concerns raised by UNEP will also impact upon tourism futures. Consumption of water across the globe is growing at double the rate of population growth and tourism is a voracious consumer of natural resources such as energy and water. In the future this will have to be carefully managed as the days of abundant energy dwindle and water becomes a precious asset in some regions of the world: indeed estimates suggest that, by 2025, 1.8 billion people will live in areas of absolute water shortage (see Gössling *et al.*, 2015). As we reach the years of 'peak oil' when the maximum amount of oil is being extracted from the earth, there is a growing dialogue supporting the transition to a low-carbon economy. This will depend upon development of renewable energy technologies for tourism operations and 'fossil fuel free' efficient and smart transport systems (Becken, 2015). Biodiversity, too, is being impacted upon by development in many regions of the world, and by climate change. For an industry that depends upon natural resources as part of their attraction this remains a serious issue for tourism.

Technological Drivers of Change

The UNWTO has stated that the world in the year 2020 will be characterised by the penetration of technology into all aspects of life. Tourism futures will be determined and facilitated by technology, and where, to paraphrase the well-known commentator on technology trends, Donald Norman (2007), the most successful technology will be invisible to the user and, where it does interface with the user, the experience will be organic. It is when we think of technology that we realise how unpredictable the future can be; for example, in the 1970s the Internet was not even predicted. The following quote from Lewis (2002) brings home the impact of the Internet on tourism futures:

> 'Wide-eyed amateurs, 15 year old teenagers and outsiders can nonchalantly take on the professionals, insiders and establishments and drub them into submission' (p. 117).

This quote underlines the fact that the Internet has levelled the playing field for tourism marketing. A good website means that small remote destinations can compete equally with the giants of tourism such as Spain (see, for example, visitandorra.com), whilst SMEs can take on large corporations.

The fusion of information and communication technologies (ICTs) will allow tourism enterprises to become more efficient and competitive, not simply by lowering costs and facilitating market access, but also by allowing them to network and integrate with other enterprises – and their consumers. Indeed, everything and everyone will be connected in the future. ICTs and big data will increasingly allow customisation of products and real-time access to demand allowing flexible pricing and segmentation almost down to the individual. In the market we are also seeing the growth of online tourism communities; here, the evolution of the Internet will transform the way that business is done and for tourism the fusion of Internet technologies with social activities such as blogging will facilitate content-rich sites and enable networked online tourism communities. By enhancing user-generated content this will displace more traditional ways of seeking information about tourism. New generations of the Internet will advance booking systems and consumer access by introducing intelligent systems and enabling personal travel advisors and intelligent recommendation systems delivering tailored informa-tion – TripAdvisor, for example, could evolve into a professional information hub employ-ing content moderators and peer reviewers (Dwyer *et al.*, 2007; Future Foundation 2015). Effectively, technology has increased the connections between the actors in the tourism system. However, as authorities become concerned at the openness of the Internet, there is a danger that in the future, 'Balkanisation' of the Internet will create regional closed versions – in, say, Russia or China – curtailing the international nature of the medium. In the next case study we examine the furthest extreme that technology can take the tourist – into virtual reality.

Mini Case Study 14.1
Virtual Tourism

In the realm of science fiction we find virtual reality (VR) has been talked about – a completely immersive digital world that is neurologically indistinguishable from the outside world. There is an ongoing debate as to whether VR may one day replace the authentic travel experience all together; indeed, the very nature of tourism as an 'experience' lends itself perfectly to VR – virtual reality is simply a further step along the road of engineering tourist experiences and one that reinforces the trend of leisure activity based upon the home with, say, gaming. It is, for example, already possible to take a virtual tour of Tutankhamen's tomb or Stonehenge, or to view hotel properties before visiting (www.shangri-la.com).

Proponents say that as 'cocooning' behaviour increasingly places the home as a central and secure base for leisure activities, VR may depress demand for the real thing. And, of course, the impacts are minimal: no environmental degradation, carbon emission, cultural demonstration effect or risk of disease. However, opponents contend that VR will simply whet the appetite for more travel through enhanced exposure to, and awareness of, the product, as VR is used simply as an advanced form of tourist brochure.

There is no doubt that truly immersive VR is some years away, but the development of products such as Okulus Rift is bringing the reality closer. Okulus Rift delivers a 3D immersive experience for the user and such is the promise of the technology that it has been purchased by Facebook and is expected to be on sale in early 2016. As would be expected, Okulus Rift has inspired rivals such as Samsung's gear VR headset. However, there are still technological issues to overcome as the headsets can create nausea, they are ugly and cumbersome to wear and the current tech-nology does not allow interaction with other users.

Nonetheless, VR is already being used in a variety of ways for tourism – planning and management, marketing, entertainment, education, accessibility and heritage preservation (Guttentag, 2010). But, of course, the key question is just how easily will the market accept VR substitutes for the real thing – if, for example, VR is to be used to protect heritage by diverting visitation from authentic heritage?

DISCUSSION QUESTIONS

1. Expand on the above list of the 'pros' and 'cons' of virtual tourism.
2. Debate in class whether you think VR will ever replace authentic travel.
3. Is VR the most sustainable form of tourism – visitation without impact?

Sources:
Guttentag, D.A. (2010) Virtual reality: applications and implications for tourism, *Tourism Management* **31**(5), 637–651.

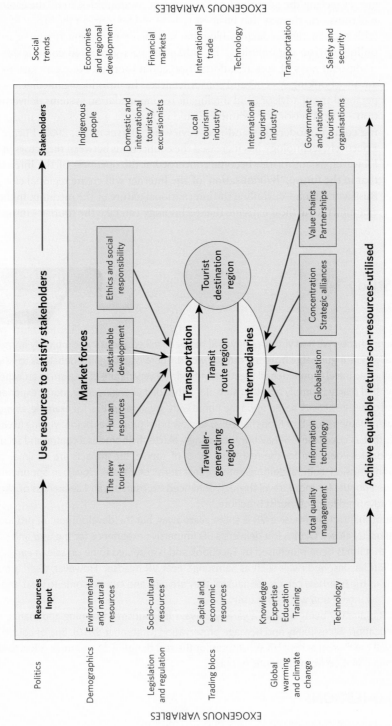

Figure 14.1 A framework for tourism trends analysis

The Response – Tourism Futures

Given the drivers of change identified above, we now turn to examine how they will shape tourism futures. This section returns to the elements of Leiper's tourism system introduced in Chapter 1. Leiper's system recognises the complexity of tourism and the need to match up trends both on the demand side in terms of markets and consumer behaviour, with trends on the supply side in terms of product developments and the destination. To consider any one of these elements in isolation would provide an unbalanced assessment of tourism futures. And, of course, the tourism system itself does not operate in isolation and is subject to a number of cross-cutting influences such as climate change and technology (Figure 14.1).

Tourism Market Futures

In Leiper's 'traveller generating region', the demographic and social trends identified above have combined to change both the scale and nature of tourism markets, facilitated by technology and the economy, but tempered by crises and environmental and ethical concerns. Future tourism markets will be dominated by technology, characterised by fragmentation and they will be borderless. Many tourism futurists have suggested that the maturing of the tourism market is creating a 'new tourist', or a 'post-tourist', characterised as experienced, sophisticated and demanding. This means that the traditional annual family holiday mostly spent in a beach resort may be gradually superseded by multi-interest travel and a range of creative and innovative travel experiences – and, of course, holidays will be seen as a time to detox from the digital world. These trends will see the relative importance of conventional packaged tours decline in favour of independently organised tourism, often using 'dynamic packaging' or a more bespoke form of tourism.

The New Tourist

The new consumer of tourism will demand more. They will be knowledgeable, networked, discerning, seek quality and participation and, in the developed world, be increasingly drawn from an older age group (Yeoman, 2008). Motivations for travel are moving away from passive sunlust towards educational and curiosity motives. At the same time, travel will be facilitated by flexible working practices. Tourists from the major generating regions of the world have become frequent travellers, are linguistically and technologically skilled, and can function in multicultural and demanding environments overseas. Add to this media and Internet exposure of tourism destinations and the reduction of perceived distance to reach such places and the stage is set for a reappraisal of holiday formulae. Education, too, has played a part, together with enhanced communications, and has led to more sophisticated requirements from holidaymakers who are now looking for new experiences combined with rewarding activities, but never too far from a wireless hotspot. Here, the emergence of the knowledge-based society is significant for tourism as travel products are merged with education and entertainment to create 'info-tainment' or 'edu-tainment' at many destinations. As technology has constantly improved the quality of entertainment, visual images and sound in our own homes, so we have come to expect a similar level of quality of our tourism experience. Pine and Gilmore (1999) have taken this one step further by suggesting that in the future consumption will be driven by 'experiences' and that suppliers will 'engineer' these experiences. Tourism is perfect for this approach as, for the new tourist, travel is less about being at the destination and more about the experiences associated with being there as travel becomes the medium for personal fulfilment and identity. Indeed, many commentators suggest that the 'experience' will increasingly drive the decision to purchase a holiday, rather than the 'destination' itself. Here, the Future Foundation (2015) has created six future traveller tribes for 2030 based on personality and the psychology of travel, influenced by 'social media, ethical concerns and a desire for well being' (p. 3). The tribes are fluid and consumers may identify with more than one. They are:

1. simplicity searchers based on ease and transparency in travel;
2. cultural purists immersing themselves in the destination;
3. social capital seekers seeking social reward from travel;
4. reward hunters seeking a return on their travel investment;
5. obligation meeters such as business travellers; and
6. ethical travellers shaped by their conscience.

The new tourist though will differ from earlier travellers in their embrace of ethical travel and their concern for the destinations and communities who live there. We will see an increase in philanthropic, conscientious travel and the growth of fair trade tourism as the tourist recognises their responsibilities to the destination (Hall and Brown, 2008). Here, however, the consumer psychology of tourism will be critical in determining whether tourists really care about climate change enough *not* to fly. In recognition of this trend, the World Committee on Tourism Ethics was inaugurated in 2008 to track implementation of the UNWTO's Global Code of Ethics for Tourism (http://ethics.unwto.org/en/content/world-committee-tourism-ethics), whilst in 2009 Tourism Concern issued a hard-hitting report on tourism and human rights (Tourism Concern, 2009) (www.tourismconcern.org.uk). In response to this trend, new forms of tourism such as volunteering (volun-tourism) are growing whilst suppliers are embracing the idea of corporate social responsibility (CSR) particularly with respect to local communities. This in part is facilitated by the Internet as online communities of new tourists are created as in the case study below.

Mini Case Study 14.2
Networked New Tourists

Introduction

As we have seen, the 'new tourist' seeks authenticity in their experiences, increasingly relying upon other travellers for validation and recommendation facilitated by Internet sites such as www.raveable.com or www.expedia.com. Social networking sites have embraced tourism, creating online communities of like-minded travellers. This case outlines two such communities as examples of how the Internet is providing the perfect medium for 'new tourists' to network and exchange travel ideas.

The True Travellers Society

Launched in 2006, the True Travellers Society (TTS) is a Canadian, Internet-based not-for-profit organisation. The site aims to help new tourists 'truly travel' by sharing travel stories, blogs and adventures of people 'truly travelling'. TTS is 'dedicated to providing free information that will help independent travellers get the most out of their experiences' and operates as a membership-based website allowing the sharing of:

'information about no or minimal fee meaningful travel and volunteer travel opportunities. These opportunities can include anything from volunteering at an orphanage, to a festival, to wildlife conservation'.

This is effectively a networked online community of 'new tourists' who, as in the philosophy of TTS, believe that 'travelling is more than simply visiting a country and taking in the sites with other tourists' – in other words, travel away from 'tourist traps'. As such, *truly* travelling 'involves immersing oneself with the local people, activities, and environment'.

The site has evolved into a resource for 'volun-tourism' with opportunities and resources to help travellers find volunteering opportunities.

VirtualTourist

VirtualTourist is another worldwide travel community where travellers and locals share real travel advice and experiences from an 'insider's perspective'. It provides unbiased, user-generated 'travel advice from people behind the places'. It demonstrates clearly both the popularity of this type of community, and also the evolution towards a professional and organised traveller presence on the Internet. VirtualTourist is hugely popular with impressive statistics:

- 1.3 million registered members from more than 220 countries and territories;
- 1.8 million travel tips on more than 72,977 locations worldwide;
- 3.7 million photographs; and
- 63,000 destination tips.

The site was launched in 1999 with the objective of bringing people together to share their travel experiences and in 2008, almost 10 years later, it became part of the TripAdvisor Media Group (see case study in Chapter 12). It is therefore interesting to see the evolution of online communities of tourists who were once an ad hoc and somewhat 'fringe' group to ones that are now mainstreamed into the tourism sector and increasingly commercialised. As they have matured, sites such as VirtualTourist have offered travel tools, staged events, and provided lists of 'top picks and selections'.

DISCUSSION QUESTIONS

1. Does the 'institutionalisation' of these groups reduce the credibility of their recommendations?
2. Take a destination that you are familiar with and look it up on VirtualTourist. Do you think the advice is accurate?
3. Draft two advertisements for a niche tour operator seeking to gain a presence on both websites. How would the two advertisements differ?

Sources:
www.TripAdvisor.com
www.truetravellers.org
www.virtualtourist.com

We can see from this case that online communities are having an increased impact upon the tourism product itself and the tourists trust each other in preference to advertisements or company endorsements as 'e-word of mouth' grows in importance. Of course, there will be an increased requirement for high standards of product design, efficiency and safety, but more importantly through user-generated websites such as TripAdvisor, the tourist is more critical and aware of the product and can compare offerings. At the same time, as the new tourist is conscious of value for money rather than simply price, other elements of the marketing mix will become important. In particular, this will mean that 'quality' will remain a key attribute in tourism product development and customer convenience in all its forms will be demanded by the new travellers. The issue of quality is increasingly important because the consumer is time poor and will increasingly demand that the products they purchase will be quality controlled and reliable.

Approaching Future Markets

Every new tourist is different, bringing a unique blend of experiences, motivations and desires and the use of big data will allow creation of a 'market of one'. Tourism will therefore increasingly follow the trend of other industries towards customising. Here, technology enables products to be tailored to meet individual tastes. This means that the way that these markets are approached will be different in the future:

- We are seeing the growth of the idea of 'co-creation' of tourism products where the customer helps to formulate the product along with the supplier.
- Technology, through the use of social media, has seen power shifting to the customer; they are knowledgeable and engage with products and services in real time and businesses will engage with the customer to engineer their brands.
- We are rethinking approaches to tourism market segmentation and moving towards deep and meaningful research to understand tourism behaviour (as we saw in Chapter 13).

Destination Futures

For Leiper's 'tourist destination region', there is no doubt that destinations of the future will need to be better planned and managed and show more concern and respect for their environment and host community. Indeed, everyone involved in tourism will have to take increased responsibility for social and environmental issues. In the future, the focus of tourism will be on the destination as new intelligent management systems and techniques are adopted and the attention to volume will give way to concepts of visitor experience and value. These concerns will be addressed by enhanced tourism planning and visitor management techniques and a clear agenda to involve local communities in the futures of their destinations. In this way, the imperative will be for the sustainable management of tourism destinations and the conservation of their unique characteristics. Examples here include the management of UNESCO world heritage sites such as Machu Picchu in Peru or Mount Everest (http://.unesco.org/en/list/274).

The central issue is the gradual shift from short-term to longer-term thinking and planning in tourism. It is no longer acceptable for the industry to exploit and use up destinations and then move on; indeed we are already seeing the results of this in the demise of some of the mass-tourism resorts built in the 1960s and 1970s – Acapulco in Mexico (www.acapulco.com/en/) and Benidorm in Spain (www.benidorm.com/) are examples here. The concepts of the tourism area life-cycle and strategic planning provide a much-needed long-term perspective in this respect. This means that destinations can decide to remain at a particular point on the life-cycle by using marketing and planning approaches, rather than being inexorably driven to grow – or decline. On the demand side there are also drivers of sustainability as consumers place pressure upon the industry and destination managers to behave in a responsible manner; if they do not then their destination may be shunned as environmentally unacceptable to visit.

Managing the Destination of the Future

Destinations are responding to these demands in a variety of ways. Resource-based destinations are adopting sophisticated planning, management and interpretive techniques to provide both a welcoming and a rich experience for the tourist, while at the same time ensuring protection of the resource itself. The innovative use of technology is assisting here, as in virtual 'itours' (see http://itoursaustralia.com.au/).

Enterprises at the destination are also responding to the drive for sustainable destinations in three ways:

1. The tourism industry is anxious to demonstrate that it is both responsible and acting to curb some of the excesses of past development. Increasingly, sustainable tourism practices are being adopted as guidelines and manuals; certification and eco-labelling

are examples here. They encourage tourism enterprises to 'raise their game' in terms of sustainability and allow the consumer to discern those enterprises that are attempting to be sustainable in their practices. Indeed, it could be argued that sustainability will become a driver of innovation in the tourism sector with the larger companies adopting three guiding principles for their actions:

- sustainability is driven by business imperatives such as competitiveness;
- all the organisation's stakeholders are involved – including customers and suppliers; and
- sustainability is underpinned with detailed and research and to guide decisions.

An example of this trend is Green Tourism, who offer independent guidance on sustainability to tourism businesses (www.green-tourism.com).

2. Destinations will benefit from future trends in the tourism supply chain. In the past, this was a combat zone with each member feeling they had to compete. For destinations, this resulted in exploitation by tour operators who failed to recognise that the resort was, in fact, their product. In the future, tourism businesses will begin to recognise the importance of working with other members of the chain and this will include tour operators investing in the destination.

3. Networks or alliances of businesses and consumers along value chains will increase business efficiencies and improve communication. This trend is critical for the tourism sector and is leading to a shift in thinking away from management of individual sectors of the industry to the concept of integrated management.

So what of the future for tourism destinations? We can discern two clearly different and divergent trends:

1. The first is the trend towards the use of artificially, technologically enhanced destinations such as theme parks, cruises and resorts. Examples here include Las Vegas (www.visitlasvegas.com/), the Disney theme parks and Carnival Cruise Line (www.carnival.com). The product is unashamedly artificial, creating a fantasy world that will be increasingly part of the 'experience' economy. Technology plays a major role here with theme parks re-engineering their parks to be computer interfaces to communicate with visitors' devices such as wrist bands.

2. The second trend is for authentic, well-managed contact with nature and indigenous communities. Here, ecotourism and heritage tourism are the obvious examples with sympathetic encounters with wildlife (gorilla encounters in Rwanda) or native peoples (meeting with Maori in New Zealand). This type of destination demands a different type of management to the artificial fantasy destination, as here it is the resource that is paramount in delivering the experience.

Transport Futures

By its very definition, tourism is a transport-intensive activity and is therefore exposed to changes in energy and fluctuating oil prices. Historically, change in tourism has been closely linked to transport innovations in Leiper's 'transit route region', but in the future, the influence of transport will be diluted by the emergence of other new drivers of change. At the same time, transportation itself will benefit from technological change that will improve the speed, reduce the cost, improve fuel consumption and most importantly improve the environmental efficiency of travel. Nonetheless, the influence of transport as a driver of tourism futures should not be underestimated. Tourism remains dependent upon transport technology. This applies especially to new developments such as tourism in space. Equally, tourism may also be constrained by transportation in the future as old systems fail to accommodate increased levels of demand, or travellers perceive the security risks of travel as too great, or the environmental cost too onerous. The inadequate capacity of transport infrastructure will act as a real constraint upon tourism growth in the future, particularly in Europe and the USA.

The future will also see a change in the management and approach of transport enterprises with an emphasis on both marketing and the building of strategic alliances to gain market share. The airline sector, for example, was very heavily affected by the downturn in travel following 9/11, and has seriously rethought its response to future markets and patterns of travel. Here there are two schools of thought. Boeing sees the future in medium-sized aircraft that can operate flexibly between hubs and also secondary regional airports (www.boeing.com/). Airbus, on the other hand, sees the future in larger aircraft, with a longer range that will dominantly ply long-haul routes (www.airbus.com/). The key here will be to adjust the capacity and range of aircraft to 'match' market demand.

Environmental factors, too, will be an increasing concern for all transport modes in the future, particularly as in the case of air transport, emissions are unlikely to be reduced in the medium term. Indeed, the Intergovernmental Panel on Climate Change estimates that air transport accounted for 2 per cent of total carbon emissions in the early years of the century and will rise to 3 per cent in 2050 (www.ipcc.ch/). Environmental factors may bite in two ways:

1. The consumer has an increasing concern for energy consumption and this may lead to a gradual modal shift in transport away from air and towards surface modes.

2. This trend may be reinforced by the imposition of environmental taxes on both air and car travel, which will prompt further changes in choice of transport mode as tourism is asked to pay its way.

In response, the industry is developing more environmentally efficient, high-capacity, high-speed passenger vehicles. As a result, competition between transport modes will increase in the future, characterised by improved rail services and products, the realisation of the environmental advantages of rail and continued technological developments in the area of high-speed train networks. A magnetically levitated (Maglev) fast train service is already operating in Shanghai (www.smtdc.com/en/) and commentators suggest that by 2030 Maglev technology may be replacing more traditional forms of traction. Road transport has not escaped this revolution with driverless cars and traffic prediction enabled by Wi-Fi and sensors and, of course, hybrid and electric cars increasing in popularity as battery technology improves. Forecasts of international transport predict that technological developments, use of aviation bio fuels, increased airline efficiency and labour productivity savings will offset any rises in aviation fuel prices. This is supported by the fact that on short-haul routes the low-cost carriers are gaining market share from the traditional 'scheduled' carriers.

Future Tourism Products

The key to understanding Leiper's framework of tourism, and indeed the study of tourism, is that all elements of tourism are interlinked. This is clear when we consider the question: What will tourism products look like in the future? To answer this question we could, of course, revert to the hype of commentators with their flying cars, but in fact it is more helpful to understand the underlying process of how these products will merge. This involves the concept of 'product markets' (introduced in Chapter 13).

In the future, tourism products and markets will remain inextricably linked. As we saw in Chapter 13, the 'product market' concept helps explain how markets function and will evolve in the future, and therefore helps us to understand different types of future tourism products and how they can be classified (Cooper and Hall, 2008). The concept is based upon the 'exchange' between tourists and suppliers and how the two partners in this exchange will change in the future. For example, we have already seen that:

- the consumer will be more demanding but also more concerned about issues such as CSR, fair trade and ethical consumption; whilst
- suppliers will use technology to engineer experiences for the tourist and provide 'immersive previews' of their products so that you can 'try before you buy' (Future Foundation, 2015).

This evolving exchange will lead to the creation of new types of tourism into the future. These will range from the emerging products of today such as dark and adventure tourism through to products that will characterise tourism futures – such as space tourism and virtual reality, as we saw in the case study. For professional futurists, it is not so much the list and type of these new product markets that is important but, rather, the underlying approach of analysing how they will emerge. Here, in each product market, *tourists* can be classified by their behaviour and involvement, as their 'wants' will tend to cluster, whilst *suppliers* will tend to specialise in particular product markets. Taking space tourism, for example:

- In terms of the characteristics of the market, demand will depend upon price, the length of stay in space, motivations and the associated facilities (Cater, 2010). Also, medical advances, such as drugs to combat motion sickness, would make space tourism more appealing. On earth, demand will be stimulated by the development of spaceports and space-tourism centres – such as Florida's 'Space Coast' – where prospective tourists can experience simulated space flights.
- In terms of the product, accommodation may be on orbiting hotels which offer views of the earth, astronomy, space walks and activities designed to make use of micro-gravity, such as swimming, diving or gymnastics.

Cross-Cutting Issues for Tourism Futures

The final section of this chapter examines the response of the tourism sector to four cross-cutting issues that will have considerable impact upon tourism futures.

Risk and Security

Safety will always be a paramount consideration for the traveller. Despite the economic growth scenarios outlined above, tourism is vulnerable to natural and man-made crises, unexpected events that affect traveller confidence in a destination, whether the risk is real or perceived. Already the events of the twenty-first century have tended to focus attention on security risks to travel associated with terrorism (or by the future threat of cyber-terrorism and acts of war), and political groups such as ISIS creating effective 'no-go' areas for tourism (Piekarz *et al.*, 2015). However, tourism is affected also by natural disasters such as pandemics, tsunami, earthquakes, floods, volcanoes and avalanches. The impact of the wild card event will vary according to its duration and also the degree of preparedness of the destination. And, of course, these events are more significant because society is more mobile and therefore more exposed, whilst destinations are often in locations vulnerable to earthquakes and hurricanes and avalanches (Ritchie, 2009).

The UNWTO defines a crisis as:

'Any unexpected event that affects traveller confidence in a destination and interferes with the ability to operate normally'.

These 'wild card' events have changed the way that we travel. Within a few weeks of the attacks of 9/11 the tourism sector had adopted a new vocabulary, including phrases such as 'risk management', 'destination recovery' and 'crisis management'. As the sector has become more resilient to and experienced in dealing with such events it is clear that 'time is of the essence' and this shaped the evolving approach (UNWTO, 2011b) (Figure 14.2). Bierman (2002) has coined a new scale for tourism to describe the magnitude of a crisis that can have an impact upon a destination. He calls this the DESTCON scale, with DESTCON 1 the most severe crisis that tourism can experience down to DESTCON 5, when normality resumes.

International travel can also be a bio-security threat as it facilitates the spread of infectious diseases as well as the introduction of alien species into countries. As a result, quarantine, customs and bio-security procedures have been increased at many borders – a contradictory trend to the 'borderless' world of globalisation. Threats such as bird flu or the African Ebola outbreak prompt the UNWTO to establish a bio-security procedure. This procedure is advantaged by the fact that epidemics are crises that can be predicted, unlike terrorist attacks, which are not predicable.

Elsewhere, disease and decreasing levels of safety will constrain the uninhibited expansion of tourism. The spread of AIDS, for example, may render some otherwise attractive destinations no-go areas while increasingly vociferous campaigns against sex tourism may also alter tourism flows and motivations. For the developing world there is a fine balance between reporting of such occurrences and protecting their income from tourism.

Finally, tourism is vulnerable to other forms of crisis such as the severe economic downturn of 2008/09. This economic crisis was one of the worst since the 1930s and its 'systemic' nature will impact upon both consumer spending on tourism and the sector's ability to invest, particularly SMEs.

Climate Change and the Green Economy

Growing recognition of the seriousness of climate change has prompted tourism policy and management intervention as well as a call for the tourism sector to embrace the 'green economy'. At the international level, various agencies have been active in promoting concerns through meetings, reports and calls to action. This has led to a series of meetings and declarations by the major intergovernmental and private sector organisations and all the international agencies now have reports on tourism and climate change which can be accessed on their websites.

For the future, the solutions are challenging. One of the ways that tourism contributes to climate change is through carbon emissions from tourism-related activity such as transportation. Whilst approaches such as green taxes on carbon emitters, or carbon trading

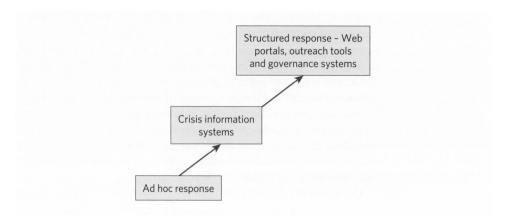

Figure 14.2 The evolving response to crises in the tourism sector

schemes, will undoubtedly target tourism in the future, carbon offsetting has emerged as a popular but controversial way to neutralise the greenhouse gases emitted by travel. For the future, solutions will coalesce around four areas:

1. consumer education with a view to adapting behaviour;
2. destination adaptation to climate change;
3. reduction of carbon emissions and adoption of carbon trading schemes; and
4. scientific advances in the use of alternative energy forms and the sequestering of carbon through natural 'sinks' such as forests.

All of these solutions combine to demand that tourism embraces the principles of the 'green economy'. This can be achieved by the sector mainstreaming policies and technologies that change the way tourists and the industry operate, adopting a quadruple bottom line where climate is added as the fourth element, and accounting for the carbon footprint of tourism using contemporary approaches such as the tourism satellite account.

Technology

The creative use of technology has allowed the tourism sector to add value, reduce costs and build a close relationship with their customers. Yet, it is interesting that the major innovations in the use of technology have come from outside tourism. It was the computer industry that devised the concept of e-intermediaries, for example, a concept that has revolutionised how tourism is sold as we saw in the previous chapter. Technology, too, is allowing the creative use of databases and big data to individualise tourist experiences, understand patterns from social media posts and to develop sophisticated customer relationship management. Of course, technology also gives the tourist much greater control over how they interact with enterprises and purchase their travel. Shirky (2010), for example, says that the Internet creates engaged, connected consumers who share experiences as time online through social media increases and passive activities such as watching TV decreases. Tourism enterprises will increasingly use technology to reduce operating costs and, as a result, their structures will change, becoming flatter and more networked organisations.

Technology will also impact upon tourism futures in two further ways:

1. There will be a mushrooming of embedded technology in cities and destinations allowing, for example, hand-held devices for guides and navigation (such as nodeexplorer.com). When combined with mobile computing and the growing participatory media culture this means that managers will be able to track a tourist's digital and contextual footprint to communicate market opportunities, facilitating dynamic destination management. At the same time, tourists will be able to communicate with each other through geo-social networking sites such as www.Foursquare.com, www.Gowalla.com and Yelp.com. These sites allow tourists to find out who is nearby, make recommendations and play interactive games.
2. Technology is empowering the consumer in the marketplace to reverse the traditional supply chain from *company-to-customer* to *customer-to-company*. Here, the customer drives the relationship with the tourism enterprise, turning marketing on its head with the customer in control, co-creating products with the sector and forming 'customer managed' relationships with companies. So powerful is this trend that companies will evolve their brands in tune with shifting consumer opinion, monitored by posts on social media.

Human Resources

Many of you reading this book will be looking towards the tourism sector for a career. Indeed, the challenges facing the tourism sector will only be met successfully by a well-educated, well-trained, bright, energetic, multilingual and entrepreneurial workforce who understand the nature of tourism and have a professional training. A high quality of professional human resources in tourism will allow enterprises to gain a competitive edge and deliver added value with their service. This book has outlined a professional and analytical approach to tourism; an approach that demands high standards of professionalism and education. Achievement of many of the best practices that we outline will only be possible with a well-trained tourism workforce.

Tourism is a high-touch, high-tech, high-involvement industry where it is the people that make the difference. Yet, in a number of countries, an acute shortage of trained manpower and skills are impacting upon the growth of tourism, hence the move to using robots in Japan. The ability to succeed and the future performance of tourism and related activities will depend largely upon the skills, qualities and knowledge that managers will be able to bring to their business (Lee Ross and Pryce, 2010).

In the past, tourism has been characterised by a lack of sophistication in human resource policies and practices, imposed by outmoded styles of human resource management and approaches to operational circumstances. This leaves tourism vulnerable to ideas, takeovers and domination by management practices found in other economic sectors. Indeed, practices that are commonplace in other service industries – comprehensive induction, regular appraisal, effective employee communications – are underdeveloped in many tourism and leisure businesses.

A high-quality tourism workforce can only be achieved through high standards of contemporary tourism education and training. Tourism education and training involves the communication of knowledge, concepts and techniques that are specific to the field of tourism, but which draw upon the core disciplines and themes of areas such as geography, finance and marketing. The future of tourism education will lie in changing the modes of delivery of courses by using blended approaches through technology, making material available through 'massive online open access courses' (MOOCS), greater customisation of education to meet the needs of particular student groups, and a rethink of the content of tourism courses, which currently have become mired in twentieth century thinking. This brings us back to the influential Tourism Education Futures Initiative (www.tourismeducationsummit.com), which we showcased in Chapter 1. TEFI is attempting to draft tourism education approaches for a changing world, stressing skills such as managing change and environmental stewardship.

SUMMARY

The futures of tourism are exciting but we must guard against being too confident in predicting the future. This chapter has examined the key reports on tourism futures, which confirm the fact that tourism is a difficult sector to predict. Each of the drivers of the future that we identify in the chapter is influential in its own right, but when combined they deliver a powerful force shaping the futures of tourism. Futurists counsel against predictions of a single 'future of tourism', but we can begin to see some of the possible scenarios. We discussed the type of tourist we may expect to find in the future and how they will differ from the tourists of today. Future markets, too, will be more fragmented and dominated by technology and new products, including trips to space. At the same time, the destination will come under increasing pressure and will need careful and appropriate management, whilst transportation will be greener and more efficient. The chapter closed by examining cross-cutting issues that will be of key concern in the future.

Of course, tourism cannot control all the forces that impact upon it. However, the message of this book has been that, whatever tourism futures bring, tourism will only be successful if we take a scientific and disciplined approach. We offer you the challenges of tourism management and an exciting future as you become 'future makers'.

Discussion Questions

1. If the 'new tourist' were truly concerned about climate change they would not travel at all. Debate this contentious statement in class.

2. Critically review the key drivers of tourism futures and show how they are related.

3. How can destination marketing organisations leverage from the content available on mobile devices?

4. Write a report on how you see the tourism labour market developing in the future. How can companies prepare for this new market?

5. In the future, ethical consumption of tourism and CSR concerns will be increasingly important. Discuss this statement in the light of the need for companies to make a profit and return on investment.

Annotated Further Reading

1. Buckley, R., Gretzel, U., Scott, D., Weaver, D. and Becken, S (2015) Tourism megatrends, *Tourism Recreation Research* **40**(1), 59–70.
   Contemporary review of futures' drivers.

2. Cetron, M.J., DeMicco, F.J. and Davies, O. (2010) *Hospitality 2015: The Future of Hospitality and Travel*, American Hotel & Lodging Educational Institute, Orlando, FL.
   A perspective on the future from the hospitality perspective.

3. Dwyer, L., Edwards, D., Mistilis, N., Scott, N., Cooper, C. and Roman, C. (2007) *Trends Underpinning Tourism to 2020: An Analysis of Key Drivers for Change*, STCRC, Gold Coast, Australia.
   An authoritative and comprehensive review of drivers of the future and their implications for tourism.

4. Nordin, S. (2005) *Tourism of Tomorrow – Travel Trends and Forces of Change*, European Tourism Research Institute, Östersund.
   A wide-ranging and visionary report based upon the techniques of futures research.

5. Pine, J.B. and Gilmore, J.H. (1999) *The Experience Economy*, Harvard Business School Press, Boston, MA.
   A visionary book, casting glimpses into the way that tourism products will be engineered and themed as 'experiences' in the future.

6. Ritchie, J.R.B., Mair, J. and Walters, G. (2014) Tourism crises and disasters: moving the research agenda forward, Chapter 49 in Lew, A.L., Hall, C.M. and Williams, A.M. (eds) *The Wiley Blackwell Companion to Tourism*, Wiley, Chichester.
   Contemporary review of the impact of crises on tourism.

7. www.spacetourismsociety.org
   A comprehensive website covering all aspects of space tourism.

8. UNWTO (2011) *Tourism Towards 2030 – Global Overview*, UNWTO, Madrid.
   A report delivering a thorough analysis of future markets and products.

9. VisitScotland (2005) *Our Ambition for Scottish Tourism: A Journey to 2025*, VisitScotland, Edinburgh.
   An example of a national tourism agency building scenarios for the future

10. Yeoman, I. (2008) *Tomorrow's Tourist*, Butterworth Elsevier Heinemann, Oxford.
    A visionary book by one of the leading futurists working in tourism.

References Cited

Becken, S. (2015) *Tourism and Oil*, Channel View, Clevedon.

Bierman, D. (2002) *Restoring Tourism Destinations in Crisis: A Strategic Marketing Approach*, CAB, Wallingford.

Buckley, R., Gretzel, U., Scott, D., Weaver, D., and Becken, S (2015) Tourism megatrends, *Tourism Recreation Research* **40**(1), 59–70.

Cater, C.I. (2010) Steps to space: opportunities for astrotourism, *Tourism Management* **31**, 838–845.

Cooper, C. and Hall, M. (2008) *Contemporary Tourism*, Elsevier Butterworth Heinemann, Oxford.

Dwyer, L. (2014) Transnational corporations and the globalization of tourism, Chapter 15 in Lew, A.L., Hall, C.M. and Williams, A.M. (eds) *The Wiley Blackwell Companion to Tourism*, Wiley, Chichester.

Dwyer, L., Edwards, D., Mistilis, N., Scott, N., Cooper, C. and Roman, C. (2007) *Trends Underpinning Tourism to 2020: An Analysis of Key Drivers for Change*, STCRC, Gold Coast, Australia.

European Tourism Futures Institute (2014) *The Future of European Tourism*, ETFI, Leeuwarden.

European Travel Commission (2006) *Tourism Trends for Europe*, ETC, Brussels.

Forum for the Future (2009) *Tourism 2023*, Forum for the Future, London.

Future Foundation (2015) *Future Traveller Tribes, 2030*, Future Foundation, London.

Gössling, S., Hall, C.M. and Scott, D. (2015) *Tourism and Water*, Channel View, Bristol.

Hall, D. and Brown, F. (2008) The tourism industry's welfare responsibilities: adequate response? *Tourism Recreation Research* **33**(2), 213–218.

HM Treasury (2006) Stern Review on the Economics of Climate Change, HMSO, London.

Kaku, M. (2008) *Physics of the Impossible*, Doubleday, New York.

Lee Ross, D. and Pryce, J. (2010) *Human Resources and Tourism: Skills, Culture and Industry*, Channel View, Bristol.

Lewis, M. (2002) *Next: The Future Just Happened*, Coronet Books, Philadelphia, PA.

Nordin, S. (2005) *Tourism of Tomorrow – Travel Trends and Forces of Change*, European Tourism Research Institute, Östersund.

Norman, D.A. (2007) *The Design of Future Things*, Basic Books, New York.

Piekarz, M., Jenkins, I. and Mills, P. (2015) *Risk and Safety Management in the Leisure, Sport, Tourism and Events Industries*, CABI, Wallingford.

Pine, J.B. and Gilmore, J.H. (1999) *The Experience Economy*, Harvard Business School Press, Boston, MA.

Ritchie, B.W. (2009) *Crisis and Disaster Management for Tourism*, Channel View, Bristol.

Scottish Tourism Alliance (2013) *Tourism Scotland 2020*, Scottish Tourism Alliance, Edinburgh.

Shirky, C. (2010) *Cognitive Surplus*, Allen Lane Harmondsworth.

Tourism Concern (2009) *Putting Tourism to Rights*, Tourism Concern, London.

UNEP (2002) *Global Environment Outlook 3 – Past, Present, and Future Perspectives*, United Nations Environment Program, New York.

UNWTO (2001) *Tourism 2020 Vision*, UNWTO, Madrid.

UNWTO (2007) *Tourism Market Trends*, UNWTO, Madrid.

UNWTO (2010) *Demographic Change and Tourism*, UNWTO, Madrid.

UNWTO (2011a) *Tourism Towards 2030 – Global Overview*, UNWTO, Madrid.

UNWTO (2011b) Toolbox for Crisis Communications in Tourism – Checklists and Best Practices, UNWTO, Madrid.

WTTC (2002) *Increasing Mobility, Expanding Infrastructure*, WTTC, London.

WTTC (2013) *Tourism for Tomorrow*, WTTC, London.

Yeoman, I. (2008) *Tomorrow's Tourist*, Butterworth Elsevier Heinemann, Oxford.

Yeoman, I. (2012) *2050 – Tomorrow's Tourism*, Channel View, Bristol.

Major Case Study 14.1
Tourism Futures Scenarios

Traditional Scottish landscape.
Source: © hstiver/Fotolia.com

Futurists say that the future cannot be predicted, but alternative futures can and should be forecast, and that to be useful, futures studies should be linked to strategic planning and policy. Scenario planning is an approach that is being increasingly used in tourism to predict alternative destination futures and to assist agencies in planning.

Scenario planning was developed by the oil company Shell in the 1960s and has grown out of future studies and strategic analysis. It is a tool that assists in understanding the meaning of business environments and develops a range of pictures and stories of multiple, plausible futures, constructed using future-shaping drivers and trends. Scenarios help to link the future with decisions that need to be made in the short term by asking 'what if' questions.

Scenario planning uses a systems approach that recognises the interconnectedness of tourism. For example, in Australia, the Tourism Futures Simulator has been created that views tourism as a complex system (Walker *et al.*, 1998). By applying systems thinking to tourism, scenarios of the future can be built utilising all of the elements of the system and their relationships to see how destinations and their markets might evolve. The advantage of this approach is that it prevents agencies focusing on a single issue – such as terrorism – and that the individual issues can be located within the wider system and the policy response can be more effective and less 'reactive' to single issues.

Scenario planning is a process rather than an answer and has to be deeply rooted in research. The scenarios are not forecasts, nor are they one-off exercises, but they develop and evolve. Organisations can then gain a competitive edge by utilising the scenarios to think and act in a particular way and to develop a strategic 'conversation' with stakeholders. This allows the organisation to understand the future and to develop plans and policies accordingly to align themselves with the future scenarios. There are a number of examples where tourism has used scenario planning:

- Scotland has led the world in developing scenarios of tourism futures. Their approach uses a variety of data sources and models and a process of triangulation to develop scenarios. The exercise is led by the 2025 Scenario Planning Group, formed to find out and understand the future strategic direction of the sector. Four future scenarios for Scottish Tourism were developed with time horizons of 2015 and 2025. Each scenario describes a very different world and tourism future (VisitScotland, 2005). These scenarios are a way of thinking about tourism futures in Scotland, showing how tourism can follow different trajectories. Importantly, they assist VisitScotland to plan ahead by taking strategic actions and developing policies that anticipate the scenarios. (It is interesting to compare the predictions made for 2015 with what has actually transpired.)

- The European Tourism Futures Institute (2013) has developed four scenarios to examine how sustainable tourism will develop in Europe by 2040. This was done using rounds of Delphi surveys with experts (see Chapter 12). The four scenarios are:

  - **Back to the seventies,** where European economic growth has been rapid and demand for energy outstrips renewable sources, leading environmentalists to worry that the ecosystem will be damaged. Management of mass tourism is seen as preferable to developing low-impact tourism.

  - **Captured in fear,** where the European economy lags behind its neighbours and begins protectionist measures. This reduces innovation in technology placing the environment at risk.

  - **Shoulders to the wheel,** where the European economy is competitive and successful, leading to an inventive, innovative tourism sector majoring on sustainability.

  - **Unique in the world,** where Europe believes it can gain competitiveness by focusing on sustainability. Small-scale tourism is preferred.

- The Forum for the Future (2009) has developed scenarios for UK tourism to 2023. Again the scenarios were created using expert input, focusing around whether international travel will be constrained or encouraged, and whether environmental sensitivities will curtail international travel. The scenarios are:

- **Boom and bust** with extensive travel, although questions remain as to how long it can continue.

- **Divided disquiet,** where wars and devastating climate change severely curtail travel.

- **Price and privilege,** where oil prices have rocketed and the price of travel has devastated the industry and few people can afford to travel.

- **Carbon clampdown,** where tradable carbon allowances are in place for everyone and domestic travel therefore becomes popular and a more ethical approach to travel is seen.

In the scenario building approaches above it has been important to incorporate the views of stakeholders and experts from the outset. In this way, the process creates an adaptive learning organisation where a focus on the future is embedded within the processes and management of tourism organisations. Finally, the scenarios can be used to examine issues such as:

- **climate change** – scenarios of climate futures how should tourism adapt;

- **the future tourism consumer** – their profiles, tastes and motivations and just how the products can be developed to meet their future needs; and

- **technology** – scenarios of future technologies and their impact on consumer purchasing patterns.

The scenario planning approach is a fascinating one, creating multiple futures and ensuring that organisations adapt their planning to the future.

DISCUSSION QUESTIONS

1. Many organisations find it difficult to break out of thinking about the present, and projecting their thinking into the future. Draft an event brief for a seminar to bring together destination stakeholders and showcase the scenario building approach to them.

2. Taking the socio-cultural drivers of the future identified in the first part of this chapter, draft a scenario of the tourism consumer in 2025.

3. Thinking of a destination that you are familiar with, identify the key drivers of the future that could form the basis of a scenario building exercise.

Sources:

European Tourism Futures Institute (2013) *Sustainable Tourism 2014: A Manifesto*, ETFI, Stenden.

Forum for the Future (2009) *Tourism 2023*, Forum for the Future, London.

VisitScotland and Future Foundation (2005) *Our Ambition for Scottish Tourism: A Journey to 2025*, VisitScotland, Edinburgh.

Walker, P.A., Greiner, D., McDonald, D. and Lyne, V. (1998) The tourism futures simulator: a system thinking approach environment, *Modelling and Software* **14**(1), 59–67.

Yeoman, I. (2008) *Tomorrow's Tourist*, Butterworth Elsevier Heinemann, Oxford.

Yeoman, I. and McMahon-Beattie, U. (2005) Developing a scenario planning process using a blank sheet of paper, *Tourism and Hospitality Research* **5**(3) 273–285.

INDEX

Universal Declaration of Human Rights
(UDHR) 269
Universal Studios 158
university accommodation for tourists 178
unstable demand 58
UNSTAT (United Nations Statistical
Commission) 16
UNWTO *see* United Nations World
Tourism Organization
urban detailing 81
urbanisation 325
Urry, J. 101
US Tour Operators Association
(USTOA) 203
USA *see* United States
user-generated content sites 276
user-generated reviews 276
user-oriented attractions 153–4, 159
user pays approach 250
USTOA (US Tour Operators Association)
203
utilities 40
Uysal, M. 269

V
value chains 335
value marketing 296
value statistics 60
Vargo, S.L. 296–7
variable costs 35, 225–6
Venice 82
vertical conflicts, distribution channels 199
vertical coordination of policies and
actions 247
vertical integration, distribution channels
201, 209
vertically integrated tour operators 311
very strong sustainability 129
very weak sustainability 129
VFR (visiting friends and relatives) 22, 179
VICE model 54–5
Vienna 264–5
Vietnam 151
viral campaigns 309
virtual itours 334
virtual reality (VR) 329
virtual tourism 329
VirtualTourist 333
visas 248
visioning 46
visiting friends and relatives (VFR) 22, 179
visitors
attractions *see* attractions
control 138–9

economy 62
impacts, Galapagos Islands 95
international 17
management 136–41, 166
payback 80
profile statistics 60
satisfaction 125
VisitScotland 344
Voase, R. 166–7
Volga 240
volume statistics 60, 61
volun-tourism 313
voluntary instruments 133
volunteer tourism 313
VR (virtual reality) 329

W
Wales 51, 108
walking 39
Wall, G. 44, 62, 77, 79, 92, 101, 105–6, 108,
113, 232–3
wanderlust 273–4
Wanhill, S. 66, 154, 164, 166, 201, 247, 250
Warsaw 157
waste management 132
water-borne transport 236–40
water consumption 328
water management 132
water stress 88
water supply and quality 88
waterbuses 240
wave-piercing catamarans 236
the way, transport 223
weak sustainability 129
web portals, destinations 254
websites
customer-driven distribution 311
tour operators 204–5
wellbeing, subjective 125
West Edmonton Mall, Canada 157
whale watching 85
Wheeller, Brian 78
Whitbread 135
Whitford, M. 41–2
whole of destination approach 122,
131, 256
whole of destination management 135
wholesalers 202
wider impacts 67
wild card events 337
wildlife 44, 85–7, 335
Williams, A. 20
Wirksworth 108
Witt, Stephen 66

women
empowerment, READ global project
110
status and influence 326
wonder attractions 154–5
Woodside, A.G. 275
working conditions 74
World Bank
poverty definition 117
World Commission on Environment and
Development 125–6
World Committee on Tourism Ethics 332
world heritage sites 163, 334
World Summit on Sustainable Development
(Johannesburg, 2002) 6, 117
World Travel and Tourism Council (WTTC)
5, 6, 62, 67
climate change 83
Hotel Carbon Measurement
Initiative 83
Tourism for Tomorrow 323–4
World Wildlife Fund (WWF) 133
wotif.com 185, 189
WTTC *see* World Travel and Tourism
Council
Wuzhen, China 106
WWF (World Wildlife Fund) 133

X
X, Generation 325
xenophobia 100

Y
Y, Generation 325
Yangtze 240
Yellowstone 156
Yelp.com 339
Yemen 50
Yeoman, I. 324
yield management 189, 203, 226
Yokohama Hakkeijima Sea Paradis,
Japan 160
young adults determinants of
demand 282
YouTube 299, 309

Z
Z, Generation 325
Zeithaml, V. 186–7
Zelinsky, W. 20
zero emissions 235
zones, capacity 138
zoning 36
zoos 157

'Chris Cooper's second edition of the *Essentials of Tourism* covers all of the "essentials" a reader new to the study of tourism could possibly need plus so much more. The inclusion of "classic papers" which synthesise the seminal work in the field are wonderfully positioned alongside the latest research in the field and international case studies which are both contemporary and engaging. This is certainly one of the most "classroom ready" introductory texts I have come across and is unquestionably a "must-have" for introductory undergraduate and postgraduate tourism courses.'

Associate Professor Lisa Ruhanen, UQ Business School, The University of Queensland, Australia

How has a family-run hotel in Jamaica become one of the leading sustainable tourism projects in the world? How has the rise of social media impacted upon tourism market research? And just how effective are crowd-sourced destination strategies? For answers to these and many other contemporary tourism questions, simply turn to the second edition of *Essentials of Tourism* by Chris Cooper. From digital marketing to assessing the impact of events, every tourism student will find this book essential reading not only for grasping the key issues, but also for applying them to real-world problems faced by professionals in the tourism industry. The book includes many new case studies from every continent around the world, including cases from Australia, New Zealand, Sri Lanka, Austria, Cambodia, South Africa, India and Bulgaria to give you a truly global perspective on how tourism theory can be applied in an international context. This is combined with a lively and accessible writing style which will support and guide you through how tourism has been affected and will continue to be shaped by technology, changing government policy and sustainability concerns.

Key features:

- Fully updated content throughout, including sustainable tourism, marketing, industry sectors and how social media is impacting upon tourist behaviour.
- Comprehensive coverage of the essential elements of tourism, including the social and environmental consequences of tourism, events, transport, accommodation and special interest tourism.
- Each chapter identifies an important *classic paper* which has acted as a milestone in tourism thinking.
- The academic theory is strongly supported by three case studies per chapter and is accompanied by stunning colour photography and figures helping students to apply their knowledge to real tourism situations.

Chris Cooper is an experienced author and Professor of the Business School at Oxford Brookes University, UK.

ISBN 978-1-292-08838-9

9 781292 0883

www.pearson-books.co